This third Companion is devoted to ancient theories of language. The chapters range over more than eight hundred years of philosophical enquiry, and provide critical analyses of all the principal accounts of how it is that language can have meaning and how we can come to acquire linguistic understanding. The discussions move from the naturalism examined in Plato's *Cratylus* to the sophisticated theories of the Hellenistic schools and the work of St Augustine. The relations between thought about language and metaphysics, philosophy of mind and the development of grammar are also explored.

The essays will interest those studying ancient philosophy and philosophy of language, the history of thought about language, and linguistics.

COMPANIONS TO ANCIENT THOUGHT: 3

Language

Companions to Ancient Thought

In recent years philosophers have radically reappraised the importance and sophistication of the philosophical texts of the ancient world. This new series of Companions is intended particularly for students of ancient thought who will be reading the texts in translation but approaching them with the analytical skills of modern philosophy and with an eye to their contemporary as well as their historical significance. Each volume is devoted to a specific field of philosophy and contains discussions of relevant ideas of all the major philosophers and schools. The books do not attempt to provide a simplified conspectus of ancient views but rather critical discussions of the central and therefore representative arguments and theories.

A particular feature of the series is its exploration of post-Aristotelian philosophy, which has been shown by recent scholarship to be both philosophically exciting and historically important.

Already published

1 *Epistemology*

2 *Psychology*

COMPANIONS TO ANCIENT THOUGHT: 3

Language

Edited by Stephen Everson
Lincoln College, Oxford

Published by the Press Syndicate of the University of Cambridge
The Pitt Building, Trumpington Street, Cambridge CB2 1RP
40 West 20th Street, New York, NY 10011-4211, USA
10 Stamford Road, Oakleigh, Melbourne 3166, Australia

First published 1994

Printed in Great Britain at the University Press, Cambridge

A catalogue record for this book is available from the British Library

Library of Congress cataloguing in publication data

Language / edited by Stephen Everson.
p. cm. – (Companions to ancient thought; 3)
Includes bibliographical references and indexes.
Contents: Plato on understanding language / David Bostock – Cratylus' theory of names and its refutation / Bernard Williams – Aristotle on names and their signification / David Charles – Epicurus on mind and language / Stephen Everson – The Stoic notion of a *lekton* / Michael Frede – Parrots, Pyrrhonists and native speakers / David K. Glidden – Analogy, anomaly and Apollonius Dyscolus / David Blank – Usage and abusage: Galen on language / R. J. Hankinson – Augustine on the nature of speech / Christopher Kirwan – The verb 'to be' in Greek philosophy / Lesley Brown.
ISBN 0 521 35538 9 (hardback) ISBN 0 521 35795 0 (paperback)
1. Language and languages – Philosophy – History. 2. Philosophy. Ancient. I. Everson, Stephen. II. Series.
P106.L3127 1994
401–dc20 93-27234 CIP

ISBN 0 521 35538 9 hardback
ISBN 0 521 35795 0 paperback

SE

Contents

I

Introduction

STEPHEN EVERSON

Contemporary historians of philosophy write in a philosophical culture in which the analysis of language has been given a dominant position. It now seems quite natural to pursue questions which were once treated as those of metaphysics, say, or the philosophy of mind as lying rather within the philosophy of language. Instead of asking whether there are private mental states or events such as sensations, one asks whether there could be a private language; instead of asking whether there are numbers, one asks whether every mathematical statement must be true or false; instead of asking whether there are events and what sort of thing they are, we investigate the logical form of action sentences and determine the ontological commitments of our talk about the things that happen. The hope is that, as Donald Davidson says, in 'making manifest the large features of our language, we make manifest the large features of reality'.[1]

This approach to philosophical enquiry is, of course, characteristic of what has come to be called 'analytical philosophy', and its motivation can itself perhaps be seen to rest on a particular view of language. So, if we follow Michael Dummett, we will take the distinguishing feature of analytical philosophy to be its giving language explanatory priority over thought.[2] According to Dummett, three theses are essential for the analytical philosopher: '(i) an account of language does not presuppose an account of thought, (ii) an account of language yields an account of thought, and (iii) there is no other adequate means by which an account of thought may be given'.[3] The analytical philosopher proceeds by analysing language because, on this view, it is only by means of such analysis that one will be

[1] Davidson [483], 199. Not all who have taken 'the linguistic turn' have shared Davidson's own claim that 'in sharing a language . . . we share a picture of the world that must, in its large features, be true'.

[2] For a brief discussion of what motivates this, see the first section of ch. 5 below.

[3] Dummett [487], 39.

able to analyse thought itself. On this account, analytical philosophy rests on a thesis *about* the nature of language – that linguistic meaning is not to be explained in terms of its standing as a code for thoughts which have their content independently of their having linguistic expression.

If Dummett is correct in his characterisation of analytical philosophy, then it is a relatively recent philosophical development.[4] Certainly, there is no ancient philosopher who explicitly espouses anything like Dummett's three analytical principles, and most of the ancients would deny at least the first of them. Nevertheless, there is an important strand in ancient theorising about language in which words are taken to have their semantic properties independently of their functioning as signs of thoughts and according to which the analysis of language is a precondition at least for being able to say true things about the world. This strand is most perspicuous in Plato's *Cratylus* (*Crat.*), in which Socrates, Hermogenes and the Heraclitean Cratylus are represented as debating whether names are merely conventional or have a natural standard of correctness. Cratylus adopts a strenuously naturalistic position: 'he says that [names] are natural and not conventional – not a portion of the human voice which men agree to use – but that there is a truth or correctness in them, which is the same for Hellenes as for Barbarians' (*Crat.* 383a). Hermogenes, in contrast, argues for a conventionalist theory:

> Any name which you give, in my opinion, is the right one, and if you change that and give another, then the new name is as correct as the old . . . For there is no name given to anything by nature, all is convention and habit of the users. (384d)[5]

This, however, is challenged by Socrates, who asks Hermogenes to consider what sort of skill (*technē*) is required for assigning names:

> Then, as to names, ought not our legislator also to know how to put the true natural name of each thing into sounds and syllables, and to make and give all names with a view to the ideal name, if he is to be a namer in any true sense? . . . Then, Hermogenes, I should say that this giving of names can be no such light matter as you fancy, or the work of light or chance persons. And Cratylus is right in saying that things have names by nature, and that not every man is an artificer of names, but he only who looks to the name which each thing by nature has, and is able to express the true forms of things in letters and syllables. (389d; 390d)

[4] Dummett describes Frege as the 'grandfather' of analytical philosophy – [487], 60–1, [488], 196. For doubts about Dummett's characterisation of analytical philosophy, see Cohen [480], ch. 1.

[5] Jowett's translation, from [96].

Having established at *Crat.* 386d that things 'must be supposed to have their own permanent essence (*ousia*)', Socrates presents the task of whoever assigns names to be to capture that essence. If a name is to be correct, then it must somehow reflect what it refers to: what it is to be that thing must be expressed in the name assigned to it. On Cratylus' view, what is required of a name, if it is to fulfil that function, is that it should stand as some sort of likeness of what it refers to. Socrates has little problem in showing that this is not a satisfactory position[6] and the dialogue ends aporetically, without Hermogenes' question having received an answer.

Although Cratylus' brand of linguistic naturalism is not one which will be attractive to contemporary readers – as it was not to Plato – the thesis is not without its interest.[7] For one thing, it provides an early attempt to explain how language is meaningful without seeing it simply as a code for thought.[8] Secondly, it is representative, in a somewhat extreme form, of a more general sophistic concern with determining standards of correctness for language. So, in Plato's *Phaedrus*, Protagoras is credited with originating *orthoepeia*, 'correct diction' (267c), and both he and Prodicus are reported in the *Cratylus* as being concerned with *orthotēs onomatōn*, 'the correctness of names'.[9] Our evidence for how either of these sought to determine the correctness of words is slight, and there is no reason to believe that they shared Cratylus' belief in a natural correctness secured by a likeness between a word and what it refers to. Nevertheless, Protagoras is cited in the *Cratylus* as someone who had put forward claims as to what constituted the natural standard for linguistic correctness – but we are not told what he took that standard to be. Even if he would not have subscribed to Cratylus' particular way of determining linguistic correctness, it would seem that any theorist who maintained that there are standards for correctness which are independent of conventional usage would have to accept something like Socrates' version of the name-giver's task.

What the naturalist was looking for was a language which is fit for the description of the world – which is such as to be used to say things about the world without imprecision. The importance of this goal could be recognised without the commitment to naturalism, however. Correct speech – that is, linguistic precision – can, of course, be achieved without the aid of words

[6] See Bernard Williams' chapter below.

[7] Discussion of other varieties of linguistic naturalism can be found in chs 5 and 9 below, pp. 91 f. and 167 f.

[8] Compare Dummett on Frege: 'His semantic theory made no appeal to an antecedent conception of thoughts . . . that is why [he] is regarded as the grandfather of analytic philosophy' [488], 196. At least in this, Frege was not without his predecessors.

[9] See Kerferd [66], ch. 7 for a useful introduction to sophistic linguistic speculation.

whose structure somehow reflects the form of what they refer to.[10] Prodicus' method for achieving *onomatōn orthotēs* was to provide careful distinctions either between words which might easily be taken to be synonyms or between different senses of the same word. So, in the *Protagoras* (*Prot.*) Prodicus is represented as distinguishing between attending to the speakers in a discussion impartially and attending to them equally: 'the two things are not the same: they must hear both alike, but not give equal weight to each. More should be given to the wiser, and less to the other.' He then encourages Protagoras and Socrates to engage in a discussion rather than a dispute (the former is between friends, the latter between rivals) so that they will earn esteem rather than praise (praise can be fake, whereas esteem cannot) and produce enjoyment (*euphrainesthai*) in their audience rather than pleasure (*hēdesthai*) – pleasure is restricted to bodily activities, whereas enjoyment is not.[11]

The passage is ironical: Prodicus is depicted as being unable to say anything without contrasting it with something else. In the *Charmides*, Socrates complains about the 'endless distinctions which Prodicus draws about names' (163e). In this case, however, we are likely to side with the target of Plato's irony rather than with Plato himself. In however jejune a fashion (and we have little evidence which is independent of Plato to judge him on this), Prodicus was pursuing a project which has been characteristic of philosophy to this day – that of trying to get clear what our words mean in order that we do not create unnecessary confusion when we use them to describe the nature of things.

Socrates follows his jibe in the *Charmides* by saying that he has 'no objection to your giving names any signification which you please, if you will only tell me to what you apply them'. It might be tempting to see in this a forerunner of the sort of complaint which was made against what was called 'ordinary-language philosophy' – that too much effort was spent analysing the intricacies of idiomatic usage and too little actually in using language to reflect on the nature of things. There is indeed in Plato a move from linguistic analysis to more straightforward metaphysical speculation, but his own work, as well as that of Aristotle and the philosophers who followed him, shows a recognition that one cannot properly engage in such speculation without simultaneously subjecting the language one uses to critical scrutiny. It is more than likely that Prodicus applied his method with too much zeal, and no doubt with insufficient depth, but that method imposed a discipline on philosophical argument without which it could not have achieved even the success it has.

[10] For Hellenistic discussions of this issue, see R. J. Hankinson's essay, ch. 9 below.

[11] *Prot.* 337a–c [=D–K 84A13].

For one does not have to accept any particular thesis about the relation between language and thought to recognise that linguistic confusion breeds bad philosophy. It is not only analytical philosophers who (should) recognise the importance of analysing the words we use to express our thoughts and to say things about the world. In truth, both 'analytical' philosophers and philosophers of other kinds are likely to concern themselves with questions about the meaning of words and with questions about the nature of what those words refer to. Any difference is likely to be mostly a matter of emphasis.[12] So, when Davidson, in the paper cited earlier,[13] describes and defends the project of pursuing metaphysics by studying 'the general structure of our language', he acknowledges that that project is not a novel one:

> This is not, of course, the sole true method of metaphysics; there is no such. But it is one method, and it has been practised by philosophers as widely separated by time or doctrine as Plato, Aristotle, Hume, Kant, Russell, Frege, Wittgenstein, Carnap, Quine and Strawson. These philosophers have not, it goes without saying, agreed on what the large features of language are, or on how they may be best studied and described; the metaphysical conclusions have in consequence been various.[14]

It may be that analytical philosophers have particular theoretical reason for the pursuit of metaphysics by means of the analysis of language, but nevertheless, as Davidson says, that pursuit is one in which philosophers have been engaged since antiquity.

Parmenides' arguments against plurality and change, for instance, provide an early example of a philosopher's drawing metaphysical conclusions from claims about language. 'What is said and thought must needs be', he states in fr. 6, and then, in fr. 8, he employs this principle to draw very bold conclusions:[15]

> It never was nor will be, since it is now, all together, one, continuous. For what birth will you seek for it? How and whence did it grow? I shall not allow you to say nor to think from not being for it is not to be said nor thought that it is not; and what need would have driven it later rather than earlier, beginning from the nothing, to grow? Thus it must be either completely or not at all. (fr. 8, 5–11)[16]

[12] See Cohen [480], ch. 1, for the application of this to analytical philosophy.

[13] See above, n. 1. [14] Davidson [483], 199.

[15] The idea that a word must refer if it is to be meaningful is one which plays a key role in much early Greek theorising about language, and was used, for instance, to support the striking claim that falsehood was impossible. See Denyer [22] for a study of this issue.

[16] The translations are from Kirk, Raven and Schofield [43].

From the claim that what is non-existent is both unthinkable and unspeakable Parmenides infers that what exists must always have existed, since to say that it came into being would require saying that it came into being from nothing, and this would require what is impossible – speaking of the non-existent.[17]

Plato, too, moves from claims about language to strong metaphysical conclusions. As David Bostock argues below, at least part of Plato's motivation for positing Forms was in order to explain our ability to understand such terms as 'good', 'just' and 'large'.[18] To understand 'good', for instance, one must know what it is for something to be good, and this is not knowledge which could be obtained merely empirically.[19] The explanation of our linguistic abilities is taken to require an account of concept-possession, and this, in its turn, requires a particular theory of the world which will allow the subject to acquire the concepts needed for the understanding of language. Unless there were Forms of goodness and beauty, perfect exemplars of those properties, one would not be able to understand the terms 'good' and 'beautiful'.

The theory of Forms is rejected by Aristotle, who is duly attentive to the dangers posed by insufficient attention to the details of linguistic usage. So, in his attack on the Form of the good, in the first book of the *Nicomachean Ethics* (*EN*), he objects that Plato's theory rests on a false assumption of the unity of goods:

> Further, since things are said to be good in as many ways as they are said to be (for things are called both in the category of substance, as God and reason, and in quality, e.g. the virtues, and in quantity, e.g. that which is moderate, and in relation, e.g. the useful, and in time, e.g. the right opportunity, and in place, e.g. the right locality and the like), clearly the good cannot be something universally present in all cases and single; for then it would not have been predicated in all the categories but in one only. (*EN* 1,6.1096a25–8)[20]

Aristotle's diagnosis of Plato's error is, in essence, that he was misled by linguistic appearances: whilst the same term ('good', *agathon*) is used whenever we describe something as good, in fact the things to which we can apply the term differ so widely that it is not sensible to think of there being a single property which they all share and in virtue of which they can be

[17] For discussion of Parmenides' use of the verb *einai*, 'to be', see Lesley Brown, ch. 11 below and also Barnes [40], I, 157–72. [18] See ch. 2 below.

[19] In ch. 7 below, David K. Glidden discusses the problems raised by the sceptics over linguistic understanding.

[20] (Ross/Urmson translation from [230]). Note that what is to be predicated here is the good and not the term 'the good'. For some remarks on predication in Aristotle, see Michael Frede's chapter below, pp. 114 f.

described as good. Aristotle moves in this chapter, as so often, between questions about how words are used and questions about what the words are used to describe.[21] His opening question in the corresponding chapter in the *Eudemian Ethics* (*EE*) is, appropriately, 'We must then examine what is the best, and in how many senses we use the word' (*EE* 1,8.1217b1). Aristotle was not an analytical philosopher, at least in Dummett's sense. He did not articulate the ambition to give a theory of thought *by* providing an analysis of language, and took language to work because sounds can function as 'symbols' or 'signs' of thoughts.[22] Nevertheless, the fact that we are able to communicate our thoughts linguistically ensures the importance of being clear about what we are saying.

For Aristotle, the ability to express our thoughts to one another is part of what makes us human. So when, in book 1 of the *Politics*, he presents his argument for the claim that humans are by nature political animals, part of that argument rests on the human capacity for language:

> Now, that man is more of a political animal than bees or any other gregarious animals is evident. Nature, as we often say, makes nothing in vain, and man is the only animal who has the gift of speech. And whereas mere voice is but an indication of pleasure and pain, and is therefore found in other animals (for their nature attains to the perception of pleasure and pain and the intimation of them to one another and no further) the power of speech is intended to set forth the expedient and the inexpedient, and likewise therefore the just and the unjust. (*Politics* 1.2)

For Aristotle, the sign of man's distinctiveness as a political animal is that only humans are capable of speech (*logos*). The ability to communicate thoughts, rather than merely to express pleasure and pain, is something which sets humans apart from other animals.

Aristotle himself does not provide any sustained discussion of the relation between language and thought. Both at the start of the *Metaphysics* (*Met.*) and at the end of the *Posterior Analytics* (*An. Post.*), he discusses the differences in the cognitive abilities of humans and animals, but does not proceed to consider how these are related to what secures the ability to communicate linguistically. Nevertheless, there is in Aristotle at least the

[21] Cf. 1096b27 f.: 'But in what way are things called good? They do not seem to be like the things that only chance to have the same name. Are goods one, then, by being derived from one good or by all contributing to one good, or are they rather one by analogy?'

[22] Cf. *de Interpretatione* (*Int.*) 1.16a3 ff. What spoken sounds are said to be symbols of are 'affections of the soul (*psuchē*)' – but it seems from what follows that these are thoughts, *noēmata*: 'just as some thoughts in the *psuchē* are neither true nor false while some are necessarily one or the other, so also with spoken sounds' (*Int.* 116a9–11). The passage is discussed by David Charles in ch. 4 below, as well as in ch. 5, pp. 90–1 f. For Augustine's treatment of words as signs, see ch. 10.

material for an account of what sort of psychology is required for a creature to use and understand a language, as well as the beginnings of an answer to the question which must lie at the centre of philosophical speculation about language: how is it that sets of marks or sounds can have significance? Just as the theorist will be concerned to show what is required of a creature for it to be a *speaker* of a language, so he will also be concerned to show what is necessary for sounds (and marks) to be able to be used as (part of) a language. We communicate linguistically by uttering sounds and making signs, and it needs to be determined what constraints there are on the sounds and signs we produce if our production of them is indeed to function as linguistic behaviour. The animals in *Politics* I are caused to make sounds because they are in pain, but such sounds are not linguistic, even if, it seems, they have a communicative function.

For the Stoics also, animals are not capable of speech since they are not capable of thought: 'They say that it is not uttered speech but internal speech by which man differs from non-rational animals; for crows and parrots and jays utter articulate sounds.'[23] The consequence of this is that animal utterances are, strictly speaking, not linguistic at all:

> An animal's utterance (*phōnē*) is air that has been struck by an impulse, but that of man is articulated and issues from thought (*dianoia*) . . . Utterance (*phōnē*) and speech (*lexis*) are different, because vocal sound is also an utterance, but only articulated sound is speech (*logos*). And speech is different from language because language is always significant (*sēmantikos*), but speech can lack significance, e.g. '*blituri*', whereas language is not like this at all.[24] (Diogenes Laertius (D.L.) VII.55; 57=LS 33H; 33A)[25]

Earlier in Diogenes' report of Stoic doctrine, we find the claim that 'thought (*dianoia*), which has the power of talking, expresses in language (*logos*) what it undergoes (*paschei*) by the agency of the perception' (VII.49=LS 33D).

Whereas Aristotle's account of the relation between thought and language is schematic, the Stoics provided a much more systematic treatment of the matter, introducing propositional items, *lekta*, to mediate between the two. In *adversus Mathematicos* (*M*) VIII, Sextus Empiricus contrasts Stoic with Epicurean doctrine. Whereas Epicurus allowed only words and objects, the Stoics postulated three items; words, objects and *lekta*:

> three things are linked together, the 'signification', the 'signifier' and the 'name-bearer'. The signifier is an utterance, for instance 'Dion'; the signification is the actual state of affairs revealed by an utterance, and

[23] Sextus Empiricus, *adversus Mathematicos* (*M*) VIII.275=LS 53T.

[24] Presumably, the Stoics' attention here is focused on the sounds which animals make naturally, without being trained.

[25] 'LS' indicates a reference to Long and Sedley [308].

> which we apprehend as it subsists in accordance with our thought, whereas it is not understood by those whose language is different although they hear the utterance; the name-bearer is the external object, for instance, Dion himself. Of these, two are bodies – the utterance and the name-bearer, but one is incorporeal – the state of affairs signified and sayable (*lekton*), which is true or false. (*M* VIII.11–12 = LS 33B)

When someone speaks, what is true or false is not the set of sounds he makes but rather what is said in making the utterance. This is the *lekton*, which also stands as the content of the speaker's psychological state.[26] Whilst there is at least an apparent problem in Aristotle's theory over why those animals which are capable of memory should not be able to express the content of their perceptions linguistically, the Stoics avoid this by distinguishing between the psychological states of rational animals, whose content can be linguistically articulated, and those of irrational animals. For the Stoics, what is required if an animal is to possess a language is the ability to have mental states with content. As long as an animal is a rational animal, even its perceptions will have content which is linguistically expressible[27] – and, as we have seen, the content of a speaker's intentional states is prior to the content of the utterances he makes in expressing them. Utterances can have content only because mental states do.

Ancient philosophers, then, like their modern successors, were concerned to answer various sorts of question in their study of language. At the most basic level, they attempted to provide an analysis of the structure of language – to distinguish between subjects and predicates, nouns and sentences, and so on[28] – and to clarify the meaning of individual expressions. Secondly, they set out to give accounts of how it is that sounds and marks can be meaningful. Thirdly, they dealt with the question of how a speaker can come to understand a language. In answering all of these, the study of language could not be dissociated from questions to do with the nature of the mind and the world. Even if the ancients did not share the presuppositions of the contemporary analytical philosopher, neither their interests in the explanation of language nor their methods of general philosophical enquiry will prove alien to those brought up to take those presuppositions almost for granted.

[26] See Michael Frede, ch. 6 below, for a systematic discussion of the Stoic theory of *lekta*. The implications of the Sextus passage for the understanding of Epicurus are reviewed in ch. 5, pp. 84 f.

[27] This is not to imply that Aristotle thought either that perceptions do not have content or that one cannot express that content in language. What is at least initially puzzling on his account is, given this, why one needs a high-level faculty such as *nous* in order to speak a language at all.

[28] David Blank, in ch. 8, describes the relation between philosophy and grammar in the Hellenistic period.

2
Plato on understanding language

DAVID BOSTOCK

In Plato's early dialogues Socrates is portrayed as specially concerned with questions of ethics, and in particular with the concepts of goodness, virtue, courage, justice, temperance, piety, and so on. He perpetually asks what these things *are*, thinking that if we cannot say what they are then we will not know how to set about pursuing them, and therefore will not know how we ought to live. But also, in those early dialogues, Socrates is regularly shown as unable to find any satisfactory answers to his 'what is *x*?' questions. Although there are many who think that they can say, for example, what virtue is, on investigation their answers all turn out to be mistaken in one way or another, and no correct answer ever emerges. It is perhaps not completely clear what Socrates *would* have counted as a correct answer to one of his 'what is *x*?' questions, but at least there is no doubt about this: the question asks for some description or account of the *one* thing that is common to all the *many* instances, examples or cases of *x*, and it is not to be answered just by giving a list of such examples. This one thing that is common to all the many examples Plato came to call the Form of *x* (*eidos*, *idea*), or 'the thing that *x* itself is' (*auto ho esti x*), and he evidently thought that it was crucially important to be able to provide a suitable account of it.

Now some 'what is *x*?' questions appear simple enough to handle. For example, the question 'what is quickness?' can be answered by saying that quickness is doing a lot in a little time (*Laches* 192a–b), the question 'what is shape?' can be answered by saying that shape is the limit of a solid (*Meno* 76a), and Plato evidently supposes – rather to our surprise – that there would be no particular difficulty in finding an adequate answer to the question 'what is a bee?' (*Meno* 72b–c). But the cases that actually concerned him seemed very much more difficult, and Plato must, I think, have asked himself why this is. What makes the difference between a question such as 'what is shape?', which we can answer readily enough, and a question such as 'what is virtue?', which defeats all our efforts? Why is it that in the one case we can, and in the other we cannot, discern the *one* thing common to all the *many* examples?

Reflection on this question appears to have led Plato to believe that the reason for the difficulty is that, in the important cases, the examples themselves are defective, ambiguous and inadequate. Thus if one is looking for examples of beauty one might perhaps suggest that gold is a beautiful material, or that bright colouring is beautiful, or that that girl over there is beautiful. But always one has to admit that this holds only in some ways and to some extent. For example, the famous gold and ivory statue of Athena in the Parthenon at Athens is *more* beautiful because the flesh is done in ivory and *not* gold (*Hippias Major* (*Hipp. Ma.*) 290a–b); similarly bright colouring may be beautiful for some objects, or in some settings, but in others it is not (*Phaedo* 100c–d); or again, a girl may be beautiful for a girl and yet be merely plain beside a goddess (*Hipp. Ma.* 289a–c). To generalise, each of the many things that we call beautiful may equally, and just as correctly, be called not beautiful (*Republic* 479a), and the same would equally hold – Plato supposes – of what we call good, or just, or virtuous, and so on (*Republic* 479a, *Phaedo* 75d).

Indeed, Plato came to believe that the same situation held with many other words too. In a crucial argument at *Phaedo* 73c–76e his example is equality. We do (in a way) know what equality is, and that knowledge does somehow depend upon our experience of equal sticks, equal stones and other such perceptible examples. Yet this is puzzling, for anything that is equal will also 'seem to be', or 'be seen to be', unequal. Unfortunately, the interpretation of this phrase is disputed, since the Greek word in question (*phainetai*) may take either meaning. On the first reading, Plato is saying that equal sticks may seem to one man to be equal and to another man to be unequal. But I believe that the second reading is correct,[1] and if so then his point is that a given stick will be seen to be equal to one thing but not equal to another, just as it will also be seen to be large in relation to one thing but small in relation to another, or heavy in relation to one thing and light in relation to another (*Republic* 479b). That is, he is not saying that people can make mistakes over equality, or even – mysteriously – that they can disagree about it without either side being wrong. There are, after all, perfectly familiar ways of settling such a dispute (*Euthyphro* 7c). Rather, he is saying that the same stick may quite *correctly* be called both equal and unequal, as it may also quite correctly be called both large and small, both heavy and light. It exemplifies both opposites at once, just as what is beautiful is also ugly, what is just is also unjust, and so on.

[1] I have argued this at length in my [144], 72–94.

The numbers appear to provide yet another example of the same phenomenon. Thus a finger is no doubt unambiguously a finger, but should it be called one thing or many? Plato's answer is 'both', for what is one finger will at the same time be *three* joints, and no doubt many *hundreds* of cells (*Republic* 523d, 524e–525a; *Parmenides* 129c–d). But this at once introduces a suggestive contrast, for the number one that the mathematicians speak of is just one, and is not also many of anything. (Plato will not allow the number one to be, say, two halves; he insists that it has no parts.) Similarly one might find it plausible to say that the number two is just two, and is not also one, or three, or any other number.[2] But these 'numbers themselves' that we are speaking of are clearly not perceptible objects, and should rather be classed as intelligible objects (*Republic* 525d–526a). So one might make this suggestion: whereas a perceptible object that exemplifies one number will also exemplify other numbers too, it appears that an intelligible object, and in particular a 'number itself', will be an instance of that number only, and of no other.

It is not clear how soon these thoughts about the numbers themselves influenced Plato. The passage from the *Republic* that I have been drawing upon was evidently written some time after it had first struck him that there were no adequate examples in this world of beauty, goodness and justice, or even of equality, largeness and smallness. But Plato did draw a similar conclusion for these other cases too: *wherever* we cannot find adequate perceptible examples in this world, we must posit the existence of special intelligible examples, which really do exemplify just one concept, without also exemplifying its opposite. To see why, let us return to the problem that underlies *Phaedo* 73c–76e.

If we raise the question of how one comes to understand a word such as 'red', then everyone will say that an important part of the process is that one is shown examples of red things, and taught that the word is correctly applied to these things. Without such examples, it is very difficult to see how the word could ever be understood. But now, consider the word 'equal'. In an ordinary and everyday sense we do understand this word – we do know what equality is – and yet we have just said that there are no unambiguous examples to which this word applies. That is, any perceptible object that one might adduce as an example of an equal thing will *also* be an example of an unequal thing, so it will illustrate the meaning of the word 'unequal' just as much as it illustrates the meaning of the word 'equal'. But it is obvious that these two words do not have the same meaning, so one must conclude that

[2] Later, when he had seen the error of his ways, Plato did grant that the number two was *one* number (*Parmenides* 144a–c).

neither of them can be understood simply on the basis of perceptible examples. So, *retaining* the view that examples are required for understanding, Plato is led to suppose that there must be some suitable *imperceptible* example that we are somehow aware of. There must *be* something that is equal, without also being unequal, only it cannot be a perceptible thing, but must be grasped by the mind alone. And the same must hold for all those other words – 'beautiful', 'good', 'just', 'large', 'small', and so on (*Phaedo* 75c–d) – where all the perceptible examples are at the same time examples of their opposites. The special and unambiguous example of *x*, imperceptible but intelligible, Plato *also* called the form of *x* (*eidos, idea*), or 'the thing that is *x* itself' (*auto ho esti x*).

Naturally, one wants to know how the mind does grasp these special and imperceptible examples, and here Plato calls upon another line of thought which, I suspect, he had first elaborated for a different reason. I imagine that he had for some time believed in the immortality of the soul, and had taken this to imply that just as the soul is never destroyed, so also it was never created. His picture was that the soul is periodically reincarnated, living a succession of earthly lives with periods 'in Hades' in between. In the earlier dialogue the *Meno* it had occurred to him that this picture may be put to work to explain (what *we* call) *a priori* knowledge. In some cases – and Plato takes an example from geometry – it appears that we are able to 'draw knowledge out of ourselves', without any explicit teaching. To explain this, it must be supposed that the knowledge was already latent within us, and this in turn will be comprehensible if we can suppose that we existed before this present life began, and originally acquired the knowledge at some earlier stage (*Meno* 81a–86b).[3] From the context in which this discussion is set, it is clear that Plato wishes to apply it to the vexing question 'what is virtue?', for we can at least hope that the answer to this question too is latent within us, and can be brought to the surface by an appropriate enquiry. But the *Meno* gives us no direct reason to suppose this, and this is where the *Phaedo* adds to, and strengthens, the argument.

Since we do understand such words as 'equal' and 'virtue', at least in an ordinary and everyday sense, we must somehow be acquainted with a suitable unambiguous example. But as no such example can be perceived in this world, it must lie in another world, to be perceived with 'the eye of the mind' rather than 'the eye of the body'. It is reasonable, then, to extend the theory of the *Meno* about *a priori* knowledge, and to suppose that our original acquaintance with the imperceptible and unambiguous example

[3] The *Meno* is somewhat evasive about when exactly this knowledge was first acquired, and in fact it ends by suggesting that the knowledge has 'always' been in the soul (86a–b).

also lies in a previous, and unbodily, existence. It will then follow[4] that we do have latent within us a knowledge of what virtue is, and what equality is. At present we 'recollect' that knowledge only in a dim way, which explains why in an ordinary and everyday sense we *do* know what equality is – i.e. we do understand the word 'equal' – whereas in a stricter and more philosophical sense we do *not* know what equality is, i.e. we cannot actually answer the Socratic question 'what is equality?' (*Phaedo* 74a–b and 76b–c). The problem for the philosopher, then, is to bring to the surface this latent knowledge of such important things as goodness, beauty and justice. We must have such knowledge, for otherwise one could not explain how exposure to the defective examples of this world could trigger the ordinary understanding of language that we all possess. But philosophical understanding will not be achieved by engaging upon a more searching scrutiny of those examples. Rather, as with other cases of *a priori* knowledge, we must seek to bring out what is in a way already in us; we must seek to 'recollect'.

Such, then, is Plato's position in the *Phaedo*, and it is fascinating to see what a remarkable theory has been elaborated from a puzzle about how we understand our language. Preoccupied at first with notions such as goodness, Plato is struck by the point that there are not in this world any unambiguous examples of things that are good. Considering, then, how we come to understand the word 'good' in the first place, he is led to claim that there must be an unambiguous example in another world, that we must once have apprehended it, now dimly recollect it, and should therefore be able to attain a full knowledge of what goodness is if only we can learn how to turn our attention away from the things of this world and focus upon what is already in us. Now in the case of a word such as 'good' there is indeed a sense in which Plato's premise is correct: there are no unambiguous examples in this world. (That is, of any proposed example it may be disputed whether it is an example, without our having to conclude that the disputants do not mean the same by the word 'good'.[5]) But his theory is now by no means confined to such evaluative words. He extends it to words such as 'large', 'small' and 'equal', which *we* recognise as words for relations, and to the number-words, which *we* (taught by Frege) recognise as introducing second-level concepts. We can therefore say that Plato has misunderstood how these words function, and is therefore looking in the wrong place for his 'unambiguous examples'. Accordingly our reaction is that Plato's theory

[4] This assumes that a previous acquaintance with a Form (*qua* perfect example), if fully recollected, will enable us to give an account of that Form (*qua* common characteristic). The assumption is, to say the least, questionable.

[5] This is a *version* of Moore's celebrated 'open question' argument: it shows that the word 'good' cannot be *defined* by examples.

has a philosophically respectable foundation only in the case of such rather special words as 'good'.

But evidently Plato saw things the other way about, and he came to feel that *all* general words were in much the same position. Even in the *Phaedo* there are some indications that he was inclined to extend his theory in this way,[6] and by the time that we come to book x of the *Republic* this extension is explicit. He announces there that *wherever* we have several things all called by the same name there is a corresponding Form (596a), even in the case of such things as beds and tables, but these Forms are still thought of, apparently, as imperceptible and intelligible examples of what a bed or table really is. At any rate, they are thought of as the kind of thing that God could *create*, and the beds and tables that we create are copies or imitations, *resembling* the Form (597a–c). (The idea is perhaps this: we can tell the difference between a good bed and a bad bed, which shows that we know not just what beds usually are but also what they *ought* to be. But such knowledge is not to be gained simply by perceiving the actual examples of beds in this world.) So Plato comes to adopt the very general view that *every* general word applies *primarily* to a Form (construed as an imperceptible and intelligible example), and only secondarily to the familiar, ordinary and perceptible examples around us: the latter are 'called after' the former.

It is not completely clear how much of this theory survives into the later dialogues. First, it seems to me very probable that Plato quite soon abandoned the theory of recollection. Even in the *Republic* the theory is never mentioned, though the *Republic* still retains the idea that knowledge is to be gained by turning the eye of the soul in the right direction, away from the things of this world and towards the Forms (518b–e). Some have seen an allusion to the theory at *Timaeus* 41d–e, but that must be regarded as very doubtful. In fact the only other dialogue where the *Phaedo*'s theory is clearly repeated is the *Phaedrus*, for there again we are told that every human soul must once have seen the Forms, at a time before it came to be embodied, since otherwise it would not be capable of understanding language (249b–c). But it is well to remember that this passage occurs within Socrates' long and fanciful speech in praise of love, and there are indications in the remainder of the dialogue that we should treat the details of this speech with some caution. Thus at 265b it is said that the speech is 'mythical', and 'perhaps attains some truth, but perhaps goes astray in other places'. And certainly it is itself an example of that writing which, at the end of the dialogue, we are told never to take seriously (277d–e). So it may not be unreasonable to surmise that at this date Plato regarded the theory of

[6] I have discussed this in my [144] 196–201.

recollection as an attractive conjecture, but one that he would not strongly insist upon.[7]

More significant is the way that this theory fares in the *Parmenides* and the *Theaetetus*, the two dialogues that open Plato's 'late' period. In the first part of the *Parmenides* various objections are raised against the view of Forms to be found in the *Phaedo* and the *Republic*, and the last of these is an argument purporting to show that even if there are Forms we could not know anything about them (133b–134e). It is true that this argument is, as it stands, wholly unconvincing, and when Plato introduces it as 'the greatest difficulty' (133b) he may possibly be speaking ironically, and suggesting to us that it is in fact the easiest to resolve (cf. *Theaetetus* 165b). Nevertheless it would still be somewhat surprising that he should give us no hint of the theory of recollection at this point, if that were still his own way of overcoming the problem; and certainly no such hint is given.

By contrast, the recollection theory is hinted at at one point during the *Theaetetus*. In an attempt to show how false belief is possible, Plato introduces the idea that the mind may be viewed as a wax tablet (191a–196c), containing impressions of what we have perceived and remember. But this wax tablet is also said to contain impressions of the Forms themselves – for example of the Form of man, and of horse, and of the numbers (195d–196a) – which are *not* imprinted by perception. Although nothing is said about how these imprints are in fact formed, it would seem to be quite a natural view that they were formed by some previous contact with the Forms themselves, as the recollection theory requires. However, this image is then rejected as unhelpful – it will not, after all, explain how we can have false beliefs about the numbers themselves – and Plato proposes a new image which seems incidentally to deny the theory of recollection. (The mind is compared to an aviary, the various birds in it corresponding to our knowledge of the various numbers, and it is said that the aviary is at first empty, but comes to be stocked as a result of teaching. Moreover this teaching is conceived as 'handing over' knowledge, from one person to another, and not at all a matter of encouraging someone to look in the right direction (197e–198b).) We may say, then, that during this part of the *Theaetetus* an image is proposed which does *suggest* the theory of recollection, though it does not affirm it, and this is then replaced with another image which incidentally denies recollection. But in the end that too proves unable to resolve the problem about false belief, and so both are rejected. As I shall argue shortly, the *Theaetetus* does still retain the view that understand-

[7] One might extend the same surmise to the tripartite theory of the soul. (270d–e strongly suggests that this theory needs to be re-examined.)

ing language requires a grasp of the Forms, but it tells us virtually nothing about how this grasp is achieved.

I think we can reasonably infer from this that Plato was at least doubtful about the recollection theory at the time when he was writing the *Parmenides* and the *Theaetetus*, and since he never once recurs to the theory thereafter it is very probable that he abandoned it. For example, the theory is not even mentioned as part of the doctrine of the 'friends of the Forms' who are criticised at *Sophist* 248a–249d, though their position is evidently very close to that of the *Republic* (and the *Timaeus*), and part of the argument is about what happens when a Form becomes known (248a–e). Again, the theory is not mentioned at *Statesman* 285c–286a, which aims to justify the procedure of seeking for an 'account' (i.e. definition, *logos*). There we are told that some things have sensible likenesses[8] which it is easy to point to, and by means of which they may be grasped without an account. But for the most important things there are no such clear images, and they can be revealed only by an account. We must therefore practise giving accounts in *all* cases, for even in a case where it is not essential it is a necessary training for the important cases where it is essential. Evidently there is no suggestion here either that recollection will aid us in searching for accounts, or that recollection will make it clear to us when a proposed account is indeed a correct account. But those were precisely the functions that the theory of recollection was meant to serve, when it was first introduced in the *Meno*. Finally, if we may assume (which is disputed) that the 'philosophical digression' in the *Seventh Letter* is by Plato, or at least is a fair report of what Plato himself had said on some occasion, then we can certainly infer that Plato no longer held the recollection theory at the end of his life. There he twice tries to describe how it is that genuine knowledge is at last attained (341c–d, 344b), but can speak only metaphorically in terms of illumination, and a light being kindled which then 'nourishes itself'. He would surely have said that what is illuminated will strike one with the familiarity of a memory, if that were what he still believed.

Supposing, then, that Plato did abandon the theory of recollection, we may ask *why* he did. It was surely not because he ceased to believe in the immortality of the soul. A likely explanation is that he came to abandon the view of Forms which had initially made the recollection theory seem attractive. The theory is supposed to explain how it is that we do, in a way, have knowledge of the Forms, although they cannot be perceived in this world. And the suggested explanation is that the Forms are not in this world but in another, that once upon a time we too were in that other world, and

[8] I discuss the implications of this phrase below.

that while there we did 'perceive' them. So the Forms must be thought of as the kind of thing that one could in principle 'perceive', so long as one is in the right 'place', and this picture may indeed seem to make some kind of sense when Forms are construed as special and unambiguous *examples*, which the things in this world *resemble*. But the *Parmenides* very clearly exposes this view of the Forms as a confusion: Forms cannot *both* be universals – i.e. the one thing common to *all* the many instances – and at the same time be themselves (special) instances of those universals.

If Forms are to be special and unambiguous examples, then evidently the Form of largeness must itself be a large thing and incapable of being small, and similarly the Form of smallness must be a small thing and incapable of being large, while the Form of equality must be an equal thing and incapable of being unequal. But, as Plato points out, this view of Forms clearly cannot be combined with the view that large things are large by having the Form of largeness *in* them (131a–e, 150a–d), though this is just what Plato does want to say of the universal. Furthermore, irrespective of how exactly it is that large things are related to the Form of largeness, if the Form is itself another large thing, then apparently[9] we shall need yet *another* Form of largeness to be the characteristic common both to the Form and to the large things we began with. And if this second Form of largeness is again a large thing, we shall be launched upon an infinite regress of Forms of largeness, which is absurd (131e–132b). To generalise this point, whatever the relation between Forms and particulars is, it cannot be that particulars *resemble* Forms (132d–133a). Now, a close analysis of these arguments shows that their real force is to demonstrate that a Form cannot *both* be a common characteristic *and* a (special) instance of it. Since Plato clearly does not want to give up the view that a Form is a common characteristic, he must therefore abandon the claim that they are also special and unambiguous examples. This leaves him the option of continuing to suppose that such special examples do exist, so long as he no longer identifies them with the Forms themselves. But no one would maintain that he ever did embrace this option, and it seems very probable that he himself thought of these arguments as showing that there were no such special examples. Moreover, he was evidently right to view these supposed entities with great suspicion. For example, how could there be an equal thing that was so unambiguously equal that it was not unequal to *anything at all*?

To delve more deeply, the original reason for supposing that the Form of F-ness was itself a special and unambiguous example of an F thing would

[9] As Vlastos has pointed out in [228], the argument needs a supplementary assumption (of 'Non-Identity') at this point. But I doubt whether Plato noticed this, as he does not point it out to us.

lead to the conclusion that this Form exemplified F-ness but exemplified no other Form whatever. It is something that is 'of one Form only' (*monoeides*), and does not exhibit *any* opposite characteristics (129c–130a). (If the Form of F-ness were also an example of G-ness, then when faced with it I might take it as an example of G-ness and not of F-ness. In that case, my acquaintance with it would not explain how I understand the word 'F'. That is, in order to be a genuinely unambiguous example there can be only one characteristic that it is an example of.) But it is a consequence of this that no Form, other than the Form of sameness, can exemplify sameness, which is to say that no such Form can be the same as anything, not even itself. Equally, no Form, other than the Form of otherness, can exemplify otherness, which is to say that no such Form can be other than anything, not even the things that are other than it. But these consequences are manifestly absurd (139c–e). Indeed we may apply the reasoning in this way: no Form, other than the Form of existence, can exist (cf. 141e–142a). This is a *reductio ad absurdum* with a vengeance. Clearly we must say that everything that exists participates in existence (and oneness, 144b–e), and in both of the 'opposites' sameness and otherness, and even imperceptible things are no exception to this. So there simply cannot be such 'unambiguous examples' as the theory of the *Phaedo* required.

It may be conjectured that Plato was first led to see that something must be wrong with the *Phaedo*'s theory by his new-found interest in such 'all-embracing' Forms as being, sameness and otherness. It is, after all, quite obvious that the theory cannot be consistently applied in these cases. But whatever the source of his insight, he certainly gives us, in the *Parmenides*, some very cogent objections to his earlier theory, and I believe that he was well aware of this himself. Accordingly, I believe that he thereafter abandoned the theory of the *Phaedo*, and ceased to think of Forms as unambiguous examples of themselves. The difficulty for this claim is that there do appear to be some passages in dialogues later than the *Parmenides* which reaffirm the old theory. One such stumbling-block is the *Timaeus*, which undeniably adopts a view of Forms very similar to that in the *Republic* and the *Phaedo*, and yet the orthodox dating for the *Timaeus* places it after the *Parmenides*. But we may deal with this objection by questioning the orthodox dating. The only positive reason for placing the *Timaeus* later than the *Parmenides* is its literary style, but I do not myself believe that stylometric criteria are at all reliable as evidence for chronology, and there are besides several quite independent reasons for placing the *Timaeus* in Plato's middle period.[10] I shall therefore say no more of this issue here. But

[10] The classic statement of the case is Owen [114]. I have added some further considerations in my [180], 7–9, 22–30, 146–50.

undoubtedly the *Sophist* and the *Statesman* are later than the *Parmenides*, and if these dialogues reaffirm the old theory, then Plato cannot have drawn from the *Parmenides* the moral that I am supposing.

There are a few places in the *Sophist* where Plato seems, at first glance, to be still assuming (illegitimately) that a Form is an instance of itself, but closer scrutiny soon dispels this appearance. The first occurs during the criticism of Parmenides' 'One Being' at 244b–245d. At one point in that discussion Plato observes that what has several parts may have oneness as an attribute (*pathos tou henos echein*), but cannot be 'the one itself' (*auto to hen*), since what is genuinely one (*to alēthōs hen*) must be without parts (245a). This appears to assume that the Form of oneness must itself be a thing that is supremely one, to such an extent that it has no parts at all. But it is very difficult to believe that this is Plato's own position in the *Sophist*. At any rate, he is going to tell us in the more positive part of his discussion that the Form of otherness (or not being <so-and-so>) is divided up into numerous parts, one of which is, for example, the part comprising those things which are other than beautiful (i.e. not beautiful) (257c–258a, 258d–e). So one would certainly expect the Form of oneness to be similarly divided, perhaps with a part comprising those things that are (say) one *finger*, or possibly with a distinguishable part for *each* thing that exists (since whatever exists is one), as at *Parmenides* 144c–e. Bearing this in mind, I think it more plausible to say that Plato is not committing *himself* to the view that the Form of oneness cannot have parts, but is making use of the fact that his adversary Parmenides is committed to this. As Plato saw it, Parmenides denied any plurality at all (244b–d) and must therefore have identified his 'One Being' both with oneness and with being, denying parts to any of them. Or perhaps it is enough just to say that Plato's overall purpose in this part of the dialogue (242c–250e) is simply to persuade us that we understand the notion of being no better than the notion of not being, and he is not necessarily committed to the validity of any of the arguments he uses. (Certainly he is not committed to the validity of the arguments he uses earlier when trying to persuade us that we do not understand the notion of not being, 237b–241b.)

This last plea cannot, of course, be used when we turn to the more positive part of the discussion, from 251a. Yet here too we find Plato affirming, for example, that rest cannot be in motion (presumably because it must be at rest), and that motion cannot be at rest (presumably because it must be in motion) (252d, 254d, 255a). But, as Vlastos has pointed out,[11] Plato's words here are ambiguous, and may perfectly well be taken to mean that

[11] Vlastos [213].

whatever is at rest cannot be in motion, and *whatever is in motion* cannot be at rest. Moreover, it makes very much better sense of the argument if we do interpret them in the latter way. (The same applies to other similar passages in this part of the *Sophist*, notably 258b–c.) In fact I have argued elsewhere[12] that we cannot understand Plato's argument in the *Sophist* unless we do see that his statements of the form 'F-ness is G' *must* sometimes be interpreted in the generalising way, as meaning 'whatever is F is G', though on other occasions they *must* be interpreted as singular statements about the Form (or kind) F-ness itself. Indeed, Plato slips from one use to the other in a very disconcerting fashion. I think we may conclude that he is now so little inclined to view Forms as 'separated' from their instances in this world that he even fails to distinguish clearly between statements about the Forms themselves and statements about all their instances.

Whereas the *Sophist* is clearly much concerned with the metaphysical status of the Forms (or kinds) that it treats of, the *Statesman* is largely neutral on such issues. For the most part, its recommendations on how to seek for an adequate 'account' of statesmanship (or anything else), and its suggestions on how simple examples may be used to guide us in more complex cases (277d ff.), have no metaphysical implications at all. But the brief passage at 285d–286a, which explains why it is necessary to seek for 'accounts', would appear to be an exception. As Cherniss has pointed out,[13] this passage apparently speaks of the instances of a Form as its *likenesses*, or *images*, which is standard terminology in the dialogues of the middle period, but which presupposes just that view of the nature of Forms that the *Parmenides* has so convincingly attacked. As a matter of fact the details of the passage are somewhat peculiar. It tells us that some things (*ta men tōn ontōn*) have perceptible likenesses through which they may be explained to an enquirer, but the greatest and most important things (*ta megista kai timiōtata*) have no such images clear to men. The incorporeal things (*asōmata*), which are the important ones, can only be revealed by an account. What is odd here is the implication that the things that do have suitable perceptible likenesses are *not* incorporeal, for in that case it would seem that they cannot be Forms (though it is not clear what else they might be). The incorporeal things no doubt are Forms, but it would be possible to take the statement that they 'have no images made clear to men' as true simply because they have no images at all. On this view the passage states, in contradiction of the theory of the middle period, that no Forms have images. But I confess that I do not find this interpretation very convincing, and Cherniss is no doubt right to compare the passage with *Phaedrus* 250b, where it is implied that important

[12] Bostock [190]. [13] Cherniss [115].

Forms such as justice do have images in this world, but these images are not clear to us, and fail to remind us of the Form itself. (By contrast, the images of beauty in this world are clear to us.) I think it more likely, then, that Plato is indeed meaning to speak of Forms throughout, and wishes to say that some can in practice be grasped well enough by pointing to their instances, though others cannot.[14] He is, no doubt, speaking carelessly when he suggests that the former are corporeal, and I would suggest that he is speaking equally carelessly when he refers to the instances of a Form as likenesses or images of it. This is the terminology of the middle period, and I imagine that Plato has slipped back into it because he has no other handy and familiar general term for the instances of a Form. But the doctrine which once made this terminology appropriate is I suspect absent;[15] certainly the *Statesman* does not repeat the imagery of the *Phaedrus*, whereby the Forms are in one world and their instances here are in another.

Let us recapitulate. Plato began with the belief that where we have a general word, truly applied to a number of things, there is some one thing, a Form, that all those many things share. He was also apt to suppose that we do not understand the word unless we can *say* what it is that all these instances have in common. At first he applied this view mainly to the central concepts of ethics, and he seems to have supposed that in other cases there is not much difficulty in saying what a number of instances have in common. But further reflection on the ethical problem led him to believe (rightly?) that in this case there was a serious difficulty over the instances themselves, and he then (wrongly) came to see the same difficulty in many other cases too. This leads him to the theory of the *Phaedo*. To resolve the difficulty we must postulate the existence of special unambiguous examples, available only to the eye of the mind and not the eye of the body, which we have 'seen' in a previous existence and now dimly recollect. So he presents us with what clearly is a theory about how we understand our language, and which allows him now to distinguish between two levels of understanding. The ordinary understanding of general words that we all possess rests on the fact that we have a dim recollection of those special and unambiguous examples, and it does not presuppose an ability to *say* what these words mean. But what we should strive for is a deeper and properly philosophical understand-

[14] From the context, it would seem that the Form of weaving is one that can be grasped well enough from its instances, though we must practise giving an 'account' of it, as a guide for the Form of statesmanship, which can only be grasped by an 'account'.

[15] I would say the same of the *Seventh Letter*, which also refers to instances as images (342b ff.).

ing, to be attained by the mind alone and without help from the senses, which will enable us to provide definitions or analyses of the concepts concerned.

In setting out this theory Plato fell into a logical confusion. The special and unambiguous examples that it postulates he called Forms, while at the same time he continued to think of a Form as something common to its many instances. Thus the Form is inconsistently viewed as a special and unambiguous example of *itself*. In the *Parmenides* Plato has certainly seen that this theory runs into difficulties. The arguments in the first part of that dialogue do very clearly show that, if we hang on to the view that Forms are common characteristics (as Plato does), then we cannot *also* say that they are special and unambiguous examples. These arguments do not by themselves show that there cannot be such special examples at all, though it is not altogether clear that Plato realised this, but they do at any rate point to problems with this conception. Moreover, there are arguments in the second part of the dialogue which can clearly be applied to show that the conception is indeed an incoherent one. At the very least, we can certainly say that in the *Parmenides* Plato expresses very serious doubts over the theory of the *Phaedo*.

I believe that this in fact led him to abandon the theory. He continues, certainly, to believe in Forms as universals, and he continues to view the philosopher's task as that of gaining improved and explicit understanding of these Forms. But if we take the view that the *Timaeus* belongs to his middle period, then we can say that the later dialogues show hardly any trace of the theory of special and unambiguous examples. (The exception is *Statesman* 285d–286a, which I take to be a merely verbal echo of the earlier view.) Certainly, we hear no more of recollection, and – more importantly – we hear no more of the separation of the Forms from the changing things of this world. On the contrary, the *Sophist* appears to take the view that to talk about the Forms just is to talk generally about their instances, and the *Statesman* acknowledges that a philosophical enquiry may perfectly well make use of such a grasp of Forms as perception may provide. The author of the *Phaedo* would hardly have approved of these sentiments.

Yet there is one aspect of the *Phaedo*'s theory which does survive, and this brings us back to the topic of how we understand our language. Plato still supposes that a general word has meaning by standing for a Form, and hence that to understand the word is to have some kind of grasp of the Form in question. So language presupposes the existence of Forms. This he reaffirms at the end of the first part of the *Parmenides*, where we are told that, despite the difficulties which have just been developed about the Forms, they must nevertheless exist. For one who denies this 'will completely destroy the power of discourse' (135c). In the *Sophist* too language is said to require Forms, 'for it is through the combination of Forms, one with another, that a statement (*logos*)[16] comes to exist' (259e).[17] But the point is perhaps best illustrated from the course of Plato's argument in the *Theaetetus*.

The first part of that dialogue ends with an argument to show that perception by itself is never knowledge (184b–186e). It is claimed that being is not a perceptible thing, so perception by itself cannot reach being, whereas knowledge pertains only to what is true, and truth always involves being. Hence perception cannot reach truth, and so cannot be knowledge. The interpretation of this argument is disputed, but I see no viable alternative to that given by Burnyeat,[18] which takes the claim that truth always involves being as a claim that every (true) statement can be regarded as containing the verb 'to be', no doubt as a copula.[19] If this is right, then Plato's thought is that a statement (whether true or false) always involves the notion of being, and to understand that statement one must therefore grasp the notion of being, but since being is not a perceptible thing, perception cannot provide us with the relevant understanding. (As to how we *do* grasp the notion of being, Plato tells us only that it is done by the mind, operating independently of the senses, but gives no further elucidation (185c–e).) The general theory behind this argument is, then, that a statement consists of several terms, that one does not understand the statement until one grasps each of these terms individually, and at least one of these terms – namely being – will be a Form (i.e. an imperceptible item).

The second part of the dialogue, while not questioning this result about perception, *does* put in question the assumption that whatever is known must be a truth, and hence a statement. It begins at once with a puzzle about the relationship between one who believes some statement and the *terms* of that statement, for it seems very natural to say that he must *know* these terms, but that then makes it difficult to see how his belief could nevertheless

[16] *Logos* very clearly means 'statement' at 260c, so it should bear the same meaning at 260a, and hence also at 259e.

[17] There is a well-known puzzle here. Plato appears to imply that *every* statement asserts a combination of Forms, and yet goes on to consider the statements 'Theaetetus sits' and 'Theaetetus flies', which seem at best to assert a 'combination' of Form and particular, rather than of Form and Form (263a ff.). It is difficult to see what to say about this, but see n. 19 below.

[18] Burnyeat [181]. (I have discussed alternative interpretations in my [180], 110–42.)

[19] *Perhaps* this is the answer to the problem of n. 17 above. Even the simple verb 'sits' is held to involve the notion of being, as revealed in its paraphrase 'is sitting'. (Cf. Aristotle, *de Interpretatione* 21b9–10.) Hence 'Theaetetus sits' asserts of Theaetetus a combination of the Forms being and sitting. (Note that at 263b this statement is said to assert 'things that are' (plural) of Theaetetus.)

be false. While Plato can provide an explanation (in terms of 'the wax tablet') of how one's beliefs about perceptible objects can be false, he cannot see how to extend this to encompass false beliefs about imperceptible objects (particularly the numbers), so this puzzle remains unresolved (188–200). But, at least as I interpret the dialogue,[20] it continues still to be concerned with the relationship between the judger and the *terms* of his judgement in what follows.

As we have said, this appears on the face of it to be a case of non-propositional knowledge, and therefore a kind of knowledge that does *not* 'reach truth', in the sense used at the end of the first part of the dialogue. But during the discussion of false belief it has been pointed out that when the item concerned is a perceptible item, then one is in a position to make judgements about it if one can perceive it, and merely perceiving the item can certainly be distinguished from knowing it (191a–194b). On the other hand, Plato has not seen how to draw an analogous distinction where imperceptible items are concerned (195d–196c), and accordingly the final section of the dialogue is, I believe, mainly concerned to discuss one's knowledge of these imperceptible items, i.e. Forms.

At least since the *Phaedo* Plato has seen that we must allow for two levels of understanding: there is the ordinary understanding of language that we all possess, and there is the deeper philosophical knowledge that we aspire to, and which manifests itself in the ability to 'give an account', i.e. a definition or analysis. We may hope, then, to reserve the title of knowledge for the latter, which will allow us to maintain that this knowledge does 'reach truth', namely the truth expressed in the account. But now Plato notices a very awkward objection to this view: the theory of 'Socrates' Dream' (201c–202d) brings out the fact that a definition of one thing will explain it in terms of *others*, and these other things will have to be *known* if mastery of the definition is to manifest knowledge of the thing defined. But if this means that these other things in turn have to be defined, a vicious regress apparently follows. In short: definitions must eventually end in indefinables; if the definitions are to manifest knowledge, then the indefinables must be known; and hence there must be a kind of *knowledge* which does not involve any such 'account'. We may hope to evade this result by varying what we will allow as an 'account', but at least in the *Theaetetus*[21]

[20] Evidently this interpretation is somewhat speculative. I have defended it in greater detail in my [180].

[21] Fine has argued [182], that Plato's way out of the problem is to allow accounts to go round in circles, in that the account of A will mention how it combines with various other items, including say B, and the account of B will similarly mention how it combines, *inter alia*, with A. But while this may perhaps be Plato's *later* position, it is not to be found in the *Theaetetus* itself.

Plato does not see a way of doing this (206c–210a), and so the result of the second part of the dialogue is that the conclusion of its first part is undermined. We cannot keep our 'two levels of understanding' separated, and we must admit that there is a kind of knowledge which does not 'reach truth', namely the judger's knowledge of the (imperceptible and indefinable) terms of his judgements. (This knowledge we can perhaps describe as the ability to recognise the item, and distinguish it from others, in all its various combinations. Just this is what we do count as 'knowing the letters' (206a–b); it is a possible way of understanding what it is to 'know Theaetetus' (209c); and it is what the *Cratylus* has often said to be the role of a name in language (e.g. 388b, 422d, 428e). It does not, however, involve any kind of 'account' of the thing in question.)

Thus the problem that underlies all of the second part of the *Theaetetus* is one that stems from Plato's basic assumption that general words have meaning by standing for Forms (and hence to understand the word one must in some way 'grasp' the Form). In the *Theaetetus* he tells us nothing very much about the nature of the Forms (except that they are imperceptible), and nothing much about how we do come to grasp them (except that it is done by the mind alone, independently of the senses). As I have argued, there is no reason to suppose that he still endorses the theory of the *Phaedo* on these topics, but at the same time he does not appear to have any other positive theory with which to replace it. Nor do later dialogues seem to shed any light on the problem of how we first manage to acquire that grasp of the Forms that is manifested in our ordinary understanding of language (though they do, of course, have more to say on how to seek for the deeper philosophical knowledge that we aspire to). But it seems clear that Plato never allowed this gap in his overall position to disturb his confidence in the basic assumption: the role of a general word is to stand for a Form, and since we do understand general words, we must have some kind of access to the Forms they stand for.

This assumption one might well regard as Plato's main and most enduring contribution to the theory of language. I hope that it hardly needs saying these days that the assumption is wholly mistaken. To put matters in our terminology, the role of a predicate is not to *stand for* any kind of abstract object, and it is quite misleading to construe our understanding of predicates as some kind of 'acquaintance' with the 'objects' they allegedly denote. The point is just that a predicate is used to *say* something of a subject, and not to *name* anything. It is remarkable that this insight too is Plato's. Distinguishing names (*onomata*) from verbs (*rhēmata*), he observes in the *Sophist* that neither by itself *says* anything, and even the shortest sentence must have one of each. Such a sentence 'not only names, but completes something, weaving together a name and a verb' (262d). Thus verbs do *not* function in the same way as names do; they have quite a different kind of role.

Unfortunately Plato never followed through this extremely significant point. It did not occur to him to argue that since the verb 'is' does *not* function as a name, we do not need to postulate an abstract object, being, to be what the verb does name, an object which every competent user of 'is' has access to. It certainly did not occur to him to extend this thought to the claim that *all* general words function more as verbs than as names, and so are to be assigned a predicative rather than a naming role. (Nor, of course, could anyone else see how to extend the thought in this way, until first Frege and then Russell had made clear how natural language conceals quantificational structure.) As a result, people laboured for centuries with the model that Plato first introduced: general words stand for abstract objects (universals), and anyone who can talk must therefore have some kind of access to these objects, however mysterious this supposed 'access' may seem to be. Yet we should recognise that it was Plato himself who first pointed to a feature of language which has ultimately led to the rejection of that model: we do not need to suppose that all words function essentially as names. But neither Plato nor his successors saw the full significance of that crucial observation that verbs are not names, and every sentence must contain a verb.

3

Cratylus' theory of names and its refutation

BERNARD WILLIAMS

At the very beginning of Plato's *Cratylus* Hermogenes explains Cratylus' view by saying that it supposes there to be a certain natural correctness (*orthotēs*) of names; that this correctness is the same for all linguistic groups; and (very strongly) that it has nothing to do with what name anyone actually applies to anything – so that, he is quoted as saying to Hermogenes, 'your name would not be Hermogenes, even if everyone called you that' (383b). This last point implies something which explicitly emerges later, that, for Cratylus, the question whether some word '*N*' is the *correct* name of a given item is the same as the question whether '*N*' is that item's name at all.

The assumption that the answers to those questions must be the same is not shared by everyone in the dialogue. It is shared by Hermogenes, for reasons which are (roughly) the opposite of Cratylus'. It is not shared by Socrates, whose final position requires us to distinguish the questions; or rather, to put it more precisely, it requires us to make a distinction which can be handily put by us in terms of a possible divergence between *the name of* X and *the correct name of* X, and is often so put in the dialogue, but which can also be expressed, as we shall see later, in terms of two kinds of correctness.

In trying to give some account of Cratylus' theory of names, I shall particularly emphasise that distinction and Cratylus' denial of it. Some of what I include in that theory is not advanced by Cratylus in the dialogue, but by Socrates in the course of his attempt, with Hermogenes, to elaborate a notion of 'the correctness of names' (see 391b for the start of their enquiry); but Cratylus fully adopts their theory (428c), and, whatever other status these conceptions may have, they are (at least in outline) consequences of the general views which are refuted in the argument against Cratylus at the end of the dialogue. Whether Plato displays any independent attachment to them is a question I shall touch on at the end.

According to Cratylus, then, if '*N*' is not the name of a given item, it makes no difference if people call it '*N*' – or, perhaps, try to call it so: the embarrassment at this point will grow into an objection. Equally, if it is the name of that item, it makes no difference if people do not so call it. The name-relation is purely binary, relating a word and an item. Names can, of course, be of different kinds, and while the first examples are proper names of people, this is not the basic case, and the theory applies to general terms; indeed, it applies to proper names because it applies to general terms. Exactly what kind of item is named by a general term is a question on which the dialogue gives us no help, and it need not concern the present discussion.

What could such a binary relation be? The first level of discussion which contributes to answering the question gives us the principle that if '*N*' is the name of a given item, and '*N*' can be resolved etymologically into other names, then the combination of those names must be appropriate to the item. But this, clearly, only raises another question; we eventually have to invoke a theory of elements, and these achieve their relation to what is named through imitation (*mimēsis*) (422 seq.), the basic idea, sketchily enough conveyed, being that the action of producing a certain vocal sound resembles some process in the domain of what is to be named. This theory, elaborated in detail through the labours of the etymological section, and presented with an immense degree of irony by Socrates to Cratylus, is agreed by him to represent his view (428c).

We originally saw that Cratylus holds

(1) If '*N*' is the name at all of an item, it is the correct name of that item.

We have now learned

(2) If '*N*' is the name of an item, '*N*' bears a certain complex relation to that item.

Let us call that relation *the Φ-relation*. The relation is to be explained in terms of the procedures for resolving names into other names, and, ultimately

(3) the Φ-relation is grounded in the idea of an element of a name being a *mimēma* (430a9) of a process or natural feature.

There is a difficulty lurking in this which Plato seems to mark without pursuing. (3) requires that there should be elements of names which are related to reality through *mimēsis*, but it does not require that they should themselves be names: indeed they are not, and an elementary name – the simplest thing which is itself a name – is, relative to these elements, itself a complex.[1]

[1] The point is discussed by Norman Kretzmann in his [166].

While the theory permits this, there seems no reason why it should actually require it. Socrates is obviously right in saying at 422b that the correctness of those names that are elementary will have to be tested 'by some other method' – i.e. not by etymological resolution; but it does not follow that they must be resolved into something other than names. They might be names whose correctness is to be tested by a method which does not involve resolving them at all.

It is unclear why the theory should not yield this outcome. There is indeed the point that the ultimate simples are sounds, which, except for the vowels, cannot be uttered by themselves: the nearest we can come to isolating them in speech is to add further and arbitrary elements to make them pronounceable. This point is, of course, made at 393e, merely in order to illustrate, early in the argument with Hermogenes, the general idea that the addition or subtraction of some elements need not destroy the effect of a name. But the status of the elements surely raises a question about the theory of the *Φ*-relation. Why is it that the ultimate elements, when made with a little assistance into isolable names, turn out to be the names of those sounds (or letters), and not names of the natural features to which they are linked by *mimēsis?* The problem for Cratylus should not just be that the word for hardness can be either *sklērotēs* or *sklērotēr* (434c), but that it is not *rh(ō)* itself.

When Cratylus enters the dialogue at 428, he asserts claim (1) of his position in the strongest possible terms, resisting at the same time Socrates' suggestion that 'legislators' (*nomothetai*), regarded as originally imposing names, might be expected to have done their work better or worse. 'So are all names correctly applied (*orthōs keitai*)?', Socrates asks, and Cratylus answers, 'Inasmuch as they are names' (429b10–11). In reply, Socrates makes explicit the distinction denied by (1), in the form of distinguishing between the view that the name 'Hermogenes' does not apply (*keisthai*) to the third person present, and the view that it does apply, but 'not rightly'; and Cratylus says that it does not apply to him at all, but is rather the name of someone who has the appropriate nature, i.e. to whom that name bears the *Φ*-relation.

Socrates' essential step in refuting these claims is to show that they leave Cratylus with nothing coherent to say when one introduces the dimension of what speakers actually do with names, a dimension necessarily left out by any view which finds the whole account of naming in the *Φ*-relation, since that relation is simply a relation between words and things. Socrates' first example (429e) ingeniously introduces the act of addressing someone (*proseipein*) with the wrong name. The example is of one who, in foreign parts, greets Cratylus and says 'Welcome, Athenian visitor, Hermogenes, son of Smikrion!'[2] The question is, does he not even *address* Cratylus, but rather Hermogenes? Or no one? When Cratylus replies that such a person would seem to him *phthegxasthai allōs*, 'to speak' – one could take it to mean – 'to no purpose', his answer leaves Socrates still with the room to ask (rather oddly) whether what he spoke was true or false; but this elicits the explanation that he would be making a noise, like someone banging a pot, and this retrospectively offers the possibility of a different reading for *allōs*: he would *merely* be producing speech.[3]

This conclusion can be related quite simply to Cratylus' position. It is important that Cratylus does not have to say (what would be simply false) that the speaker addresses Hermogenes rather than Cratylus. He can reasonably say that there is a speech-act, which may be called 'addressing someone by name', such that there are two separate necessary conditions of its being true that *X* addresses *Y* by name:

(i) *X* addresses (speaks to, directs words to, etc.) *Y*;
(ii) In the course of (i), *X* uses a name which is a name of *Y*.

It will follow that in the situation which Socrates puts to Cratylus, the speaker does not address anyone by name: not Cratylus, because of condition (ii), and not Hermogenes, because of condition (i). If the purpose of his speaking was to address someone by name, then indeed he spoke *allōs* – even if Cratylus' final gloss on that failure is a little exaggerated.

However, that does not get Cratylus very far, and once the speech-act aspect of the question is raised at all, Socrates is in a position to show that even to understand Cratylus' theory requires one to understand possibilities which Cratylus denies. He shows this, first, with regard to mistakes, and, ultimately, with regard to convention.

Cratylus denied that, in the imagined situation, the speaker addressed anyone by name, since he did not satisfy both the conditions of doing that with respect to any one person. But he cannot deny that the speaker satisfied condition (i) with respect to the man in front of him: he certainly, for

[2] Hermogenes' father's name was Hipponikos: 384a8, 406b8. It has been conjectured that Cratylus really was son of Smikrion: cf. Diels–Kranz (D–K), *Die Fragmente der Vorsokratiker* (6th edn), II.65.1 and note.

[3] This sense of *allōs*, for instance in Sophocles, *Philoctetes* 947, 'a mere image', is admittedly well attested only where *allōs* occurs with a substantive (see Jebb, *ad loc.*). But the reading suggested, besides tying up with Cratylus' later remark, has the advantage that it gives him a reply which relates to, and undercuts, *all* the alternatives that Socrates presents in his question. *Phthegxasthai* is, of course, a standard term not only for human sounds, but for animal cries (see Aristotle, *Historia Animalium* 535a30) and for noises from inanimate things – for instance, a pot when struck, *Theaetetus* 179d. (I am grateful to Malcolm Schofield and Martha Nussbaum for comments on this matter.)

instance, spoke to him. Moreover, he used a particular name in relation to him; and Cratylus must know all that, or he could not diagnose the situation as he does. So Cratylus must accept that the speaker performed *some* speech-act in relation to the man in front of him, and indeed he must know what it is for *X to call Y* '*N*'. But if so, then he must know what it is for *X* to call *Y* '*N*' although '*N*' is not *Y*'s name, and he is in a position to recognise mistake. Moreover, he must know what it is for almost everyone usually to call *Y* '*N*', and he is in a position to recognise convention.

The argument about mistake is developed in terms of the allocation (*dianomē*) of names. One can identify *Y* and a particular name independently of one another, and one can bring that name to *Y*'s attention (431a1–2, cf. 430e6–7, very forceful expressions of perceptual confrontation), just as one can bring to his attention a certain picture; and one can claim that what is displayed is his name or picture. Whatever relation constitutes a particular name's being his name – if, for instance, as Cratylus believes, it is much the same relation as constitutes a picture's being his picture – that claim may be false. Even when it is, there has certainly been an allocation; hence there are mistaken allocations of names.

It is important to see what a *dianomē* is. It is an activity which can be performed on either names or pictures in relation to their objects, and, according to Socrates' introduction of it (430d), it has the properties that, in the case of a picture, if the picture is allocated to a person of which it is the picture, then the *dianomē* is correct (*orthē*), while in the case of a name, if it is allocated to the person of which it the name, then the *dianomē* is both correct and true. This suggests that the *dianomē* does not simply involve the claim 'this is your picture (name)', for in any sense in which that is true or false, as well as right or wrong, with names, it is equally so with pictures. We should rather expect that *dianomē* is an activity which, when done with a name, yields a *logos*, something that can be true, and when done with a picture, does not. We can imagine a wordless *dianomē* of a picture – handing it to the subject, for instance; and we can imagine a partly worded one, in the form of someone's saying, for instance, 'You are . . .' and presenting a picture. The analogy to this in the case of names would be saying 'You are . . .' and presenting a name. But 'presenting a name' is itself a linguistic activity (cf. 387 c6, 'naming is part of speaking'); and saying 'You are . . .', followed by presenting '*N*', comes to saying 'You are *N*', which, unlike its picture analogue, can be true as well as correct.[4] Of course, there is also a kind of statement that is available in both cases: that statement which

[4] Cf. the formulation at 429c6 of the question to which the discussion of *dianomē* helps to give an answer: 'Is someone not mistaken who says *that he is Hermogenes?*'

Socrates gives, and which in the name case takes the form 'this is your name'.

Nothing here, any more than elsewhere, restricts the discussion to proper names. Indeed, in the picture case it seems that the pictures can be taken as ascribing the general properties of male and female (431a3–4). The model therefore has some potential to destroy those general arguments against the possibility of falsehood, naturally associated with Cratylus' position, which put in an appearance at 429d; and that is recognised, in a rather sketchy way, at 431b. Those arguments rest, in one way or another, on the idea that an expression '*E*' cannot misfit reality, since it must be allocated either to nothing, or to whatever it is that it fits. But this critic must have some conception of what counts as 'fitting', as I have called it, and of what it is that a given '*E*' would fit. But then he has an understanding of some (at least) statements of the form '"*E*" fits *that*', an understanding which allows also for the possibility of such a statement's being false; and that possibility is the same as that of '*E*' misfitting reality.

This has the same structure as the *dianomē* argument in the *Cratylus*. Of course, the potential for destroying the argument against falsehood cannot be fully realised until a *general* way is found of locating independently the item which '*E*' fits or misfits, and this is not achieved until the *Sophist*, if then. The point that the *Cratylus* does not achieve this has been made by John McDowell,[5] who points out that 'the function of indicating what is being talked about is not credited to a constituent in the account' but has to be discharged by an act of confrontation. (A similar limitation, it may be said, can be found in the account given by the *Theaetetus*, in so far as that is even partly successful, of false identity statements.) The *Cratylus*, however, disclaims any attempt to give a general answer (429d7–8), and what it does say perhaps has a greater potential for being generalised than the criticism allows. McDowell also objects that the *Cratylus*' contribution is not merely limited but misguided, on the ground that it tries to assimilate falsehood to partial accuracy, as though an expression could be discovered to misfit reality only if its general shape were right but other features wrong. But this is to connect the discussion of *dianomē* too closely to what follows. That discussion lasts to 431c3, and indeed relates, though not in very general terms, to the puzzles of falsehood; from 431c4, Socrates takes off on a further discussion (*au*, c4), designed to deal with the Φ-relation itself.

This discussion reverts to issues of name-*giving*, and the activities of a *nomothetēs*. Plato might be thought to invite confusion by moving so easily between name-giving and the use of established words, since the possibili-

[5] McDowell [177], 236

ties of mistake are evidently so different in the two. But – as Plato clearly sees – they are different only if certain assumptions are made, assumptions which are denied by Cratylus. According to Cratylus, there is no act which a *nomothetēs* or anyone else can perform to *make* '*N*' the name of *Y* – '*N*' either bears the required *Φ*-relation to *Y* or it does not. Hence what is called 'name-giving' will be merely a trivial variant on describing. The distinction between name-giving and using an established name will collapse also at the other end of the spectrum, with that radical Humpty-Dumpty view which Hermogenes offers early on (384d1–2, 385a) as one version of what he opposes to Cratylus. As Cratylus assimilates name-giving to describing, so this assimilates describing to name-giving. The view, opposed to both of these, that what is *Y*'s name depends on 'agreement and custom',[6] precisely leaves room for the distinction, since there is an important difference between following a practice and trying to initiate one.

In his attack on the *Φ*-relation itself, Socrates first shows that there is a conflict between Cratylus' faith in *mimēsis* (his thesis (3)) and the all-or-nothing view that he takes of the name-relation, since *mimēsis* depends on resemblance, and resemblance is a matter of degree. The very notion of one thing's being an *eikōn*, a representation, of another, involves this point; for the only *absolute* notion of resemblance that could be used is that of indistinguishability, but an item indistinguishable from Cratylus would not be a representation of Cratylus, but 'another Cratylus'. The very idea of a representation of *X*, such as Cratylus takes a name to be, already implies at least a selection among the properties of *X*. The following argument, including the examples at 434–5, works from this point to show that we can recognise that '*N*' is the name of *Y* independently of the exactness of its representation, and this, like the argument about *dianomē*, undermines thesis (1). But it goes further, for the same considerations show that one can recognise '*N*' as the name of *Y* independently of resemblance altogether. (3) is wrong, and, as Hermogenes said (414c2), getting resemblance to do this job is a sticky business,[7] and we have to fall back on agreement. It is merely custom and agreement that makes a given name the name of a given item, and this excludes not merely this particular candidate for the *Φ*-relation but any kind of *Φ*-relation as constituting the name-relation itself.

The conclusion may be put in terms of the conditions for something's being a name; and that could leave it open whether there was some further question about the correctness of the names which, as things are, we use.

[6] *Sunthēkē kai ethos*, the standard phrase in the dialogue: cf. *ethei tōn ethisantōn*, 384d8. As Robinson pointed out, it is only in that passage and in conjunction with that phrase that *nomōi* in this dialogue expresses the contrast to *phusis*: see his [173], 112.

[7] 435c4–5.

Alternatively, the conclusion may itself be expressed in terms of correctness, as it is at 435c. In those terms, the conclusion will be that agreement and custom govern everyday correctness – they will be the determinants of whether someone has correctly used a name which we have in our language. In that case, the further question that might possibly arise would be about the correctness of our language. We may then distinguish two ways in which questions about correctness may be raised. There are certainly questions of internal correctness, to be settled by reference to our linguistic practices. There may or may not be a question of external correctness, a question about the correctness of our linguistic practices.

Socrates agrees with Hermogenes that custom and agreement are the sole determinants of internal correctness. Hermogenes, however, thinks that there is no further question of external correctness, while Socrates thinks that there is: there are requirements on what a language has to be, which follow from what it has to do. This is the point of the tool analogies at 387 seq. But this, as Kretzmann[8] has made very clear, has nothing to do with any idea of the material properties of words resembling the world, as was claimed in the theory of the Φ-relation. The resources of the language can be better or worse adapted to the requirements of dialectic, and that will make it better or worse in an external sense, but it will be so only in virtue of its structural properties and the semantic relations of its terms to each other, and not in virtue of their shape or sound or any such feature.

Socrates, then, differs from both Hermogenes and Cratylus in thinking that there are two questions, of internal and external correctness; or, in the alternative formulation, that there is one question about what the name for a given item is, and another about whether the practices that undoubtedly assign it that name are correct. Hermogenes thinks that there is only one question, settled by the appeal to our practices. Cratylus thinks that there is one question, to be settled by the basically external device of the Φ-relation; but Socrates' own answer to the external question will be on totally different lines from that.

Socrates' conclusions are not formally inconsistent with claiming that names do as a matter of fact possess some mimetic features; nor do they strictly exclude the aim of remodelling the language so that names acquire such features. Many have thought that Plato does show some real attachment to the mimetic principle. But, so far as the actual language is concerned, the treatment of the etymological enterprise as a whole, and particularly the mimetic aspect, is loaded with irony and warnings (cf. 426b1, the reference to the expert; 428d, Socrates' doubts; and many other

[8] Kretzmann [166], especially 135. But see Schofield [174], 61–2, n. 2.

passages); while it is a notable fact that Socrates is prepared to rerun the entire diagnosis of the language on lines opposite to the Heraclitean principles which he and Hermogenes have used. He indeed says at 435c2–3 'it pleases me that names should be as far as possible like things', a formulation neutral between explanation of the actual language and aspiration for a better one; but it is permissible to take this as referring to what Socrates indeed claimed long before, that the structure of language should represent the structure of things.

Certainly that is all we should expect Plato to find important. Here one must bear in mind not just the conclusions already discussed, but the powerfully demystifying arguments towards the end of the dialogue about what might be learned from language. Cratylan *mimēsis* is not what makes our names function as names, and, if they display such features at all, the question arises of how they came to do so. They will, at best, be a flickering record of observations made by the *nomothetēs* (as one might say, by human experience). As a recipe for linguistic improvement, again, the mimetic principle has nothing to offer. The functions of language, and the purposes for which it might be improved, are to teach, learn, inform, divide up reality. The knowledge required for that can appear in language only if someone possesses it already; and while there might be point in making that knowledge appear structurally, and thus improving language dialectically, there can be no such point to altering it in the direction of Cratylan *mimēsis*.

Even if it is not formally inconsistent with them, an attachment to Cratylan *mimēsis* is in fact banished by the conclusions of the *Cratylus*. This brilliant, tough-minded and still underestimated dialogue does not only show that the idea of language's having mimetic powers could not explain what language is; it leaves the belief in such powers looking like what it is, a belief in magic.

4

Aristotle on names and their signification

DAVID CHARLES

I Introduction

Aristotle's discussion of names (*onomata*) and their meaning or signification (*sēmainein*) is part of his general account of linguistic signification, definition and thought. This is still a somewhat neglected area of study. Some have doubted whether he was interested in *meaning* at all.[1] Others have suggested that he developed an account of the meaning of natural kind terms of the same general form as that suggested by Hilary Putnam in his papers in the 1960s and 1970s.[2] Still others have represented Aristotle as proposing an anti-realist account of meaning of the type recommended by Michael Dummett or Hilary Putnam in the 1980s.[3] Philosophers who read Aristotle are confronted with a disagreeable dilemma: either he had no account of meaning or he had one similar in basic respects to certain proposals which have gained currency in recent years. Either way his account does not greatly advance our philosophical understanding of these complex issues. In this paper, I shall challenge both these claims by suggesting that Aristotle had (at least) an account of the meaning of *names*, which differs in several basic ways from these twentieth-century proposals, and is worthy of philosophical assessment in its own right.

My starting-point will be Aristotle's discussion of the signification of names and 'name-like expressions' in the *Posterior Analytics (An. Post.)* and *de Interpretatione* (*Int.*). While he comments on these issues elsewhere (for example in the *Topics, Categories (Cat.), Metaphysics* (*Met.*), *Physics* (*Phys.*) and *Poetics*), *de Interpretatione* and the *Posterior Analytics* suggest the basis for a relatively systematic view, which is clearly connected with his account of definition and thought (*noein*). It may well be that at other times Aristotle held other views on the same topics. But I shall focus mainly on *de*

[1] For example, Irwin in his [257]. I shall use 'meaning' and 'signification' interchangeably in this essay unless a contrast is explicitly signalled.

[2] Thus, Bolton in his [255]. [3] Thus, Nussbaum in her [262].

Interpretatione and the *Analytics*, and not attempt an overall survey of all his writings on these issues. The account which he offers there is a striking one which plays a major role in shaping his discussion of other central issues.

In this paper, I shall outline Aristotle's discussion of accounts of what names signify in the *Analytics* (section 2), and of names and similar expressions in *de Interpretatione* (3). This sketch will bring into sharper perspective his discussion of empty names and existence (4), and of permissible substitutions in knowledge (and belief) contexts (5). From this vantage-point, I shall seek to articulate some of Aristotle's views on the interconnections between signification, thought and definition (6). In the final sections (7) and (8) I shall make a few remarks about the role his account of signification plays in motivating certain of his other views, and about the philosophical problems which it faces. These final sections do not attempt an exhaustive treatment of the issues they raise, but aim merely to suggest avenues for further investigation.

2 'Stage-one accounts' in *An. Post.* II.7–10

The opening lines of II.10 run as follows:

> Since a definition is said to be an account given in reply to the 'What is—?' question, it is clear that one kind of definition will be an account given in reply to the question 'What is it that a name or name-like expression signifies?' An example of such a question is 'What is it that "triangle" signifies?' When we grasp that what (it is that) is signified exists, we seek the answer to the 'Why?' question. It is difficult to understand in this way (*viz.* through gaining an answer to the 'Why?' question) things which we do not know to exist. (93b29–35)

In the first three sentences, I take Aristotle to commit himself to a three-stage view of successful scientific enquiry (93b29–32). The passage distinguishes three stages as follows:

Stage one: this stage is achieved when one grasps an account of what a name or name-like expression signifies;

Stage two: this stage is achieved when one grasps that what is signified by a name or name-like expression exists;

Stage three: this stage is achieved when one grasps the essence of the object/kind signified by a name or name-like expression.

These stages are analytically separable even if they are not always chronologically distinct.[4] But if they are chronologically distinct, they occur in this order.

In Aristotle's own examples (thunder (93a22–3, b8–13, 94a2–9) and

[4] Stages two and three occur 'at the same time' on occasion (93a16–20, 35–6).

triangle (93a33–4, b31–2)), the enquirer reaches stage one when she knows an account of what the term signifies. At this point she might know that 'thunder' signifies the same as 'a certain type of noise in the clouds'. At stage two, she comes to know that thunder exists, and at stage three she discovers the basic cause of noise belonging to the clouds in the relevant way. This is achieved by the empirical discovery of the relevant causal connection between *noise* and *the clouds*.

If this is correct, two consequences immediately follow:

(a) it will not be an essential part of knowing an account of what a name or name-like expression signifies that one knows that the kind exists;[5]

(b) it will not be an essential part of knowing an account of what a name signifies that one knows the essence (for example: efficient cause) which is grasped at stage three.

In this account, knowledge of accounts of what names signify will not require knowledge of the *existence* of the kind signified. (This is achieved at stage two.) Nor will knowledge of such accounts *require* any knowledge of the essence of the kind signified (if it exists). When the kind exists, the latter is gained at stage three. But there can be accounts of what names signify even when the kind does not exist, and so lacks an essence. Hence, knowledge of such accounts cannot require knowledge that the kind in question has an essence (yet to be discovered). Accounts of what names signify cannot require knowledge that the kind exists or that it has an essence. (See also section 6 for further discussion of these issues.)

The three-stage view of scientific enquiry is (I believe) one of Aristotle's major proposals in *An. Post.* II.8–10.[6] In it, there can be accounts of what

[5] For a contrasting view, see Bolton [255], 523 ff.

[6] I argued for the 'three-stage view' in my paper 'Aristotle on Meaning and Natural Kinds', presented to the St Louis meeting of the Society for Ancient Greek Philosophy in 1986. The arguments, which I summarise here, are given in more detail in that paper and in my forthcoming book: *Aristotle on Meaning and Natural Kinds*. Acceptance of the three-stage view is consistent with thinking that either all or only some accounts of what names signify are definitions (or definitions of a kind). Thus, Aristotle could have accepted the three-stage account, and still regarded only some accounts of what names signify as *definitions*, provided that what makes them definitions (for example that they are of genuine kinds) is independent of what makes them *accounts* of what the terms signify. In my view, Aristotle took all accounts of what names signify to be definitions of a kind (cf. 93b29–32), but distinguished these from *genuine* definitions (93b37–94a13), which meet further conditions. The issues are complex and require detailed discussion (see 'Aristotle on Meaning and Natural Kinds'), but they lie outside the scope of this paper. D. Devereux and D. de Moss accept my arguments for the three-stage view, but doubt whether all accounts of what names signify are definitions [256]. A similar view was taken earlier by Sorabji [252], 196–8.

names like 'goatstag' signify, even when there is no corresponding kind in reality (92b5–8, 25–9). The enquirer can possess accounts of what names signify when beginning to enquire into the existence or essence of certain phenomena (93a29–36; cf. the example of the void: *Phys.* 214a16–17). Knowledge of what terms signify is rigorously separated from knowing that the kind signified exists (71a11–17, 72a19–24; cf. the examples used in *An. Post.* II.1: centaur, eclipse, etc.). Such accounts do not assume 'one or other part of a contradiction' (72a19–24, cf. 93a33–5). They appear rather to be of the form:

> the void is a place, if there is one, deprived of body. (*Phys.* 214a16–17)

As such they do not require knowledge of the existence or essence of the kinds signified; instead they set the target for an enquiry into essence and existence.

If this is Aristotle's view, what follows for his treatment of the signification of names? He makes several important claims on this and related issues in *An. Post.* II.7–10 and 13.

CI] *Accounts of what names signify* signify the same as *names*. In 92b26–7 Aristotle writes that if definition were to establish what the name signifies, 'it would be an account signifying the same as a name'. And this can only be because he assumes that accounts of what names signify signify the same as the relevant names.

C II] There can be several different accounts of what one name signifies ('pride' might be taken as 'not tolerating insult' or 'indifference to fortune', 97b21 ff., even if pride were just one condition). This is because accounts of this type pick on necessary properties of a kind (93a20–4), and there can be several distinct necessary properties of a given kind.

C III] What is signified by a term at stage one can be the very same thing as what is discovered (in some cases) to exist at stage two (93b32: 'when we discover that *what* is signified exists': cf. 71a15, 'triangle' signifies *this* (sc. triangle)).

C IV] There are accounts of what 'goatstag' signifies (92b6–7, cf. 93b35–7: these would be accounts 'stitched together' by us).

C V] Accounts of what terms signify play a role in guiding enquiry at stages two and three (93a29–36, b29–34).

There are several points of apparent conflict between these claims. If the three-stage view is correct, understanding an account of what a name signifies cannot involve knowing of the existence or essence of the kind in question. But if C III] is correct, names on occasion signify what exists. How is this possible? And how does 'goatstag' get its significance if there are no goatstags (C IV])?

'The account of what "triangle" signifies' signifies the same as 'triangle' (C I]). But there can be several different accounts of what 'triangle' signifies which pick out different necessary properties of triangle (C II]). How is this possible? Does it require that 'triangle' is ambiguous?

The *Analytics* passages, and the three-stage view they contain, raise rather than resolve these issues. At most these five claims set targets which Aristotle's view of the signification of names and accounts of what names signify should meet.[7] But they do not state in explicit terms Aristotle's account of these issues; nor do they show how these targets are to be achieved. Is there further evidence that Aristotle held C I]–C V]? Did he actually possess a coherent account of these matters in which C I]–C V] are vindicated?

3 Simple names and signification: *de Interpretatione* chapters 1–2

Aristotle's remarks near the beginning of *de Interpretatione* suggest a starting-point for an affirmative answer to these questions. There he writes.

> Spoken sounds are symbols of affections in the soul, and written marks are symbols of spoken sounds. And just as written marks are not the same for all, neither are spoken sounds. But what these are in the first place signs of – affections in the soul – are the same for all; and what these affections are likenesses of – things in the world – are indeed the same for all. These matters have been discussed in the work *On the Soul* (*de Anima*), and do not belong to the present subject. (16a3–8)

Written marks and spoken sounds are signs – *in the first instance* – of affections of the soul, which appear to be thoughts in this context (16a10,14).[8] Names are signs for thoughts which are not yet combined with other thoughts, for which verbs are signs, to make affirmations,

[7] This view of *An. Post.* II.8–10 represents a mid-position between two opposed interpretations. Bolton [255] took these chapters to present Aristotle's explicit account of the signification of kind-terms; however, Ackrill [269] was unconvinced that any general account of signification was even assumed in these texts. In my view, such an account is presupposed but not made explicit in these chapters.

[8] On this account, written and spoken expressions are *conventional* signs of states of the soul: 16b10,19. They are conventional signs of such states because they are *both* signs (*sēmeia*) and symbols (*sumbola*). There may be signs which are not symbols and hence non-conventional (for example natural signs), and symbols

capable of truth and falsity. In what follows I shall focus on this case which is central to Aristotle's account of affirmation (see section 8).

Let us begin with *simple* names, successfully applied to objects or kinds: 'Cicero' or 'man'.[9] The written mark 'a' is a sign – in the first instance – of a given thought, the thought of Cicero or of man. The meaning of 'a' is fixed by the thought with which it is conventionally correlated. The identity of thought is determined by its object or content (or in Aristotle's terms, the relevant Form received: see below.) So, the meaning of 'a' is fixed by what the thought with which it is correlated is about: its object or content.

What, for Aristotle, determines the identity of the object or content of a given thought? In this passage, Aristotle confines himself to saying that at least some thoughts are *likenesses* of things in the world (*homoiōmata*), and noting that this issue is further discussed in *de Anima* (*DA*). So this points us elsewhere for the account we seek.

An overview of *de Anima*'s discussion of thinking confirms the major role Aristotle gives to the idea of *likeness*. In cases of successful thinking (as in perceiving) objects in the world *liken* the thinking faculty to themselves. This is a causal process in which the starting-point is the object in the world.[10] When it occurs, the Form is transferred from the object in the world to the thinking faculty. This transference explains the general nature of the

which are not signs because not semantically significant. Aristotle's mixture of conventional (*symbolic*) and non-conventional (*likening*) relations is his attempt to disentangle two separate strands which are confused by Plato in the *Cratylus* (for example 430d5 ff., cf. 386c ff.). For a contrasting view, see Kretzmann [258]. Parts of Kretzmann's view are convincingly criticised by Tselemanis in [260]. I consider the remainder of his view in discussing the notion of *likeness* below. Aristotle says practically nothing in *de Interpretatione* about the conventional aspect of significance, and I will follow his example in this paper.

[9] Aristotle's category of *names* includes proper names and common nouns (for example 'man', 'horse', 'Socrates'). Simple names have no relevant internal semantic structure (*Int.* 16a20–6): see section 4. It is very important to note that Aristotle does not say that *all* affections of the soul are likenesses of things in the world. He confines himself to saying 'what affections are likenesses of are things in the world' (16a7–8), which leaves open the possibility that *some* affections (for example those concerning goatstags) are *not* likenesses of anything (see section 4). In particular he does not say that *all* names are related to affections which are likenesses of things in the world.

[10] For perception, see (for instance) *DA* 418a3–6. For thought, *DA* 429a13–18, 430a3–4, 417b16–19. Aristotle applies his 'likening model' in both cases. This is a specific *causal relation* in which the cause 'likens the effect unto itself' (cf. *de Generatione et Corruptione* (*GC*) 324a9–11) so that the effect is 'made like' the cause. In this way, the wax which receives the imprint of the ring is *likened* to the ring which produces it. This means more than that it resembles the ring. For that would be true also of marks which happened to look like the ring, but were not produced by it in this way. I defend this interpretation in more detail in *Aristotle on Meaning and Natural Kinds*.

relevant thoughts – *viz.* their content. So the identity of the thought is fixed by its content, and this in turn is fixed by the thought being 'likened' to certain objects in the world in the *Form-transferring way.*[11] And this is what makes the thought (with its content) the one it is.

The meaning of a simple linguistic expression 'a' is fixed in the first instance by the content of the thought with which it is conventionally correlated. In those cases where the thoughts are likenesses to things in the world (in this way), the content of the thought is fixed by that object which causes it to occur in the likening (*Form-transferring*) mode. In such cases, therefore, the meaning of 'a' is fixed, in the *second* instance, by the objects in the world which cause in the *Form-transferring way* the thought with which 'a' is conventionally correlated. The second relation is fundamental to determining the meaning of 'a' in this case: for it is this which fixes the content of the relevant thought, which in turn determines the meaning of 'a', whether or not it is a significance relation.

In considering this range of cases, I shall take two phrases in the opening lines of *de Interpretatione* as fundamental: 'first' (16a6) and 'likeness' (16a7). In grasping their role and significance we see that for simple names successfully applied to objects or kinds:

> 'a' signifies the kind K_1 if and only if K_1 produces the thought θ_1 (with which 'a' is conventionally correlated) by *the Form-transferring route.*

When this occurs, θ_1 will be likened to K_1 in the *Form-transferring way*. Thus, there are two semantically relevant relations:

> 'a' signifies IMMEDIATELY θ_1 if and only if θ_1 is the thought-content with which 'a' is conventionally correlated.

This scheme says that the meaning of 'a' is fixed immediately by what θ_1 is about. This will be common to all cases of meaning, and is the prime object of signification. In certain cases (for example) where thoughts are produced in the Form-transferring mode by a kind in the world:

> 'a' signifies MEDIATELY K_1 if and only if K_1 produces θ_1 (with which 'a' is conventionally correlated) in *the Form-transferring mode.*

[11] Brentano ([249]) clearly saw these two separate elements in Aristotle's account of perception and thought, but emphasised only the first (*viz.* that of the thought 'becoming identical with its object') at the expense of the second (*viz.* the role of the efficient cause). However, if one takes both its elements together one finds Aristotle's answer to Brentano's problem: what makes my thought about Cicero a thought about *Cicero?*

In these cases, the latter relation is fundamental because it is this which determines the content of θ_1 with which 'a' is conventionally correlated. What is signified mediately fixes what is signified immediately by 'a'.

This account provides a starting-point. To complete it one needs to know what the relevant *Form-transferring route* is, and what occurs when there can be no such route because there is no object or kind in reality (for example in the case of 'goatstag': 16a16, which also has significance).

The full elucidation of Aristotle's account of this *Form-transferring route* is a major undertaking which lies outside the scope of this paper. There are several ingredients, however, which constitute the basis of his account:

(i) the route involves a given object/kind as the efficient cause of θ_1;[12]

(ii) the efficient cause explains the relevant general features of θ_1: *viz.* what it is about, i.e. its object;[13]

(iii) the relevant causal process is one guided by *teleological* principles and occurs only when the organism is functioning correctly;[14]

(iv) the goal of the thinking faculty is *understanding* of an independent world-order organised on intelligible principles.[15]

Each of these features, and their interconnection, requires detailed examination. But the following at least is clear. In the cases under discussion,

'a' signifies $_{\text{MED}}$ K_1 if and only if K_1 produces θ_1 (with which 'a' is

[12] This is implicit in Aristotle's account of 'likening': see n. 10 above. I am further assuming that for Aristotle the efficient cause is *constitutive* of the processes it causes (cf. *Met.* 1041a29–32). The result could not be thunder/a thinking of Cicero (of this type) unless it was caused by fire being quenched/Cicero (cf. *An. Post.* 94a5–6, 93b10–19).

[13] Aristotle's efficient or 'making' causes (for example the art of housebuilding) make the effect be a certain way (for example be organised in given ways), and do not merely bring the effect into existence. They make objects have given properties ('A causes B to be G'), where the latter are capable of having those properties (cf. *Met.* 1049a5–8).

[14] The goal is *knowledge* of the intelligible world-order, as the goal of visual perception is to see coloured objects (*DA* 417b20–7). The latter goes wrong when the sense is stimulated inappropriately (*On Dreams* 460b24–6), and one fails to act appropriately. The idea of an intelligible world-order is the basis for Aristotle's discussion of *thought* in *An. Post.* (100a10–b2: cf. b13). The goal of understanding such an order is suggested by the linguistic comparisons between the role of active thought and Plato's Form of the good (*DA* 430a14–16).

[15] This is the achievement of those who know the causes of certain (for example) illnesses generally specified, and do not merely know by experience that *this* medicine works for *this* illness (*Met.* 981a8–12, 27–31). In grasping the relevant cause one locates the illness in its appropriate niche in an intelligible world-order (generally specified). This differs fundamentally from having a purely practical grasp on what the illness is, which would be exhausted by being able to tell (for example) who has it when they are brought into your surgery.

conventionally correlated) as its efficient cause in a way which meets conditions (ii)–(iv).

In such cases θ_1 will be the thought it is precisely because it is produced by a route of this kind. The efficient causal component is constitutive. Further, to have this thought the thinker needs to be able to locate K_1 in an independent, intelligible, order of this type. So while it will be constitutive of possessing a thought of 'man' that it is a thought caused by the kind/man, to have such a *thought* (properly speaking) will also require that one thinks of man as a certain kind of animal (for example featherless) located on a genus/species tree. If one lacks this kind of understanding one will not have a thought (properly speaking) of *man*, although one may have some less demanding doxastic attitude towards the kind (for example: imagination: cf. *DA* 432a11–14. See also section 8).

In these cases, what is signified by a term is what is discovered to exist at stage two in the enquiry. This is because what is signified$_{MED}$ by the term is a kind in the world, and this partially fixes the signification$_{IMM}$ of the term. Further, in these cases, the account of what the name signifies will include the conjectured location of the kind in an objective and intelligible world-order. Thus, 'man' will signify the kind *man*, and the account of man will specify *man* as 'animal of a certain type: for example biped'. Armed with such thoughts one can begin to search for the essence of man – the search for something which explains why men are animals of this type (in Aristotle's terms, why the property of being a biped belongs to animal). In this way, C III] and C V] in section 2 are satisfied. One can have such thoughts about man and understand the name 'man' without knowing that the kind exists. This will be possible because one need not know at stage one that the signification of the name is in fact fixed in the *Form-transferring way* by objects or kinds in the world. Thus, for example, I may have thoughts about thunder or man provided I meet these conditions, and not yet know that the relevant kind exists. For I may not know what brought about these thoughts, or that there is one unified phenomenon that did so. (They might turn out to be distinct phenomena: see the inconclusive discussion of *pride*: *An. Post.* 97b13 ff.). Thus, I may understand the name, but not yet know whether the kind in question exists. (In this way C I] and the *Analytics* three-stage view of enquiry are accommodated in a direct and simple way).

An account of what a name signifies requires certain specific information about the kind in question. In particular, it requires information about what are, in fact, necessary properties of the kind. Such accounts place constraints on the type of information required if the thinker is to have an account of what the name signifies. But at stage one she will not know whether the kind exists (or has an essence). In order to discover this, she needs to know that she is confronted with an organised unity, and so with an existing kind (stage two). At stage one she will lack knowledge both of the existence and of the essence of the kind, which is achieved at stage three. (See C V] in section 2.)

The account of what the name signifies should reflect this ignorance of the existence of the kind. The cases under discussion may be represented diagrammatically as follows:

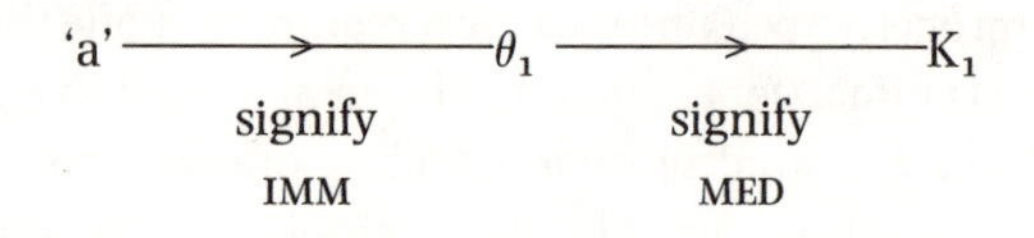

The content of the thought θ_1 is determined by the kind that is signified immediately, but the thinker's knowledge need not extend as far as knowing of K_1's existence. In having a thought of K_1, one thinks of K_1 as possessing certain features which locate it in an ordered world. But this thought need not involve knowledge of K_1's existence; rather it should be of the form:

> *man* is a certain kind of bipedal animal, if there is such a kind,
> *thunder* is a kind of noise in the clouds, if there is such a distinctive kind,
> *void* is a place deprived of body, if there is such a place (*Phys.* 214a16–17)

which reflects the thinker's lack of knowledge of the existence of K_1. The signification-relation in these cases extends further into the world than does the knowledge of the thinker.

In grasping the thought *man*, the thinker grasps that man is a kind of animal. Names and accounts of what names signify signify the same in Aristotle's account. How can this be, if the relevant account does not commit the thinker to knowledge of the kind, but the name could not have that signification unless the kind existed? Aristotle's answer is to propose that names and accounts signify the same provided that they both signify the same objects or kinds in the world non-accidentally. This will only occur if the kinds or objects in question have the same essence (stage three discovery). If they do not, names or accounts will not signify the same – even if they are true of objects or kinds which always co-occur.[16] So, 'possessor of weight' and 'occupier of three-dimensional space' will not signify the same

[16] For Aristotle, objects are described as 'being named together' (*synōnymous*: *Cat.* 1a6) provided that they have the name 'in common' and 'the definition which *corresponds* to the name is the same'. Thus two token names ('a_1', 'b_2') are 'common' provided that they refer non-accidentally to the same objects and the definition which answers 'What is a_1?' is the same as that which answers 'What is a_2?' Since common names cosignify, two different names (e.g. 'cloak', 'garment') will cosignify under these two conditions. Similarly with 'man' and

kind even if they are always in fact true at the same time of the same objects. For the essence of one kind is not the same as the essence of the other, and hence what the two terms signify non-accidentally is different. Conversely,

'noise in the clouds'

and

'noise accompanied by lightning'

will both signify the same as 'thunder', provided that they are true only of the same kinds with the same essence (for example quenching of fire). Similarly,

'noise in the clouds caused by quenching of fire'

will signify the same as 'thunder'. But 'thunder' will not signify the same as 'the quenching of fire in the clouds', which is its efficient cause, and gives the answer to the 'Why?' question. For the efficient cause and its effect are distinct objects. Thus, 'thunder' and 'a certain kind of noise in the clouds, if there is one such' will signify the same provided that there is one kind in the world which both signify. In the case of substances, 'man' will signify the same as 'biped animal with a given essence: for instance being rational/ having a soul of a given kind, if there is such a kind'. But it would not signify its essence, *soul of a given kind*, since the enmattered kind and its essence are different, and 'man' in its basic use signifies the composite species (matter and form/shape) and not its form/shape or essence alone (*Met.* 1043b2–4, a30–6). So while simple names of this type do signify kinds (or species) with essences, it is not correct to say that they signify that essence. For that requires a distinct name with this specific significance.

On this view, two names ('a', 'b') have the same significance if and only if they signify the same objects or kinds, and this will be so only if the answer to the question 'What is *a*?' is the same as that to 'What is *b*?'[17] Accounts of

'biped animal'. Thus, names and definitions may signify the same, without names having to signify the essences which are the subject-matter of those definitions. For they will signify the same provided that both signify non-accidentally the same kinds (for example the kind *man*), and the answer to the question: 'What is man?' is the same as the answer to the question: 'What is biped animal?' (cf. *Met.* 1041a19–23).
For a contrasting view, see Irwin [257], 246. Irwin's argument for the conclusion that names signify essences is ably criticised by Tselemanis in his [260].

[17] This account suggests that the following expressions will have the same significance:
'Cicero': 'Tully'
'gold': 'the substance whose essence is atomic number 79'
'man': 'biped animal' (see also section 5).

what a name signifies signify the same as the name provided that they signify the same objects non-accidentally, and the answer to the question 'What is thunder?' is the same as 'What is a kind of noise in the clouds?' This will be so if the answer to the question:

> Why does noise belong in the clouds?

points to the essence of the phenomenon: *fire being quenched*. But this will occur only if the terms which figure in the account specify a non-accidental property of thunder. For if they did not do so, the answer to the relevant 'Why?' question would not point to the essence of the phenomenon. Hence, it is a condition of adequacy for a proper account of what a name signifies that it specifies some non-accidental properties of the kind. If one fails to meet this condition, one lacks a proper account of what the name signifies.[18] Failure to do this means that one lacks a genuine thought of the kind: for one has failed to locate it in a well-defined slot in an intelligible ordered world. The terms one uses to mark out the kind need to be such as to capture the objective grid of kinds in the world. If one lacks an account of this type, one does not think of *thunder* (as such), although one may have some lesser doxastic attitude towards thunder or something *thunder-like* which happens to occur when thunder occurs: for example noise which frightens sheep (for there will be other sheep-frightening noises).

The thinker will not know that the account of what the name signifies in fact selects a necessary property until she knows the essence of the phenomenon; for this allows her to establish which properties are necessary. But the account will only be a proper account of what the name signifies in these cases if when it predicates one thing non-accidentally of another it specifies necessary properties of the kind.

This is the basic case in Aristotle's discussion of names. It encounters problems at various points:

(a) how do names (like 'goatstag') for non-existents have significance?
(b) how are statements about existence to be understood?
(c) how are statements involving propositional attitudes to be understood?

In considering these difficulties, we see some of the basic components of Aristotle's philosophy of language. But they rest in turn on his views in

[18] See, for instance, *An. Post.* 93a24–6. It is difficult to advance at all in scientific investigation when one possesses a grasp of only the accidental properties of thunder (93b31–5). One can, of course, say things about thunder, and be in contact with thunder, but one still lacks thoughts about thunder if one only possesses an accidental account of thunder.

philosophical psychology and metaphysics which I shall outline in the final sections.

4 Goatstags, non-simple names and existence

There can be accounts of what 'goatstag' and 'void' signify (if the previous section is correct) along the following lines:

> the void is the place, if there is one, deprived of body (*Phys.* 214a16–17), and

> the goatstag is the kind of animal, if there is one, which is the offspring of goat and stag.

But this does not indicate how the signification of these names themselves is fixed. This clearly cannot be determined by the process of 'likening' of thoughts to kinds in the world, as this can occur only when the kind in question exists. So how do 'goatstag' and 'void' have significance, if there is no kind in existence to which the relevant thought is likened?

Aristotle begins *Int.* 2 by stating that names themselves have no parts which signify 'in separation' or 'in their own right' (16a20–1). His evidence for this is that in names like 'Callippus' or 'Whitfield' the parts such as '– field' do not signify in the way they would in the phrase 'the white field' (16a21–2). He then adds:

> It is not, however, the same for compounded names as for simple ones. In the latter there are no parts which signify anything. In the former, the parts do have meaning (*bouletai*), but they signify nothing when separated, as, for example, 'boat' in 'pirate-boat. (16a23–6)

Elsewhere he notes that in 'double-words' parts do signify (*sēmainei*), but not 'in their own right' (16b32–3). It is not immediately clear whether 'Callippus' is used as an example of a simple name (Ammonius) or a compounded one (Ackrill). However, the basic distinction is between simple names which have no parts which signify anything (in the context of this name), and compounded names (like 'pirate-boat' or 'goatstag') whose parts do have some meaning but do not signify anything 'in their own right' in this word when separated from the other parts. Thus, in compounded names the function of the relevant parts is not to signify (for instance) boat or goat as they would if 'boat' or 'goat' stood alone, but the parts are none the less semantically significant and play some role in determining the meaning of the whole.

Aristotle does not expand this account of compounded names further, but his brief remarks indicate (at least) that the parts contribute to the meaning of the compound whole, which is determined by the significance of the parts *plus* their mode of combination. For example, the significance of 'goatstag' is fixed by the significance of 'goat-' and '-stag' plus their combination to form (for example) 'offspring of goat and stag', or 'part-goat, part-stag, animal'. One could not understand the contribution of 'goat-' to the compound 'goatstag' solely in terms of what it signifies when used in isolation. The significance of 'goat-' is dependent on what the simple name 'goat' signifies, but its meaning-contribution in the compounded name is not exhausted by this. Indeed, when viewed as an element separated from the compounded name (*viz.* 'goat-'), it signifies by itself neither goat nor any particular combination of goat and anything else. Thus, in a clear sense, 'goat-' in this context signifies nothing by itself.

Compounded names require the existence of simple names as the basic case; for if there were no simple names, there would not be the relevant parts for compounded ones. But in the case of compounded names the significance of the whole is not determined by the 'likening' relation to things in the world as in the case of simple names; for that relation is blind to the internal semantic complexity of the name. If this is so, the term 'goatstag' can have significance in virtue of the semantic contribution of its parts, even if there is no kind in the world to which it is likened.

Aristotle does not spell out in any detail how this proposal is to work for compounded names. His focus is mainly on simple names, and he is not concerned to develop a theory for less central cases. But in one version it would look in outline like this:

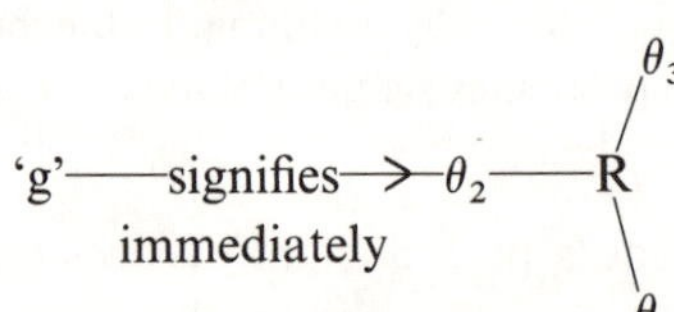

The significance of 'goatstag' is determined by the content of the compounded thought (θ_2), which in turn is fixed by the thought-contents of simple thoughts θ_3 and θ_4 standing in relation R (for example offspring of). While θ_3 and θ_4 have their content because they are (in the basic case) 'likened' to things in the world, the content of θ_2 depends on the contents of θ_3 and θ_4 *thus connected*, and is not itself directly dependent on a likening relation between it and a specific kind in the world (*viz.* goatstag). Indeed this is precisely what distinguishes simple and compounded names. Aristotle need go no further than this in specifying precisely how the elements in the compounded name make their semantic contribution. It is enough that he has preserved the centrality of the likening-relation for simple names, while indicating the general outline of what is required in a distinct account of compounded names.

From this viewpoint, the significance of 'goatstag' is partially fixed by the thoughts of simple kinds which give rise to it in the favoured way. And these will when combined yield the account of what 'goatstag' signifies: *viz.* a kind of animal, if there is one, which is the offspring of goat and stag. Given that there is no further likening relation in this case to things in the world, there will be nothing more to the significance of the name 'goatstag' than what is given in the account of what the name signifies.

This account will apply to those empty names which like 'goatstag' are semantically compounded. But it cannot apply in this form to all empty names, since not all empty names are compounded in this way: for instance 'Pegasus', 'void', 'Socrates' (if Socrates does not exist: *Cat.* 13b31). Does Aristotle have a strategy which applies to these also?

He considers a semantically simple name of the relevant type in *Int.* 8. There he writes:

> If one name is given to two things which do not make up one thing, there is not a single affirmation. Suppose, for example, that one gave the name 'cloak' to man and horse. Then
>
> 'Cloak is white'
>
> would not be a single affirmation. For to say this is not different from saying
>
> 'Horse and man is white',
>
> and this is not different from saying
>
> 'Horse is white and man is white.'
>
> So if this signifies many things and is more than one affirmation, clearly the first signifies either many things or nothing. For there is nothing which is a man and a horse. (18a18–26)

The crucial idea in this passage is that if one name is not given to *one* thing, there is not a single affirmation (18a18–20). And this will be true in any case where there is not one thing which is the subject of the affirmation. Thus, Aristotle writes (*Int.* 20b13–16) that there is not a single affirmation even if there is one name in cases where there is not *one* thing which it signifies. So if a name 'cloak' is given to *horse and man*, there is no single affirmation made when one says:

'Cloak is white.'

This will be equivalent to

'Man is white and Horse is white',

and has significance (if it does) by being correlated with the distinct objects it signifies: man, horse. For it cannot have significance in any other way, since there is nothing which is both *a man and a horse* (18a24–6).

In this passage, Aristotle indicates that the thought

'Cloak is white'

can be complex in cases where the apparently simple name 'cloak' is not given to one thing. He does not even say that this name is significant, but only commits himself to the more cautious claim that *if* it is significant, this is because its significance depends on its being correlated with many objects (in a given relation). So we can in turn conclude only this: within the class of non-compounded names, some are given to one thing, and others (like 'cloak') are not. In the latter case, their significance (if they have one) depends in some way on the significance of the complex expression like 'man and horse' with which they are correlated (see also *Met.* 1045a25–7). This latter class must include all non-empty names, because in their case there is not one thing in the world to which they are given. Thus 'void' and 'Pegasus' turn out to be dependent for their significance on complex thoughts with which expressions such as 'place deprived of body' and 'winged horse, offspring of . . .' are correlated. And this must be so because in these cases there cannot be the relevant likening relation to *one* thing in the world of the sort which links 'man' or 'Pericles' to the appropriate kind or object.

If this is correct, there cannot be *single* affirmations if the grammatical subject, even if non-complex, does not signify one existing object or kind. And this is because the signification of empty names is determined in a way which rules out these being used in single affirmations, since in these cases there is no one object with which they are correlated and which produces the relevant affection of the soul.[19] All significant empty names must therefore be semantically complex (like 'goatstag') or dependent for their signification on complex expressions (like 'cloak'). In either case, their significance is dependent in some way on that of the simple names which form constituent parts of the relevant complex name or expression. And the latter's significance is fixed in the ways indicated in section 2 by the likening relation to objects and kinds in the world.

Aristotle, armed with these resources, can allow us meaningfully to say:

'Goatstags do not exist' (21a32–3)

and

'Pegasus does not exist',

because the significance of 'goatstag' and 'Pegasus' is fixed in a way which

[19] This will be so also if there is no proper unity referred to by a given term. Thus, 'pride is F' would not say *one* thing of *one* thing, if there were more than one thing which was pride (97b14–24). Some complex names can also signify one thing in the required way: see *Int.* 20b15–18.

allows these sentences to retain their significance, even when it is discovered that goatstags and Pegasus do not exist. The first sentence would be equivalent to:

> 'It is not the case that the property of being the offspring of both goat and stag belongs to animal',

and would be true. In a similar way

> 'Goatstags are found in Bosnia'

would be false, as this would be equivalent to the conjunction:

> 'Being the offspring of goat and stag belongs to animal *and* (that) animal is found in Bosnia.'

And since the first conjunct is false, the whole expression is false.

In single affirmations in *de Interpretatione*, one thing is predicated of one actual thing (non-accidentally). Thus, in singular cases, it will follow from

> 'a is F'

that

> 'a exists'.

Similarly, from plural affirmations of this type such as

> 'All As (men) are F'

it will follow that

> 'Some As (men) are F',

since in this case also one thing (being F) is predicated of *one thing* (for instance the class of men or the kind man). In both cases of single affirmations the subject term must refer to one actual thing (individual, class or kind). If there had been no such class or kind, there could not be a single affirmation of this form. And in this case, 'man' would have been dependent for its significance on a complex thought in the way in which 'void' is.[20]

[20] This account of one basic ingredient in Aristotle's logical square of opposition does not require that the language as a whole contain no empty terms, only that single affirmations do not. (To complete it one requires a detailed specification of what is signified by 'All As . . .' But that lies outside the scope of this paper). It should be contrasted with Smiley's approach to these issues in his [534]. Smiley preserves the logical square by employing a 'many-sorted' logical system in which every subject term refers to an existing object. But this, at a stroke, banishes such empty names as 'goatstag', 'void' or 'Socrates' from the language, contrary to Aristotle's explicit examples in *de Interpretatione*, *Categories* and *Physics*.

These existential consequences can only be avoided if the sentences

'a is F'

and

'all As are F'

are, despite their initial appearance, not single affirmations. 'Cloak' and 'goatstag' provide examples of terms which cannot fit into single affirmations. Other somewhat similar cases are suggested by a further type of complexity in the subject-place which arises when the object specified is not a proper unity (cf. *Int.* 20b15–17). An apparent example of this is:

'Homer is F (for example a poet)' (*Int.* 21a24–5).

Aristotle claims that in this case it does not follow that

'Homer exists',

because 'is F' is not predicated non-accidentally of *Homer* 'in his own right' in the original sentence (*Int.* 21a25–7). In that sentence 'is F' is predicated non-accidentally of (perhaps)

'Homer the poet . . .'

but not of Homer himself (as 'good' is predicated of A-the-shoemaker and not of A himself in the sentence 'A is a good shoemaker' *Int.* 21a14–16). Alternatively in this sentence 'is F' might be predicated non-accidentally of *the poet* and not of *Homer* (as Ammonius suggested). Thus, while it may follow that

'The poet of this book exists'

or

'Homer, i.e. the poet of this book, exists',

it does not follow that

'Homer exists.'

Aristotle does not say in general under what conditions this type of rephrasing is required. Presumably he thinks that in this case 'Homer' is correlated with a complex thought whose content is fixed not solely by Homer himself, but by his (for instance) being the author of the *Iliad*. And this is because 'is a poet' is predicated essentially of the poet or of Homer the poet, and not of Homer. But he gives no indication of why this is so.[21] (Perhaps he thought that if 'is F' was predicated of Homer in his own right, one would need to make sense of doubtful possibilities such as 'Homer might not have written the *Iliad*.' But this is only a conjecture.)

In the case of genuinely single affirmations,

> 'Thunder is loud'

will entail

> 'Thunder exists.'

And this reflects the fact that if one has a simple thought of thunder, thunder must exist. But the speaker who possesses this thought of thunder need not know (in Aristotle's view) that thunder exists. For she need not know that her thought is produced in the appropriate way. Thus, while she understands the term 'thunder', and possesses an account of what it signifies (for example 'thunder' signifies a type of noise in the clouds), she need not yet know that it exists. To establish that it does exist she has to establish that noise does, in fact, belong to the clouds in the appropriate way, by proving that thunder is a genuine unity. While she may in this way come to discover that

> 'Thunder exists',

[21] The variety of cases of names which Aristotle discusses in *de Interpretatione* alone ('Callippus', 'Homer', 'goatstag', 'cloak') makes it unprofitable to ask whether *all* Aristotelian names are existence-presupposing. (See, for example, Michael Wedin's and William Jacobs' discussions of the claim that all singular affirmative sentences imply the existence of a bearer of the grammatical subject of the sentence ([294], [293]). There is a rich variety of cases, which can be classified initially as follows:

	Names which can occur in a single proposition (which says one thing of one thing)	*Names which can occur only in complex expressions*
Simple names	'Callippus' 'Man'	'cloak' 'Pegasus' 'void'
Complex names	'pirate-ship' 'Rational biped' (Name-like expressions)	'Homer the poet' 'Goatstag'

Simple names in single propositions presuppose the existence of their bearer. Any name which can occur in a single proposition entails the existence of its bearer. But there are simple and complex names ('Pegasus', 'goatstag', etc.) which do not entail or presuppose the existence of their bearer, even if they occur in singular (but not *single*) affirmative sentences of the form 'a is F'. Earlier discussions of these topics appear to overlook these complexities in Aristotle's account.

knowledge of its existence was not part of her original understanding of the term 'thunder'. So this sentence will not be a 'referential tautology', nor will its denial be a 'referential contradiction', as it would have been if knowing the meaning of 'thunder' had required her to know that it exists.[22]

Aristotle's dependence on such single affirmations is reflected elsewhere by his insistence that for every affirmation, 'there is one opposite negation, and for every negation an opposite affirmation' (17a32–4). He defends this in *de Interpretatione* with explicit reference to affirmations in which one thing is predicated of one thing (18a13–14). In these cases, it is clear that there is one negation of

'Socrates is sick',

because

'Socrates is not sick'

and

'It is not the case that Socrates is sick'

entail one another. So here there is only one negation, and either it or the original affirmation is true (and the other is false): see *Cat.* 13b29–31. But is this principle generally true? Does it apply to the case of empty names?

In *de Interpretatione*, Aristotle modifies this principle for cases like 'cloak', if this signifies man and horse. For it is not necessary in this case that one of

[22] These issues require further detailed discussion elsewhere. On the view sketched here, existence *can* be a property of objects or kinds (in Aristotle's account), and need not in general be a property of properties. For a contrasting view, see Owen [300]. Owen mistakenly 'entangled' himself in most of these snares because he did not grasp Aristotle's view of accounts of what names signify. For Aristotle 'ice' would signify the same as 'solid water'. To establish that ice exists is to establish that *solidity* belongs to *water* (in which one thing is predicated of one thing, and the thing of which the predication is made is not itself ice). So to establish that ice exists is not to establish that *solidity* belongs to *ice* (or solid water). Equally, to deny that ice exists is to assert that *solidity* does not belong to *water*. It is not to assert that *solidity* does not belong to *solid water* (ice), which (as Owen correctly notes) is a contradiction. If so, there need be no difficulty in understanding *exists* as a predicate of *ice*, or in taking Aristotle's existence-proof to establish that ice exists by establishing that *solidity* belongs to water. Owen can only undermine this view by substituting *ice* (or solid water) for water in the sentence: '*Being solid* belongs to *water*.' But this is to misunderstand Aristotle's rules for substitution (cf. *An. Post.* II.8:93a20–5, 93b9–12). It is only if one succumbs to this misunderstanding that one is tempted to interpret 'exists' in Aristotle as equivalent to the existential quantifier, and treat 'ice exists' as saying that the property of *icehood* is instantiated ([300],82 ff.).

'cloak is white

and

'cloak is not white'

is true and the other false (18a25–6). For both could be true if (for instance) men were white and horses were not white. But while this modifies the principle in the case of some complex affirmations, it does not show how it can be applied to empty names such as 'goatstag' or 'void'.

Aristotle addresses this issue in *Cat.* 13b32 ff., but his discussion is somewhat elusive. He claims that if Socrates does not exist, 'Socrates is F' is false and 'Socrates is not F' is true. However, since in the immediate context there is less explicit discussion of the signification of names than in *de Interpretatione*, it is correspondingly difficult to determine how the empty name 'Socrates' is to be understood. If it is treated along the lines suggested above,

'Socrates is F'

might be analysed as (for example)

'The property of (for example) being the offspring of A and B belongs to an animal, and that animal is F'

and will be false since the first conjunct is false. But what of 'Socrates is not F'? Why is this true? Why is there only *one* negation of 'Socrates is F'? Indeed there seem to be two non-equivalent negations:

'The property of being the offspring of A and B belongs to an animal and that animal is not F'

and

'It is not the case that being the offspring of A and B belongs to an animal and that animal is F.'

The latter is true (if there is no Socrates), but the former is not. For the former entails

$\exists x[\text{Offspring } x \mathbin{\&} \neg Fx]$,

which is false, while the latter entails

$\neg\exists x[\text{Offspring } x \mathbin{\&} Fx]$,

which is true.

In *Cat.* 13b32 ff. Aristotle replies to this question by (in effect) insisting that the negation which contradicts 'Socrates is well' is 'It is not the case that Socrates is well', which he distinguishes both from its opposite 'Socrates is ill' and its privation (for example) 'Socrates is deprived of health' (13b15–17, 22–7). In the latter two cases, if Socrates does not exist, the sentence is false. Thus Aristotle distinguishes the privation 'Socrates is unwell' (which is entailed by 'Socrates is ill') from 'It is not the case that Socrates is well', and treats the last sentence alone as the denial of 'Socrates is well' relevant to its contradiction (13b27–32, 34–5). And it is this sentence which will be true if Socrates does not exist. Where a modern logician would speak of the *scope* of negation, Aristotle separates distinct types of *opposite* (12b26 ff.). This suggestion is clear also in *Int.* 19b25, where Aristotle distinguishes

'A is not just'

from

'A is not-just' (*viz.* unjust)

and regards the former as the negation of

'A is just'

and the latter as its privation.[23] Thus, in developing his defence of the principle that for every affirmation there is one opposite negation, he shows how he intends to understand the negation of 'Socrates is F', when there is no Socrates. The crucial point (for our purposes) is that there are always two non-equivalent types of *opposite* in the case of empty names, while in the case of non-empty names the two are (generally) equivalent: cf. *Cat.* 13b19–21. And in single affirmations, this equivalence will be maintained because there one thing is predicated of one actual thing (unaccidentally).

When negation in contradictions is understood in this way, it is unproblematic to deny existence. 'Pegasus does not exist' will be understood as

'It is not the case that Pegasus exists',

which in turn will be understood (given the account above) as

'It is not the case that being a winged horse belongs to animal.'

There is no temptation in Aristotle's account, once privation and negation are separated, to conclude that Pegasus must exist because he is thought about and said not to exist or not to walk. Non-existence is not the privation

[23] In the context of single affirmations in which 'one thing is said of one thing', if 'It is not the case that Socrates is wise' is true, then so is 'Socrates is not wise' (*Int.* 20a24–6). But this is not a general rule, but applies only to names in single affirmations of the relevant type.

of a positive state (*hexis*) of the subject (*Int.* 21a32–3; cf. 17a26–32).[24] Although 'existence' can be a predicate of individuals in this account (see n. 22 above), it does not specify a positive state they possess.

5 Knowledge, belief and substitution

Names and expressions ('a', 'b') signify the same if and only if they signify the same objects and the answer to the question: 'what is a?' is the same as to 'what is b?'. In this case, the objects designated by 'a' will be essentially the same as those designated by 'b'. What does this say about the belief and knowledge contexts? Does it follow from Aristotle's account that if John believes that the Greeks are advancing, he also believes that the Hellenes are advancing, even if he is unaware that the Greeks are the Hellenes? Does Aristotle have any way of avoiding this conclusion or alternatively making it less counter-intuitive?

Aristotle's remarks are brief and fragmentary. In *de Sophisticis Elenchis* 179a35–8 he appears to allow that if two objects or kinds are the same in essence, then whatever is true of one is true of the other. Thus, if Coriscus had been the same in essence as the man approaching, and if S had known that the man approaching was hooded, he would have known that Coriscus was hooded.[25] But since Coriscus and the man approaching are not essentially the same, S can know that the man approaching is hooded, but not know that Coriscus is hooded.

This suggests that Aristotle accepted the following substitution principle:

S knows that Fa
a is the same in essence as b
———————————————
S knows that Fb.

Indeed, given that for Aristotle 'a' and 'b' signify the same provided that they signify the same objects non-accidentally and the answer to 'What is a?' is the same as to 'What is b?', it is difficult to see how he could have avoided accepting this inference pattern.

[24] On this view, Meinongian realms of possible individuals only enter the picture if one fails to separate negation and privation in such sentences as 'Pegasus does not exist.' The Aristotelian diagnosis of the error made by thinkers as diverse as Parmenides, Plato (in the *Sophist*) and Meinong is that they fail to distinguish between the negation of affirmations and individual objects being deprived of properties.

[25] At this point I am indebted to Sandra Lynne Peterson's excellent discussion ('The Master Paradox', Princeton University D.Phil. thesis, 1969). She, however, does not discuss the relation between this substitution principle and Aristotle's account of signification.

However, the resulting position appears paradoxical. 'Cicero' and 'Tully' will have the same significance on this account, and so will 'man', 'biped animal' and 'featherless biped'. But someone may know that men are rational, but not know (it appears) that featherless bipeds are rational, because they are ignorant of the fact that men are featherless bipeds (even if they grasp the significance of each). And this even if they know that men are biped animals. So it appears that Aristotle's substitution principle falls prey to obvious counter-examples. In the grip of these examples, one might wish to challenge (in a Fregean spirit) Aristotle's substitution rule, and the account of meaning which underlies it.

Aristotle's alternative appears to be to divide types of knowledge, separating accidental from non-accidental knowledge. Thus, he writes in discussing intentional action in the *Ethics* (*Nicomachean Ethics* (*EN*)/ *Eudemian Ethics* (*EE*) 1135a24–30):

> I call 'intentional' an action within one's power where one acts knowingly and not in ignorance of who is being affected, with what, and for what good – and one knows each of these non-accidentally . . . for it is possible that the person struck is one's father, and one know that the person is a man or one of the bystanders, but be ignorant that it is one's father.

In this case one knows *non-accidentally* that one is striking a bystander or a man, but only knows *accidentally* that it is one's father. This type of ignorance (accidental knowledge) is to be distinguished from cases where one has no idea one is striking anybody at all (blind ignorance). In this case, Aristotle accepts that one knows *Fb*, because one knows *Fa*, and a = b, but separates different types of knowledge. And this could be so even in cases where a and b are essentially identical. So in these cases, while the following inference will be valid

S knows that Fa
a is the same in essence as b
S knows that Fb,

the premise will concern non-accidental knowledge, while the conclusion will be about accidental knowledge.

What is accidental knowledge? It appears to allow for a way in which one can know *Fb*, even when one is not aware that one does so. The substitution principle is valid, so one does know *Fb* even though one does not know *Fb* in the way in which one would know this proposition if one acted intentionally on it. Thus, one may know *Fb* accidentally if one knows *Fb* in a way which does not allow one to use this knowledge in one's practical reasoning. Accidental knowledge involves *a way of knowing* the simple proposition *Fb* which is consistent with not being aware of it *as* the proposition that *Fb*.[26] More needs to be said about what these ways of knowing are. But the salient fact, for present purposes, is that Aristotle permits the substitution of 'a' and 'b' (when they have the same meaning) in unqualified knowledge contexts because they non-accidentally designate the same object with the same essence.

To grasp the significance of 'a' one must at least know non-accidentally *some* account of what 'a' signifies. But it is not a requirement for knowing the significance of 'a' that one knows *every* account of what 'a' signifies. So one can know non-accidentally that men are rational, but not know non-accidentally that featherless bipeds are rational even though men are non-accidentally featherless bipeds. Accidental knowledge (thus understood) can be of non-accidents. (If this is correct, there can be failures of substitution in the context 'S knows non-accidentally that . . .').

6 Signification and definition

On Aristotle's view, what is signified$_{\text{IMM}}$ in every case is a thought in a thinker's mind, and what determines what is signified in this way is what fixes the contents of these thoughts. In some cases, the content of the thought will be determined by the kind in the world which causes the relevant thought in a *Form-transferring way*. If there is no such kind, the content will be fixed in the different ways outlined in section 4. The ways in which the content is fixed differ in these cases, as the types of thought differ in virtue of the differing ways in which they are produced. While there is a feature common to the signification of 'goat' and 'goatstag' (*viz*. both

[26] Accidental knowledge need not require different objects of knowledge, as accidental causation need not require distinct processes separate from essential causes. See my [251], 50–1. Accidental causes *can* be the same processes as essential causes, but merely be differently described if (for example) Polyclitus, the sculptor, sculpts. At this point, one can see analogies between Aristotle's strategy and recent responses to Frege's puzzle: for example Salmon [529]. Aristotle's *ways of knowing* simple propositions correspond in some measure to Salmon's *guises*. Both at least are non-identical with Fregean senses: see below. But there are also differences, since Aristotle appears to allow free substitution only within certain propositional contexts (for example 'know'), and not within others (for instance 'know non-accidentally'). Hence, his motivation for permitting certain substitutions seems to be specific to certain propositional attitudes, and is not simply the general outcome of the sameness of significance of certain singular terms and a compositional semantics for attitude ascriptions (as in Salmon's proposal). Thus non-accidental knowledge is (for example) of the proposition known when it is seen or grasped in a given way (*viz*. in the manner distinctive of non-accidental knowledge). Since the issues here are complex, and Aristotle's own remarks fragmentary (because he focuses on the central case and ignores peripheral details), a full discussion lies outside the scope of this paper.

signify$_{IMM}$ a relevant thought in the thinker's mind), this similarity is comparatively superficial since the way in which the thought's content is fixed varies considerably between the two cases.

In Aristotle's view (as outlined in section 3) to have a thought of *thunder* is to have a thought caused in the Form-transferring way by thunder. For this to be a thought, one needs to grasp an objective location for thunder in an intelligible world as *a certain kind of noise in the clouds*. The latter gives an account of what the name 'thunder' signifies which has the same significance as 'thunder'. One needs both this account and a thought caused in the right way to have a proper thought of thunder.

This view has important implications for Aristotle's theory of definition. Stage-one accounts of what the name signifies constitute a preliminary and partial definition of 'thunder'. In grasping such an account, one need not know that the kind exists. Nor need one be able to fix the extension of the kind in a way which distinguishes it from other kinds of noise in the clouds. For what makes this an account of 'thunder' is not (for instance) our abilities to discriminate thunder from other noises but rather how the thought itself is caused: *viz.* by thunder. Nor is such an account a dictionary definition of 'thunder', since it fails to give necessary and sufficient conditions for something being thunder.

This type of account need not involve any reflection on what holds the relevant kind together, or indeed on whether the kind has an essence at all. It could be grasped by one who thought that this term marked out an objective kind ('cut the world at its joints'), but had no views about whether (for example) kinds have essences or underlying structures. Its role is rather to hold up a kind for further scientific enquiry into its nature. Such introductory accounts play an important role in enquiry but need not themselves give the materials uniquely to identify the relevant kind. The latter work is done as a result of the thinker's epistemic contact with the kind, leading eventually to a completed definition which fully identifies the kind:

> 'thunder is the noise in the clouds caused by quenching of fire'.

This final definition, while it signifies the same as the name (and introductory account), introduces material which considerably exceeds what is understood in grasping the name or the account of what the name signifies. This is because it contains an answer to the 'Why?' question which is asked, but not resolved, in the initial stages of enquiry. And this is what enables one who possesses the final definition to determine the extension of the term 'thunder'.

The final definition is a full account of what is signified by the name, and thus replaces or completes the initial partial definition. The definitions have the same significance because they both signify non-accidentally the same essential kind. It is this fact alone which is sufficient to account for their shared significance. What fundamentally determines that terms signify the same is how things are in the world, not what thinkers believe or think at different stages in scientific enquiry. In Aristotle's account, it is not our beliefs or practices that determine sense, or sense that determines reference. The pattern runs in the opposite direction. It is how things are in the world and not our practices that fixes the signification of our terms.

The signification of 'thunder' is determined independently of whether we are prepared to defer to experts in using it, whether we can fix the extension of the term or believe that it has an essence (yet to be discussed). For these practices and beliefs emerge in our employment of the thought thus acquired, and do not constitute our possession of it. Naturally, we will be prepared to defer to experts, examine thunder for its essence and search for its extension. But these will be elements in our subsequent enquiry into thunder, and not the basis for our initial understanding of the term. In this way, the 'signification relation' puts us in cognitive contact with a genuine kind which we proceed to investigate. But the *use* to which the thought (or term) is put is not an element in the *meaning* of the term itself. Aristotle rejects output or 'meaning as use' theories of signification at their base.[27]

This general orientation is especially vivid at the beginning of *de Interpretatione*. The world determines what thoughts we have, and these are (in favourable conditions) the same for all (16a6–8). The relevant thoughts cannot be determined by anything narrower than what is specific to humans. Indeed, the account appears not to be limited even to our species, but might include (for all that is said) gods or other animals, who have the relevant psychological states. In any event, the signification of a term is determined independently of any particular features of our own social practices or forms of everyday life. With one bound, Aristotle is free (from taking) social or practice-based elements as constitutive in his account of signification. The contents of Aristotelian thoughts, which are the basis for linguistic meaning, are determined not by our distinctive ways of life or shared social activities, but rather by the way in which kinds in the world imprint themselves on our psychological states. At the centre of his account

[27] For a contrasting view, see Nussbaum [262]. She ties our understanding of linguistic expressions to the distinctive ways of life in our (or similar) communities (pp. 275–6). I find no evidence for this Wittgensteinian reading in the *Analytics* or *de Interpretatione*, which are the basis of my paper.

of signification is a strongly realist view in which the world determines the nature of the thoughts and linguistic expressions we have.[28]

This perspective motivates several of the specific features we have so far noted, and distinguishes Aristotle's account *au fond* from the Fregean theory of sense.[29] Given that names have their significance in this way, it is unsurprising that Aristotle accepts the principles of substitution in knowledge contexts noted in section 5. In his view, terms 'a' and 'b' will have the same significance whether or not a thinker knows that they do. The thinker's preparedness to doubt that $a = b$ in no way undermines the claim that 'a' and 'b' have the same significance. Conversely, 'a' and 'b' can have the same significance, and the thinker know the meaning of both (for example 'being a featherless biped' and 'being a rational biped') but not know that they have the same significance because she does not know that they have the same essence. For it is this which determines whether or not (for instance) 'pride' is univocal (*An. Post.* 97b15–25). Since the thinker may not know whether pride has one essence (or more than one), she may not know whether she is using a 'univocal' term.

Accounts of what names signify are for similar reasons non-equivalent to Fregean senses. They articulate something that has to be grasped if one is to have a genuine thought about (for instance) 'thunder', but they do not give the full significance of the term or sufficient conditions for its successful

[28] His account also differs from joint input and output theories, in which the signification is determined both by what causes the thought *and* by the discriminating knowledge it permits. On a mixed view, one could not have thought of water unless one were able to discriminate samples of water or fix the extension of the term 'water'. Aristotle, if I am correct, would see these latter abilities as ones which one would acquire when one knew the signification of 'water', but not as constitutive of that knowledge. In this respect (among others) Aristotle's view differs from the account of the meaning of such terms formulated by Hilary Putnam in his [521]. I discuss these differences in greater detail in *Aristotle on Meaning and Natural Kinds*.

[29] I take 'Fregean sense-theories' to be committed to the following claims:

(a) to grasp the sense of a term is to grasp something which determines its reference;

(b) senses are *transparent*: if two senses are the same, and one grasps both, one is able to grasp that they are identical without further reflection;

(c) senses are *not* object-dependent (with the exceptions of the senses of 'I', 'now', 'this'); one can grasp the sense of a name and there not be an object to which the name refers.

See, for instance, Dummett [486]. There is currently much controversy over whether Frege himself held all of (a)–(c); the 'new Oxford Fregeans' (for example Evans [496]; McDowell [515]) debate whether, and in what form, he held (a) and (c). However, since Aristotle's view of signification seems to differ on each of these points from Fregean sense theories, distinctions between species of the latter genus are not relevant for our purposes.

application. Rather, they give a partial and incomplete account of the thing which the name signifies, which provides the required starting-point for an enquiry into its essence. However, one cannot (*pace* some contemporary anti-Fregean direct reference theorists) have a genuine thought about 'thunder' without thinking of thunder as an objective kind occupying its own space in an intelligible world. If one lacks this, one may say the word 'thunder', but will not have genuine thoughts about the phenomenon. Belonging to a community where 'elm' is used to signify a kind of tree is not sufficient to give each of its members genuine thoughts about elms, if they lack sufficient distinguishing information about the kind of tree in question. Such people can (for example) ask questions about elms, but do not as yet have Aristotelian thoughts about them.

To have a genuine thought about thunder or man requires that one thinks of the relevant phenomenon as having its own position in an intelligible world: (for instance) as occupying some definite place in a genus/species tree. Thus, thoughts of thunder or man are thoughts of thunder as a type of noise in the clouds, or man as a type of animal. This is why accounts of what the term signifies (in these cases) need to specify a non-accidental property of the relevant kind. For if the property had been accidental, one would have failed to locate the kind in an appropriate manner in its proper slot in the genus/species structure of the world. (This does not require that in knowing such an account one knows that the property is a necessary one. It is sufficient, in Aristotle's view, that the property is *in fact* a necessary one.) The world itself has to possess an intelligible structure of this kind if it is to be the object of our thoughts, and the systematic mode of description essentially involved in thinking. And this is why we cannot *think* of man save as a kind occupying its distinctive slot in this intelligible structure.

There are indications that Aristotle went further than this. On occasion, he suggests that the world itself could not lack this type of intelligible structure because it is essentially identical with the divine mind, and as such essentially an ordered cosmos, governed by the same constraints as thought itself (*DA* 430a15–21). In this account, the components of the *world* must be interconnected as ordered elements in a coherent whole in the same ways as the elements of our thought are. Indeed, it is because the world is thus ordered that our thoughts are similarly organised. If this is so, *man* (*viz.* the kind) could not exist without being placed where it is in its genus/species tree. The kind has to occupy this slot in the same way as our thought of 'man' has to be located in its own slot (as the thought of an animal of a given kind) in our thoughts of the world. Therefore, 'man' will only have the significance it does if it signifies the kind which is essentially an animal of a given kind with its own unique position in the metaphysical structure of reality.[30] At this point Aristotle's account of significance rests on his distinctive version of essentialist metaphysics.

While Aristotle's account of names differs in these ways from some twentieth-century accounts, he is seeking to explain how thoughts and expressions are regulated in such a way as to distinguish between their correct and incorrect application.[31] Thus, 'goat' is on occasion correctly applied to goats, provided that it is goats and not sheep which originally produced the relevant thought in the *Form-transferring way*. 'Goatstag' is incorrectly applied to goats, provided that it is both goats and stags which produced the relevant thought in the relevant way (and not goats). In this sense, Aristotle is offering an account of the *meaning* of names, although its nature differs sharply from the majority of twentieth-century theories.

7 Further metaphysical and epistemological consequences of Aristotle's account of signification

Aristotle's assumptions about the significance of names are to the fore in his discussion of other basic issues. For example, in this defence of the Principle of Non-Contradiction (PNC) in *Met.* III.4 he argues as follows:

> if 'man' signifies one thing (as it does), let this be two-footed animal. I mean by signifying one thing this. If 'man' signifies one thing, *viz.* A, if anything is a man, its being a man will consist in its being A.

In this passage, Aristotle is imposing conditions on 'man' signifying one thing: if it does this, whenever it is used (it signifies) one kind with its own essence (i.e. not by picking out the kind in virtue of some accidental feature it possesses: for example being pale).[32] It is important that 'man' signifies one such kind *non-accidentally* in this manner. If 'man' does signify one kind with

[30] These remarks require much more development and scrutiny. For fuller discussion of the roots of Aristotle's metaphysical essentialism, see my 'Aristotle on Meaning and Natural Kinds'.

[31] For a contrasting view which appears to confine a theory of meaning to (for example) giving dictionary definitions, see Irwin [257], 241–3. Irwin's paper, in effect, challenges one to say how Aristotle can be offering an account of meaning (if he is not (for instance) aiming to give dictionary equivalents). I have been much helped at this point by discussions with Michael Morris.

[32] In this passage, Aristotle does not say 'signifying something by "man" is signifying what it is to be a man'. He is rather imposing conditions on 'man' signifying one thing: if it does this, then it signifies some kind which has an essence. ('Pale', by contrast, will not signify one thing, as there is no kind of this type which it designates.) But this only supports the stronger claim if one adds the following premise: to signify a kind which has an essence is to signify the essence itself. However, this is clearly a further highly controversial step, and there is no sign that Aristotle took it in this passage. For a contrasting view, see Irwin [257], 261–2.

one essence in this way, 'being a man' cannot signify the same as 'not being a man'. For if this happened, 'man' would not signify *one* thing, as it would signify the same as 'not-man'. But this is not the case. Nor could it be. For if it were, there could be no rational discourse or thought about man (1006b9–11).

This argument rests on three major assumptions.

[A] 'Man' signifies one thing.
[B] [A] is possible only if 'man' signifies one kind *non-accidentally* (in contrast with 'pale' and 'educated':1006b14–16).
[C] 'Man' signifies one kind non-accidentally because the kind it signifies (unlike 'pale' or 'educated') has *one* essence of the appropriate type.

[A], [B] and [C], however, do not demand that the name 'man' itself signifies the essence. All that they require is that the name signifies something which has an essence (if it is to signify *one* thing).[33] And this is an advantage in the dialectical context of *Met.* III.4. For if the sceptic about the PNC could only be defeated if he already accepted that names signify essences, it would have been easy for him to escape refutation by accepting that

[A] 'Man' signifies one thing,

while denying that what it signifies is an essence. It might, for example, signify a substance which has an essence, but not the essence itself. Or the composite. In these ways, the term 'man' would have significance without its signifying an essence at all.

[A], [B] and [C] are important in this argument because they show that

[33] This is also true of Aristotle's subsidiary argument in *Met.* 1006b28–34. This runs as follows:
(1) What 'man' signifies is two-footed animal.
(2) Necessarily, if a is a man, a is a two-footed animal.
(3) It is not possible that if a is a man, a is not a two-footed animal.
The transition from (1) to (2) is valid (given [A] and [B]) without requiring that 'man' signifies the essence of man. All that it presupposes is that 'man' signifies a unity which has a given essence ('This – *viz.* a two-footed animal – was what "man" signified' 1006b29–30). And this seems the correct way to take this in the light of the cautious (extensional) interpretation of 'signifying one thing' offered in 1006a31–4. The transition from (1) to (2) is interesting in its own right, for it sharpens the constraints on 'signification' in line with [B]. This requires that if 'gold' signifies gold, it is necessary that gold is gold. So what is signified cannot be an accidental feature of gold (so specified). If the necessity is *de re*, what is signified cannot be an accidental feature of gold (*that* very stuff). But this does not require that what is signified is the essence of gold. For it could be the substance (gold) which is signified, which has an essence which (in Aristotle's view) it could not lack.

Aristotle's defence of PNC is addressed to opponents other than the small group of ultra-essentialists who happen to accept the somewhat implausible premise:

[D] 'Man' signifies the essence of man

while rejecting

[E] 'Man' signifies a substance, which has an essence.

[E] is both semantically shallower and more plausible than [D]. Since Aristotle is concerned to give a general defence of PNC, it is 'man' in the sense of [E] with which he must be principally concerned (cf. 1043a28–32). In this understanding, the significance of 'man' and 'the essence of man' are distinct [1043b2–3).[34]

Aristotle envisages that his opponent will deny [B] by denying [C]: all predication is accidental, because there are no distinct essences of the type envisaged in [C] (1007a34–5, 20–2).[35] Aristotle replies that if there are no essences, there will be no basic subjects for sentences such as

'Man is F',

because the subject term will dissolve into several parts said accidentally of each other. And this will go on indefinitely, each new subject term dissolving in turn in this way (1007a35–b1). But this (according to Aristotle) is not possible as accidents can only be predicated of each other if both belong to one substance with one essence (1007b3–5, 15–16). There must be simple sentences in which 'one thing is said of one thing' at the basis of any such predication-tree, where the latter one thing in this case is a kind with its own essence.

[34] For a contrasting view, see Irwin [257], 262–5. It is a merit of Irwin's discussion that he focuses on the relation between signification and essence in *Met.* III.4.

[35] Those who take this line (according to Aristotle) must say that there is 'no such thing as what it is to be man . . . For this phrase ['*what it is to be a man*'] signifies one thing, and this is the essence of something. And to signify an essence is [to signify] that there is nothing else which is what it is to be that thing' (1007a21–7). So these people must give up talking of *what it is to be a man* (and so reject [C]). In this passage the focus of the discussion is on the significance of the phrase: *what it is to be a man* (1007a22, 23), and this must be the subject of '*it* signifies one thing'. This argument therefore is not connected directly with the issue of the significance of '*man*', since '*man*' and '*what it is to be a man*' differ in significance (1043a29–32, b3–4). A more cautious opponent would deny [C] without claiming that everything is said accidentally. He would rather account for 'signifying one thing' in a way which is neutral with respect to the existence or non-existence of essences. But this opponent is not on stage precisely because he is objecting to Aristotle's basic semantic assumptions which underlie this argument (*viz.* [A] and [B]).

In this reply, [B] is particularly important. Aristotle is, in effect, supposing that 'man', if it signifies one thing, signifies one kind non-accidentally. 'Man' has its significance because it signifies that kind on all occasions when it is coherently uttered. Its significance cannot be fixed by a description accidentally true of man. Thus 'signifying one thing' requires that the term designates the same kind of object whenever it is used with this significance. It could not maintain its self-same significance and apply to a different object or kind. There is no possible case in which 'man' or 'Cicero' has the significance it actually does and signifies a different object or kind from the one it actually does. This is ruled out by Aristotle's understanding of 'signifying one thing', and the *likening account* of thought (see section 3) on which it is based. Further, 'man' signifies one kind non-accidentally because (in Aristotle's theory) the kind has its own essence of an appropriate type in virtue of which it occupies a distinctive slot in the metaphysical structure of reality ([C]: see section 6). Possession of this essence is what makes the kind the one it is. Aristotle's metaphysical theory is introduced to legitimise his account of non-accidental signification. Given that 'man' has the significance it does, it must signify the kind *man* with its own distinctive essence.

So strong is Aristotle's attachment to [B] that he cannot envisage that one might accept [A] and reject [B] by allowing that 'man' *happens* to signify one thing because only one thing in this world happens to satisfy some relevant definite description. For this alternative would allow [A] to be true without [B] or [C] being accepted. It is because Aristotle is committed to [B] that he thinks that if kinds lacked essences, terms would cease to signify one thing. Aristotle's defence of PNC shows how firmly he is wedded to semantic claims [A] and [B], and to his attendant understanding of basic simple affirmations. His method is to argue that if someone signifies something, there must be objects signified non-accidentally by names in their basic propositions (1006a21–3, 31–b12). In effect, Aristotle takes [A] and [B] as his starting-point, together with the assumption that there is significant discourse, and then proceeds to give an account of substance and essence which legitimises these semantic assumptions.[36]

[36] In particular, Aristotle needs to show what type of object is signified in the relevant basic propositions, and how they are connected with their essences (*Met.* VI.6,17; VII.2,3,6). Thus, his metaphysical account is one part of his attempt to vindicate his assumption that basic names signify kinds in nature. In addition, he had to spell out how we are in fact in cognitive contact with such kinds (see section 3). Aristotle undertook both these tasks. However, the crucial point from his viewpoint is that both projects were ones he shared with anyone who successfully engaged in significant discourse, and wished to explain how this occurred. For the relevant assumptions are common ground for all who participate in significant discourse.

Aristotle's theory of signification is a realist one. The signification relation in the basic case of non-complex names in single affirmations attaches us to kinds in the world with their distinctive essences. Given that such non-complex names signify, there must be genuine kinds in the world with which we are in appropriate causal contact if we are to have thoughts at all. It is small wonder that, armed with this view of signification, he was untroubled by 'global scepticism' about the existence of an external world containing natural kinds. There had to be such a world, with which we are in cognitive contact, for the basic expressions of our language to signify at all, or for us to have the thoughts we need intelligibly to raise (for example 'Cartesian') sceptical doubts. It was only with the emergence of a different, and less plausible, set of semantic assumptions that global sceptical doubts of this kind could be coherently raised.

In the light of this theory of signification, widely held or authoritative opinions cannot constitute truth. The testimony of the many, or of relevant experts, is to be accepted because they are in close, and reliable, contact with the kinds they study. Aristotle required an account of the precise nature of epistemically relevant contact necessary for *knowledge*. But this account was not the basis for his positive views about *truth*. Realism was presupposed at the first stage in his account of the signification of names. Terms have their significance, and can be used to express truths, whether or not we can know such claims to be true. Truth is not constituted by our knowledge of the world, nor is it posited as the best explanation of why we all believe certain things to be true.[37] From Aristotle's viewpoint these options appear unattractive because they both ignore the prior commitment to a realist account of truth already implicit in his account of thought and signification. Whatever the role of dialectic may be in Aristotle's epistemology, it does not provide either his answer to scepticism or the basis of his theory of truth. For these are already presupposed in his account of signification.

8 Problems and possibilities

At the base of Aristotle's account of language there are semantically simple names (including proper names and common nouns) in single affirmations which signify individual substances and kinds. Complex names and complex expressions depend for their significance on the existence of

[37] In this, Aristotle is not an 'internal realist' for whom 'truth is inside the circle of our lived experiences of the world'. For a contrasting view, see Nussbaum [262], 290–2.

semantically simple names, whose significance in turn is determined by the thoughts with which they are correlated being intrinsically *likened* to substances and kinds in the world (see section 2). These simple names, and the single affirmations in which they prominently figure, shape central elements of Aristotle's logical, metaphysical and epistemological theory (see sections 4, 6 and 7).

Aristotle's reliance on the relation of *likening* of thoughts to substances and kinds is the first central feature in his account, and one which underlies his discussion of simple and non-simple names, existence, negation and knowledge. His confidence in this relation enabled him to allow the thinker using simple names cognitive contact with kinds and substances in the world, even if she had no knowledge of their existence and no views at all about their internal structure. It is because Aristotle conceived of the *likening* relation in this way that he was under no pressure to treat ordinary names and common nouns as complex, or to limit his simple names to (for example) sense-data or some set of phenomena with privileged (for instance incorrigible) epistemic status. Nor did Aristotle's simple names attach to indefinable, primary elements of which nothing further could be said.[38] For terms like 'man' are attached to kinds whose internal natures are discoverable, and whose connections with other kinds ('*animal*', etc.) are discernible in grasping the account of what they signify. There is a limited holism involved in grasping the relevant thoughts of *man* and *animal* at the outset (*An. Post.* 100a10 ff.). In these ways Aristotle's account of the bearers of simple names differs fundamentally from (for example) Russellian basic 'individuals', or the simples of the *Theaetetus* (compare Wittgenstein, *Philosophical Investigations* 1.46, commenting on *Theaetetus* 201e2 ff.). But in turn it rests on his account of the *likening* of thoughts to substances and kinds. The most pressing philosophical and scholarly question in this area is to examine how far this fundamental relation is well defined and properly motivated. But the answer requires a full understanding of Aristotle's account of the content of *thought* in *de Anima*, which lies outside the scope of this paper.

The general shape of Aristotle's account of names, built on this foundation, is a distinctive one. His emphasis on *likening* makes his theory superficially like those anti-Fregean direct reference accounts which pro-

[38] It was only when thinkers like Russell attached simple names to items of which one has immediate knowledge that it becomes attractive to limit the reference of such names in this way. See Russell [525]. The interconnections between Russell's views and Plato's *Theaetetus* are discussed by McDowell in his [183].

mote a speaker's causal contact with the object or kind as constitutive of the semantic significance of the name.[39] However, unlike such accounts, Aristotle also requires that the speaker, if she is to have *thoughts* about *man* or *elms*, should possess enough information to locate the kind in an objective grid of the genus–species type (see section 2). Causal contact – even of the likening kind – is not enough to give a speaker *thoughts* about man unless she also possesses an elementary account of what 'man' signifies. But, in Aristotle's account, although such accounts are required for *thoughts* about kinds or individuals, and they have the same significance (in Aristotelian terms) as the relevant names, they do not constitute Fregean senses (for the reasons given in section 6). In this respect Aristotle's account represents an interesting and unoccupied mid-position between Fregean and direct reference theorists.

This paper has focused on Aristotle's account of names used in affirmations as signs of thoughts about objects and kinds in an objective world. But it might seem completely magical that people come to have such thoughts or express such affirmations. Does not the mastery of such names require the thinker already to possess a rich web of linguistic knowledge, which is not itself explained in Aristotle's picture? Is Aristotle not vulnerable in this way to the very objections which Wittgenstein pressed against Augustine's apparently Aristotelian account of signification (*Philosophical Investigations* 1.1–3, 31–3)? These questions are of the first importance in reaching a balanced evaluation of Aristotle's views. But it should be noted at the outset that in his account the emergence of thoughts about *man* or *gold* is the product of a long and complicated process which essentially involves previous *experience* of (for example) pieces of gold or particular human beings of the type a skilled artisan or doctor might have (*Met.* 981a10 ff., *An. Post.* 100a3–14). Such people are guided by *imagination* but may none the less lack Aristotelian thoughts, and fail to make Aristotelian affirmations (*DA* 432a11–13) or grasp names of kinds in the ways we have so far considered. Their understanding of terms like *man, illness* or *gold* appears to be exhausted by their practical ability to discriminate particular cases of each when they are confronted by them (cf. *Met.* 981a5–12), without requiring any theoretical or explicit grasp on the kind itself. In Aristotle's view, such people can have a practical grasp on natural kinds before they have objective thoughts about them. Thus he did not take *thought* as the unexplained starting-point in his account of the signification of names, even

[39] As discussed in Evans [496], 64ff.

if (Wittgenstein's) Augustine did. His emphasis on the importance of a prior practical grasp on natural kinds[40] opens up rich areas for further study, but they lie outside the scope of this paper.[41]

[40] If a skilled craftsman does grasp the *same* term 'gold' or 'man' as the fully conceptual thinker, it is clear that the content of the latter's thought cannot be constitutive of the significance of the name 'gold'. For one could grasp the natural kind term 'gold' without having any such thought or account of what the name signifies. The alternative possibility is to admit that there are no genuine Aristotelian *names* for kinds at the pre-conceptual level. Both philosophical and exegetical issues are complex at this point and require further detailed investigation.

[41] I have gained from discussion of these topics with Jonathan Barnes, Robert Bolton, Tyler Burge, John Campbell, Kei Chiba, Stephen Everson, Michael Frede, Montgomery Furth, Tomomasa Imai, Shigeru Kanzaki, Atsushi Kawatani, Stephen Law, Gavin Lawrence, Mario Mignucci, Michael Morris, Pantazis Tselemanis, Thomas Upton, Jiro Watanabe and Timothy Williamson. An early version of some of these ideas was contained in my paper 'Aristotle on Meaning and Natural Kinds'. Later versions were read at a conference on Aristotle's Biology at La Rochelle (1987), at UCLA, UC Irvine and Stanford (1989), at Villanova University (1990), and at Tokyo University and Trinity College, Dublin (1991). I am indebted to critical audiences on each of these occasions. Michael Morris' unpublished papers on Aristotle on Meaning greatly assisted me in thinking about these issues.

5
Epicurus on mind and language

STEPHEN EVERSON

In his rather sharp review of the first (and, as it turned out, the only) volume of Husserl's *Philosophie der Arithmetik*, Frege complains of 'the devastation caused by the irruption of psychology into logic' – something he characterises as 'a widespread philosophical disease'.[1] The source of Husserl's particular infection was, according to Frege, that of taking words to designate ideas rather than objects:

> Here [in the conception of number as an aggregate] one feels the need to cleanse things of their peculiarities. The present attempt belongs to those that carry out the cleansing operation in the wash-tub of the mind. The advantage this offers is that the things in it assume a quite peculiar pliancy; they no longer knock so hard against each other in space and shed many of their bothersome peculiarities and differences. The mixture of psychology and logic, which is so popular nowadays, yields a strong lye for this purpose. First everything is turned into ideas. The meanings of words are ideas. Thus the thing to do with e.g. the word 'number' is to point to the corresponding idea and to describe its origin and composition. Objects are ideas. Thus J. S. Mill, to the author's applause, allows objects ('whether physical or mental') to enter into a state of consciousness and to form part of this state of consciousness. But would not, e.g., the moon sit a bit heavy on the stomach of one's state of consciousness?[2]

Once objects have been turned into ideas, so that the terms 'A' and 'the idea of A' are taken to designate the same thing, the investigation of those objects becomes a branch of psychology.[3] As Frege points out, 'if a geographer were given an oceanic treatise to read which gave a psychological explanation of the origin of the oceans, he would undoubtedly get the impression that the

[1] Frege [498]. [2] [498], 316. Translation from [517], 197.

[3] 'The circumstance that expressions like "moon" and "idea of the moon" are never clearly distinguished, spreads such an impenetrable fog that the attempt to get clear . . . is doomed to failure' ([498], 329 ([517], 207)).

author had missed the mark and shot past the thing itself in a most peculiar way'.[4]

Clearly, to treat oceanography as a species of psychology would be a gross confusion, as it would be to think that numerical terms *refer* to psychological states. Quite rightly, in the introduction to his own *Grundlagen der Arithmetik*, Frege sets out as two of his three fundamental principles 'always to separate sharply the psychological from the logical, the subjective from the objective' and 'never to lose sight of the distinction between concept and object'. It has become customary to apply the term 'psychologistic' to discussions, whether of mathematics or of anything else, in which these principles are not respected. Now, whilst the confusion which consists in conflating concept and object – in treating the terms '*A*' and 'the idea of *A*' as if they had the same reference – is a straightforward one, it is possible to find in Frege's work the diagnosis of what some have taken to be an even more insidious confusion of the psychological and the non-psychological.

So, in his essay 'Über Sinn und Bedeutung', Frege distinguishes the reference (*Bedeutung*) of an expression from its sense (*Sinn*). Two expressions may share the same reference but still differ in sense: although 'The evening star' and 'The morning star' both refer to the same thing (the planet Venus), it is possible to understand them without knowing that they do refer to the same thing. The sense of an expression is, to use Dummett's phrase, its 'cognitive value'.[5] The sense of a sentence is what one grasps when one understands it – it is the content of a thought. What is important here is that both the reference *and* the sense of an expression are further distinguished from any associated idea (*verknüpfte Verstellung*) which people have.[6] Whilst the last is subjective, both of the first two are objective – that is, whilst the idea of, say, the moon may differ between individuals, neither the reference nor the sense of the term 'the moon' will so differ. As Frege puts it, using a different example,

> A painter, a horseman, and a zoologist will probably connect different ideas with the name 'Bucephalus'. This constitutes an essential distinction between the idea and the sign's sense, which may be the common property of many people and so is not a part or mode of the individual mind . . . In the light of this, one need have no scruples in speaking simply of *the* sense, whereas in the case of an idea one must, strictly speaking, add whom it belongs to and at what time.[7]

[4] [498], 332. Translation from [517], 209. D. Bell, in his [475], 59 f., attempts to defend Husserl against Frege's reading of him. See Dummett [491], 19–21 for a defence of Frege on the point.

[5] See Dummett [486], 94.

[6] Frege [499]. See 43–6.

[7] Translation by M. Black in [517], 160 (=[499], 44).

The point is that whereas it is possible for the same sense to be grasped by two different people, it is not possible for them to share the same idea. Whilst what it is to entertain a thought is to grasp the sense of a sentence, that sense remains objective in that it is independent of its being grasped by any particular thinker.[8]

Sense thus plays a key role in Frege's explanation of linguistic understanding, and it is plausible to see in his doctrine of sense, with its detachment of the contents of thoughts from the ideas which are relative to particular episodes of thinking, the reversal of the traditional attempt to explain the meaning of language by reference to the contents of thoughts, *independently and antecedently conceived*. That is, rather than trying to explain the meaning of language by reference to the content of thoughts, where these are dependent upon particular acts of thinking, Frege provided the means, by first determining the senses of sentences, to specify the contents of thoughts. In this way, Frege's explanation both of language and of thought stands opposed not merely to a psychologism which fails to respect the distinction between concept and object but to one in which the theory of meaning is treated as itself a branch of psychology.

So, according to Michael Dummett, the effect of Frege's doctrine was to make possible adequate theories both of language and of thought precisely because it allowed the theorist to construct a proper account of understanding:

> Thoughts – the senses of sentences – are, on his account, intimately connected with the notion of truth – a notion belonging to the theory of reference. Our grasp of the sense of an expression is our way of apprehending what its reference is – a particular way, out of various possible ways; and our grasp of the thought expressed by a sentence is constituted by our apprehension of the condition for it to be true. The notion of understanding – of a grasp of sense – is of crucial importance to a philosophy of either thought or language . . . We can arrive at a plausible account of sense only if we first have a workable conception of content – of that which is grasped; and this is why Frege arrived, for the first time in the history of philosophical enquiry, at what was at least the beginnings of a plausible account of sense, and thus of understanding. Those who *started* with the conception of the inner grasp of meaning floundered in confused descriptions of irrelevant mental processes, achieving nothing towards explaining either the general notion of meaning or the meanings of specific expressions.[9]

[8] Cf. [517], 369: 'The grasp of a thought presupposes someone who grasps it, who thinks. He is the owner of thinking, not of the thought.'

[9] Dummett [491], 15.

On Dummett's view, the theorist of thought must *begin* with the specification of the meanings of sentences – a specification which should make no reference to the psychological states of those who understand the sentences. Only once this has been achieved can one begin to provide a theory of thought by using those specifications. Any theory, either of thought or of language, which does not respect the explanatory priority of language to thought will be psychologistic and hence unsuccessful.[10]

Whether or not Dummett is correct in his contention that an account of linguistic meaning which makes use of psychological notions must thereby fail, his deployment of Frege's distinction in this context can be taken to have set up a challenge to any theorist who does bring psychological states or acts (such as thought or belief or intention) into the explanation of linguistic meaning.[11] Such a theorist will need to establish at least two things if his theory is to succeed. First, it must be possible to get some grip on the content of thought independently of that content's finding linguistic expression – otherwise the theory will be circular (and the circle will be too restricted to do any significant explanatory work). Secondly, it must be shown how a public language is possible. The danger of allowing the meaning of linguistic expressions to be determined by the content of thoughts is that one will no longer have the means to establish the distinction between a thought and a thinking – and so linguistic meaning will itself become subjectivised. It was for this reason, as we have seen, that Frege distinguished between the contents of thought and subjective ideas.[12] By taking the former to be specified by giving the sense of a sentence, already determined by its way of fixing its truth-condition, he was able to treat the content of a thought as independent of any particular act of thinking in which it is grasped. Anyone who reverses the direction of explanation will need to secure the objectivity of language in some other way.

Confused or not, the attempt to explain linguistic meaning by reference to the intentional content of the psychological states of speakers has proved attractive since the earliest linguistic theorists. We find, for instance, the following account of the relation between words and mental states at the beginning of Aristotle's *de Interpretatione*:

[10] Dummett has pursued this theme throughout a series of writings. See, for instance, his [486], 157–9, [489] and [488].

[11] Of course, the fact that a theory of the sense of sentences has to serve as a theory of understanding can properly place constraints on how it is derived – hence Dummett's own worries concerning the Davidsonian project of deriving it from the truth-conditions of sentences, when truth is realistically conceived.

[12] The idea of subjectivity here imports no more than that ideas, unlike thoughts, will be individuated by reference to the subject who has the idea.

> Spoken sounds are symbols (*sumbola*) of affections in the soul (*psuchē*) and written marks are symbols of spoken sounds. And just as written marks are not the same for all men, neither are spoken sounds. But what these are in the first place signs (*sēmeia*) of – affections of the soul – are also the same for all; and what these affections are likenesses (*homoiōmata*) of – actual things (*pragmata*) – are also the same. (16a3–8)

Words, which are conventional, stand as signs for mental states – which have their intentional properties in virtue of being 'likenesses' of objects in the world. The structure of Aristotelian semantic theory is to provide an account of the content of thoughts, or concepts, and then to view the semantic properties of words as derivable from this.

The question of whether and, if so, how Aristotelian psychologism could meet Dummett's Fregean challenges lies outside the scope of this paper. What will concern us is to determine whether Epicurus' semantic theory is psychologistic and, if it is, whether it is confusedly so. I shall take it that a semantic theory is psychologistic if it accepts that in specifying the meaning of sentences or the reference of words (or in explaining how particular linguistic items have the semantic properties they do) the theorist must make reference to the content of the psychological states of speakers. A theory, such as Husserl's, which takes, say, mathematical words actually to refer to ideas will count as psychologistic, but so will any theory in which words and sentences have their semantic properties in virtue of the semantic or intentional properties of mental states.

Whereas 'psychologism' is generally used now as a term of abuse, implying the *confusion* of the psychological with the non-psychological, it need not carry this implication. Certainly a psychologistic mechanics would rest on confusion, but so, equally, would a non-psychologistic theory of action.[13] We should not treat it as decided in advance that if Epicurus is committed to a psychologistic theory of language, this must be the result of confusion on his part.

[13] There is room for caution here, however. John McDowell in his [516], 225–6, actually complains of Frege's 'psychologistic conception of the psychological', in which 'the domain of the mental is marked out by the line between the inner and outer', so casting 'psychological facts about other people . . . to utter unknowability'. McDowell's hope is that by cleansing psychology of this conception of the psychological, one need not root out 'everything psychological from our account of how language works' in order to avoid psychologism. In the present discussion, however, I assume no particular conception of psychological states and McDowell's very subtle discussion would still count as psychologistic, as that term is employed here.

What underlie the utterances

After some introductory remarks, Epicurus begins the summary of his physical doctrines, the *Letter to Herodotus* (*Hdtm.*), with some advice about method:

> First, then, Herodotus, we must grasp the things which underlie utterances (*ta hupotetagmena tois phthongois*) so that we may have them as a reference point against which to judge what is believed or investigated or puzzled over, lest everything be undiscriminated (*akrita*) by us, as we attempt infinite chains of proofs, or we have empty utterances. For the primary concept[14] (*prōton ennoēma*) corresponding to each utterance (*phthongos*) must be seen and need no additional proof, if we are going to have something to which to refer what is investigated or puzzled over or believed. (*Hdtm.* 37=LS 17C[15])

Although Epicurus' primary concern here is with how to ground one's beliefs, the references to language are suggestive – and, given the paucity of our evidence for Epicurus' theory of language, commentators have had to treat it as being of some importance for the reconstruction of that theory. What we learn from the passage is that every utterance is related – 'corresponds' in Long and Sedley's translation – in some way to an *ennoēma* and that (or in that) these *ennoēmata* 'underlie' utterances.[16] This, as it stands, is not very helpful. What needs to be determined if the passage is to cast light on Epicurean linguistic theory is, first, what an *ennoēma* is, secondly, what is the relation in which *ennoēmata* stand to utterances, and thirdly, what, if anything, that relation is taken by Epicurus to explain about language. Since the passage is both important and suggestive, it will not be surprising that answering these questions has occasioned considerable disagreement amongst Epicurus' commentators. On the basis of different answers to them, Epicurus has been taken to advance a semantic theory which is psychologistic, to treat linguistic meaning as extensional and to offer no theory of meaning at all.[17]

[14] I have retained Long and Sedley's 'primary concept' as the translation of *prōton ennoēma*, although, as will become clear, this is controversial. Unfortunately there is, I think, no neutral translation available.

[15] Somewhat altered.

[16] 'Utterance' is intended to be a reasonably neutral translation of *phthongos*. It is not clear quite what sort of item is to be counted as a *phthongos*: the term could refer to any uttered sound, or to words, or to parts of words, or even possibly to sentences. As I shall argue later, there is some reason for taking *phthongoi* to be semantic units (or parts of such units), but this question should be treated as open for the moment.

[17] For these views, see respectively Long [364], De Lacy [362] and Glidden [363].

So, in their *The Hellenistic Philosophers*, Long and Sedley claim that what are said to underlie utterances in this passage are 'preconceptions' (*prolēpseis*), which they take to be 'generic notion[s] of any type of object of experience, the concept naturally evoked by the name of that thing' and that here they appear in 'their guise of the meanings underlying words'.[18] It is not entirely clear, perhaps, what this latter claim amounts to. In talking of something which, in its different 'guises', can apparently be both psychological and semantic, it might seem as if Long and Sedley are thinking of *prolēpseis* as similar to Fregean senses: a sense, after all, is the meaning of a sentence and is what is grasped in thinking. It is not obvious, however, that this is what they have in mind and, in any case, *prolēpseis* are not well suited to play the role of the senses either of words or of sentences. In an earlier piece, Long had similarly claimed that 'the meaning of a word is primarily the *prolēpsis* or concept which it brings to mind', where *prolēpseis* are 'fine aggregates of atoms which present themselves to consciousness as images'.[19] According to Long and Sedley, then, the meanings of words are firmly psychological entities – concepts or mental images – and it is these to which the natural scientist must look when pursuing his investigations. The theory of meaning which results from this interpretation is quite clearly a psychologistic one. It may be that Long and Sedley are rash to claim that *prolēpseis are* the meanings of words on this picture but words will have meaning in virtue of corresponding to psychological states which have intentional properties because they are images. The reference of a term is determined by what its associated *prolēpsis* is a *prolēpsis* of. Semantics becomes dependent upon psychology, and determining the meaning of words becomes a matter of determining the intentional properties of the psychological processes or states to which they correspond. *Prolēpsis* will play the same role in Epicurus' theory that the relevant 'affections of the soul' apparently do in Aristotle's.[20]

In contrast to this psychologistic reading of *Hdtm.* 37 is one offered by David Glidden, who argues that what we should understand to underlie utterances are not psychological entities such as speaker's concepts but rather 'the referents of our utterances, the things in the world voiced sounds identify'.[21] If this is right, then the *prōton ennoēma* which corresponds to an

[18] Long and Sedley [308], I, 89 – see also p. 101. Strictly, they claim that these are 'almost certainly what Epicurus also calls "preconceptions"'. In his [324], 14 f., Sedley argues that Epicurus' introduction of the term *prolēpsis* post-dates the writing of the *Letter to Herodotus* (except the discussion of time in 72–3, which, he argues, was a later addition).

[19] Long [364], 120. [20] The parallel is claimed by Long himself: *ibid.*, 121.

[21] Glidden [363], 198.

utterance will also need to be removed from the realm of the mind: it will not be, as Long and Sedley translated the term, a 'primary *concept*'. Accordingly Glidden takes it not to be 'some subjective mental representation . . . but rather some feature of reality one has become cognizant about by means of using one's sense organs, which provide a physiological and physical link between observers and the world'.[22]

Indeed, not only, on Glidden's view, are meanings not to be identified with mental states, but they play no role in Epicurean linguistic theory at all. The meaning of a word does not determine its reference, and there is no role for the study of semantics as such: 'just as Wittgenstein's *Investigations* do not present a theory of linguistics so much as some assorted views concerning how speech acts are used, so we should understand the Epicurean account of language as a theory of behaviour at best'.[23] What distinguishes Epicurean linguistic theory from that of, say, Aristotle is precisely the lack of any role for mental states in the determination of the meaning, or the reference, of words: 'Words do not acquire their use as referring expressions on the basis of some prior conceptual recognition which mediates between the sound and its reference. Rather, reference succeeds because of natural utility, where human sounds label things in response to sensory stimulation just as animal sounds do.'[24] Rather than a word's referring to something in virtue of corresponding to or signalling the speaker's concept of that thing, it does so in virtue of being elicited by the action of its referent on the speaker's senses.

It can be said immediately that Glidden's reading of *Hdtm.* 37 – at least in its understanding of *prōton ennoēma* – is far from natural. The word *ennoēma* is not a common one: it is cognate with *ennoein*, 'to think', and thus with *nous*, 'mind'. It appears once before, in the first book of Aristotle's *Metaphysics*, where it clearly refers to a type of mental item,[25] and was to become something of a technical term in Stoicism for general concepts.[26] This provides at least strong external evidence against taking Epicurus to use the term to refer to things outside the mind – certainly given the absence of any apology or embarrassment. To counter this objection, Glidden tries to palliate his reading of *ennoēma* by comparing it with the term 'bit of information' as used in 'computer language'. Both terms, he claims, 'divide [their] reference between some physical state of the organism, or machine state, and the state of the world that the organism, or machine, is attending to'.[27] 'Divided reference' here seems to signify little more than ambiguity –

[22] *Ibid.*, 196. [23] *Ibid.*, 202. [24] *Ibid.*, 201–2.

[25] 981a6: 'Art comes about when from many notions (*ennoēmata*) gained through experience, one universal judgement about similar objects is produced.'

[26] See Long and Sedley, section 30. [27] Glidden [363], 197.

and a dangerous ambiguity at that: 'bit of information' may refer to a state of the machine or it may refer to what that state is about. There is certainly no reason to think that *ennoēma*, at least, is ambiguous in this way – or, I suspect, that 'bit of information' is. No doubt one can specify a piece of information either syntactically (as a series of digits) or semantically (as being the information that *p*), but in both cases the reference is firmly to a state of the machine. There is no 'division' of the reference of the term between the machine and the world.[28] 'Bit of information', like *ennoēma* when taken naturally, refers to a state which has content and not to what that state is about.[29]

What seems to spur Glidden into his anti-psychologistic reading of *Hdtm.* 37 is the thought that, as a materialist, Epicurus should have no business talking of mental states at all. So, he writes:

> If we take Epicurean materialism seriously, the *ennoēma* as an organic episode (an act of attention) or, in its primary use, as referring to what one is attending to surely cannot be something mental, neither a mental act (i.e. non-physical) nor a mental object. And if we are to take Epicurus' injunction [to see the *prōton ennoēma* corresponding to each utterance] as urging us to observe [*sic*] the 'brain state' correlated with every utterance, then it would seem that every utterance concerns ourselves alone (specifically our physiology). It is far more likely that what we are to observe is what that 'brain state' is attending to in the world.[30]

The advantage of taking *ennoēma* to refer to what is observed in the world rather than to some mental state which is about what is observed in the world is, on this view, that one can remove from Epicurus' account of cognition and language items to which, as a materialist, he should not offer house room. Glidden acknowledges that his account of Epicurus has not removed all potential for materialist embarrassment – in particular the talk of 'attending to' some object is, he thinks, 'difficult for a materialist to use' – but at least in avoiding taking *ennoēma* to refer to a mental entity, he has rid Epicurus' account of something 'whose very existence . . . contradicts materialism'.

Now, it is almost a commonplace amongst contemporary philosophers that the price of adopting a materialist metaphysics is the need to reject

[28] See Dretske [485], 5 f., for a discussion of information bits.

[29] In its standard use, the notion of divided reference is applied to general terms in contrast to singular and mass terms: thus Quine [523], 90–1: 'a singular term names, or purports to name, just one object, though as complex and diffuse an object as you please, while a general term is true of each, severally, of any number of objects'. In this sense, the *terms ennoēma* and 'bit of information' will indeed divide their reference, but hardly in the way Glidden requires.

[30] Glidden [363], 197, n. 37.

items which have intentional or semantic properties unless those properties can be shown to reduce to properties recognised by physics.[31] We can leave to one side the question of whether this commonplace amounts to much more than prejudice and rest content for the moment with noting that the urge either to secure the mental by showing that (and how) it can be reduced to the physical or, failing that, to eliminate it altogether is indeed a contemporary and not an ancient one. Epicurus was certainly an atomist, convinced that 'the totality of things is bodies and void' (*Hdtm.* 39 = LS 5A1) and that all phenomena could be explained in terms of the movement of atoms through the void. His writings, however, are shot through with mentalistic idioms, and he shows no sign at all of embarrassment in this.[32] There is certainly no overt contradiction between Epicurus' atomism and his taking *ennoēmata* to be mental items: he need be committed to no more than that any *ennoēma* has both a mental and an atomistic description. An *ennoēma* will then be both a concept of something, or belief about it, and also an arrangement, or movement, of atoms.

So, whether or not Epicurus' materialism should have led him to give up mentalistic explanation (or, indeed, vice versa), it did not in fact do so – and so there is no pressure from that source to read the remarks in *Hdtm.* 37 in such a way that Epicurus is denying that words correspond (in some way or other) to psychological states of speakers.[33] If there is to be such pressure, it will need to come from elsewhere.[34]

Words and objects

There are two possible sources of such pressure: first, there are two passages from later authors in which Epicurus' semantic theory is contrasted, explicitly or implicitly, with that of the Stoics. Secondly, there is Epicurus' own account of the origins of language, which will be examined in the next section.

[31] See Quine [523], 219–21. The literature on this topic is now, of course, immense.

[32] See Annas [310], 84 f., for the contrast between Epicurus and contemporary psychological materialists. Sedley [356] argues against taking Epicurean materialism to involve reductionism.

[33] And that they do gains some further support from Epicurus' *de Natura* 28 (fr. 13VII.4, Sedley), in which false belief (*doxa*) is said to be subordinate to words (*pseudēs hupotetachthai tais lexesin ekeinais doxa*) – so that it was clearly, at least at the time of the *de Nat.*, consistent with Epicurean doctrine to treat mental states as being 'subordinate' to words. See also Philodemus, *de Rhetorica* B261.10–14 (Sbordone).

[34] Glidden's claim is that if we take *ennoēmata* to be mental items, this will have the effect of making every utterance concern ourselves is easily dispatched: it does not follow from the fact that an utterance corresponds to a mental state that it refers to, or is about, that state.

Plutarch's *adversus Colotem* (*adv. Col.*) is an attack on the work of Epicurus' disciple Colotes. At one point he ridicules Colotes' rejection of the Megarian philosopher Stilpo's abolition of predication. According to Stilpo, predication as such is impossible because one can only couple two expressions by means of the verb 'to be' (*esti*) if the referents of the expressions have the same essence.[35] Effectively restricting the function of the verb 'to be' to the signalling of identity, Stilpo denied that such sentences as 'Socrates is human' could be true, or even, perhaps, well formed.[36] Reasonably enough, Colotes had objected that such a restriction would unduly impair our ability to say true things about the world. Plutarch is contemptuous of this response:

> Indeed if mere linguistic confusion of this sort is ruinous to our lives, who is more in error than you [Epicureans] about language? You completely abolish the class of sayables (*lekta*), to which language (*logos*) owes its existence, leaving only sounds (*phōnai*) and things (*ta tunkanonta*[37]), and denying the very existence of the intermediate states of affairs signified, by means of which learning, teaching, preconceptions (*prolēpseis*), thoughts, impulses and assents come about. (*adv. Col.* 1119F=LS 19K)

Stilpo might have denied the possibility of predication, but, on Plutarch's view of the matter, the Epicurean account of language was such as to make language impossible tout court. In denying the existence of (what the Stoics called) *lekta*, it discarded precisely what made language language.

Plutarch's account is, of course, polemical, but some confirmation, and clarification, comes from a more dispassionate, if still concise, discussion in Sextus Empiricus' *adversus Mathematicos* (*M*) VIII. Here the Epicurean theory of signification is explicitly contrasted with that offered by the Stoics:

> There was another disagreement [concerning truth]: some took the sphere of what is true and false to be the signification (*to sēmainomenon*), others the utterance (*phōnē*), and others the process that constitutes thought (*hē kinēsis tēs dianoias*). The Stoics defended the first opinion, saying that three things are linked together, the 'signification', the 'signifier' and the 'name-bearer'. The signifier is an utterance, for instance 'Dion'; the signification is

[35] For a consideration of ancient discussions of *esti*, see ch. 11 below. There is a brief discussion of Stilpo in Denyer [22], 33 f.

[36] 'If we predicate good of man or running of a horse, the predicate is not the same as the subject, but the formula that defines the essence of man is one thing, while that which defines the essence of good is something else again . . . Therefore they err who predicate one thing of another, as if the essence of both were the same.' *Adv. Col.* 1120a (translation from B. Einarson and P. H. De Lacy, *Plutarch's Moralia*, XIV (London/Cambridge, Mass., 1967)).

[37] Einarson's translation of *ta tunkanonta* as 'facts' is particularly unfortunate, importing as it does intensional items.

> the actual state of affairs revealed by an utterance, and which we apprehend as it subsists in accordance without thought, whereas it is not understood by those whose language is different although they hear the utterance; the name-bearer is the external object, for instance, Dion himself. Of these, two are bodies – the utterance and the name-bearer, but one is incorporeal – the state of affairs signified and sayable (*lekton*), which is true or false . . . But Epicurus and Strato the physicist, as they leave only two of these – the signifier and the existing thing – appear to hold the second view and to ascribe truth and falsity to the utterance.
> (*M* VIII.11–12 = LS 33B, 13)

On the Stoic view, it is not an uttered sound itself which has semantic properties, but rather what is said by uttering that sound. Thus, any meaningful utterance will involve three items: the sounds uttered, what is referred to or described by the utterance and an incorporeal item, the *lekton*, which the utterance 'reveals'.[38] The Epicureans, in contrast, recognise only two of these – the uttered sound, which itself is true or false, and what it refers to or describes. *Lekta* are left out of the account.

The Stoic theory of *lekta*, of course, post-dates Epicurus' own work, and whatever Plutarch and Sextus are reporting, it cannot have been any explicit denial on Epicurus' part of the role of *lekta* in the explanation of linguistic meaning (although later Epicureans may well have made the denial explicit).[39] Rather, we have to take it that Epicurus' account of how words get their meaning was not hospitable to items which played the role given to *lekta* within the Stoic theory. Now one thing we know about that role is that *lekta* were taken to be the contents of intentional states: the Stoics 'say that a *lekton* is what subsists in accordance with a rational appearance, and a rational appearance is one in which what is apparent can be exhibited in language' (*M* VIII.70 = LS 33C).[40] Perhaps, Epicurean semantic theory would not allow the introduction of *lekta* because it denied a place to the states which, in Stoic psychology, have *lekta* as contents. *Lekta* could have no role because states with content – thoughts, beliefs, 'rational appearances' – have no role. As support for this line of speculation, one could perhaps press Sextus' claim that Epicurus includes only two of the items posited by the Stoics (the utterance and what it refers to) and see in it an

[38] The implications of this passage for Stoic semantics are discussed by Michael Frede below, pp. 118 f.

[39] Thus, we should be cautious, for instance, of Annas' formulation of the disagreement when she says that 'Epicurus thinks that *lekta* are metaphysically objectionable entities, and that there are no such things' (Annas [310], 168).

[40] SVF II.187. See also LS 33D: 'For the appearance arises first, and then thought, which has the power of talking, expresses in language what affects it by the agency of the appearance' (DL VII.49 = SVF II.52).

Epicurean denial of the revelance of anything further – including, for instance, the 'affections of the soul' posited by Aristotelian semantic theory. An account of signification which made mention only of linguistic expressions and what they refer to would not qualify as a psychologistic one.

Indeed, to anyone versed in contemporary semantic theory, the idea that Epicurus may have restricted the items relevant to providing such a theory to words and their referents will be highly suggestive. Following Frege's rejection of psychologism, there has been much work on the project of explicating semantics without recourse to the psychology of the speakers of a language. So, it was specified above that what it is for a semantic theory to be psychologistic is for it to make use of psychological notions in the explanation of how expressions have their semantic properties. Thus, if one were to claim that the name 'Epicurus' refers to Epicurus *because* it is associated with a speaker's concept of Epicurus, or that the sentence 'Epicurus is difficult' means what it does *because* it is such as to express the belief that Epicurus is difficult or *because* it is such as to communicate the thought that Epicurus is difficult, then one's explanation of the reference of 'Epicurus' or the meaning of 'Epicurus is difficult' would be psychologistic. The explanations cited all make essential use of psychological notions – those of concepts, beliefs and thoughts. A non-psychologistic theory, in contrast, will make no such essential use of psychological concepts. Of course, such a theory will not deny that the sentence 'Epicurus is difficult' *is* such as to express the belief that Epicurus is difficult, but will not make use of this fact in order to explain why the sentence means that Epicurus is difficult. The order of explanation will indeed be reversed: on the non-psychologistic account, it will rather be *because* the sentence has the meaning it does that it is such as to express the relevant belief. Similarly, it will be *because* 'Epicurus' refers to Epicurus that it can be used in sentences to express beliefs about Epicurus.

To characterise a non-psychologistic theory as one that does not make essential use of psychological notions in its explanation of the semantic properties of linguistic expressions is, of course, merely to characterise it negatively: it gives no hint as to how such a theory will in fact work. The approach which has proved most fruitful in achieving this has been to see how one might provide a theory of meaning for a particular language:

> If there can be such a thing as a theory of meaning for any language, meaning cannot be anything but what such a theory is a theory of. Hence a clear and convincing description of the shape which such a theory of meaning for any language would take, not itself uncritically employing the notion of meaning, ought to remove all perplexity about the nature of meaning in general.[41]

[41] McDowell [514], 42.

The projected form of such theories has been to specify, for every sentence of a language, the conditions under which that sentence is true.[42] In order to get to this stage, the theorist will have to state the 'semantic value' of the expressions of the language and show how the meaning of sentences is determined by the semantic values of the constituents of those sentences.[43] This will require the theorist both to show *how* any sentence is constructed – and thus to provide a syntax for the language in question – and to specify the semantic values of the basic expressions of that language. So, one will need to construct a theory of reference for that language in which it is stated what its referring terms actually refer to.[44] This can be simply done. For instance, one of the axioms of the theory for English will be

'Dion' refers to Dion.

This is all that needs to be known in order to know what the term 'Dion' contributes to the truth-conditions of the sentences of which it is a component.[45] The only items it refers to are a word and an object in the world.

The purpose of showing what the axioms of such a theory would be like is not actually to construct a complete theory of meaning for a language – the thought is rather that, as Dummett puts it, 'the correct methodology for the theory of meaning is to enquire into the general principles upon which a meaning-theory is to be constructed', where a meaning-theory is 'a complete specification of the meanings of all words and expressions of one particular language'.[46] In the theorems and axioms of a meaning-theory, no reference is needed to the mental states or the conceptual abilities of speakers (except, of course, for those terms which refer to mental states).

It should now be more obvious why the testimony of Plutarch and Sextus should prove suggestive – what is suggested is the recognition that in explaining the meanings of words, Epicurus dispensed with anything other than their referents. Whereas the Stoics brought in propositional items and Aristotle correlated words with psychological affections, Epicurus, in allowing only 'the signifier and the existing thing', showed himself to be an early

[42] See Davidson [481].

[43] The term 'semantic value' is Dummett's. See, for instance, his [492], ch. 1, in which he defines it thus: 'the semantic value of an expression is that feature of it that goes to determine the truth of any sentence in which it occurs' (p. 24).

[44] One may also have to provide a theory of sense for the expressions of the language – although it may be that in providing a theory of reference for a language, one thereby provides a theory of sense for its referring expressions. Contrast McDowell [515] with Wiggins [536].

[45] The theorem is not as trivial as it may, at first inspection, look. Note that, as McDowell points out ([515], section VI), the knowledge that 'Epicurus' refers to Epicurus is more substantive than simply knowing that '"Epicurus" refers to Epicurus' is true. I am ignoring the problems created by intensional contexts.

[46] Dummett [492], 22.

adherent of the view that one can specify the meaning of linguistic items without having to make mention of the psychology of the speakers of a language.

Tempting as it might be to accept this suggestion, it rests on an interpretation of Plutarch and Sextus which is by no means forced on us. For Sextus, after all, does not say that Epicurus allowed only two sorts of items into his account of signification – merely that he allowed in only two of the items posited by the Stoics. What is in question is whether we should see this as the result of his also leaving out of his account the psychological states included within the Aristotelian theory. If we should, then this will provide reason against reading *Hdtm.* 37 in such a way that 'what underlie utterances' refers to *prolēpseis* (or *prolēpsis*-like items) – although this, as was argued above, is the most natural way to take it.[47] To use Plutarch and Sextus to provide such reason, however, requires identifying *lekta* with thoughts or perceptions. This is unwarranted – and rests on the confusion of particular mental acts or states with the content of those acts or states. *Lekta* are not thoughts themselves but rather their contents.[48]

With this distinction in hand, we do not have to take either Plutarch's or Sextus' account of the Epicurean theory as evidence that Epicurus denied a role to thoughts or beliefs in the explanation of linguistic meaning. Rather, the Epicurean's disagreement with the Stoics could be construed as concerning the existence of *propositions*: whereas the Stoics allow that there are incorporeal entities which are grasped by thought and expressed in language, the Epicurean would hold to a more restrictive ontology which would exclude anything other than corporeal items – which he would take to include beliefs.[49] Plutarch's attack on this theory could then be seen to be drawing what would be an unwelcome *consequence* for the Epicurean. It is important to recognise that his charge goes beyond the claim that by denying *lekta* he makes language impossible – psychology itself becomes untenable. Without *lekta*, there could be no 'learning, teaching, preconceptions (*prolēpseis*), thoughts, impulses and assents'. The claim would be that *lekta* are required for these psychological states to occur – in effect, that one cannot have propositional attitudes without accepting propositions. What

[47] See above, pp. 81–3.

[48] See Annas [310], 98–9. Frede, ch. 6 below, provides a much more nuanced account of these matters than is possible here.

[49] One might draw the contrast by saying that whereas the Stoics would have been prepared to quantify over propositions, the contents of thoughts and utterances, the Epicureans would not, but would have stuck at the level of quantifying over beliefs and utterances themselves. See further Annas [310], 98 ff. for the disagreement between Epicurus and the Stoics over the placing of content within psychological theory.

would be at stake here would be just the issue raised earlier about whether Epicurus can consistently both maintain that there are no other entities than atoms (and systems of atoms) and void and allow that people can have mental states with propositional content. Given that the Epicurean does maintain the existence of mental states, his implicit denial of *lekta* does not in itself show any unwillingness to make use of them in the explanation of how words get their meaning.

It might be thought, however, that to construe the differences between Epicurus and the Stoics in this way is to fall into an anachronism warned against earlier. For, whilst we are not required to take Epicurus to have said anything against the existence of *lekta* as such, it does seem that the interpretation needs him to have denied the existence of propositions – and, prior to the Stoics' espousal of *lekta*, there would have been little call for him to have done so. It is no more plausible, that is, to find Epicurus denying propositions than *lekta* themselves.

So, if this minimal reading of Plutarch and Sextus does require that Epicurus explicitly denied the ontological propriety of propositions, this would be sufficient to make it highly suspect. Fortunately, it does not make this necessary, since it is quite clear from established Epicurean doctrine that Epicurus would not have permitted abstract objects such as propositions into his science. To see this, one only has to consider the embarrassment which the support for *lekta* caused the Stoics themselves. Whilst committed to the thesis that only corporeal things exist and can act and be acted upon, they admitted into their ontology incorporeal items (void, place, time and *lekta*): these are said to 'subsist' (*huphistasthai*) rather than to exist. As Annas says, the difficulty for the Stoics with the doctrine of *lekta* is that although it enables them to talk about the contents of perceptions and thoughts, it does so 'at the cost of making central use of items which are not physical and do not exist'.[50]

Epicurus would certainly have had no truck with entities of this sort. Of course, if talking of propositional attitudes did commit one to the existence of abstract objects such as propositions (as Plutarch's charge seems to assume), then either his account of the mind or his materialism would have been in trouble. This, however, remains a live issue[51] – and was so even once the Stoic theory was in place. For instance, in Ammonius' commentary on Aristotle's *de Interpretatione*, written sometime during the fifth–sixth centuries A.D., he reports Aristotle as claiming that words 'primarily and immediately' signify thoughts (*noēmata*) and, through these, things. He continues:

[50] Annas [310], 98.

[51] See Davidson [482], 165–6. Davidson's 'sententialist' theory is attacked in Schiffer [530], ch. 5.

'And it is not necessary to conceive of anything else additional to them, intermediate between the thought and the thing, which the Stoics postulated and decided to name a *lekton*' (*On Aristotle's de Interpretatione* (*In Ar. de Int.*) 17, 26–8 = LS 33N). Epicurus would have agreed wholeheartedly with this. The fact that he would not have countenanced *lekta* does not mean that he would have given up talking about perceptions and beliefs and *prolēpseis* – and neither Plutarch nor Sextus provide us with reason to believe that he denied such states a role in his semantic theory.

The point can perhaps be clarified in the light of the sort of meaning-theory canvassed earlier in the section. Such a theory will deliver a set of theorems in which the meanings of the sentences of the relevant language are specified. It will be able to do this because it will also contain a specification of the syntax of the language, together with a set of axioms specifying the semantic values of the primitive expressions of the language. So, one axiom of the theory for English will thus be

'Dion' refers to Dion,

since the theory will require an axiom for each name of the language, pairing the name with the object it refers to. As said before, it is tempting to find in Sextus' contrast between Stoic and Epicurean doctrine the recognition, on Epicurus' part, that to give the meaning of, say, 'Dion', what one has to do is to specify what it refers to. Even if this is true, however, it does not by itself bear on the question of whether he thought that words have the semantic values they do in virtue of standing in some relation to the psychological states of speakers. Clearly, someone who accepts a psychologistic semantic theory is under no pressure to deny the truth of '"Dion" refers to Dion': a theory which denied that 'Dion' refers to Dion would be absurd. What will distinguish, for instance, a psychologistic theory of reference will be that the theorist thinks both that it is necessary to specify quite generally what it is for a term to refer to an object and that to do this will require some reference to the mental states of speakers.[52]

So, having specified at the start of the *de Interpretatione* that words are significant because they are symbols of affections of the psyche, Aristotle can proceed to discuss the semantics of words directly. So, a name 'is a spoken sound significant by convention, without time, none of whose parts is significant in separation' and a verb 'is what additionally signifies time, no part of it being significant separately' (*Int.* 16a19–21; 16b6–7). Whilst he accepts that names and verbs are significant – that is, perhaps, that they

[52] So, one might suppose that a name '*a*' will refer to an object if '*a*' is associated with beliefs about that object. On this account, people's holding beliefs about objects would be explanatorily prior to names' referring to objects.

have semantic values – Aristotle also recognises that one cannot say anything merely by uttering a name or a verb by itself:

> A sentence is a significant spoken sound some part of which is significant in separation – as an expression, not as an affirmation. I mean that 'animal', for instance, signifies something, but not that it is or is not (though it will be an affirmation if something is added); the single syllable of 'animal', on the other hand, signifies nothing. Every sentence is significant (not as a tool but, as we said, by convention), but not every sentence is a statement-making sentence, but only those in which there is truth or falsity.
> (*Int.* 16b26–17a3)[53]

One could accept all of Aristotle's analysis of the relation between the parts of sentences and their functions without accepting that words are significant because they are symbols of thoughts.

So, both Aristotle and Epicurus believe that both spoken sounds and mental states can be true and false,[54] and neither's theory introduces propositional items to stand as the content of both mental states and utterances. What still needs to be determined is whether Epicurus follows Aristotle in treating linguistic significance as being derived from the content of intentional states or whether he rests content to treat the semantic properties of linguistic items as being either prior to, or at least autonomous of, the content of perceptions and thoughts.

Linguistic naturalism and the origins of language

There is one certain and important difference between Aristotelian and Epicurean accounts of language – and this is that whereas Aristotle takes words to be conventional, Epicurus believes that some words at least are naturally significant. When, in the *de Interpretatione*, Aristotle defines a name as 'a spoken sound significant by convention', he proceeds to connect the claim that names are conventional with their role as symbols of thoughts: 'I say "by convention" because no name is a name naturally, but only when it has become a symbol' (*Int.* 16a26–8). If Epicurus denied Aristotle's claim that there are no natural names, then he may also have denied that names have significance only because they correspond to psychological states.[55] It would have been open to him to have taken

[53] Translation from Ackrill [253]

[54] 'Just as some thoughts in the soul are neither true nor false while some are necessarily one or the other, so are spoken sounds (*houtō en tēi phōnēi*).' What are true or false are those sentences which say that something does or does not hold – such a sentence is a 'simple statement' (*haplē apophansis*: *Int.* 5.17a23–4).

[55] For the potential opposition between naturalism and psychologism, see the Introduction above, p. 3.

language to be such as to communicate thoughts because it is naturally significant rather than accepting the Aristotelian position that linguistic items are significant because they symbolise thoughts. To see whether Epicurus' naturalism did lead him to a denial of psychologism, one needs to consider what form that naturalism took.

It seems that one reason for the claim that certain names are naturally names was the thought that if all words were conventional, this would require an inventor of language – something which the Epicureans took to be absurd.

> To think that someone in those days assigned names to things, and that is how men learnt their first words, is crazy. Why should he have been able to indicate all things with sounds, and to utter the various noises of the tongue, yet others not be supposed to have had that ability at the same time? Besides, if others had not already used sounds to each other, how did he get the preconception of their usefulness implanted in him? How did he get the initial capacity to know and see with his mind what he wanted to do? Again, one person could not subdue many and compel them to want to learn the names of things. Nor is it easy to find a way of teaching and persuading a deaf audience of what needs to be done: they would utterly refuse to tolerate any further his drumming into their ears the unfamiliar sounds of his voice. (Lucretius V.1041–55 = LS 19B3–5)[56]

The hypothesis of an original language-giver is taken to be implausible on at least two counts. The first is that for someone to have formed the idea that it would be useful to have words for things, he would have had to have acquired a preconception, *prolēpsis*, of the usefulness of language. Since the acquisition of a *prolēpsis* of something requires perceptual experience of it, one would only be able to appreciate the usefulness of language once one had already had experience of a working language. Thus, until a language had come into operation, no one would have been able to have appreciated its usefulness. Moreover, even had someone been able, *per impossibile*, to work out the advantages of introducing a language, he would not have been able to communicate his discovery to other people, since they would have been unable to recognise the point of what the putative language-giver was attempting to do as he made sounds at them. Although they would have heard him making sounds, they would have been deaf to their significance.[57]

What, then, is Epicurus' explanation for the origin of language?

[56] See also LS 19C (Diogenes of Oenoanda 10.2.11–5.15).

[57] Diogenes of Oenoanda makes the point that he would not even have been able to summon people 'by edict'.

> We must take it that even nature[58] was educated and constrained in many different ways by objects (*pragmata*), and that its lessons were later made more accurate, and augmented with new discoveries by reason – faster among some people, slower among others, and in some ages and eras, owing to <individual needs, by greater leaps>, in others by smaller leaps. Thus, names too did not originally come into being by coining, but men's own natures received sense-impressions (*phantasmata*) and were affected in ways which varied peculiarly from tribe to tribe, and each of the affections and impressions caused them to exhale breath peculiarly, according also to the racial differences from place to place.
> (*Hdtm.* 75 = LS 19A1–2)[59]

Epicurus denied the need to posit an inventor of language because he denied that language is an invention. People make (some of) the particular sounds they do because they are affected in particular ways by the objects in their environment.

Although Epicurus' interest here is in the origin of language, it does not seem over-adventurous to find in it at least the basis for an account of how sounds can have significance. For although Epicurus allowed that languages could develop from the stage described here, there is no indication that this stage is less than fully linguistic. It is not clear whether the original speakers were actually caused to utter complete sentences – but they were certainly caused to utter sounds referring to the objects around them.[60] The explanation Epicurus offers is not just of why people should make sounds, but of why they should produce words, i.e. sounds which have significance. No more is cited in that explanation than that people are disposed to make certain sounds in response to particular stimuli. Words thus stand in a non-conventional relation to what they denote. That a word has the extension it does is to be explained by reference to the causal history of its utterances. Not only is it not necessary to postulate an inventor of words, but it will not be necessary to explain how individual speakers acquire the ability to speak a language either. Linguistic ability (of a rather basic sort) is innate and consists just in the disposition to utter sounds when affected by external objects.

This suggests a way of explaining why terms have the reference they do without making reference to the psychological states of speakers. Take, for instance, the explanation of the fact that 'cow' refers to cows. The Aristotelian explanation for this would presumably be that 'cow' refers to

[58] Presumably human nature.
[59] The translation has been slightly adapted.
[60] There is no mention of the original speakers uttering sentences in either Epicurus or Lucretius – but nor is the regimentation of the original words into sentences given as one of the developments from the original language.

cows because 'cow' is a (conventional) symbol for a certain psychological affection and that affection is a likeness of cows. The Epicurean explanation, in contrast, might be the following: 'cow' refers to cows because people (of a certain race) are caused to utter 'cow' when they are affected by the streams of atoms (*eidōla*) emanating from cows.[61] This, of course, can be generalised: a term will refer to whatever it is that causes people to utter that term as a response to the stimulus of being affected by the atoms which emanate from it. This provides an account of reference which makes no use of psychological notions. Epicurus can be seen to be offering an explanation of signification which uses only the resources of atomic causation. Understandably, Glidden finds support in Epicurus' account of the origin of language for his non-mentalistic interpretation of Epicurean linguistic theory: 'The cries which result, at this stage of language, are like the cries of animals: spontaneous, noncognitive responses which can also be used to signal their cause.'[62]

The trouble, of course, is that it is not at all obvious that Epicurus does offer such a stimulus–response model of utterance – and pretty obvious that, if he does, his account is too crude. What that account is intended to secure is a uniformity of verbal response among the members of particular races to the presence of objects in the world. It is such a uniformity of response that provides (some of) the materials for a public language. We thus have a correlation between three things: the atoms which come from objects and which strike the senses, the affection which is produced by the impact of those atoms and the verbal response elicited by that affection. What is not yet clear is how the second and third of these are to be described if the theorist is to capture the relevant causal regularities. Is what the affections have in common that they have a similar atomic structure or that they have a similar intentional content? Is it that a relevant type of affection will cause people of the same race to produce the same *word* or the same sort of noise? Depending on how these questions are answered, Epicurus will be seen to offer rather different sorts of theory. If the affections produced by the impact of atoms are described intentionally – that is, as states with content – then the explanation of signification will not avoid making use of psychological notions. If the response elicited by the affection is described not as a noise but as a word, then Epicurus will have failed to explain the genesis of language.

This last point itself provides compelling reason to accept that, according to Epicurus, when people (of the same race) are relevantly affected by an

[61] According to the Epicurean theory of perception, we perceive when our senses are hit by *eidōla*, the streams of atoms which are constantly emanating from solid objects. For this theory, see my [357], 174–9 and Asmis [350], ch. 6.

[62] Glidden [363], 200.

object of a certain type, they will make sounds of the same sort. The effect of the affection is to cause the subject to 'exhale breath' in a particular way – that is, to make a certain kind of sound. The account is intended to explain how names come into being without their being coined (and in the absence of a pre-existing language), and this is achieved because there is a causal explanation for why people should make the sounds they do – a causal explanation which requires no reference to language itself. To speak of 'names' or 'words' is to employ linguistic notions: to speak of 'sounds' is not. It is because people naturally make similar sounds in response to the same sort of object that those sounds function as a name for that sort of object. The uttered sounds are words, but it is not because they are words that they are (originally) uttered. Linguistic items are thus explained without reference either to other linguistic or semantic items or, perhaps, to the presence of communicative intentions more generally.

So, it is important to Epicurus' account of the genesis of language that the sounds people are caused to utter are described initially just as sounds and not as words. What, then, of the affections which give rise to those sounds: do these stand in causal relations to particular sounds under atomic or under intentional descriptions? Glidden's characterisation of the utterances as 'spontaneous non-cognitive responses' would seem to require that the affections are not described intentionally. Glidden goes on to contrast what Epicurus says with Augustine's distinction between *signa naturalia* and *signa data*: whilst the former are produced unintentionally and without the desire to signify anything, the latter (which include all linguistic symbols) 'communicate to another mind the intention in the mind of the person who makes the sign'.[63] According to Glidden, whilst Augustine is unsure how such things as animal noises and cries of pain fit within this distinction, since they 'express the motion of the mind without intention of signifying', this did not worry the Epicureans, 'since they maintained that at least some voiced sounds are both natural signs and linguistic elements as well'.[64]

One should note the shift here from the claim that the compelled utterances of early men were 'non-cognitive' to the rather different claim that they were unintentional (at least, they were made without the intention to communicate). The first claim, however, is independent of the second. Even if these cries were made without the intention to signify anything by doing so, they may still have been caused by the cognitive states of their utterers. This takes us back to the question of how the affection produced by objects is to be characterised. This is important because it bears directly on the question of whether Epicurus' account of signification should

[63] Glidden [363], 202. The reference is to Augustine, *de Doctrina Christiana* II.1.1–2.
[64] Glidden [363], 203.

be construed non-psychologistically. So, a non-psychologistic explanation of signification was offered above: a term will refer to whatever it is that causes people to utter that term as a response to the stimulus of being affected by the atoms which emanate from it. This, however, is crucially vague as to what sort of affection is in question.

It clearly cannot be the case that Epicurus believed that people will utter a particular cry no matter how they are affected by an object: the *eidōla* which stream off a cow and hit the back of my head will produce no response at all. If the relevant sounds are to be made, then one will have to be affected in the right way – and this must be perceptually. In *Hdtm.* 75, people are said to exhale breath in particular ways because they receive *phantasmata*, i.e. affections of the senses which represent the world as being in a certain way.[65] What will cause utterances of 'cow' will be *phantasmata* of cows – and there is no reason to think that Epicurus maintained that all *phantasmata* of cows are type-identical as arrangements of atoms.[66] What cause the people to make the sounds they do are indeed cognitive states – their perceptions of the world around them. In order to accommodate this, and to remove the vagueness from the earlier explanation of signification, one would need to expand that explanation so that a term will signify whatever causes people to utter that term as a response to the stimulus of being *perceptually* affected by the atoms which emanate from it. This is no longer a non-psychologistic explanation of signification.

The point is that although Epicurus' account of the origin of language does postulate a mechanism for how certain sounds can be significant by nature rather than by convention, it is human nature rather than the nature of the sounds which is used to secure this. Certain patterns of sounds naturally refer to particular types of objects because of their causal history – but that history must include the cognitive states of people. If Epicurus, in showing how some of the sounds people make when they do not know a language can nevertheless be 'linguistic items as well', is indeed providing an embryonic causal theory of reference, then it will still be a psychologistic theory of reference. What will make a sound, or pattern of sounds, significant is that it is caused by a relevant psychological state (a perception,

[65] *Phantasmata* are assessable for truth – they have truth-conditions.

[66] Compare Searle's point that a causal theory of reference will not avoid intentional causation and so will not provide 'an external causal account of the relation of name to object': 'Of course, in such cases [when an object is identified perceptually] there will also be an external causal account in terms of the impact of the object on the nervous system, but the external causal phenomena will not by themselves give an ostensive definition of the name. To get the ostensive definition the perceiver has to perceive the object and that involves more than the physical impact of the object on his nervous system' (Searle [532], 235).

say); what will make it have the significance it does will be that the psychological state which causes it has the content it does.

That it is the differences between the different psychic affections which are relevant to the explanation of the different noises which are produced is confirmed by what follows Lucretius' report of the origins of language:

> Lastly, why is it so surprising that the human race, with its powers of voice and tongue, should have indicated each thing with a different sound to correspond to a different perception? After all, dumb animals, tame and wild alike, regularly emit different sounds when afraid, when in pain and when happiness comes over them. (Lucretius V.1056–61 = LS 19B6)

So, the sounds dogs make differ depending upon whether they are in a rage or fearful or affectionate; stallions make different noises when they are libidinous from when they are frightened. Given the variety of sounds made by animals, that humans should be able to make a sufficient variety of sounds to be able to indicate different types of object is unsurprising:

> If, then, different perceptions compel animals, dumb as they are, to emit different sounds, how much more likely is it that mortal men at that time were able to indicate different things with different sounds?
> (V.1087–90 = LS 19B7)

The variety of sounds caused in animal species by different emotions would only be relevant if emotions and perceptions were taken to be relevantly similar – and that relevant similarity is, of course, that they are all psychological affections. Just as the noises of animals correspond to different emotions, so the noises made by humans correspond to different perceptions and thereby to different objects. This directly follows Epicurus' claim in *Hdtm.* 75 that '*each of the affections* and *phantasmata* caused them to exhale breath peculiarly'. The exhalations will all reveal the psychological affections of the speaker – it is just that in the case of perceptual affections, the affections will themselves be related to particular types of object in the world.[67]

Such a reading of the doctrine of *Hdtm.* 75 is not forced on us, however. Certainly neither Epicurus nor Lucretius provides any explicit formulation of a causal theory of signification, and we should perhaps be cautious of detecting any such constitutive explanation of signification in those passages. For Epicurus does not claim that when people were caused to make sounds on perceiving objects they were thereby caused to utter the names for those things. What he does claim is that (certain) names are natural

[67] For the importance of recognising perceptions to be a species of affection, see my [421], 132 ff.

rather than conventional and that the reason for this is that the members of the same race will be caused to make the same noises when they perceive objects of the same type. This is consistent with the claim that those noises are names, but does not entail it. To see why, it is helpful to examine the beginning of Lucretius' discussion of the naturalness of language:

> It was nature that compelled the utterance of the various noises of the tongue, and usefulness that forged them into the names of things. It was rather in the way that children's inarticulacy itself seems to impel them to use gestures, when it causes them to point out with a finger what things are present. (Lucretius V.1028–32=LS 19B1–2)

Lucretius here contrasts the contribution made by nature with that made by utility. Nature is responsible for the noises (*sonitus*), whilst the names of things (*nomina rerum*) are produced by utility. The idea seems to be that the need to pick out different things (presumably communicatively) caused people to make use of the sounds which were already associated with them. Just as the child who cannot speak will point to things, so the articulate adult will utter those sounds which are naturally associated with the type of object which he wishes to distinguish. If a certain sound is associated with a belief about, or perception of, a certain type of object, then making that sound will be an obvious way of bringing that object to the mind of someone else. Sounds, on this view, would not become names until they were used as such.

What would be on offer now would not be any constitutive explanation of how certain sound-types are significant but rather an explanation of how people could have come to use sounds to name things without the prior existence of a language. Certain sound-types would be naturally such as to call certain types of object to mind – but the making of those sounds would not constitute naming things until people found themselves doing so because they wished to indicate the objects to other people. In the absence of pre-existing linguistic conventions, the sounds would function as *signa data* because they were *signa naturalia* – but without the intention to signify, they would not be linguistic items.[68]

That this is the right way to construe the explanatory ambition of Epicurus' account of the origin of language is perhaps confirmed by the fact that there is no suggestion that all words are to be explained in this way.

[68] Epicurus assumes, I think, a much greater sonic similarity between the utterances of words than in fact exists. When someone from Kensington, say, says 'power', this will be much closer sonically to the 'par' of received pronunciation (RP) than it will to the 'power' of RP. Nevertheless, it is still 'power' that is uttered, and not 'par'. For the difficulties of identifying word-types, see Kaplan [510].

Once 'nature' had done its work, 'its lessons were later made more accurate, and augmented with new discoveries by reason'. This is vague as it stands, but is amplified as the passage continues:

> Later, particular coinings were made by consensus within the individual races, so as to make the designations less ambiguous and more concisely expressed. Also, the men who shared knowledge introduced certain unseen entities, and brought words for them into usage. <Hence some> men gave utterance under compulsion, and others chose words rationally, and it is thus, as far as the principal cause is concerned, that they achieved self-expression. (*Hdtm.* 76 = LS 19A3–5)

Epicurus complicates his account in two ways. First he allows that a word can refer to an observable entity even if it does not consist of the sort of sounds which are produced in a speaker when he is perceptually affected by that object. Languages have evolved so that some words for which there is a causal explanation of the sort offered above have been replaced by others – either, it seems, because the original word was longer than was convenient or because more than one (type of) object elicited the same, or perhaps very similar, verbal response, so giving rise to problems of ambiguity. The second complication is that many words in a language cannot be explained as the result of perceptual stimulation because what they refer to is not observable – i.e. not such as to produce any perceptual stimulation at all. However the utterance of these is to be explained, it will not be by reference to our responses to perceptual stimuli. Once Epicurus' account of the origin of language has been seen to be an explanation of how people could have come to use organised sounds to communicate with each other, rather than as an attempt to provide a constitutive explanation of linguistic signification, then there is no tension between what Epicurus says about the first stage of language use and the recognition that that was merely the beginning of the development of language proper.

Belief and language

So far, then, our evidence for reconstructing Epicurus' account of signification is pretty slim. It is not that there is conflicting evidence for his understanding of the relation between language and thought but rather that the evidence so far has been indeterminate on the question. The reports of Plutarch and Sextus do not, on reflection, weigh either way; the Epicurean theory of the origin of language can be read to suggest psychologism but is more plausibly taken not to bear on the question at all, and *Hdtm.* 37, even if it postulates a relation between mental states and utterances (and it has been disputed that it does), does not say that utterances are significant *because* they stand in that relation. The problem is that there is simply nothing in what survives of Epicurus' writings in which he addresses the question of how sounds are significant in the way that, say, Aristotle does at the start of the *de Interpretatione*. Given this, and given the elusiveness of our other ancient evidence for Epicurean semantic theory, any reconstruction of that theory is bound to be speculative. Nevertheless, I think, there is still some reason to direct that speculation one way rather than the other.

There is one further passage which has yet to be canvassed. In his précis of Epicurus' philosophy, Diogenes Laertius gives the following report of the role of *prolēpseis*:

> *Prolēpsis*, they say, is, as it were, an apprehension (*katalēpsis*), or correct belief, or conception (*ennoia*), or universal stored notion (that is, memory), of that which has frequently become evident externally: e.g. 'Such and such a kind of thing is a man.' For as soon as the word 'man' is uttered, immediately its delineation also comes to mind by means of *prolēpsis*, since the senses give the lead. Thus what primarily underlies each name is something evident. And what we inquire about we would not have inquired about if we had not had prior knowledge of it. For example 'Is what's standing over there a horse or a cow?' For one must at some time have come to know the form of a horse and that of a cow by means of *prolēpsis*. Nor would we have named something if we had not previously learned its delineation by means of *prolēpsis*. Thus *prolēpseis* are evident. And belief depends on something prior and evident, which is our point of reference when we say, e.g., 'How do we know if this is a man?'.
> (D.L. x.33 = LS 17E)

Diogenes here provides an explicit link between the psychology of speakers and the use of language. *Prolēpseis* underlie names: without *prolēpseis* there would be no names. Earlier, in the consideration of *Hdtm.* 37, we saw that Long and Sedley took the reference there to 'the things which underlie utterances' to be to *prolēpseis*, and this passage provides confirmation of that. Long and Sedley also took the reference to be to *prolēpseis* in 'their guise of the meanings underlying words'. The evidence of Plutarch and Sextus will have shown that this latter claim is misguided: it is words themselves that have semantic properties, and not something underlying them. There is no evidence at all that Epicurus introduced a set of meanings, in some way separate from the words we utter. For a sentence to be meaningful, there does not have to be a meaning to which it somehow corresponds.[69] Nevertheless, we can perhaps capture what Long and Sedley

[69] Cf. Davidson [481], 20–3. Glidden [363], 189 f., rightly objects to taking *prolēpseis* to be meanings: his conclusion that there is nothing which corresponds

have in mind if we reformulate the point by saying that, according to Epicurus, it is in virtue of standing in the relevant relation to a *prolēpsis* that a word has the significance it does.

Does D.L. x.33 provide any confirmation of that psychologistic thesis? Not straightforwardly. Whilst there is obviously nothing in the passage which would be inconsistent with a psychologistic semantics, such a position is not demanded by it. There is certainly no explicit statement of the thesis that what makes a name significant is that it has a *prolēpsis* underlying it. Rather, what we are given is an account of what sort of psychology is required if someone is to be able to use words – and one which is more detailed than was given in *Hdtm.* 75. There, Epicurus explained the first utterances simply as the result of a reaction to perceptual stimuli. Here we learn that in order to use words which refer to objects of a certain type, the speaker must be able to recognise objects as being of that type – and this requires that he possess the relevant *prolēpsis*. So, in order to be able to identify cows, one must have acquired a (or, perhaps better, the) *prolēpsis* of cows. To be able to utter 'cow' so as to refer to a cow, it is not sufficient that one be, or have been, perceptually affected by a cow: one must also be able to recognise the cow as such. The role of *prolēpseis* also extends to the explanation of understanding the utterances of other people: one understands someone else's utterance of 'cow' to refer to cows because the word calls to mind the form, or 'delineation', of cows. As we have seen, at the first stage of the development of language, the sound of a word will be naturally associated with a particular recognitional ability – at later stages, the association can be a conventional one.

All this is quite compatible with a non-psychologistic semantic theory. To accept that a speaker will only understand sentences which include the word 'cow' if he knows what a cow is, or can recognise cows, is not to make the reference of 'cow' dependent on the content of thought. It is helpful to look back again to the sort of meaning-theory discussed in the previous sections. So, the theory of meaning for English will contain the axiom

> '"Dion" refers to Dion.'

Knowledge of this would be sufficient to understand the name 'Dion' – that is, to know what it contributes to the sentences in which it occurs. In order to understand that axiom, however, one would need to have some beliefs about Dion: it is no help to be told that 'Dion' refers to Dion if one has not the

to the meaning of a term in Epicurus encourages his claim that 'Epicurean linguistics shows little concern for how words acquire meanings and thereby describe what is happening in the world' (p. 187). One does not need to postulate meanings in order to show how words are meaningful.

slightest idea who Dion is.[70] Similarly, to know that 'cow' refers to cows (or that what fall within the extension of the predicate – 'is a cow' are all and only cows) one needs to have some beliefs about cows – and this, according to Epicurus, requires that one possess a (or the) *prolēpsis* of cows.[71]

However, if D.L. x.33 is, on the face of it, compatible with a non-psychologistic semantics, the relation between thought and language which it postulates is certainly one which is at the least congenial to psychologism. For the linguistic identification of objects is presented as only one species of a more general identificatory ability. If one has a *prolēpsis* of cows, then one will be able to form beliefs about cows and also, given suitable other knowledge, to say things about them: 'Nor would we have named something if we had not *previously* learned its delineation by means of *prolēpsis*.' The ability to use 'cow' to refer to cows rests on knowing the 'delineation' of cows, and this knowledge is antecedent to the linguistic ability both temporally and in order of explanation. One does not have to make reference to the linguistic ability in order to define the possession of the relevant *prolēpsis*. (Of course, we shall have to use language in order to define it – but that is not to the point.) We saw in the first section that one of the claims of those who reject psychologism is that it is only by doing so that one can develop a satisfactory account of *thought* itself. The idea is that unless the theorist treats language as being explanatorily prior to thought, it will not be possible to characterise thoughts in such a way as to make manifest their contents.[72] In treating the possession of concepts and propositional attitudes as being either explanatorily prior to, or merely autonomous of, the semantic properties of language, Epicurus' theory lacks what is perhaps the primary motivation for a non-psychologistic theory.

What a psychologistic explanation of linguistic significance requires, if it is to avoid the confusions with which the Fregean charges it, is a way of showing how one can attribute the same concept or propositional attitude to different speakers without appealing to their disposition to use the same words in a similar way or to utter sentences in relevantly similar circumstances. If the theorist is to maintain, say, that 'cow' refers to cows because it is related in some way to the concept of a cow or that the sentence 'Cows are herbivores' means that cows are herbivores because it expresses the thought that cows are herbivores, he had better be able to give an account of what it is to have the concept of a cow or to have the thought that cows are

[70] Cf. McDowell [515], 150.

[71] For this discussion, I shall treat general terms such as 'cow' as if they refer to objects of a certain type, as names refer to particular objects. Not to do so would be to complicate the discussion irrelevantly. Their proper treatment, however, is indeed complex: see, for instance, Quine [523], ##19–20 and Wiggins [537].

[72] See the passage from Dummett given above, p. 76.

herbivores. Such an account will only avoid circularity if it does not make reference to the ability to use the word 'cow' to refer to cows or the ability to use the sentence 'Cows are herbivores' to express the thought that cows are herbivores.

It is at this point that it becomes important to focus on the fact that what underlies an utterance on the Epicurean account is not just any belief but a *prolēpsis* or, in the terminology of *Hdtm.* 37, a *prōton ennoēma*. Now, *prolēpseis* function, along with perceptions and the 'primary affections' (pleasure and pain), as the criteria of truth for Epicurus.[73] In judging, say, that the object I see is a man, the truth of my judgement will be guaranteed as long as I refer the content of the perception to the content of the relevant *prolēpseis*.[74] What distinguishes *prolēpseis* from other beliefs,[75] and what guarantees their truth, is that they are perceptually acquired:

> *prolēpsis*, they say, is, as it were, an apprehension (*katalēpsis*), or correct belief, or conception (*ennoia*), or universal stored notion (that is, memory), of that which has frequently become evident externally.
> (D.L. x.33 = LS 17E1)[76]

To acquire the *prolēpsis* of a cow, one must have perceived cows, and to acquire the *prolēpsis* of a man, one must have perceived men. The content of a *prolēpsis* is, moreover, restricted to what is perceptually apparent: there will not be *prolēpseis* of any entities which do not feature in the content of perceptions, and properties which are not apparent will not feature in the content of *prolēpseis*.[77]

The fact that *prolēpseis* form only a sub-set of beliefs, and presumably only a sub-set even of putatively identificatory beliefs, makes it slightly puzzling

[73] See D.L. x.31 = LS 17A. Of course, if Sedley is right (see n. 18 above), Epicurus had not introduced the term *prolēpsis* at the time of writing *Hdtm.* 37 itself: even so, it is clear that the *prōton ennoēma* is already playing a criterial role.

[74] D.L. x.33 = LS 17E6–7: 'Thus *prolēpseis* are evident. And belief depends on something prior and evident, which is our point of reference when we say, e.g., "How do we know if this is a man?".'

[75] Accepting Diogenes Laertius' report that *prolēpseis* are 'correct beliefs'. This is confirmed, for instance, by *Letter to Menoeceus* (*Ep. Men.*) 123–4 = LS 23B: 'The impious man is not he who denies the gods of the many, but he who attaches to the gods the beliefs of the many about them. For they are not *prolēpseis* but false suppositions (*hupoleipseis pseudeis*), the assertions of the many about gods.' It would be odd if Epicurus were to suggest that one could confuse *prolēpseis* with false beliefs if they were not the same type of mental item.

[76] If it is true that the term *prolēpsis* was introduced towards the end of Epicurus' career, this would help to explain why Diogenes presents a list of different characterisations. *Ennoia* may well correspond to the *ennoēma* of *Hdtm.* 37; the use of 'perception' perhaps picks up *Hdtm.* 82, where Epicurus talks of 'universal affections' as distinct from particular ones.

[77] See Glidden [358] for this point.

that in *Hdtm.* 37, the cost of not grasping *prolēpseis* is not merely that one will make false statements and hold false beliefs but that everything will be undiscriminated (*akrita*) or utterances will be 'empty'. We can leave to one side, for the moment, the unpacking of Epicurus' metaphor of 'empty utterances': what is fairly plausible is that whatever empty utterances lack is some semantic property. It is not that, if one fails to grasp *prolēpseis*, one will hold false beliefs about things and make false statements about them. Rather, it seems, one will not succeed in distinguishing anything to hold beliefs or make statements about. If for an utterance to be empty is for it to lack the relevant semantic property, then utterances which do not have *prolēpseis* underlying them will either not refer to anything (in which case Epicurus' metaphor will match the contemporary one of 'empty names') or be nonsensical.

The questions raised by this are, of course, what it is for an utterance to be empty and why the lack of an underlying *prolēpsis* should make it so. It will not be because it does not express a belief, since one can form beliefs without reference to *prolēpseis*. *Prolēpseis* function as criteria of *truth* in Epicurus' system, and his concern in *Hdtm.* 37 is indeed epistemological rather than psychological or semantic. The *prolēpseis* are the criteria against which to judge (*epikrinein*) 'what is believed or investigated or puzzled over': grasping *prolēpseis* is necessary for sifting true beliefs from false and not for forming beliefs at all. The point here is not that if we do not pay proper attention to the *prolēpseis* we will not have beliefs – but rather that we run the danger that none of our beliefs will be true. *Prolēpseis* provide a 'reference-point' for what is enquired into, puzzled over or believed. If it is possible to refer beliefs to *prolēpseis*, it must be possible to form beliefs independently of *prolēpseis*. There is no sign that Epicurus thinks that one cannot communicate false beliefs linguistically – indeed in *de Natura* 28, he seems to report as an earlier claim of his that 'all human error is exclusively of the form that arises in relation to *prolēpseis* and perceptions because of the multifarious conventions of language' (28.31.10=LS 19D). If a belief which does not rest on a *prolēpsis* can be expressed linguistically, then an empty utterance will not be senseless – which suggests that what Epicurus has in mind when he talks of 'empty utterances' are those utterances which do not succeed, or with which the speaker does not succeed, in referring to things.

This suggestion is supported by reflection on the ability of *prolēpseis* to operate as a criterion of truth. One danger of not grasping *prolēpseis* is that none of one's beliefs will be true. If that were to happen then everything would be undiscriminated – that is, we would not succeed in identifying kinds of object (or perhaps even particular objects) in the world. The most obvious way to take this is that although one may believe that there are things of a certain sort, nothing is of that sort. One will hold identificatory beliefs, but since these will be false, they will not succeed in identifying anything. The content of such an identificatory belief would perhaps be an existentially quantified definite description (of greater or lesser complexity), and so the belief would be false either because nothing satisfied the description or because more than one thing, or type of thing, satisfied it.[78] An uttered word with no underlying *prolēpsis* will then be empty because it fails – or the speaker fails – to refer to anything.

Which, though, the word or the speaker? The question is crucial because if it is the uttered words which are empty, then this provides clear evidence of Epicurean psychologism. The problem here is that, even if we are right to take 'empty' to mean 'non-referring' (and this remains interpretative), Epicurus' claim can be taken in two different ways. We can take an utterance either to be a set of sounds uttered on a particular occasion or to be an act of producing such a set. So, we can distinguish between the sentence-type 'Cows are herbivores' (which can be uttered by different people on different occasions) and a particular speaker's uttering the sentence 'Cows are herbivores.' If we take Epicurus' claim to be that it is the uttering which is empty, then he could still allow that what is uttered – a token of the sentence-type – has the same meaning as any other uttered token of that sentence-type: in effect, he would be making a distinction between word-meaning and speaker's meaning.[79] Although the speaker would have uttered a sentence which means that cows are herbivores, *he* would have failed to *say* anything about cows because he lacked the *prolēpsis* of cows. If, alternatively, we take Epicurus to be saying that it is the uttered sounds which are empty, then he is committed to a straightforwardly psychologistic explanation of linguistic signification. For whether an uttered word refers, and what it refers to, will depend on the concept which underlies it – and the nature of the associated concept can differ between individual speakers. 'Cow' may refer to cows in your idiolect but be empty in mine.

[78] So the content of the belief could be: 'There is only one thing [or type of thing] which is *F* and *G* and . . .'. For the belief to constitute a *prolēpsis*, the values of *F* and *G* would have to be such that they feature in the content of perception. There is no further requirement, however, that the subject's language should include terms suitable for expressing the belief that some object is *F*. Being *F* might well be having a certain distinctive shape which is perceptually discriminable but for which there is no term in the language. Of course once one has identified a shape as being distinctive *of* a type of object – say a cow – then one will be able to identify the shape as being the shape of that sort of object – so, one could say of something that it was 'cow-shaped'. Nevertheless, the ability to discriminate the shape will be prior to the recognition that it is the distinctive shape of a kind of object.

[79] This way of understanding Epicurus' point has been suggested to me by Jonathan Barnes. For the distinction, see, for instance, Grice [506] and Kripke [512].

The advantage of accepting the first of these interpretative options is that it enables Epicurus to recognise that the semantic values of words are objective: they do not differ between speakers. In effect, Epicurus would be putting forward the reasonable claim that if one is to succeed in using a name to refer to something, one must be able to distinguish that object or type of object from other things or types.[80] Although there is no knock-down argument against construing Epicurus' claim in this way, it is cast in doubt by the fact that in *Hdtm.* 76, Epicurus undoubtedly uses *phthongos* ('utterance') to refer to the sounds that are made and not the making of those sounds. Given that this is in any case the more natural way to take *phthongos* – and given also that Epicurus is committed to the priority of thought over language – the second interpretative option is, I think, preferable, and we should cautiously accept that the semantic values of the words a speaker utters are a function of his *prolēpseis*

If this is the correct way to construe Epicurus' talk of empty utterances, then it will be seen that he is indeed committed to a psychologistic semantics – for the semantic properties of the words uttered, and not merely whether uttering those words constitutes someone's saying something, will be determined by the content of the beliefs of the speaker.[81] What a speaker refers to by using the term 'cow' will depend on the content of the (possibly complex) identificatory belief which underlies that term – and whether that term refers to anything at all will depend on whether that belief actually succeeds in identifying something.[82] Unsuccessful identificatory beliefs will result in empty utterances, that is, words which do not succeed in referring to anything.

The effect of this would be to make the semantic properties of sounds dependent upon the psychology of individual speakers – and would thus cause problems for any attempt to provide a semantic theory for a public language. Even if someone were trained to utter the sentence 'Cows are herbivores', the set of phonemes he uttered would not mean anything (even that cows are herbivores) unless he possessed the relevant *prolēpseis*. Rather than there being word-types of a public language, whose semantic values could be specified independently of any reference to the psychological states of speakers, one would have to give the semantic values for the token utterances of individual speakers – and explicating what it is for a word to have a semantic value of whatever sort would require reference to the

[80] For this requirement on acts of saying, see Evans [494], 6–7.

[81] And where the content of the belief need not be such as to be specifiable in linguistic terms – see n. 78 above.

[82] Where, for the reasons given in the previous paragraph, the condition for identification is stronger than simply that at least one thing fits the belief.

mental states of the speaker. This is precisely the consequence of a psychologistic semantics which drove Frege to reverse the order of explanation. If words have meaning because they stand for ideas, and ideas are token states of individual speakers, then one cannot secure the objectivity of sense.[83]

Although Epicurus' theory is, on this reading, a psychologistic one, it nevertheless differs from fully intensionalist theories of meaning, as they are standardly construed.[84] For although the reference of a term will depend upon the speaker's beliefs, it will not be fully determined by those beliefs, since whether it refers at all will depend also on how the world is. At least in the case of (natural) kind terms, this is not the merely trivial point, which any intensionalist will be happy to accept, that whether a term refers depends on whether there is something for it to refer to. Of course, in the case of names, if a name refers to whatever satisfies a definite description and nothing does satisfy the relevant description, then the name will be empty. In the case of natural-kind terms, however, matters are more complicated. So, we can take the central claims of an intensionalist theory of meaning as being that, first, the intension of a term is constituted by a set of beliefs and that, secondly, a term's intension determines its extension. So, if my concept of a parrot is that of a blue and green bird which squawks, then the extension of 'parrot' in my idiolect will include all and only blue and green birds which squawk. Whatever satisfies the relevant descriptions will be included within the extension of the term.

It is this latter claim which, on the present account, would be denied by Epicurus: it is not sufficient for a natural-kind term to have an extension that there be objects which satisfy the descriptions given by the putative identificatory beliefs of the speaker. Whether a natural-kind term refers will depend not only on whether there are objects which satisfy the relevant descriptions but on whether those objects actually constitute a natural kind. It is not that if I cannot distinguish between parrots and parakeets, then 'parrot' in my idiolect will refer to both parrots and parakeets, but rather that it will not refer at all: it will be empty.[85]

Further, although Epicurus' account of semantics turns out to be psychologistic, it is not straightforwardly vulnerable to the Fregean objection that psychologism will lead to subjectivity of meaning. Indeed, it is tempting to see Epicurus' insistence on the importance of attending to the

[83] See the passage cited above, p. 75.

[84] See, for instance, Hilary Putnam's characterisation of such a theory at the beginning of his [521].

[85] There would have, then, to be some account of how such terms as 'bird', 'mammal' and 'animal' acquire their reference. This would be at least complicated and there is no sign, I think, that Epicurus recognised the need for it.

content of one's *prolēpseis* as a response to the worries which motivate that sort of objection. *Prolēpseis* function as criteria of truth because, like perceptions, they are guaranteed to report things as they are. As long as my identificatory beliefs of something are directly taken from my perceptions of it, then they will be true. They will also be such as successfully to identify the kinds into which perceived things fall.[86] Both perceptions and *prolēpseis* are able to bear this epistemological load because their content is determined by the objects of perception themselves: it is only if one starts going beyond the content of perceptions and *prolēpseis* that one risks falling into error. So long as what underlie my words are *prolēpseis* and not less secure beliefs, then my words will indeed succeed in referring to things – and so will those of other people. Just as the *prolēpsis* I acquire after repeated observations of parrots is guaranteed to pick out parrots, so is that acquired by anyone else.

For those beliefs which are *prolēpseis*, the common causal history of different people's *prolēpseis* guarantees that they do have relevantly the same content – which is why one can talk of *the prolēpsis* of something.[87] Epicurus' psychologism does not carry an inevitable danger of people's terms having different extensions because their concepts differ, since, if they follow his epistemological advice, their concepts will not differ. 'Parrot' will have the same extension in my idiolect as it does in anyone else's if it rests on the *prolēpsis* anyone will acquire in virtue of having perceived parrots.[88] Although it is a consequence of the psychologism that the meaning of words in an idiolect is prior to that of words in a common language, it is a consequence of the relation of *prolēpseis* both to experience and to language that speakers are able to make their idiolects type-identical. Epicurus, unlike later semantic psychologists, was not forced into an account of language which rendered meaning irredeemably subjective.[89]

[86] See Frede [24], 240 f. for some remarks on the relation between perception, *prolēpsis* and thought. Compare David Charles' remarks on Aristotle at the end of ch. 4 above.

[87] See Jackendoff [509], 30–1, for a somewhat similar response to this danger posed by psychologism (although Jackendoff himself takes the more extreme view that terms actually refer to entities of a mentally constructed world). His own conclusion is not un-Epicurean: 'Thus we can reasonably operate under the assumption that we are talking about the same things, as long as we are vigilant about detecting misunderstanding.' For Epicurus, that vigilance would mean ensuring that we use our terms in accordance with *prolēpseis*, and this would justify what Jackendoff takes to be an assumption.

[88] Of course, once words are determined by convention rather than by nature, there is the risk that different people may associate different words with the same concept – hence, perhaps, the warning in *de Natura* 28 (cf. above, p. 104).

[89] I am grateful to Jonathan Barnes for allowing me to see an unpublished piece of his on Epicurus' semantics and to him, Hugh Johnstone and David Charles for comments on an earlier draft of this essay.

6

The Stoic notion of a *lekton*

MICHAEL FREDE

The notion of a *lekton* lies at the very heart of the Stoic theory of language. The Stoics distinguish between an expression one utters or uses in saying something, and what gets said by uttering or using this expression. Thus they distinguish between the expression 'Socrates is ill', which is used to say that Socrates is ill, and what gets said by using this expression, namely that Socrates is ill. This kind of item, i.e. what gets said by using the appropriate expression in the appropriate way, the Stoics call a *lekton*. The notion lies at the very centre of the Stoic theory of language, because, on the basis of this distinction, the Stoics in one part of dialectic proceed to develop systematically a general theory of the kinds of things which get said, whereas in the other, or another, part of dialectic they try to develop a general theory of the expressions we use to say what we mean to say, what there is to be said (see Diogenes Laertius (D.L.) VII.62–3; 43–4). And since the Stoics assume that the primary point of using expressions is to say what there is to be said, they also, when they study expressions, study them primarily from the point of view of how they manage to reflect, to represent, to signify, to express, what we mean to say by using them. Hence, to understand the Stoic theory of language it is important to get as clear a grasp as possible on how the Stoics conceive of a *lekton*.

Perhaps the way to start is to look at the term *lekton* itself. It is a verbal adjective derived from the verb *legein*, 'to say'. In general such verbal adjectives ending in *-tos* are used in one or more of the following three ways: (i) they can indicate a passive state: thus *agraptos* means 'unwritten'; (ii) they can indicate a passive possibility: thus a *haireton* is something which can be chosen, an *aisthēton* something which can be perceived; (iii) they can have an active sense: thus *dynatos* means capable. Sometimes in late antiquity the word *lekton* is used in the active sense. In fact, some very late ancient authors, for example Philoponus, *On Aristotle's Prior Analytics* (*In An. Pr.*) 243.4 ff.; cf. Ps.-Alexander, *On Aristotle's De Sophisticis Elenchis* (*In*

S.E. 20, 28 ff.) claim that this is how the Stoics use the word. But this, obviously, is not correct. The Stoics clearly use the word in a passive sense for what gets said when we use the appropriate expression, rather than for the expression. Moreover, as we will see, the Stoics think that what gets said has some status independently of its actually being said, that it is somehow there to be said, whether or not it actually is said. And this suggests that the word *lekton* in Stoic usage has the passive modal sense of 'something which can be said'.

The next question, then, is: what is the relevant sense of 'to say' here? From what has been said earlier it should be clear that the relevant sense of 'to say' here is one in which what is said is not an expression, but rather what gets said by using the expression. To avoid any misunderstanding the Stoics systematically distinguish between saying (*legein*) and uttering (*propheresthai*), between being said and being uttered. We are told (D.L. VII.57): 'But there is also a difference between saying and uttering. It is sounds which are uttered, but things which are said; which is also why these things are *lekta*.' Similarly Sextus Empiricus, discussing *lekta*, tells us (*adversus Mathematicos* (*M*) VIII.80) that the Stoics characterise the sense of 'to say' in which *lekta* are things to say in this way: to say something is to utter an expression which is significative of the thing one has in mind. Thus there is a clear distinction between saying and uttering; it is expressions which are uttered, things, *lekta*, which are said. We should not let ourselves be confused by the fact that in Greek, as in English, what gets said can be identified in terms of the expression used. We do say 'He said: "it is getting late".' But this does not mean that what got said was the expression 'it is getting late'; it rather means that he said that it was getting late. Similarly with 'He said to him "Shut the door!"' and 'He told him to shut the door', with 'He said to him "what time is it?"' and 'he asked him what time it was'. When, then, Plutarch (*de Stoicorum repugnantiis* (*de Stoic. rep.*) 1037d) reports that according to the Stoics when we say 'Don't steal' we are saying one thing, namely 'Don't steal', ordering another thing, namely not to steal, and forbidding yet another thing, namely to steal, we should not get confused: the point is not that in uttering the expression 'Don't steal' we are telling somebody not to steal and forbid him to steal. The point rather is that in saying to somebody that he should not steal, we are ordering him not to steal and forbidding him to steal. So the relevant sense of 'to say' is one in which it is not the expressions themselves which get said, but rather what gets said by using these expressions.

Moreover the relevant sense of 'to say' is such that to say something may be a matter of making a statement or a claim, of asserting a proposition. But as the Plutarch passage shows, it may also be a matter of asking a question, or of issuing a command, or of invoking somebody, or of swearing an oath, or whatever else there may be of this kind. Thus the Stoics distinguish different kinds of things to say, or different kinds of *lekta*, depending on what one is doing in saying something (cf., e.g., D.L. VII.66 ff.; S.E., *M* VIII.71 ff.). Claims, things claimed to be the case, roughly propositions, are just one kind of *lekton*, though the most important one. But there are also questions, commands, invocations, oaths, and the like. These different kinds of *lekton*, though they have further distinguishing features, are distinguished primarily by the fact that in saying them one is doing a certain kind of thing, for example asking a question. Thus it is a distinctive feature of claims or propositions that they are true or false. But they are defined not in terms of this feature, but by the fact that they are the kind of item such that in saying this sort of thing one is asserting something (cf. D.L. VII.66; S.E., *M* VIII.71). So a *lekton*, to go just by the word, is what gets said, a thing to say, what there is to say, what can get said, in the sense indicated. And, in fact, I take this to be the primary notion of a *lekton*, at least in the context of the Stoic theory of language.

But a *lekton* is not just what gets said by using the appropriate kind of expression; a *lekton* is also made to serve two further functions. These have already been alluded to in Sextus' characterisation of the relevant sense of 'to say', mentioned above: to say something is to utter an expression which is significative of the thing one has in mind. So a *lekton* not only is what gets said, but is also (i) what is signified by the expression used to say something, and (ii) what the speaker has in mind, what he thinks, when he utters the expression. In a way it is easy to see why the Stoics identify what gets said both with what is signified by the expression used and with what the speaker has in mind. For in this way we can readily see how somebody who knows the language also knows what is signified by the expression he hears, and thus knows what gets said, and thus knows what the speaker has in mind (cf. S.E., *M* VIII.12). But let us look briefly at these two identifications separately.

A *lekton* is what is signified by the corresponding expression. Hence the Stoics also refer to the *lekton* as 'what is signified' (*sēmainomenon*), and to the expression as a 'thing signifying' or 'signifier' (*sēmainon*) (cf. D.L. VII.62-3). But there are two things to keep in mind here, if we want to get clearer about the notion of a *lekton*. First, it is not the basic meaning of the term *lekton* that a *lekton* is what is signified or meant by an expression; it only serves this function because the Stoics identify what gets said with what is signified by the corresponding expression. Secondly, though a *lekton* is something which is signified by an expression, we should not rush to the unwarranted conclusion that anything which is signified by any expression for this mere reason already is a *lekton*. Our sources often talk as if there were one distinction indifferently marked as the distinction between *lekta*, 'things' (*pragmata*), 'things signified', on the one hand, and 'sounds' or 'expressions' and 'things signifying', on the other. But this may be a rather loose way of talking, which is only roughly adequate. We will return to this point later.

The other equation we need to consider in some more detail is this: the *lekton* is what the speaker has in mind, the thing thought, when he utters an expression to say something. The Stoic view is this: like animals we do have impressions of things, for example impressions of things we look at. But because we are rational beings, because we have minds, these impressions in our case are rational impressions or thoughts (D.L. VII.51). This means that they are articulated in a certain way, namely in such a way as to represent a propositional item. Thus when we perceive a green object we tend to have the thought that the object in front of us is green. The thought itself is conceived of by the Stoics as a complex physical state. For they conceive of the mind as a physical entity and correspondingly treat its states as physical states. But the content of the thought, what it represents, is a propositional item. Thus the thought in question represents the object as being green. In this sense there is a *lekton* corresponding to every human impression or thought; and it is in this sense that the *lekton* is what one has in mind when one is thinking something and when one is saying what one is thinking. Given that different people are rather different, it is not surprising that these thoughts are very different even when they think or say the same thing, for example that the object is green. But since the propositional content, the *lekton*, is precisely the same, we can also understand precisely what somebody is saying and what he is thinking, though his thought and our thought may be very different indeed. In this way what gets said, what there is to say, the *lekton*, also serves as the content of our thoughts and as what is signified by the expression we use when we express our thoughts. So thus far we have no reason to doubt that the basic notion of a *lekton* is the notion of a thing to say, and this all the more so since not everything which gets thought gets said, and since not everything which is there to say gets thought. There are lots of things to say which never get thought or said. Nevertheless they are there to be thought or said.

Though this is the basic notion of a *lekton*, one may wonder whether it is the original notion. There is, for instance, the following possibility which, for the moment, we may just note as a possibility: when the Stoics talk about *lekta*, this not only includes propositions, but also questions, orders, invocations, and the like. The reason for this simply is that *legein* is taken to have such a wide sense as to cover any speech-act. But clearly what the Stoics primarily have in mind, and what they are mostly interested in, are propositions, things said in a narrower sense of 'to say' or *legein*, namely the sense of 'to claim' or 'to state'. Some things the Stoics have to say are more readily understood if we assume that the original notion of a *lekton* was narrower in this way and only got extended when the Stoics tried to give an account of language as a whole.

But before we pursue this any further, another fact has to be introduced. The Stoics standardly distinguish between complete *lekta* and incomplete *lekta* (see D.L. VII.63). As examples of incomplete *lekta* we invariably get what the Stoics call 'predicates' (*katēgorēmata*: see D.L. VII.63–4). These are items which correspond to the verb-phrase of a declarative sentence in the way in which a *lekton* corresponds to the whole sentence. Thus being wise and taking a walk are the predicates corresponding to '... is wise' and '... is taking a walk'. It is easy to see why they are called 'incomplete *lekta*'. To utter the expression '... is wise' is not yet to say anything; nothing gets said by just saying '... is wise' (see D.L. VII.63); to get a complete *lekton* we have to add something. It is more difficult to understand why such incomplete *lekta* would also be called *lekta*. For, strictly speaking, given the notion of a *lekton* as a thing to say, they are not *lekta* but only incomplete *lekta*, and, just as an unfinished sentence is not a sentence, an incomplete *lekton* is not a *lekton*. But Diocles (in D.L. VII.63) talks as if it were; for he reports: 'of *lekta*, the Stoics say, some are complete and the others incomplete'. Perhaps Diocles is just talking carelessly. But there is a way to explain why the Stoics may have had no qualms about also calling predicates *lekta*, 'things to say'. We will remember that Plato in some crucial passages makes the distinction between saying something and saying something about something (see, for example, *Theaetetus* 188d9–10; 189b1–2; *Sophist* 262e6–263d4). Thus somebody who is saying that Theaetetus is flying might also be described as saying about Theaetetus that he is flying. Correspondingly one might think that a predicate is a thing to say at least in the sense that it is a thing to say about something. In this way one would understand why the Stoics might be ready to extend the notion of a *lekton* to cover predicates, especially since, as we will see, *lekta* in the strict sense and predicates have a further feature in common: they are supposed to be incorporeal somethings (see below).

With this in mind let us return to the question of the origin of the notion of a *lekton*. I think there is reason to believe that this notion of a *lekton* was originally a metaphysical notion, the notion of a fact, of an incorporeal item to be contrasted with the body it is a fact about, and that the notion only in a second step got modified or construed in such a way as to serve both in metaphysical and in logical or linguistic contexts.

But let us first consider the notion of a predicate: for this notion, too, originally seems to be a metaphysical notion. What I have in mind when I talk about a metaphysical notion is this: we use the term 'predicate' to refer to a predicate-expression like 'is wise'. But in Greek philosophy there is a tradition of using the word 'predicate' to refer to an item in the ontology which is supposed to be signified by the predicate-expression. If, for example, we look at Aristotle's treatise *Categories*, we see that what is predicated is not an expression, but an entity. What is more, Aristotle clearly uses the verb 'to predicate' (*katēgorein*) in the sense of 'to ascribe a true predicate to something', i.e. a predicate is not only an item in the ontology, but an item which belongs to the subject it is ascribed to. Thus the notion of predicate here really is the metaphysical notion of an attribute. But why is it called a 'predicate'? The idea seems to be this: there are not only objects, but there are also further entities introduced by truths about the objects. To put the matter differently: Aristotle's thought seems to be that there are not only items like Socrates and Fido and a tree in our ontology; there must also be items like the species man or wisdom, because it is true to say of Socrates that he is wise or that he is a man. These further items, in Aristotle's ontology, are the predicates.

Now Aristotle has a certain view as to what is predicated when Socrates is wise: he thinks it is wisdom. This reflects the fact that his ontology is an ontology of entities rather than of facts or states-of-affairs. Thus in his ontology what corresponds to the fact that Socrates is ill is an ill Socrates, a composite of Socrates and illness.

Other philosophers, though, took exception to this. They, too, distinguished between an object like Socrates and a quality like wisdom. But they did not identify the predicate with the quality wisdom, as Aristotle and his followers did. They distinguished between wisdom, the quality, and being wise, the predicate. Seneca (*Letters* (*Ep.*) 117.11–12) not only tells us that the Peripatetics rejected the distinction, but also attributes the origin of the distinction to the 'old dialecticians' from whom, he says, the Stoics inherited it. Seneca explains the distinction in these terms: the field which a farmer has is one thing, namely something corporeal; but it is not to be identified with having the field, which is something incorporeal; similarly wisdom is one thing, namely on the Stoic view a quality and hence a body; having wisdom or being wise is something altogether different, namely something incorporeal. The point which is made here is clearly a metaphysical point: in addition to Socrates and to wisdom, both of which are bodies, there is also such an item as Socrates' being wise, which is not a body, but something incorporeal.

This metaphysical contrast between a body and an incorporeal predicate is one the Stoics rely on in various contexts. Thus, for example, in ethics when they claim that virtue or wisdom is good, but being virtuous or being wise is not (see Seneca, *Ep.* 117.1 ff.); or when they argue that we have to distinguish between the object of desire, which is a good, for instance wisdom, and what is to be desired, which is having that good, for instance to be wise, which, as they put it, is incorporeal and a predicate (see Stobaeus, *Eclogae* (*Ecl.*) II.97.15–98.6). Quite generally they say that an impulse is an impulse for a predicate (see Stob. *Ecl.* II.88.2 ff.). Perhaps the most important and most interesting use of the distinction, though, is made in the context of the Stoic account of causality. The Stoic view, attested in many places (see, for example, S.E., *M* IX.211; Stob. *Ecl.* I.138. 14 ff.), is that a cause is a body, but that what it is the cause of is not a body, but an incorporeal predicate; it is the cause for a body of a predicate, or, as we would put it, it is the cause for a body to have a predicate true of it: the sun, for example, is the cause for the wax of its melting.

Now it is clear here that we are not talking about predicates in a linguistic or a logical sense; we are rather talking about metaphysical items of a certain kind which are contrasted with bodies. But it is also easy to see in these contexts how readily one would move from the notion of a predicate or an attribute, which is something which is true of something, to the notion of a predicate which is or is not true of a given object.

With this in mind let us return to *lekta* and consider the first attested use of the word by Cleanthes. Clement (*Stromateis* (*Strom.*) VIII.9.26.3 ff.) reports the Stoic doctrine that causes are causes of predicates, but then adds that some also say that they are causes of *lekta*. And he explains this by saying that Cleanthes called predicates *lekta*. The text is problematic in various ways, but it very strongly suggests, not only that Cleanthes used the word *lekton*, but that Cleanthes, as opposed to Zeno, said that causes are causes of *lekta*. This, in turn, allows for different interpretations. Perhaps Cleanthes meant to clarify or to correct Zeno's point: wisdom, for example, is not the cause of the predicate 'being wise', but rather of the *lekton* that somebody is wise. But presumably Cleanthes was just trying to make the very point Zeno had made in a different way: Socrates is a body, wisdom is a body, but that Socrates is wise is not a body, but an incorporeal *lekton*; and it is this *lekton* which is caused, rather than the wisdom, which is a body.

But however we interpret this, here we have a metaphysical notion of a *lekton*. We are not concerned with the meaning of expressions, or the intentional objects or contents of thoughts, but with facts; whether or not anybody has thought of them or will ever think about them, whether or not they get stated is completely irrelevant. The point is the metaphysical point that there is an item like Socrates' being wise which is not to be confused with either Socrates or wisdom, but which, though not a body, nevertheless has some ontological status, since it is the kind of item of which a cause, properly speaking, is the cause. Here the notion of a *lekton* seems to be the notion of a true thing to say, just as the notion of a predicate had been the notion of a something truthfully predicated of something. And one can see why the term *lekton* would have seemed appropriate. We do not understand the world properly unless we take into account that there are not only bodies, but also truths about bodies, which themselves are incorporeal. But, again, one readily sees how one could move (or slide) from the notion of a true thing to say to the notion of a thing to say which is true or false, and how then this notion would get naturally extended to cover things to say quite generally. This, I think, is in fact what happened. But it does not matter much whether it did or not, if we want to get clear about the standard Stoic notion of a *lekton*, as it was clearly used by Chrysippus and his followers. What does matter is that even on the standard notion of a *lekton* facts, true propositions, remain paradigms of *lekta*. And this should make us hesitant about assuming too readily that the basic notion of a *lekton* is the notion of the meaning of an expression, and it should also make us hesitant about assuming too readily that *lekta* are language- or mind-dependent items.

But let us turn to the metaphysical status Stoic *lekta* are supposed to have. They are supposed to be incorporeal somethings which as such merely subsist, but do not exist. To understand this we have to take into account that the Stoic view is strikingly similar to that of the Unreformed Giants of Plato's *Sophist*. Like the Giants the Stoics believe that only bodies exist; thus they are even ready to say that the soul, virtue, wisdom are bodies. Quite generally everything which can affect something else or can be affected is counted as a body and hence as a being. But the Stoics also realise that their theory makes reference to items like the void, space, time and *lekta* which are not bodies, but which cannot be said to be altogether nothing, to have no status whatsoever. Hence for items of this kind they introduce the category of a something (*ti*) which, though incorporeal, is not nothing (see S.E., *M* X.218). Correspondingly they introduce the notion of subsistence (*hyphistanai*), as opposed to being (*einai*), to characterise the mode of existence of these items (see S.E., *M* I.17; VIII.70). The question is why the Stoics want to attribute to *lekta* an ontological status in the first place and what kind of status subsistence is.

If we return to our initial distinction between an expression used to say something and what gets said by using this expression, we might be quite ready to make this distinction, but this in itself would not commit us to the view that ontologically there are two distinct items here, an expression and a thing to say. The Stoic doctrine of *lekta* becomes controversial precisely because the Stoics assume that in some sense there are things out there to be said, items distinct both from the expressions we use and the thoughts we express. Why, then, did the Stoics attribute an ontological status to *lekta*? Given our earlier remarks the answer, in a way, should be easy. The very point, or at least a point, in introducing the notions of a predicate and a *lekton* was the metaphysical one that reality is not just constituted by bodies, that in addition to bodies there are also predicates true of bodies, propositions true about bodies. So it is not surprising that *lekta* should be accorded some status, namely precisely the status of incorporeal somethings, as opposed to bodies.

But given that we now operate with the notion of a predicate which is true or false of something, and the notion of a *lekton* which is true or false, rather than the notions of an attribute or a fact, the Stoic doctrine must be somewhat more complex. For not just attributes and facts are accorded subsistence: any predicate and any *lekton* is supposed to be a subsistent incorporeal something. Accordingly the Stoics introduce a new notion, the notion of being present or being there (*hyparchein*). And this is applied not only to *lekta*, whether complete or incomplete, but also to time. As we noted earlier, the Stoic view is that time is an incorporeal something, too, and as such only subsists and does not exist. But the Stoics go on to distinguish between the past and the future, on the one hand, which merely subsist, and the present, which is there or is present (Stobaeus, *Ecl.* I.106.18 ff.). Similarly in the case of predicates: as incorporeal somethings they subsist, but if they are true of something, they have the stronger status of being there or present (*Ecl.* I.106.20 ff.). In fact the word *hyparchein* is often used by philosophers in the sense of 'to belong', for example by Aristotle in his syllogistic when he talks of something A's belonging to something B in the sense of 'B is A.' Similarly, finally, with propositions: a *lekton*, even if it is false, is something and hence subsists; but if it is true it is a fact and is present or there (S.E., *M* VIII.10). So, though the major reason why the Stoics do attribute some ontological status to *lekta*, whether complete or incomplete, is clearly that they want to attribute some status to facts and to attributes, this cannot be the whole explanation. For this would not explain why they attribute subsistence to *lekta* quite generally and why they attribute a special status to facts and attributes, instead of merely attributing some status to facts and attributes. So why do the Stoics attribute subsistence to *lekta* quite generally?

There are various possibilities. One is that the Stoics were still concerned with the problem which had vexed philosophers for so long and which Plato had repeatedly tried to deal with, in particular in the *Theaetetus* and in the *Sophist*, namely the problem of how false statements and how false thoughts are possible, given that there does not seem to be anything there to get stated or to get thought, if they are false. And the assumption of subsistent *lekta* even in these cases would immediately take care of such problems. But, again, the explanation might be much more metaphysical. Sextus (*M* VIII.10) reports: 'According to them true is what is there and contradictorily opposed to something, and false is what is not there and contradictorily opposed to something.' This might suggest that what is false gets its status as the contradictory of what is true; the thought might be that a fact is the fact it is in part by making it not be the case that the contradictory is true, or that a claim has to be understood not only as asserting one thing, but also as implicitly denying the contradictory.

If, thus, we consider what mode of being the Stoics ascribe to *lekta* in calling them subsistent, we should be hesitant to assume that this is some mind-dependent existence, that they only exist as the actual or even the possible contents of thought. It is, of course, true that the Stoics seem standardly to have said that a *lekton* is something which subsists in correspondence to rational impression. For we find the same formulation in Diogenes Laertius (VII.63) and Sextus Empiricus (*M* VIII.70). In fact, in Sextus Empiricus (*M* VIII.12) we get the even more suggestive formulation that the *lekton* is something which we grasp as something which subsists upon our thought (*parhyphistamenon dianoiai*). But if we consider these passages without prejudice, their point rather seems to be that the *lekton*, what is true or false, should not be confused with our thought (many philosophers had assumed that it is thoughts which are true or false: see *M* VIII.11), but rather conceived of as something subsisting alongside our thought; i.e. the point is not that *lekta* only exist as the contents of thoughts, but that they are contents of thoughts or impressions, rather than the thoughts or impressions themselves. It also does not seem to be right to attribute the view to the Stoics that facts are mind-dependent. It is, of course, true that they depend on the Divine Mind, but this is clearly not what the passages in question refer to, or what we usually think of when we say 'mind-dependent'. So it is reasonable to assume that the mode of being of *lekta* is not that of mind-dependent items, at least not in the ordinary sense of the term.

With this as a background, we can now turn to what modern scholars have treated as the locus classicus for the Stoic doctrine of *lekta*, Sextus Empiricus, *M* VIII.11–12. The context is a discussion as to what is the primary bearer of the predicates 'true' and 'false'; is it an expression, or a thought, or something else? The Stoic view, according to Sextus, is this: 'Three things, they say, go together, what is signified, what is signifying, and what has it (*to tynchanon*). Of these it is the sound (i.e. the expression) which is signifying, for example "Dion"; what is signified is the thing itself which is revealed by the sound . . . what has it is the external object, i.e. Dion himself. Of these, two are bodies, namely the sound and the what has it, one is incorporeal, i.e. the thing signified and the *lekton*, and it is this which turns out true or false.'

If we take this passage at face value, it shows that the Stoics did distinguish between (i) the expression 'Dion', (ii) what is signified by this expression, an incorporeal *lekton*, and (iii) Dion himself. It thus poses a challenge to our interpretation according to which the notion of a *lekton* is the notion of something which gets said in the relevant sense of 'to say'. For to utter the expression 'Dion' is not yet to say anything in the relevant sense, and so there also should not be a *lekton* corresponding to the expression 'Dion'. On the contrary, the passage suggests that the notion of a *lekton* is a notion of the meaning of an expression. In fact, on the basis of this passage one might come to think, as, for example, Mates did in his [385], that the Stoics distinguish between the sense and the reference of an expression.

Now before we accept such far-reaching conclusions we should take note of the fact that this is the only text which attributes to the Stoics the view that there is also a *lekton* corresponding to an expression like 'Dion'. We should also note that there must be something wrong with Sextus' account: he means to tell us what it is on the Stoic view which is true or false; but instead he gives us as an example the expression 'Dion' and what is signified by it; but whichever view the Stoics may have about what is signified by the expression 'Dion', we know that this is not going to be something which is true or false. So the least that has to be said about Sextus' account is that it relies on a badly chosen example. There is a minimal textual change which would do away with this problem: if at the beginning of VIII.12 we read *Dion peripatei*, ('Dion is walking'), instead of *Dion*, the text would become perfectly satisfactory. It would completely fall in line with the passage in Seneca (*Ep.* 117.13) parts of which we considered earlier. Seneca had reported that the Stoics distinguish between wisdom and being wise, the one a body, the other an incorporeal item. He then goes on to elucidate the distinction in the following way: Cato is a body; thus when we see Cato walking we see a body; but what we have when we see Cato walking is a thought, namely the thought which is put into the words 'Cato is walking'; and what we are saying when we say this is not a body, but an incorporeal *lekton*. (Incidentally this passage shows how easily a point made in terms of the notion of a predicate can be made in terms of the notion of a *lekton*, as we saw earlier considering Cleanthes' remarks about causality; it also shows how easily we move from the metaphysical notion of a *lekton* to the logical notion.) Thus according to Seneca we have to distinguish between Cato, a body, the expression 'Cato is walking', similarly a physical item, and the *lekton* that Cato is walking. Similarly Sextus, if we accepted the textual change, would now distinguish between (i) the expression 'Dion is walking', (ii) the *lekton* signified by this expression, and (iii) Dion himself. And this would just be the distinction we are already familiar with. Unfortunately it is clear from *M* VIII.75 that the text here is not corrupt. For in VIII.75 Sextus again distinguishes between (i) the expression 'Dion', (ii) the incorporeal *lekton* signified by it, and (iii) Dion himself.

How, then, are we to deal with Sextus' unparalleled testimony? It seems that we should distinguish three questions: (i) Is Sextus right in assuming that the Stoics distinguish between the expression 'Dion', what is signified by it, and Dion himself? (ii) Is Sextus right in identifying what is signified by the expression 'Dion' as an incorporeal *lekton*? (iii) Do the Stoics distinguish between the signification of 'Dion' and Dion himself as the sense and the reference of 'Dion', respectively? There is good reason to think that the answer to the first question is affirmative, and that the answer to the third question is negative. In the end it will turn out that the answer to the second question is presumably affirmative too, though with some important qualifications; but it will be important for our topic to see precisely in what way Sextus may be right on this question too. Thus Sextus would be right in assuming that the Stoics, given an expression like 'Dion', as in 'Dion is running', make a threefold distinction. He even would be right in suggesting that the second item in the triad, what is signified by the expression, is somehow a *lekton* too. But it will be crucial to see that this can be so only in a very derivative sense of the term *lekton*. Nevertheless, it would be a mistake on our part to conclude, on the basis of this passage, that the Stoics did distinguish between the sense and the reference of an expression.

Let us turn to the last point first. It is natural to assume that the truth or falsehood of 'Dion is running' depends on whether the predicate 'is running' is true or false of Dion. And in this case Dion himself would be the reference of the expression 'Dion' in the sentence 'Dion is running.' But this is not the way the Stoics actually construe the truth-conditions for the proposition that Dion is running (cf. *M* VIII.97–8; Alexander Aphrodisius, *On Aristotle's Prior Analytic* (*In An. Pr.*) 402.3 ff.). According to the Stoics this proposition is true precisely if there is something which is Dion and it is running; if, then, Dion is already dead or Dion has not yet been born, the proposition is false, just as it is false if Dion is not running. So Dion is not the reference of the expression 'Dion', but rather that of which the predicate is true, if the proposition is true. For 'Dion' in the sentence 'Dion is running' is not treated as a referring expression. It is rather treated in the way the Stoics treat 'man' in 'man is running' (in Greek one does not standardly say 'a man is running'). They think that this sentence is true precisely if there is something which is a man and it is running. So there, too, will be the expression 'man', what is signified by the expression, and, if the proposition is true, some man of whom the predicate is true.

Let us next turn to the first question. There are good reasons to suppose that Sextus is right when he assumes that the Stoics distinguish three items, 'Dion', the signification of 'Dion', and Dion himself; there seem to be three items, at least when the proposition is true. For according to D.L. VII.58 the Stoics claim that proper names like 'Dion' reveal or signify an individual quality, whereas common nouns like 'man' signify a common quality. This view we also find in grammarians influenced by Stoicism (see, for example, Apollonius Dyscolus, *Syntax* 103.13 ff.; 142.1–2; 155.3–5; *De pronominibus* (*Pron.*) 105.18–19; Priscian II.56; XVII.34). The details of the Stoic doctrine of individual qualities are obscure, but the view seems to be that there is something about an individual which makes it the unique individual it is, and this is the individual quality, whereas the common quality makes an object the kind of object it is, for instance a human being. Now both the individual quality and the common quality characteristic of men are something an object has. It has them in a rather special sense of 'have'. For unlike other qualities, like wisdom, the individual quality and this kind of common quality are constitutive of the object. Nevertheless they are not identical with it. And hence this kind of quality can be said to be something an object has, in a special sense of 'has', which is rather different from the sense in which it has a quality like wisdom. Thus we would readily understand why the Stoics would distinguish between the expressions 'Dion' and 'man', what is signified by them, namely an individual or a common quality, and what has this quality, namely Dion or a particular man.

There is a further reason to think that the Stoics make the threefold distinction Sextus presupposes. According to D.L. VII.70 the Stoics claim that the proposition that Dion is walking is constituted by a case and a predicate. And there is reason to think that the Stoics distinguish a case both from an expression, on the one hand, and an object, on the other, so that, again, we seem to have a triad: expression, case, object. Consider, for instance, the use of the word 'case' in *M* XI.29, where Sextus discusses how the Stoics deal with a certain ambiguity in the term 'dog'. The word 'dog' (*kyōn*) in Greek is ambiguous: it might mean (i) a dog, (ii) some kind of marine animal, (iii) a cynic philosopher, or (iv) the star. Sextus puts it in the following way: the expression 'dog' signifies a case under which the dog falls, a case under which the marine animal falls, etc. So here a case is clearly something which is signified by an expression, and equally clearly it is distinguished both from the expression and from the things designated by it. It is some intermediate item. Unfortunately we do not have a clear grasp of what a case is supposed to be.

The pursuit of this question again leads us back to metaphysics. Though the evidence is very meagre, it is clear enough that there is a metaphysical notion of a case which forms part of a network of notions, the notions of an object, a universal, an attribute, a quality, of having (*tynchanein*), possessing (*echein*) and participating. Most intriguingly, there is a Platonist version of it, which may well go back to the Old Academy, as well as a Stoic version. Simplicius (*On Aristotle's Categories* (*In. Cat.*) 209.10 ff.) tells us that the members of the Academy (he must mean Platonists, given the dogmatic character of the distinction attributed to them) called dispositions (*hexeis*) 'things to possess' (*hekta*), universals or concepts 'things to participate in', cases (*ptōseis*) 'things to have', and predicates 'accidents'. It is quite difficult, given the lack of evidence, to reconstruct the underlying view. But another passage in Simplicius (*In. Cat.* 53.9 ff.) is of some help. We are given Iamblichus' interpretation of what Aristotle means when he talks about something's being predicated of something as its subject, in particular when he talks about the genus or the species being predicated of something. Iamblichus' view is that it is not, strictly speaking, the genus which is predicated of the species when we say 'man is an animal', or the species of the individual when we say 'Socrates is a man'; it is rather a case which is predicated, and he explains a case, as Simplicius puts it, in terms of 'participation in the generic (*to genikon*)', i.e. the genus or the species. The underlying view here is clearly that Socrates participates in the universal man, but that what is predicated is not the universal itself, but a case. And a case here, at least in the example 'Socrates is a man', seems to be something like an immanent, as opposed to a transcendent, Form. Thus the view attributed to the Platonists may be this: there are objects; they participate in Ideas or universals corresponding to sortal concepts; but what they have as a result (*tynchanein*) are not these Ideas, but cases, i.e. immanent Forms; but there are also attributes like wisdom; they are not Ideas, i.e. things to participate in, or immanent Forms, i.e. things to have; for they are not constitutive of an object; rather they are things to possess; the things to possess themselves have to be distinguished from the attributes, the predicates which are true of an object when it possesses a property, for wisdom and having wisdom, or being wise, are distinct. But, whether or not this is the Platonist view Simplicius is referring to, it is clear from the two passages in Simplicius that there are Platonists who use a metaphysical notion of a case and who assume that a case is to be contrasted with both the universal or the concept or the Idea and the individuals falling under the concept, as something which is had (*teukton*), rather than something which is participated in.

What, in spite of all the difficulties of detail, emerges from a passage in

Stobaeus is that the Stoics have a view which is very much like the one I have just attributed to some Platonists, in any case the Stoic version of a metaphysical theory involving objects, cases and universals. In *Ecl.* I. 136, 21 ff. we are given the Stoics' view on Platonic Ideas. It seems as if it were assumed that there are only Ideas of natural kinds. In any case, the Stoics claim that such Ideas are mere concepts (*ennoēmata*), not conceptions or mental items, but their counterparts, mental constructs of some kind. Nevertheless, being concepts of natural kinds they have some status: they are quasi-somethings and quasi-qualified. Stobaeus then tells us (137. 3 ff.): 'Of these [sc. the Ideas] the Stoic philosophers say that they do not exist, and that we participate in the concepts, but have (*tynchanein*) the cases, which they call appellations.'

So it seems that, right down to the terminology, the Stoics have a view quite like the Platonists considered earlier, except that the Stoics replace Ideas by concepts. The case is distinguished, on the one hand, from the particular objects which have it, and, on the other, from the concept, the generic, man in general, or animal in general. Thus it seems that a case is something like the Stoic counterpart of an Aristotelian form or of a Platonist immanent Form, as opposed to the transcendent form participated in: i.e. it should be something like a common quality or an individual quality. And this is exactly, as we saw, what according to the Stoics is signified by a proper name or a common noun (see D.L. VII.58).

There is a good deal of further evidence that the Stoics distinguish the case both from the object which has it and from the generic or the concept it falls under. As to the first, the distinction would explain why the Stoics standardly call the object which has the predicate true of it, if the proposition is true, *to tynchanon*, i.e. 'what has it' (see, for example, Plutarch, *adversus Colotem* (*Adv. Colot.*) 1119f; Philop. *In. An. Pr.* 243.2; Ps.-Alex., *In S.E.* 20, 27 ff.), as, in fact, Sextus does twice in the passage under discussion (*M* VIII.11; 12). As to the second contrast, it is clearly what Ammonius (*On Aristotle's de Interpretatione* (*In de Int.*) 43.9 ff.) and others (see Stephanus, *In de Int.* 10.28–9) have in mind when they try to explain the Stoic use of the word 'case': a case is supposed to be something which falls under, or from, a universal as a concept. And it is also this contrast which Simplicius is referring to when (*In Cat.* 105.7 ff.) he reports the Stoic view as to whether a genus or a species can be called a 'this'. He points out that in this connection we have to take into account what the Stoics have to say about generic qualia (i.e. items like man in general, the universal man) and about cases. Presumably the view he refers to is this: generic qualia, i.e. universals, are not a this, not even a something, whereas cases are.

So there is a Stoic metaphysical notion of a case. It is called a 'case' because it falls under the concept of an object. But, unlike the Peripatetics and most Platonists, the Stoics distinguish between general concepts, which they also call 'genus' (D.L. vii.61) and individual concepts, which they call 'species' (D.L. vii.61). So what is ordinarily called 'the species man' the Stoics call 'the genus man', whereas Socrates, i.e. the individual concept of Socrates, will be a species (D.L. vii.61). Correspondingly we have cases both of general concepts and of individual concepts. And I take it that these cases are just the common qualities and the individual qualities respectively. This, then, is the metaphysical notion of a case. Hence the case signified by 'man' in the true statement 'man is running' is a common quality in virtue of which a particular man is a man, for example the common quality in virtue of which Socrates is a man. But, given this, it should be clear that, unlike what we may at first have thought, the common quality 'man' is not a universal, something all you share; it is rather something which in a particular case falls under this universal: it is a case of man.

Now, consider the statement 'man is in Athens' (in English, but not in Greek, one would ordinarily say 'a man is in Athens'). What is signified by 'man' here? It seems that Chrysippus used the argument 'if something is in Athens, it is not in Megara; man is in Athens; hence man is not in Megara' to show that it is not the universal man, but a case, namely a case of man, which is signified by 'man'. For it does not follow from the fact that a particular man, and hence that man is in Athens, that it is not the case that man, and hence any man, is in Megara. And he explained this, it seems, by pointing out that the universal man is not a something, let alone a this, and hence not covered by the range of 'if something . . . it . . .', whereas a case is a something. So it is a case, more specifically a case of man, which is signified by 'man' in 'man is in Athens'; in fact it is a body, namely a common quality. Does this mean, though, that it is some particular case of man, some particular body, which is signified? Obviously not; for otherwise the truth of the statement would depend on whether or not there was something with this particular (instance of the) common quality which was in Athens, when, in fact, the statement is true as long as there is any man in Athens. Moreover, one thing we can learn from the sophism mentioned above is that 'man is in Athens' and 'man is in Megara' can both be true, though it is a case which is signified, because it is no case in particular which is signified, let alone the same particular case, whereas 'man is in Athens' and 'he is in Megara' cannot both be true, because the same case is involved in both.

This may become a bit clearer if we consider an analogy. If I want a bicycle, I want a certain kind of physical object. There are any number of objects of this kind. Does this mean that I want any one of them in particular? Obviously not. Does this mean that what I want is not a particular physical object of this kind, after all, but some other kind of item, that the object of my want is some kind of intentional object? There is no need to say this. To say that one wants a bicycle is to say that one has a want which is satisfied if there is a bicycle which one has. And the bicycle which one has, if one's want is satisfied, is indeed a particular physical object. Similarly with signification. To say that 'man' in 'man is in Athens' signifies a case is not to say that there is a particular case which is signified; it rather is to say that, if what is claimed to be true is true, there is a particular case such that something has this case and it is in Athens. And this particular case is a particular quality, a particular body. So even if there are no men at all, either because they have all gone out of existence or because men have not yet come into being, what is signified by 'man' in 'man is in Athens' will be a case, though the quality does not exist at all. For, to say that a quality or a case is signified is not to say that there is a quality or a case there to be signified, just as to say that one wants a bicycle is not to say that there is a bicycle there to be wanted (bicycles, by chance, may all have gone out of existence). It is just to say that, if things are such as to make the claim true, there is a quality or a case there. This does not mean that, if the claim is false, 'man' does not signify a case. If you want a bicycle, this does not mean, either, that there is a bicycle which you want. And conversely, if there is no bicycle which you want, if perhaps there is no bicycle at all, it does not follow that what you want is not a bicycle, or that it is not a bicycle which you want.

So we might attribute to the Stoics the view that, though an expression like 'man' or 'Dion' signifies a case, this does not mean that there has to be a case there which is signified by the expression. And on this view we can straightforwardly identify the cases with the constitutive qualities of an object. So this is one notion of a case, the metaphysical notion, and we might try to reconstruct the Stoic position in terms of this notion along the lines indicated. But it seems that the Stoics, after all, do want to attribute some status to cases even if the proposition is not true. And the reason for this, presumably, is that they want to say that a *lekton*, even a false one, even one which is false because there is no Dion or no man, is constituted by a case and a predicate (see D.L. VII.70).

At this point it might help to remember, to understand the Stoic view, though perhaps not to support their position, that, as we pointed out earlier, the Stoics not only distinguish between subsistence (*hyphistanai*) and existence (*einai*), but also introduce an intermediate notion, which, for the lack of a better word, we called the notion of being present or being there (*hyparchein*). This allowed us to say that even false *lekta* and predicates in false *lekta* have some status, though they are not facts or attributes. Perhaps the Stoics dealt with cases in an analogous way. The case signified in a true statement is a body, a quality of the relevant kind. But if the statement is false, because there is no Dion or there is no man, there is still a case signified by 'Dion' or 'man', but one which merely subsists and does not exist. Put differently: there is the metaphysical notion of a case which is the notion of a certain kind of quality. But, as with *lekta* and predicates, we move from this metaphysical notion to a logical notion. We thus get the notion of something signified by an expression like 'Dion' or 'man', which, if the proposition is true, is a quality of this kind, but which, if the proposition is not true, merely subsists. A *lekton*, even if it is false, is something and hence subsists; but if it is true, it is a fact and obtains (see S.E. *M* VIII.10). A predicate, even if it is not true of something, is something and hence subsists; but if it is true of something, it is an attribute of what it is true of and obtains (see Stobaeus, *Ecl.* I. 106, 20 ff.). We might say that the metaphysical notion of a *lekton* is the notion of, for example, a fact, but that we get the logical notion of a *lekton* by moving to the notion of something which if true is a fact. Similarly we might have the metaphysical notion of a predicate which is the notion of an attribute, but we get the corresponding logical notion by moving to the notion of something which if predicated truly of something is an attribute. Correspondingly we deal with cases. There is the metaphysical notion of a case which is the notion of a certain kind of quality. But we get the logical notion of a case by moving to the notion of something which if signified in a true proposition is this sort of quality. In the first two cases, that of a *lekton* and that of a predicate, the item signified subsists; if the proposition is true, this very item not merely subsists, but is present, though it still does not exist, because it is not a body. With cases, too, the item signified would subsist, but it would exist, namely as a quality, if the proposition were true.

This might all seem unduly cumbersome and obscure, but it might help us to understand one particular detail of Stoic doctrine which otherwise is difficult to account for. One easily sees why the Stoics formulate the truth-conditions for 'Dion is in Athens' and 'man is in Athens' the way they do: 'there is something which is Dion (or man) and it is in Athens'. We want these statements to be false if Dion is dead or man is extinct. But if Dion is dead or man is extinct, the individual and the common quality do not exist either. Hence, though we do not have a problem about what is referred to by 'Dion' or 'man' in the original statement, we still have a problem as to what is signified by 'Dion' and 'man' in the statement of the truth-conditions. This will be no problem if we assume that there is at least a subsistent case to be signified, even if the proposition is false.

There are various bits of evidence, apart from Sextus' testimony and the fact that propositions like 'Dion is walking' are supposed to be constituted by a case, which would suggest that this is the Stoic view. Thus Clement, for example (*Strom.* VIII.9.26.5), distinguishes between a house and the case which a house has (*tynchanei*), and he says of the case that it is incorporeal, whereas the expression uttered, 'house', and the house are bodies.

With this in mind we are ready to consider the remaining question: is what is signified by 'Dion' an incorporeal *lekton*, as Sextus claims? We have worked out two notions of a case, of which we favoured the second. On the first notion a case is a quality; thus it is a body and cannot be an incorporeal *lekton*. On the second notion it is some incorporeal item of a curious kind, which, if the proposition is true, turns out to be a body after all. So Sextus may be right in assuming that what is signified by 'Dion' is some incorporeal item which subsists. But is it a *lekton*?

If this is, indeed, what the Stoics said, it seems to me that the easiest explanation for it is this: there are *lekta*, things to say, for instance that Socrates is wise. They are *lekta* in the strict, basic sense of the word. There also are predicates, for example 'being wise'. We call them 'incomplete *lekta*'. This can be understood in two ways: (i) they need to be completed to be *lekta*, i.e. they, by themselves, are not yet *lekta*. So to be an incomplete *lekton* is not to be one kind of *lekton* as opposed to another kind of *lekton* which is complete. (ii) In some extended sense even predicates are *lekta*; they are essentially things which get said about something, the kind of thing which is true of something. So they are *lekta* of a kind, though in an extended sense.

It should be obvious that what is signified by 'Dion' is not a *lekton* in either the strict or the extended sense, in which even predicates might qualify as *lekta*. Nor is what is signified by 'Dion' an incomplete *lekton* in the sense in which a predicate is. And it should be noted here that our sources never call cases 'incomplete *lekta*'. But we can see how the terminology could evolve in such a way that once predicates are called, not only 'incomplete *lekta*', but *lekta*, all incorporeal parts of a *lekton*, which are not complete *lekta* themselves, come to be called *lekta* in a yet wider sense. On these assumptions we can understand why a case might come to be called a *lekton*.

But even if all this were true, it would still be clear that the notion of a *lekton* involved here would be a highly derivative one. So even if Sextus were right in claiming that 'Dion' signifies an incorporeal *lekton*, we should not focus on this isolated and questionable use of the word *lekton* to determine the basic Stoic notion of a *lekton*. Hence, we should also not, relying on this passage, think that the basic notion of a *lekton* is the notion of the meaning of an expression, let alone the notion of the meaning of an expression as opposed to its reference. It rather seems, as we have been saying all along, that the basic notion of a *lekton*, as the word suggests, is that of a thing to say. That a thing to say and its parts should also be made to serve the function of being what is signified by the appropriate expressions and their parts is a derivative feature of *lekta*, though, needless to say, it is the feature which plays the central role in the Stoic theory of language. But the notions of a *lekton*, of a predicate and a case play a crucial role in Stoic philosophy outside the theory of language, in particular a metaphysical role, and this is what we always have to keep in mind when we consider their use in the theory of language.

7
Parrots, Pyrrhonists and native speakers

DAVID K. GLIDDEN

What it is to speak a language and what it is to learn a language are complementary abilities. Normally, one cannot speak a language without learning it, just as one learns a language by speaking it. Yet, I could have learned Greek without speaking it, just as my parrot may speak Greek without learning it. There are several puzzles here to serve as philosophical prey.

It might seem that the ability to speak a language, or even to express oneself linguistically with other sorts of signs, requires only that the proper mechanism be physically in place for language to arise. Function follows form. We speak because our neurons are connected in a certain way. Yet, it could also be the case that our ability to express ourselves in language presupposes some sort of innate syntax and semantics as prerequisite for linguistic competence. Only if this program functions can the mechanism speak.

Some say animals can speak, if only they can think, and animals can think, only if they think like us. In this way, thought comes first and language after. Others have less restrictive views concerning what can or cannot speak. Those who would teach a chimpanzee to sign, as well as those who study the sounds that whales make, or even noises made by chirping insects, typically conceive of language as complex behaviour, enjoying considerable diversity across the variety of species that generate such sounds or signs. The ability to use language would not then be dependent upon any single mechanism. Nor must the syntactic and semantic program be specific either, if bees are to have their language, along with porpoises and people.

Perhaps animals can speak, even if they do not think. And barnyard sounds directly attach themselves to situations, without requiring innate programmed preconceptions and syntactic rules. Sometimes, this seems to be the case with us too. Language often exhibits mechanical banality, with its words and phrases the creations of conventions, habituated over time as responses to set situations. 'How are you? . . . I'm fine' as a salutational exchange seems socially similar to the way birds sing to one another, once they land on the same tree, not to mention how dogs sniff at one another when they meet.

Those who would deny that chimpanzees can sign, the way a human language user can, insist there is something unique about our brains and the inner logic our brains use. Although such anthropocentric theorists can envisage other language users, they are thinking not of birds but of computers made by man designed to imitate the program of our minds. The hardware may be plastic, but the software does not seem to be.

Physicians interested primarily in aphasics bypass such questions altogether by focusing on the human brain, particularly on Broca's and Wernicke's areas, though other neural structures also come into play. The goal of such research, working from the bottom up, is to display how gross deficiencies in human language are a consequence of specific neurological defects. Regardless of what happens in other animals, at least we know that humans employ language, and we wonder how this is made feasible neurologically. Taking a constructive anatomical approach leaves the issue of what other things can speak beyond the realm of finite investigation.

There is one pandemic question that cannot be ignored: namely how learning is made possible at all, much less learning Greek. What it is I try to learn is either something I already know or something I am not familiar with. If it is something I already know, then there is no learning going on. If it is something I do not yet know, then I must prepare myself to learn it. Yet how can I first conceive of what it is I want to learn, prepare myself to recognise and fathom it, if it is entirely unfamiliar to me? It seems I must already be familiar with whatever I am to be familiar with, in order to become familiar with it. This paradox of recognition would be amusing if only it had a ready answer.

Taking up this puzzle, some philosophers have argued that learning language is actually impossible, unless it is another version of a language we already know: namely the language we are born with. Consequently, there is said to be only a single language we can understand: the language of our thought, proleptically divided into all the basic concepts we will ever use, such as 'dog', 'horse' or 'snow'. This language must in one way or another be already there; it must be native to us, if we are to circumvent the obstacle of familiarity.

Others reject this puzzle as subterfuge, a plot by anti-realists, who would wrongly deny that we can escape the web of our intentions. It is anti-realistic when they maintain that language, even proper names, cannot attach directly on to things, that all our words must instead be signs mediated by conceptual inventions manufactured in our minds. Such anti-realists insist that even proper names like 'Socrates' describe our intentions of the man, under some conception which we have of someone who Socratises; 'Socrates' doesn't simply name the man. Rather, it sums up in a word some conception that we have of him. The naked world is consequently nothing we can baldly signify in speech, except when what we mean by reality is only what we mean.

Realists reply that the roots of reference are in the outside world, and not only in our minds. The causal pressures of the world exerted on our brains make linguistic reference real, so that our words can actually attach to things and index portions of reality, bypassing the privacy of thought, at least in part. 'Socrates' names Socrates, not just our description of him.

The focus of this debate concerns the logic of meaning and its relationship to reference, designation and indexicality. Language signifies. And signification appears to be a mental act. So, the concept of concept or the representation of representation preoccupies the attention of philosophers of language, cognitive psychologists and artisans of Artificial Intelligence, all concerned with how significance can get attached to signs and sounds in some systematic way. And for many anti-realistic investigators it seems that representation replaces any direct demonstrative connection between words and things, turning linguistic behaviour forever inwards, as an application of an inner logic of concept and signification.

Semantic acquisition is the knot to be unravelled, if we are to understand how language and reality are connected, to the extent they are at all. Generative psycholinguists enquire how children acquire the competence to speak. But the questions these psycholinguists ask are often philosophical, addressing how the mind prepares itself to conceive of the words it is about to use. When a child learns the word for mamma, what kind of recognition must be going on? Most psycholinguists turn their attention towards conception. Very few indeed prefer to speak of stimulation and situational behaviour and leave speech entirely at that, leaving the inner life of thought for the most part unexamined, as if it were simply a case of talking to yourself.

What kind of thing can speak and how a language can be learned were also issues of great interest to the ancients. Traces can be found in Plato's writings, especially his *Theaetetus*, which first suggested that thought was inner speech, while denying that animals could think the way we humans do. Plato also questioned how communication could take place at all and language be translated, just as he made memorable Meno's paradox of familiarity. Hellenistic dogmatists took up Plato's questions and developed systematic answers on their own. Stoics and Epicureans each had their own distinctive views on whether other animals can speak and how it is we first learn a language. The Stoics advanced the conception of representational thinking as the basis for semantics, developing a psychological approach to thought and speech. The Epicureans preferred a more mechanical and behaviourist approach.

But there have always been naysayers who have found little to be gained from asking questions of this sort, whether other animals can speak or how language is first learned. Hellenistic Pyrrhonists advanced the cause of scepticism by rejecting specific answers Stoics and Epicureans gave to such puzzles over language. Yet, if we examine how Sextus thwarted the Hellenistic dogmatists of language in the name of Pyrrhonism, we can see a genuine alternative emerge. Interestingly enough, it is also an alternative recently advanced by Kripke in the name of Wittgenstein.

Can a parrot speak a language?

In his *Essay Concerning Human Understanding*, Locke insisted that our ability to think in concepts distinguishes human voices from sounds made by animals:

> *Man* therefore had by Nature his Organs so fashioned, as to be *fit to frame articulate Sounds*, which we call Words. But this was not enough to produce Language; for Parrots, and several other Birds, will be taught to make articulate Sounds distinct enough, which yet, by no means, are capable of Language.
> §2. Besides articulate Sounds therefore, it was farther necessary, that he should be *able to use these Sounds*, as *Signs of internal Conceptions*; and to make them stand as marks for the *Ideas* within his own Mind, whereby they might be made known to others, and the Thoughts of Men's Minds be conveyed from one to another. (III.1.1–2)

Elsewhere, Locke repeats the point using the same example:

> Before a Man makes any Proposition, he is supposed to understand the terms he uses in it, or else he talks like a Parrot, only making a noise by imitation, and framing certain Sounds, which he has learnt of others; but not, as a rational Creature, using them for signs of *Ideas*, which he has in his Mind. (IV.8.7, cf. II.27.8)

If we compare this passage in Locke with a passage taken from Sextus' *adversus Mathematicos* (*M*), we can see some similarity:

> Dogmatists say that man does not differ from irrational animals because of enunciated speech, since crows, parrots, and jays also enunciate articulate sounds, but rather because of native reason. Nor does he differ only

> because of simple sense impression (*phantasia haplē*), since animals too receive sense impressions, but rather because of analogical and synthetic imagination (*phantasia metabatikē kai synthetikē*). Therefore, man possesses the idea of inference and immediately grasps the concept of signification, because of such inference. (*M* VIII.275–6, cf. VII.346)

There is an ancient history to the contrast between parroting and speaking. It is evident in Sextus' *adversus Mathematicos*, as well as his *Outlines of Pyrrhonism* (*PH*), juxtaposing philosophical dogma against sceptical opposition, focusing on the same examples Locke employs.

This is no coincidence, since John Locke began the first book of his *Essay* (I.3.15) explicitly addressing a revival of the Stoic theory of common notions, recently embraced by Lord Herbert of Cherbury, who had argued that all humans hold some ideas in common, including thoughts of God. In his *New Essays on Human Understanding*, Leibniz claimed that this was old-fashioned Stoic doctrine Locke was disagreeing with (Preface, 49). In fact, Locke was closer to the Stoics than Herbert was. While denying that specific ideas were innate, Locke conceded that common conceptions many of us share are native to us, but only once we experience the requisite sense-impressions (3.15–26). Locke went on to argue that language required such native notions or ideas to differentiate itself from parroting. This was Stoic doctrine and well known as such, as Leibniz pointed out.

According to Diogenes Laertius (D.L.) VII.39–40, the Stoic Zeno of Citium was the first to divide all philosophical enquiry into three parts: the study of nature, the study of ethics and the study of *logos* – what we would now call epistemology and logic. One effect of these divisions was to establish some hierarchical order within the study of philosophy, with logic and epistemology, or *logos*, as hegemonic. For example, some Stoics compared the study of philosophy to an egg, with logic being the shell, ethics the egg-white and nature the yolk. Others compared it to a field, with logic as the fence, ethics as the crop and nature as the earth.

Zeno and Chrysippus initiated their expositions of *logos* by subdividing it in turn. One such subdivision was language. It consisted of voiced sounds, but according to Diogenes of Babylon (D.L. VII.55–7) the Stoics drew an important distinction between human voices and those of other animals. Beasts make sounds, of course, but they do so by merely beating on the air one way or another, as a result of some instinctual, natural impulse. Human voice is different. It is articulated by an act of thought, though Diogenes of Babylon points out the Stoic doctrine that the human facility for language is not fully developed until the maturity of fourteen-year-old minds. As children mature and learn to speak properly, they lose their bestiality.

All voiced sounds are material transmissions from those who speak to those who hear. But according to the Stoics a statement is a sound that signifies something transmitted by a mind. Though voices differ ethnically with dialects and mother tongues, all true speech must be conceptually articulated and anticipated, in the way a cry of pain need not be (D.L. VII.55–6). Of course, not every human sound must signify. For example, it is possible even to say a word in Greek that has no meaning. But it is not possible to fashion an entire statement out of gibberish, since in a statement things are said, which 'things' the Stoics said were incorporeal *lekta*, something like what we mean by propositions (D.L. VII.57). These 'things' the Stoics said our words express are structured mental thoughts, not objects in the world, even though we might well be thinking of the world with these thoughts and words. In this way, the sounds we make project our intentions and conceptions, instead of being merely noises responding to the situations causing us to utter them.

Over the centuries Stoics articulated this understanding of language, *lekta*, and human speech. There were Stoic grammars and Stoic accounts of propositional statements, not to mention Stoic logics. But at the heart of this approach was a theory of psychology, identifying the cognitive character of minds.[1] Humans speak because they think, and humans think in concepts. Animals do not speak, because they cannot think in concepts. And so they make noise instead.

As Diogenes reports, quoting Diocles the Magnesian, according to the Stoics concepts first come to mind in humans as a result of sense-impressions, the same sorts of sense-impressions that are inflicted on animals as well. These first impressions are physiologically stamped on to sense-organs, because of outside impulses (D.L. VII.49–53). But in the case of humans they provoke the mind to think, to formulate sophisticated impressions of its own, as rational interpretations of what is happening in our senses and in the world that affects us. In this way, appearances take on meaning, and their meaning is conceived of by the mind along the lines of the mind's own conceptual representations and inventions, in response to sense-impressions.

Concepts require experience to provoke them. Ideas are not preformed within us prior to experience. And so the Stoics are often called empiricists. They were certainly not Cartesians, for whom all ideas must be innate precisely because ideas and the thoughts that think them are sanitised from any interaction with bodily experience. On the other hand, concepts as the Stoics understood them are not themselves mechanically transmitted from the outside into us. They are not material transmissions or bodily events.

[1] See Frede [392]. For a discussion of *lekta*, see the previous chapter in this collection.

They are cognitive creations of our own which arise within our psyche, something we make up in our minds, as synthetic, conceptual responses to repeated worldly provocations (D.L. VII.52–3). So, to this extent, the Stoics agree with the Cartesians about the character of minds. Consequently, one might regard the Stoic theory of conceptual representation as a kind of nativism. Ideas are native to the mind, and it is the mind that makes them up, creates them and controls them. The senses and the outside world cannot import ideas into us, though they do occasion them and almost force the proper concepts on us on the right occasions, when the mind is properly responsive to the body and the world. Whether one wants to use the terms 'empiricism' or 'nativism', this is clear enough: according to the Stoics concepts are native to our minds and are the vehicle of thought, and thought controls speech.

It is for this reason that the Stoic distinction between animal sounds and human speech was so vital, since it marked the difference between a true mind and a more primitive psychology, one without concepts and synthetic representations as responses to the physiology of sense-impressions.[2] The conceptual foundations of Stoic thought, the safeguard of their logic and in turn their entire system, insisted upon this contrast between rational beings, articulating experiences in concepts, and mere animals who only undergo experiences without also conceiving of them. Representational thinking was the only thinking Stoics recognised as rational; the very foundations of *logos* required ideas to exist.

Notwithstanding Lord Herbert of Cherbury's use of Stoic common notions to advance the cause of a universal religion, Locke's emphasis on the role concepts play in language endorsed the Stoic doctrine of ideas. But there would not have been much point to Locke's insistence on ideas as foundations of language, distinguishing man from other animals, had not others attempted to efface this difference between human speech and noises made by animals. There were such opposing arguments, well known in the Renaissance on account of the popularity of Sextus, who recorded them in the course of advancing Pyrrhonism.

Some alternatives to Stoicism were purely argumentative. One suggestion displaced the difference between man and animals by raising animals up to our own level, claiming that animals also have a language for their thoughts, because they think in concepts too. This approach was more of an *ad hominem* argument against the Stoic exaltation of mankind. To assert that parrots also speak a language would have been abhorrent to the Stoics, who insisted on the difference between man and other animals as a means of advancing human ethics. Animals simply do not face the kinds of obli-

[2] See Inwood [384], 42–101.

gations humans do, because they lack our rational sensibility. Consequently, we live entirely different sorts of lives from animals, or at least the Stoics said we should. To suggest that animals are psychologically on a par with us was a disingenuous suggestion, more like a Trojan Horse, where Stoics might be taken in and their dogmatism brought down to scepticism.

Ad hominem alternatives to Stoicism can be seen in Sextus' *Outlines of Pyrrhonism*, where Sextus recites an argument of Aenesidemus (*PH* I.62–78) used explicitly against the Stoics' rejection of animal rationality (*PH* I.65). Aenesidemus takes two stabs at the Stoics, first arguing directly that some so-called irrational animals actually can think. His second thrust is indirect, to the effect that animal speech itself exhibits sufficient rationality to count as genuine language, so that if animals can speak like us they must think like us as well. Aenesidemus focuses on dogs, in a passage (*PH* I.67) reminiscent of Plato's *Republic* (376a–b).

Even philosophers admit dogs have more sensitive sense-organs, noses and the like (*PH* I.64). The next thing to concede is that dogs exhibit reason. And here Aenesidemus draws upon an explicitly Stoic distinction between native reason (*endiathetos logos*) and enunciated (*prophorikos logos*) speech (*PH* I.65), a distinction we have already seen above, in the passage from Sextus that I have already quoted (*M* VIII.276), in parallel to Locke. The salient characteristics of native reason are these: the ability to make decisions, the ability to recognise whatever means are necessary to achieve one's goals and the ability to exhibit self-conscious apprehension both of one's character and the condition one is in. Aenesidemus proceeds to tell dog stories portraying all three characteristics.

Dogs seek nourishment and flee the whip, thereby exercising choice. They are good trackers and hunters, thereby recognising and acquiring the skills they require for their goals. They also exhibit considerable self-awareness, caring for their bodies by licking wounds, extracting thorns and eating grass to counter indigestion, not to mention their unquestioned traits of moral character, such as giving each his due, from biting enemies to licking friends. Therefore, dogs have native reason.

Aenesidemus has other fun along the way, at the expense of the so-called Dog Philosophers, the Cynics (*PH* I.72; cf. D.L. VI.40). He also satirises an example once used by Chrysippus to demonstrate how even a dog can follow a fifth-form syllogism (*PH* I.69). Arriving at a fork in the road, this syllogistic dog smells two avenues and then promptly runs along the third, without bothering to take a sniff at all: if neither A nor B, then C. Isn't this evidence of native canine reason?[3]

[3] See Annas and Barnes [412], 39–48.

Aenesidemus next takes an indirect approach by turning to enunciated speech, and he argues that sounds animals make exhibit reason too, comparing the cries of birds and barking dogs to the speech of foreigners (*PH* I.73–7). The argument is somewhat clumsy (see *PH* I.73), but the point is clear enough: dogs and other animals respond with different sounds in distinctly different circumstances, so that it seems only proper to conclude that these animals exhibit, with their barks and cries, what the Stoics called enunciated *logos*. To take another example, birds are well known for their prophetic cries (*PH* I.77). No one would deny that birds utter special sounds under special circumstances. And if an animal exhibits enunciated *logos*, it must have native reason too (see *M* VIII.287). So birds must think as well, because their cries indicate the presence of internal reason. And the same is true of dogs and other such animals that speak.

Aenesidemus positioned these arguments that animals can think at the very end of the first of his well-known Modes of Scepticism, adding them as an afterthought (*PH* I.62, I.78). It seems likely these arguments were prefabricated and borrowed by Aenesidemus from another source, possibly from the scepticism of the New Academy, which was fond of offering Trojan Horses to the Stoics, tempting them with philosophical alternatives which would prove destructive.

In any case, Aenesidemus' indirect argument seems to prove too much, by appearing to concede that exhibitions of enunciated speech are inevitably indications of the complex kind of native reason advanced by Stoic psychology. This would require Stoics to welcome speaking animals as equals, something they could not accept. But it would also make it difficult for a Pyrrhonist himself to speak, since in enunciating speech, he would seem to concede something to Stoic dogmatism, concerning the conceptual character of his own psychology of thought (see *PH* II.130). Sextus himself presents this countervailing objection separately, in book VIII of his *adversus Mathematicos* (*M* VIII.279), before making a reply. The discussion then takes a different turn from that reported of Aenesidemus in the *Outlines*.

Sextus argues in book VIII that recognising signs and what they signify need not require the kind of complex thinking demonstrated by the Stoics in their logic. Indeed, it need not even require the self-conscious concept of judgement, so essential to the Stoic theory of inference and signification, the ingredients of thought. There are, it seems, natural signs sailors and farmers use all the time without being self-conscious about it, such as a ring around the moon meaning rain, even though such sailors and farmers lack any thought of formal inference (*M* VIII.270). Sextus goes on to argue that dogs and horses follow natural signs as well. But they do this without forming any synthetic impression or conception of what a judgement is (*M* VIII.271).

They simply put together remembered sense-impressions, associating these perceptions with each other over time. Representation and conceptual cognition are simply not required.

It turns out, or so Sextus claims, that there is a kind of natural signification that is not dependent on the conceptual constitution of the human mind, as the Stoics conceived of it (see *M* VIII.275–6). Rather, all that is required is sufficient memory to associate one thing with another over time. Upon seeing a footprint, the dog senses the animal that left the track. Upon hearing the crack of the whip, the horse leaps forward. Both the footprint and the whip signify something to these animals, but they do so only in a rudimentary, unthinking way, just the way farmers and sailors read the signs of weather (see *M* VIII.270–1, 274).

Sextus goes on to suggest that language itself might consist of such natural associations and significations, without the complex Stoic logic of analogical impressions and interpretative representations, without requiring that we self-consciously employ the concept of signification. All that is required is the experience of repetition associating one thing with another, resulting in some socially habituated sound sequence, such as 'how are you? ... I'm fine.' Exhibiting such habitudes, even purely verbal ones, is quite a different matter from forming and self-consciously employing the formal conception of connection (*M* VIII.288).

Consequently, when the dogmatist objects, questioning what the sceptic's words amount to, the sceptic is not required to concede that his words signify ideas in his mind, the kinds of ideas advanced by Stoic doctrine. Rather the sceptic's words are habituated responses associated with observed situations, brought together in his memory out of habit (*M* VIII.289). This is how in general habits act out recollections, so it is not surprising that habituations might then express themselves in speech, the kinds of habituations animals exhibit too. And if this is all that is involved in speaking, then we can speak without having to think the way the Stoics say we do. Instead of using internal preconceptions of our own invention, we make use of nature's own significations displayed to us over time, once our responses become habituated through experience (*M* VIII.289). So, it seems that a parrot, or any animal with memory, can speak a language, though Sextus does not go so far as to assert this, dogmatically. The Pyrrhonist has simply grown accustomed to customary speech, as a result of habituation.

Now it might seem that this self-defence of Pyrrhonism was designed only in dialectical response to Stoicism, after Chrysippus had turned the tables on the sceptical Carneades, putting the sceptics on the defensive, requiring them to come up with a psychology of their own to defend their own ability to speak. Perhaps this Pyrrhonist response is merely an argumentative retrenchment, itself derived from Stoicism, hearkening back to an earlier, more primitive stage of Stoic developmental theory, locating the existence of rough-and-ready language prior to fully fledged concept-acquisition. Obviously, children are able to speak some sort of language prior to coming of age at fourteen, when their conceptual apparatus was said by the Stoics to be finally fully formed. Even so, the argument Sextus employs here seems to be more than an *ad hominem* one, since by suggesting that the self-conscious application of signification is not requisite for language, Sextus' argument leaves the question vacant concerning the necessity of thinking before speaking. Furthermore, we know that the argument Sextus employs here had an independent philosophical history of its own.

For one thing, the notion of habituated observation and response had a place in ancient medicine, where physicians-against-theorising, the so-called empirical physicians, defended their own practice of medicine as an attempt to put all inference aside and to rely solely on their experience of symptoms in their patients.[4] In this way they could accept the use of nature's symptomatic signs without presupposing any theory of nature or of knowledge of their own. Consequently, empirical medicine made no commitments on the nature of disease or the nature of the mind. Empirical physicians simply saw sufficient symptoms in their practice to identify diseases on this basis, and gradually they came to associate diseases with whatever treatments seemed to work, leaving theories about phlegms to philosophers. For example, an empirical doctor would come to recognise a common cold when he saw its symptoms in a patient, simply out of habitude. And this same habitude would tell him what treatment did or didn't work. In this way, nature carried the burden of significance, not theoretical interpretations invented in the human mind.

The kind of habituation mentioned in this context was called a mnemonic signal, or *hypomnēstikon sēmeion*.[5] Natural signs were examples of mnemonic signals. Just as an empirical doctor would associate a cold with a runny nose without a fever, so any one of us could associate smoke with fire. Whenever you see one, you expect to see the other. All that was necessary to employ mnemonic signals was habituated memory, associating one thing with another over time. In this way a farmer reads the signs of weather, or a horse responds to the cracking sound of whips.

These habituated associations could also be socially induced as customs, in addition to the prognostic or diagnostic signals of natural medicine. One could associate the red colour of a flag with a warning of an enemy invasion, just as an empirical physician might identify a stab wound as the cause of

[4] See Frede [433]. [5] See Glidden [422].

death. In this way mnemonic signals were not restricted to nature's signs, but were open to the kinds of recognition induced by social habits and conventions. But this extension from nature's own mnemonic signals to purely social conventions, such as knowing how to hold a cup or pay homage to a god, ought not to obscure the continuity of customary habituation, where the agent does not interpret the significance of social acts or natural acts according to his own conceptual inventions. He simply plays his role according to what experience has shown to be the appropriate response. And Sextus next suggests that speech can be purchased cheaply in this way as well.

Sextus' appeal to natural signs and mnemonic signals borrowed something from Hellenistic medicine, if not from other sources too. Yet, his application of this argument to the use of language might appear to be unique. And it is this particular application that concerns us here, with its powerful suggestion that language in some rough-and-ready format can function independently, without self-consciously examining the inner life of the mind. Sextus suggests that we can speak regardless of the concepts we might or might not have represented in our thoughts. And he exploits this suggestion to defend his right to speak against the Stoics, who claimed that enunciated speech necessarily indicates the presence of a conceptually organised, self-conscious inner reason, applying ideas to our words, before applying words to things.

The Epicureans had already argued for something similar to Sextus' suggestion, in their own account of language acquisition.[6] Not only had Epicureans agreed that animals are sufficiently capable of habituation to use mnemonic signals and follow natural signs, but they also suggested that rudimentary animal speech could come about in this same way as well. According to Lucretius (v.1028–90), the Epicureans stressed the similarities between barnyard sounds and human speech, the suggestion being that all voiced sounds are more or less the same in natural origin, as sounds habitually established to respond to and label facts and features in the world. In this way, human speech is not, at least in its beginnings, fundamentally any different from sounds made by other animals. The foundations of language do not require idea intervention. This, of course, would have been heresy to Stoics.

In his *Letter to Herodotus* (*Hdtm.*) Epicurus described the origin of human language as a purely mechanical response to natural necessity (*Hdtm.* x.75). Lucretius put the point this way: nature forced the tongue to make the sounds it does, and utility (not conceptual invention) articulated names

[6] See Glidden [363].

for things (v.1028–9). Lucretius explicitly contrasted the forced utility of naturally articulated speech with another view, that such speech owes its articulation to a self-conscious conception (*insita notities*) of utility invented in the mind of some name-giver (v.1041–9). Lucretius rejected what became the Stoic argument that speech presupposes an *a priori*, conceptually developed native reason, complete with self-conscious inference and representation. To emphasise the point, Lucretius compared the pointing stage, before a human baby begins to speak and indicates instead by gestures, with the natural instincts of other animals (v.1030–40). Nature makes us speak, rather than speech being captive to the concepts of a human mind.

It might seem that Sextus is then taking up the Epicurean arguments and throwing them against the Stoics. There is some truth to this. Many of the examples Lucretius gives of the variegated speech of dogs, birds and horses parallel Sextus' given instances of apparently articulate animals. Even so, Sextus does not employ exactly the same argument. The Epicureans only suggested that the natural origins of language were shared with other animals. The Epicureans did not claim that concepts aren't eventually employed and introspected, once humans learn to speak. Nor did Epicureans claim that animals actually speak languages or that animals can think. Indeed, Lucretius explicitly denies that animals are language users (v.1088). An Epicurean parrot cannot then speak a language. Perhaps a Sextus parrot might, but that is an assertion only a dogmatist would make.

The Epicureans used custom and social mechanism to account for the subsequent development of language, where the Stoics used a nativism of logic and ideas. The Epicureans insisted that different tribes of humans would get together to set down rules and conventions to delineate the sounds they made; sounds would then be socialised and speech become a form of humanly organised behaviour (*Hdtm.* x.75–6). In this way, human beings part company with animals and separate tribes articulate their own native tongues, as human language comes into play, transformed from its natural origins according to the rules. Along with language, concepts would arise, to match the words we use. The Epicureans warned that empty words and empty concepts will also occur, once our speech conventions replace the natural origins of language, as simple utterances responding to set situations become obscured by customs nominally agreed upon.

Words come into use to label things. But every native speaker would have the choice of the rules he adopts to govern the sounds he uses for his words. The speaker could always disregard convention, make up his own words instead, to preserve their natural origins as indices, in defiance of the local customs. The result would be an idiolect of his own creation. It would, of course, be more convenient to speak the dialect of the local tribe. But that is a decision each of us must make. Each of us decides whether to accept the rules. Even with the Epicureans, there was at least this level of self-consciousness regarding the rules governing the words we use.

Language entry requires intervention. That, in turn, requires an individual's decision concerning the utterances he is about to speak. For the Stoics it required matching outer speech with private inner concepts and employing the concept of signification before we utter human sounds. The character of these concepts and the possibility of intentional signification naturally invited criticism, and were so challenged by the sceptics. For one thing, how are we to know whether the concepts we employ are truly representative of the experiences we've had? For another, how are we to be assured that the sounds we make stand for the concepts which we think they do? For the Epicureans it was the different matter of deciding which conventions to employ for the labels that we use. But that first required knowing that we know the rules. Despite their differences on the origins of language, both the Epicureans and the Stoics adopted an introspective strategy, comparing sounds we formulate with the intentions of our concepts or the conventions of our rules. This introspection must inevitably take place, regardless of whether whole statements that we later make are subsequently true. For both the Epicureans and the Stoics some sort of introspection of intention is required if genuine language is to be possible at all.

The Epicureans offered a somewhat behaviouristic explanation of how humans come to use a language. Such an explanation invokes the notion of mnemonic habituation, a device Sextus would employ as well. But the Epicureans also invoked the notion of following a rule. Here Sextus and the Epicureans part company. Sextus does not defend his own decision to utter the sounds he does by appealing to the rules he observes. Rather, he simply speaks the language he acquired from his youth. He does not attempt to dogmatise about the social mechanism that got his mouth to speak. He does not attempt to introspect the rules he exhibits, to reassure himself or us.

Consequently, Sextus' own defence that a sceptic can speak a language, just as we could say a parrot might, is independently adaptive, even if his arguments are retrenchments on the Stoics or borrowed from the empirical doctors or even Epicurean dogmatists. Rather, what Sextus wants to do is to defend the use of articulated speech in the language that he uses, without having to come to any conclusions whatsoever concerning what is going on inside his mind, how his speech has been articulated by some inner native reason, as the Stoics would describe it, or by some self-conscious social adaptation, as Epicurus said. We must avoid such introspective questions of intention altogether is what Sextus then suggests, in defiance of the dogmatists. Introspection of our inner thoughts or the rules we observe is better left alone, if we are to speak without being victimised by Pyrrhonism, and the same holds for Pyrrhonism too. To some this may seem to be a trick, Sextus' refusal to play along in the debate, in defending the sceptic's right to speak against the dogmatists. But even if it is a trick, something truly profound is working here, something Wittgenstein later rediscovered.

To cite a passage Kripke cites a portion of, from Wittgenstein's *Investigations* (¶154):

> If there has to be anything 'behind the utterance of the formula' it is *particular circumstances* (*gewisse Umstände*), which justify me in saying I can go on – when the formula occurs to me. Try not to think of understanding as a 'mental process' at all. – For *that* is the expression which confuses you. But ask yourself: in what sort of case, in what kind of circumstances, do we say, 'Now I know how to go on', when, that is, the formula *has* occurred to me? – In the sense in which there are processes (including mental processes) which are characteristic of understanding, understanding is not a mental process.

The kind of understanding and justification Wittgenstein recommends here is pointedly not some sort of introspective articulation by a mind about to speak but rather retrospective consideration of the circumstances of fact and situation that make such speech appropriate and taken to be such by audiences that hear and understand the speaker then. This connection with Kripke and Wittgenstein[7] will become clear, once we consider Sextus' other question concerning language acquisition: namely how a language can be learned.

The paradox of language learning

On three occasions within the corpus of his works, Sextus applies the paradox of familiarity to the impossibility of learning language: in book III of the *Outlines* and in books I and XI of his *adversus Mathematicos*. The passage in the *Outlines* goes somewhat like this: if language signifies something, it does so either by nature or convention. Yet, language cannot consist of natural signs. Otherwise Greeks and non-Greek speakers would be able to talk with one another, which they can't. But language acquisition cannot rely on conventional signs, either. Those who understand the conventions by which their words single out the appropriate things must already know the rules: that is to say, they are able to recollect and recover from their memories that this sound is supposed to represent that thing.

[7] Kripke [513].

Such persons are already familiar with the language. Speaking it is just a matter of recollecting what they know. But as for those who do not know the language yet and want to learn how its locutions work, they will not already know the rules. Nor will they be able to learn rules by demonstration, because the established convention governing the ways locutions are ordered in a particular language is not something plainly visible, something that could simply be seen, by ostension, say. Otherwise locutions would be natural signs anyone could use, Greek and Barbarian alike. And if students could not learn a language by demonstration, they could not be taught another way, since all forms of intellectual apprehension are already suspect as conceptual and private. Consequently, learning a language is impossible, because the rules cannot be taught. The conventions must already have been known (*PH* III.266–9; cf. *M* I.37–8, *M* XI.241–3).

In historical terms, Sextus is explicitly employing a version of Meno's paradox, which Plato first introduced. And so Sextus specifically alludes to Plato's doctrine of recollection with the Greek words Sextus uses here for recollecting and recovering (see *PH* III.268). Plato is a convenient source for Sextus, since Plato had previously come to the sceptical conclusion that learning is impossible and had taken up the theory of recollection as a substitute for learning. But in the wider historical context of Hellenistic philosophy, Sextus' argument would be directed not just at the Stoics, but at the Epicureans, too. It was Epicurean theory, after all, that relied on mnemonic habituation to facilitate the transition between natural signs and conventional ones, as part of their conviction that language naturally evolves from animal sounds to human speech.

Sextus' objection seizes precisely on that moment of transition, where nature is abandoned for conventionally adopted rules. Each and every native speaker must somehow understand the rules to be used that order his own tribal dialect. The Epicureans had initially relied on simple perception and ostension to facilitate initial acquaintance with these rules, as languages were being founded. Sextus objects that this won't work. Otherwise, he suggests, every native language would be readily translatable, because linguistic sounds would be as obvious as natural signs, and of course they're not (see *PH* III.266). Nor can these rules be taught, instead, because those ignorant of the rules will not be in a position to comprehend them without conceiving of them first (*PH* III.269). Sextus draws out quite effectively the introspective character of knowing a language's rules, the intentions that organise the sounds even if those intentions are socially ritualised and ruled.

Sextus' argument for the impossibility of language acquisition rests on a dilemma, how a non-native speaker is ever to learn the rules. There were various possible solutions different ancients offered to the paradox of familiarity, by appealing, say, to universal native reason to justify learning a new language or appealing to observation of linguistic behaviour. But at this point in Sextus' argument, the universal ability of native reason has already been made suspect (see *PH* III.269). Consequently, Stoic nativism cannot come into play. And the chief alternative remaining is the plain evidence of sense: hence the Epicurean model of language acquisition is examined and disposed of.

The Epicurean model proves unworkable, once it is required to answer an introspective question, namely how am I to know whether the connection that I make between some sound and the thing that sound is supposed to label is actually the connection sanctioned by the rules that I am supposed to follow? Sextus quite agrees with the Epicureans that we act on custom and habituation, but custom and habituation will itself prove unable to explain the signification of the custom. Consequently, a foreign speaker cannot understand the natives, unless he already understands the basis for their customs. And habituation will not make itself known. Custom is not something you can see.

As Sextus presents the argument, it is, on the one hand, simply a debater's device: first using the Epicureans against the Stoics to defeat nativism as the foundation of language and then employing the rational basis of Stoic nativism to undo Epicurean socially created linguistic conventions. And so the possibility of learning language is undone, and the debate is finished for the day. Sufficient to the day are the arguments thereof. But there is more to this argument than that, since the argument is given in a language for Sextus' reader to comprehend. That would prove embarrassing to Sextus only if he himself must choose between the horns of the dilemma that he cast. Sextus, as we have seen, refuses to do this, but not because there is a third philosophical alternative hiding in the wings to provide a sceptic with yet another foundation for language other than nativism or convention, Stoic or Epicurean. Sextus simply disposes of the philosophical question altogether: what are the foundations of language? He does not offer an answer; he simply uses the language that he knows, confident that we will understand him. That suffices for Sextus, and his suggestion is that it should suffice for dogmatists as well.

The dilemma Sextus cast some time ago is by now quite a familiar one. Quine's indeterminacy of translation, Goodman's dispositional sense of grue, Chisholm's revival of Brentano, Fodor's nativism all go over this same ground, as so many others have, since the days of Sextus seventeen centuries ago. Quine, for example, played Epicurus to Fodor's version of Chrysippus. 'Stimulus synonymy' attempted to fulfil the Epicurean demand for ostensibly hard evidence and failed, for reasons Sextus already understood, reasons Quine rediscovered.[8] Fodor's 'language of thought' relied on native reason, or more specifically our genes, to establish a common conceptual basis for signification and communication.[9] Sextus rejected this approach when he wrote against the Stoics' 'common notions'. There is no way of knowing that any of us employ the exact same concepts; impostors could always arise and skew communication. On the other hand, Chisholm's revival of Brentano's 'intentional inexistence' revived a medieval solution to this puzzle of translation. Following Brentano, who followed Albertus Magnus, Chisholm suggested substituting for an ignorance of reference a purely private knowledge founded on intention.[10] Chisholm's solution raised the threat of anti-realism, a spectre not even an ancient Pyrrhonist would permit. Pyrrhonists were not Protagoreans. Goodman's talk of dispositions seized upon the same aspectual character of representational diversity that generated so much of Aenesidemus' Modes.[11] However contemporary the solutions to the puzzle posed by linguistic familiarity, ancient Greek philosophers, listening from Mt Olympus, have heard all these tunes before, even if the lyrics have changed.

The question naturally arises whether this conundrum of language acquisition is worth considering yet again, not to mention whether parrots speak a language or household cats can think. Philosophical dogmatists repeat themselves as variations on a theme, as we have seen, and the Pyrrhonists long ago insisted that eventually there comes a time to stop. Philosophers cannot resolve these questions. Perhaps Sextus would not have objected to the neurological inspection of the brain, once the brain was opened to observation and the taboo of dissection disappeared; Sextus was a doctor, too. But there was something about the philosophical approach to language that bothered him as futile. For one thing traditional philosophical questions are too global, and in asking questions of this sort persistent doubts arise, which can only be ignored, but never answered. It might be better to remain naive and be reluctant to adopt global philosophical solutions, looking downwards from first principles intuited on top. It might be better, if anything, to work humbly from the bottom up, the way physicians-against-theorising did. What Sextus so objected to was philosophising itself. Even the humblest of philosophical systems, Epicureanism, fell victim to the sceptics when it came to explaining how we know we know the rules that we use, to rationalise the sounds we make.

In his *Philosophical Investigations*, Wittgenstein proved critical of philosophising too, and in particular of indulging introspection, connecting language with the inner life of thoughts. Although he was wrongly, on

[8] Quine [523]. [9] Cf. Fodor [497]. [10] Chisholm [479].
[11] Goodman [504].

occasion, taken to be a behaviourist, because of his criticisms of private languages, Wittgenstein's remarks were more fundamentally addressed, precisely because they dwelled on introspection without entirely dismissing its presence from the mind. To this extent, Wittgenstein was closer to Epicurus than to Quine. But Wittgenstein could not adopt an Epicurean solution to the origins and character of language, because scepticism would again arise, even in response to this rather minimalist version of philosophy. For instance, Wittgenstein would ask, how are we to know that we are following a rule?

Saul Kripke has written this of Wittgenstein: 'Wittgenstein has invented a new form of scepticism. Personally, I am inclined to regard it as the most radical and original sceptical problem that philosophy has seen to date, one that only a highly unusual cast of mind could have produced.'[12] I am convinced that something similar to this same sceptical problem was already discerned by Sextus. Given Wittgenstein's fondness for Pyrrhonist imagery, he probably knew of this. In any case, Kripke defines the problem this way: 'Wittgenstein's main problem is that it appears that he has shown *all* language, *all* concept formation, to be impossible, indeed unintelligible.'[13] I take it that Sextus has already argued for something similar against the dogmatists in the passage I have paraphrased. And, like Wittgenstein, Sextus continued speaking. But as Kripke pointed out of Wittgenstein, even if the solution remains suspect, the problem posed is an achievement of its own.

When Sextus' bluff was called, he responded with a sort of parrot language, one that Locke and other introspectionists reviled. Sextus said he managed to speak without introspecting conceptual inventions or linguistic rules. Locke objected that parroting was not language without the requisite self-conscious conceptual intentions. Lucretius insisted that unlike birds, we have to know the rules, once our native language has been socialised.

The solution Kripke found in Wittgenstein is this: 'Each person who claims to be following a rule can be checked by others. Others in the community can check whether the putative rule follower is or is not giving particular responses that they endorse, that agree with their own.'[14] This, of course, is not to say that the community must agree with the truth of what the speaker claimed. All they must agree on is that what the speaker claims is English, or whatever the natural language is. Kripke then goes on to elaborate on this perceived Wittgensteinean solution, incorporating what Wittgenstein regarded as criteria and agreement within the community's particular form of life. In this context, Kripke quotes this line from

[12] Kripke [513], 60. [13] *Ibid.*, 62. [14] *Ibid.*, 101.

Wittgenstein: 'If a lion could talk, we could not understand him' (*Investigations*, p. 223e). The community responds to the language it can fathom as familiar. In this way the problem of translation becomes a problem for the community, whether to expand its form of life.

Sextus did not ground his own solution to the paradox of learning language with an elaboration of his own account of customary speech, beyond describing it as parrot speech. He did not compose an essay of reflections as an alternative to philosophy, in the way the later Wittgenstein did. Instead, Sextus gave his readers an abundance of arguments designed to purge us of the urge to philosophise. But he did share a common insight with Wittgenstein's solution, as Kripke understands it.

When we consider the individual in isolation from the community of language users, problems will arise over introspective knowledge of concepts or of rules. Philosophy takes these problems seriously as endemic of something we think we need to know about the mind, just the way a psychoanalyst might speculate on some disorder hidden in the psyche that must somehow be solved. Yet, once we take the individual out of isolation, the situation changes and improves. We can all recognise a speaker whom we cannot understand, whose language is too deviant.[15] And we can do this, not because we know what happens in the mind, whether it be his or ours, but because we have got used to the way we speak and can tell when something simply does not sound right, just the way a farmer can tell when it's not going to rain.

Instead of looking prospectively from the inside out, in introspective isolation, we can adopt a different mode. As a community of language users we can look retrospectively from the outside in. Nor do we need to look too far inside. All we need to do is to tell when something's wrong, and our habits will suffice for that, just as they can tell when something's right. In this way, Kripke's understanding of Wittgenstein's solution is a lot like the habitudes established in empirical medicine, that same school of physicians-against-theorising that Sextus was a member of and so was called 'Empiricus'.

[15] *Ibid.*, 93.

8

Analogy, anomaly and Apollonius Dyscolus

DAVID BLANK

In the light of recent research it is clear that what has since late antiquity been called 'grammar' is a discipline many of whose parts and theorems had their origins in Stoic philosophy. Dividing philosophy into three parts, the physical, ethical and logical, the Stoics distinguished dialectic and rhetoric within the last, or *logikon meros* (Diogenes Laertius (D.L.) VII.41 = LS 31A). Dialectic in turn they divided into a part concerning expressions (*peri sēmainontōn*) or voice (*peri phōnēs*: VII.43) and a part concerning what is signified (VII.43) or concerning things and what is signified (*peri tōn pragmatōn kai tōn sēmainomenōn*: VII.63). The last of these parts also contains two parts, that about impressions (*peri phantasiōn*) and that about the things said which subsist upon the impressions (*tōn ek toutōn huphistamenōn lektōn*: VII.43).[1]

None of the parts of Stoic dialectic was by itself the origin of all the concerns we call grammatical. However, M. Frede has identified the first part of Diocles' description[2] of the theory of voice or of expressions (D.L. VII.55–9) as deriving from a general theory of diction (*lexis*), which can in a way be singled out as the Stoics' 'grammar'.[3] The main concern of the whole dialectical part of Stoic logic was with the shaping and correctness of thought and its expression in speech.

Grammarians, for their part, were preoccupied with other things. Reflecting its connections with Alexandrian 'philology', ancient *grammatikē* revolved around the interpretation and constitution of poetic texts. This is

[1] Cf. Frede [403] and [404]. On the Stoic *peri phōnēs* in general see now the extensive treatment by Ax in his [20].

[2] Diocles of Magnesia (floruit c. 75 B.C.) is cited by Diogenes Laertius as the author of a *Summary of the Philosophers* in at least three books. Cited frequently by Diogenes, Diocles was the source of Diogenes' lengthy account of the logical part of Stoic philosophy (VII.48 ff.). Otherwise, he is known as the dedicatee of Meleager of Gadara's 'garland' of epigrams.

[3] Frede [404], 320 ff.

clearly seen in ancient definitions of grammar,[4] as well as in lists of the 'parts' of grammar: reading aloud, poetic interpretation, analysis of glosses, etymology, analogy, judgement of poems.[5]

These 'parts' are supposed to represent the various tasks of the professional philologist. Sextus Empiricus, the Pyrrhonist philosopher of the third century A.D., makes them (*adversus Mathematicos* (*M*) I.44 ff.) the parts of grammar in the 'special' sense (*idiaiteron*), whose perfection he ascribes to Crates of Mallos (second century B.C., head of the Pergamene school), Aristophanes of Byzantium (c. 257–180 B.C., head of the library at Alexandria c. 195) and Aristarchus of Samothrace (c. 217–145 B.C., sixth head of the library at Alexandria). The ascription is interesting, since, although we know Crates was considered a Stoic philosopher, while Aristophanes and Aristarchus were the ideals of Alexandrian 'philology', Sextus does not distinguish them professionally. It is this 'special' or 'deeper' grammar which Sextus will reject as useless (the art of correct reading, writing and speaking, he says is recognised by everyone as a useful art (I.40–50)). Sextus' own characterisation of the two types of grammar is very instructive: the lower art professes to teach the elements of language (*ta stoicheia*) and their combinations and comprises generally the art of reading and writing, while the deeper art consists in investigating the origin and nature of the elements of language and also the parts of speech which are formed from the elements (I.49). Then in his attacks on various definitions of (special) grammar, Sextus draws on both grammarians and philosophers.[6]

There was no strict separation between all the concerns of grammar and philosophy in the Hellenistic period, although grammarians and philosophers were in general hardly to be confused with one another. Accordingly, philosophical concerns and terms surface throughout ancient grammatical studies. For example, the entire basis of the ancient theory of punctuation was the desire to distinguish between sentences expressing complete and incomplete *lekta*[7] and to ensure that, when spoken or read

[4] See, for instance, Dionysius Thrax ('the Thracian', although he lived in Alexandria; second century B.C.), a pupil of 'most Homeric' Aristarchus: *Μέρη δέ, αὐτῆς ἐστιν ἕξ· πρῶτον ἀνάγνωσις ἐντριβὴς κατὰ προσῳδίαν, δεύτερον ἐξήγησις κατὰ τοὺς ἐνυπάρχοντας ποιητικοὺς τρόπους, τρίτον, γλωσσῶν τε καὶ ἱστοριῶν ἀπόδοσις, τέταρτον ἐτυμολογίας εὕρεσις, πέμπτον ἀναλογίας ἐκλογισμός, ἕκτον κρίσις ποιημάτων, ὃ δὴ κάλλιστόν ἐστι πάντων τῶν ἐν τῇ τέχνῃ* (cited in Sextus Empiricus, *M* I.250).

[5] See Sextus, *M* I.91–6 as well as Dionysius, above in n. 4.

[6] Sextus, *M* I.57–90.

[7] *Lekton* ('sayable') is a term from Stoic semantic theory denoting the sense of an expression (other than a noun), the incorporeal item (in the highest genus, the *tina* or 'somethings') which is meant by an expression. A complete *lekton* is the

aloud, this distinction as well as the relation between the things said by the individual expressions was clear, making the theory of punctuation an adjunct of Stoic logic.[8]

Now, the above account sounds very different from what can be found in the standard accounts of the early history of grammatical science.[9] In those histories the Stoics are of course credited with originating the study of many of the concerns of later grammarians, but they are also given a particular theory about language, that it is full of 'anomaly'. This thesis about 'anomaly' is rarely defined for the early Stoics, but Crates of Mallos, who was known as a Stoic philosopher and was the teacher of Panaetius, is said to have developed it into the following position: precise observation of the facts of common linguistic usage shows that there is in principle no regularity of structure in Greek, especially not in its morphology – the only way to know which form is correct is to observe which form is used. This position is sometimes even taken to include the claim that there are no rules applicable to the study of Greek, and that all apparently regular linguistic phenomena are simply the result of chance.

Crates is said to have propounded his theory of anomaly in response to the theory of grammatical 'analogy' held by his enemies the Alexandrians, especially Aristarchus. They are said to have insisted that all Greek words decline according to certain patterns, and that whenever forms are found to deviate from these patterns, they should be corrected according to the analogy of other, similar words.

The conflict between the positions of Crates and Aristarchus is usually thought to have dominated the early history of grammar. Crates and his followers would, according to this story, be the last representatives of the Stoic philosophy which had given rise to grammatical theory in the first place, while the Alexandrians were pushed by their Pergamene competitors to sharpen and complete their grammatical observations and theories. In so doing, they are said to have developed grammar away from its philosophical, theoretical origins towards being an independent science, with its own principles and methods, in short, into the forerunner of modern linguistics.

The problem with this story is that it is wholly divorced from philosophical thinking. The part about Crates ignores the fact that for the Stoics language, like all products of reason, must obey rational rules. If words have changed, or if the relationship between things which can be said and words

full state of affairs meant by a complete sentence, while an incomplete one is, for instance, the predicate (*katēgorēma*) signified by a verbal expression. On *lekta*, see M. Frede's discussion in ch. 6 of the present volume.

[8] See Blank [456], esp. 59 ff.

[9] See, for example, Robins [34]. On recent changes in this picture, see Taylor [36].

has changed since the days of primitive orderliness, none the less these changes must themselves be in some way explicable: merely ascribing the changes to 'chance' (*tuchē*) will not place them outside the realm of the universal *logos*. The story about the Alexandrians has them claim that all linguistic phenomena are ordered without any reason, except perhaps some vague reference to *rerum natura* (for example Caesar, *de Analogia*, fr. 4 Klotz = Gellius, *Noctes Atticae* XIX.8.7 f.): the principle of analogy is just thought to be valid, without any theoretical basis whatsoever which might explain why grammar is regular or what makes it regular.[10]

How did such a strange story develop? The prime villain was apparently the first-century B.C. Roman polymath Varro in books 8–10 of his *de Lingua Latina*.[11] He took the discussions about method which he found in the introduction to a Stoic-influenced treatise about 'Hellenism' or the canons of proper Greek and divided them into two parts. One part contained the arguments pertaining to the regularity of inflection, which he assigned correctly to the heading of 'analogy'. The other part contained arguments pertaining to the existence of exceptions to the rules of inflection. These arguments Varro assigned to the heading of 'anomaly'. Then he staged a debate between these two sides, ascribed each side to one of two 'opposing schools' of grammatical thought, and interposed himself in his tenth book to save the day by showing the way to a reconciliation of the two camps: both notions had their place, and analogy should be used to determine the correct inflections of similar words only as far as the forms which would be suggested by analogy were also represented in common usage.

The first thing to understand about Varro's machinations is that he was wrong from the very start. When Chrysippus, 'second founder' of the Stoic school (281/77–208/4 B.C.), wrote about 'anomaly', he referred to situations in which words no longer corresponded to their meanings or their logical functions. This included our use of privative words to convey positive facts and vice versa, our use of sentences with complex meaning but containing only one word, the verb implying also the subject of the sentence, etc. (see *Stoicorum Veterum Fragmenta* (SVF) II.151, 177 f.).[12] For example, Chrysippus noted that we do not call a cow *achitōn* ('unclothed') or ourselves *anupodētoi* ('unshod') when we are bathing, for these words would imply that cows usually wore clothes and that we normally bathed with our sandals on. Also, *athanatos* ('undying'), for example, is privative in form, but positive in meaning (SVF II.52.4). It is clear enough that, used in the Stoic sense, 'anomaly' implies that there should in fact be a direct relation between the form and meaning of a word or utterance, but that this relation

[10] See Blank [455], 1–5. [11] See Fehling [458]. [12] Pinborg [33], 95.

has in some cases been disturbed. This sort of 'anomaly' could never be viewed as a general principle of the structure – or rather, the non-structure – of language.

Since Varro is the only source for 'anomaly' as a general structural principle of language, we must explain how he went wrong. There are two possibilities. He may simply have known something of the Stoic discussion of anomaly and himself expanded the use of the term from the irregular relation of utterance and meaning to the irregularity of language in general. On the other hand, he may have known empirical polemics against the validity of arts, where 'anomaly' is used to refer generally to the fact that the phenomena of life resist description and prediction by fixed rules such as technicians are fond of formulating.[13] Since he also found the same term used in Stoic discussions of language, and possibly even in the Stoic Crates, Varro may then have given the name 'anomaly' to the – supposedly Cratean – thesis that language is in principle irregular.

A look at Sextus Empiricus' book *Against the Grammarians* will strengthen the possibility that such a treatise is the source of Varro's confusion. It is often claimed that Sextus is the only Greek author to use *anōmalia* in Varro's sense of 'deviation from inflectional regularity', all other passages using the word in its peculiar Stoic sense.[14] The passage in question is *M* I.154. There Sextus is complaining about the lack of a natural explanation for certain names being singular or plural, for example Athens and Plataeae are single cities with plural names while Thebes and Mycene may be singular or plural, and he promises to deal more carefully with the *anōmalia* in these names later on. That Sextus refers with the word *anōmalia* to simple inflectional irregularity is quite unlikely, since he notes that the irregularity involves plural names for single cities and would thus seem to be of the Stoic type. In three other passages of this book Sextus also uses the adjective *anōmalos*, I.236 and 240. All of these passages refer to *sunētheia anōmalos*, also called *polueidēs* and *astatos*, the 'irregular', 'multiform', 'shifting' common linguistic usage, which is then said to be a poor basis for the discovery of *analogia*. The generality of this usage suggests that Sextus is not speaking about a specifically grammatical *anōmalia* at all, but rather about the problem which he mentions as making the life of astronomers difficult, and which he frequently says forces the sceptic to his suspension of belief, the unpredictability and variability of things and of our perceptions of the

[13] See Sextus Empiricus' books against grammarians, rhetoricians, geometers, arithmeticians, astrologers and musicians (*M* I–VI) for examples of such polemics (*anōmalia* is found at, for example, I.6). Further discussion of such polemics can be found in M. Frede's introduction to [438], XX–XXXIV.

[14] For instance Pinborg [33], 109 f.

world. The Pyrrhonians, he says (1.6), were seized by a desire to get at the truth, but they were forced to suspend their belief when confronted with the conflict of equally powerful arguments on both sides of a question and with the variability of things (*anōmalia pragmatōn*).

So Sextus does not provide support for Varro's theory of anomaly, nor does he speak of anomaly as the contrary of analogy. In Sextus analogy is the comparison of similar words (1.199: *hē analogia homoiōn pollōn onomatōn parathesis*; cf. 1.229). It is also the basis of the rationalistic art of grammar, which Sextus calls 'the analogical art' (214). Sextus produces many of the same arguments against the validity of this analogical art, as does Varro. Since we know that Epicureans and sceptical philosophers before Sextus also argued against grammar in a similar way,[15] it is likely that Varro took some of his arguments from an empirically orientated treatise against grammar. But in Sextus the contrary of analogy is not anomaly, but observation of common usage (*paratērēsis tēs sunētheias*: for example 1.153, 189, 190, 193, 209, 214, 236, 240, 241). Observation is praised by Sextus as 'non-technical and simple' (*atechnos kai aphelēs*, 1.153).[16]

There is, therefore, no principle of 'anomaly' which specifies that language – or anything else in this world – must or should be disorderly: that would, as Sextus notes, be dogmatic and unbecoming to a sceptic (cf. 1.5, where the intention of refuting the arts is called dogmatic). Rather, Sextus opposes the claim that one can and should find out the proper forms of Greek by comparing similar words and establishing regularities among them. He proposes instead (for example at 1.240) that the only basis for such comparison is observation of usage, that the irregularity of usage weakens the force of any comparisons made on the basis of usage, and that analogical comparison adds nothing to mere observation: grammar is not an art or science, a *technē*, but, in so far as it is useful, an *empeiria*, a body of experience. In this contention Sextus recalls a debate whose best-known instance is Socrates' attack on rhetoric in Plato's *Gorgias* (463a ff.).

Sextus' opponents, the advocates of the analogical art of grammar, are not just the Alexandrians, but also the Pergamenes: Crates is associated with Aristophanes and Aristarchus as perfector of the useless art of 'grammar in the deeper or special sense' (1.44), and he is associated with Chaeris' definition of grammar, which Sextus criticises (1.79). One of the targets of Sextus' criticism, as can be seen from the opposition of observation to analogy, is the degree of accuracy and completeness the grammarians claim for their analogical method. Indeed, it is obvious that one only needs

[15] See Sextus, *M* 1.1, 299.

[16] Thus we are not entitled to take large chunks of Varro's text as 'fragments' of Crates, as did H. J. Mette, in his [460], 10–55.

to postulate analogy as a criterion of correct grammar in addition to observation of common usage under two conditions: (1) one is faced with the job of correcting texts which present all sorts of unaccustomed words and forms, and one needs to make a decision in every case, or (2) one has the goal or makes the claim of being able to deal with and understand the use and formation of all words, not just those whose forms are made clear by usage. That the Alexandrians, whose grammatical studies clearly began with the textual study and explanation of Homer and other texts, needed a method to approach all textual problems is clear. An examination of the definitions of grammar criticised by Sextus will show that the claim of completeness was also topical in ancient grammatical thought.

Sextus (1.57) begins the series of definitions of grammar with Aristarchus' student Dionysius Thrax: 'Grammar is an experienced understanding of most of the things said by poets and prose-writers.'[17] Each of the other definitions cited by Sextus is presented as a reaction to the definition of Dionysius. The first critique of Dionysius' definition cited is that of Ptolemaeus the Peripatetic (date unknown). Ptolemaeus took offence at Dionysius' implication that grammar was not an actual *technē*, but merely an *empeiria*, which Ptolemaeus says would be a sort of knack, an inartistic and irrational servant, consisting in simple observation and practice (60 f.).[18]

The next critique is that of Asclepiades (of Myrleia, first century B.C.). He repeats (1.72 f.) Ptolemaeus' objection to Dionysius' use of the word *empeiria*, although as Sextus notes *empeiria* can be used in a general sense without the negative connotations which so bothered Ptolemaeus. Then Asclepiades goes on to criticise the notion that Dionysius' *empeiria* is supposed to have knowledge only of 'most' of what poets and writers say. The limitation 'for the most part', says Asclepiades, belongs to the so-called 'conjectural' arts which are subject to chance,[19] such as navigation and medicine. Grammar, on the other hand, is more akin to music and philosophy: the grammarian himself may, because of the shortness of his life, be knowledgeable only about most of what the poets say, but grammar itself is the understanding of all of it. Asclepiades' own definition, then, was: 'Grammar is an art of the things said by poets and prose-writers.'[20]

[17] *γραμματική ἐστιν ἐμπειρία τῶν παρὰ ποιηταῖς τε καὶ συγγραφεῦσιν ὡς ἐπὶ τὸ πολὺ λεγομένων*. Dionysius Thrax, *Art of Grammar* 1. Sextus version is very slightly different, having *ἐπὶ τὸ πλεῖστον* in place of *ἐπὶ τὸ πολύ*.

[18] Note that Aristotle twice said that grammar was a science (*epistēmē*): *Topics* 142b31, 'grammar is the science of writing . . . and of reading'; *Metaphysics* 1003b20, 'of an entire genus there is one *aisthēsis* and one *epistēmē*, for example grammar is one and it studies all words'.

[19] *τοῦτο μὲν γὰρ τῶν στοχαστικῶν καὶ ὑπὸ τὴν τύχην πιπτουσῶν τεχνῶν.*

[20] *γραμματική ἐστι τέχνη τῶν παρὰ ποιητῶν καὶ συγγραφέων λεγομένων.*

Chares (or Chaeris)[21] produced a definition which carried on both the above lines of criticism. He said (1.76) that 'perfect grammar was an ability technically able to discover with the utmost accuracy the meanings and the things said by Greeks, except those which fall under other arts'.[22] Here the definition of grammar as an ability seems to be an attempt to do justice to Dionysius' *empeiria* by emphasising experience, while the technical nature of grammar is introduced with regard to its diagnostic ability, the ability to tell correct from incorrect. Any possible ambiguity about whether Dionysius meant 'for the most part' to qualify the percentage of poetic and authorial utterances which grammar will explain or the accuracy with which grammar would explain these utterances is removed in Chares' definition. He says that grammar is the knowledge (*eidēsis*) of all the utterances and their meanings, not only of poets and prose-writers, but of all Greeks in general, and he claims that grammar will study these things with all possible accuracy.

The last definition cited by Sextus is that of Demetrius Chlorus (date unknown), a definition shared also by unnamed other grammarians: 'Grammatical art is knowledge of the words used by poets and in common usage.'[23] This, of course, is the most highly loaded definition of all, referring as it does to art, knowledge, poets and common usage, and claiming to know about all words universally.

The concerns of the grammarians of the second century B.C. become clear in these definitions of grammar. One is the question of the scope of grammar, whether it concerns only the works of poets and prose-writers or also the everyday language of the Greeks, and whether it will claim to be able to speak about all of the things said within its sphere of activity or about only some or most of them. Obviously, whatever Dionysius Thrax felt about this question, for we cannot assume that his definition is meant to be taken in the narrowest possible sense, his colleagues wanted to be sure to stake out as large a field as possible for their profession. Other important questions concern the type of knowledge grammar represents, how it is acquired, by

[21] We know of a Chares (the form of the name given in Sextus), but, as an associate of Apollonius of Rhodes in the late third century B.C., he seems to be too early to have responded to Dionysius' definition. Thus, it has been suggested that the name should be Chaeris, who seems to have been a pupil of Aristarchus, as was Dionysius himself.

[22] *τὴν τελείαν φησὶ γραμματικὴν ἕξιν εἶναι ἀπὸ τέχνης διαγνωστικὴν τῶν παρ' Ἕλλησι λεκτῶν καὶ νοητῶν ἐπὶ τὸ ἀκριβέστατον πλὴν τῶν ὑπ' ἄλλαις τέχναις.*

[23] *γραμματική ἐστι τέχνη τῶν παρὰ ποιηταῖς τε καὶ ⟨συγγραφεῦσι λεγομένων καὶ⟩ τῶν κατὰ τὴν κοινὴν συνήθειαν λέξεων εἴδησις* is the suggested restoration of V. Di Benedetto, 'Demetrio Cloro e Aristone di Alessandria', *ASNP* II.35 (1966), 321–4, 322, with which I do not agree.

what means and with what accuracy grammar examines utterances. Again, the grammarians correcting Dionysius were at pains to claim as much as possible for grammar, insisting that it was technical, involved with experience, diagnostic and accurate.

As the definition of Chares most clearly indicates, these two large questions are related: only a truly technical knowledge which uses accurate and methodical techniques can claim accuracy in regard to all utterances. Sextus, of course, will dispute that this is at all possible: there can never be any knowledge or science of any infinite or unlimited quantity of data (see, for example, 1.81–3), let alone of data which change, as language does. Dionysius Thrax's carefully humble formulation is perhaps written with this sort of objection in mind. The other part of the completeness claim is represented by Asclepiades and Demetrius Chlorus: grammar studies not only what is written, but also everyday spoken Greek. Clearly this claim is an attack on the empiricist view that ordinary usage is the only guide to grammaticality, a claim which will be reinforced by Apollonius Dyscolus (*de Syntaxi* (*Synt.*) 183.14, cited below). The key to the grammarians' claims of completeness must lie in postulating that there is some sort of reason to assume that all linguistic phenomena can be explained. In the language of the second-century debate, the grammarian must have principles (*archai*) and a criterion to tell correct from incorrect language. Further, if grammar is to be an art, its principles and the criterion of grammatical correctness must be technical (*M* 1.182). Finally, if the grammarian will claim that his art can correct any utterance, the criterion must be fixed. Thus, the grammarian must either decree that one person's usage, for example Homer's, will be the standard of correct speech, or he must claim that some natural law makes correct language the way it is: 'since the unclear is known from something else, one must either follow some natural criterion from which proper Greek will be recognized . . . or one must use the usage of one man who is taken to speak the best Greek' (*M* 1.186; cf. 1.153).[24]

Thus, as far as Sextus is concerned, the grammarians who argue for the existence of a useful analogical art of grammar must either adopt someone as the standard of usage, as Pindario adopts Homer,[25] or postulate that linguistic phenomena behave in the regular way they do because they follow some sort of natural law. That Sextus includes both Alexandrians and Pergamenes in this characterisation is clear from the fact that he never

[24] *ἐπεὶ τὸ ἄδηλον ἔκ τινος ἑτέρου γνωρίζεται, ἤτοι φυσικῷ τινὶ κατακολουθητέον κριτηρίῳ, ἐξ οὗ διαγιγνώσκεται τί τὸ Ἑλληνικόν . . . ἢ τῇ ἑνὸς συνηθείᾳ ὡς ἄκρως ἑλληνίζοντος χρηστέον*. See Blank [455], 11–19.

[25] Ptolemaeus Pindario was a pupil of Aristarchus. Sextus cites him as commending the usage of Homer as the norm of Greek usage (*M* 1.202, 205).

distinguishes between them, in so far as they are both proponents of rationalistic arts of grammar. This is a much more philosophically reasonable view of the two schools than that offered by Varro. Varro's picture would have the supposedly unphilosophical Alexandrians fighting for the absolute predictability of inflectional morphology, yet without giving any reason for it other than the necessity of 'analogy', while the admittedly Stoic Pergamenes have somehow forgotten that a rational nature rules the Stoic world, and they have abstracted 'anomaly' or disorderliness from linguistic observation and elevated it into a structural principle. Sextus is also clear enough about the kind of 'natural' principles assumed by the grammarians: they are wholeheartedly Stoic, as can be seen from the terminology Sextus uses to argue with them from starting-points the grammarians would accept. For example, Sextus assumes that under *logos* in the phrase 'the parts of *logos*' the grammarians must understand either the voice, which is corporeal, or the incorporeal *lekton* (1.155); thus, his argument clearly proceeds from Stoic principles.

Having laid the analogy/anomaly controversy to rest, I am now prepared to drive the final nails into the coffin of the traditional view of the early history of grammatical theory by refuting the notion that the Alexandrians developed grammatical theory into a scientific discipline independent of and ever further removed from its origins in Stoic philosophy. If such a process had taken place, it would certainly have been completed by the second century A.D., with the work of the two great *technikoi* of Greek grammar, Apollonius Dyscolus and Herodian.

Herodian's contemporary Galen wrote that, while medical experience was enough of a basis for a modest art of medicine, the whole of medical art could only be known with the help of reason (*Subfiguratio Empirica* 88.19 ff. Deichgräber). In the same way, and in the tradition of the increasingly bold claims of the second-century definitions of grammar, Herodian proclaimed that 'analogy produced predictions about every Greek word and with its art contained as if in a net the manifold utterance of human language' (*Peri Monērous Lexeōs* (*On Idiosyncratic Words*) 909.18).[26]

As for Apollonius himself, his syntax was designed to prove that logical consequence was valid in all syntactic phenomena, that rational, philosophically discoverable rules grounded in the nature of things governed syntax: 'for the rules of syntax have been demonstrated for just this purpose, so that even the unnoticed disturbances, which exist even in normal usage, may participate in the rule of regularity (*echētai tou akolouthou logou*), and lest someone assume that only those disturbances used by the poets are

[26] *ἡ πάσης λέξεως Ἑλληνικῆς πρόνοιαν ποιοῦσα ἀναλογία καὶ ὥσπερ εἰ ἐν δικτύῳ συνέχουσα τὸ πολυσχιδὲς τῆς ἀνθρώπων γλώσσης φθέγμα τῇ τέχνῃ.*

exceptional' (*Synt.* 183.14 = II.77). Apollonius assumes that language is a system all of whose parts are ordered in a logical way. Thus, the noun, which signifies a substance, is listed before the verb, which signifies a state of a substance. This is not a reprehensible retreat into 'logical' or 'non-linguistic' categories, but rather a consequence of Apollonius' rationalistic method. The builder of a rationalistic art or science must ensure that his edifice has a firm foundation by starting with principles evident to perception or to common reason (see, for example, Galen, *de Methodo Medendi* X.32.2 Kühn), and the fact that substance is prior to its states is such a principle of common reason. In his discussion of the order of the parts of speech, Apollonius criticises people with views remarkably similar to those of Sextus Empiricus:

> Perhaps some people who act ignorantly in these matters soothe their ignorance by saying that there is no 'right' or 'wrong' in such investigations, assuming that these phenomena have all been established by chance as unconnected. These people, however, will, in their general discussions, have to assume that nothing is in order and that nothing is out-of-order, which is utterly foolish; for if you admit this in one case, you must admit it in all cases. (*Synt.* 16.6–11 = I.13)

The connection between natural rule, explanation rather than mere observation, and grammar's claim to correct all utterances is made clear by Apollonius in the following passage:

> Since some constructions as these are so obvious, some people will think they can preserve correct syntax even if they do not grasp the reason behind it. They will experience something similar to those people who learn the forms of words just from experience, but not from the explanatory power of the proven usage of the Greeks and the analogy which follows from it. What happens to them is, namely, that if they err in some word-form, they are unable to correct their mistake because of the ignorance arising from their practice. Now just as the collected research on Hellenism is extremely useful, serving to correct readings in poetry and everyday language as well and even judging the imposition of words by the ancients, in the same way the present investigation of syntactical regularity will correct what sorts of mistake occur in discourse.
>
> Now there are obviously some questions which are not clearly answered by proven usage, so that people disagree as to whether *eirēkas* is the correct Greek form [for 'you have said'] or *eirēkes* with an *e*, or whether, as some claim, *Hermēi* is to be spelled with *ei*, though reason demands a spelling with *ēi*. And it turns out that the continuity of reason (*hē tou logou sunecheia*) will correct the fault of speech. Now again, this same sort of thing will be the consequence of the present endeavour too, for when some points are in doubt, the application of reason will remove the syntactical

> fault with a natural order ...[27] If poetic licence, which calls for pleonasm and ellipse, should omit to observe some rule or other, the conflicting reason will point out that which is missing or extra ... So is not reason very useful, since it fills out what is deficient without adding unnecessarily to what is not indeed defective? (*Synt.* 51.1–53.11 = I.60–2)

Here the natural order of language is the key to the grammatical system and its study, for it is the basis on which inferences about linguistic phenomena can be made and the consistency of such phenomena can be tested. What such inferences require is a knowledge of causes, of why things are as they are, and Apollonius frequently insists that the recognition of syntactical irregularities is not enough for the grammarian:

> Knowledgeable people must set out just what it is which causes syntactical irregularity, and this not by the useless collection of tropes as examples, as some did who merely noted solecisms, but did not teach what causes them. If one does not understand the cause, one will have collected all one's tropes in vain. (*Synt.* 271.6 = III.16)

Apollonius' ultimate point is that, once the cause of an irregularity is understood, the irregularity is no longer a threat to the rule, since it follows a rule itself. It is then the knowledge of the rule which gives the analogical/rational system its flawless continuity, allowing it to deduce the correct form of any and every linguistic phenomenon.

Thus, when I say that Apollonius' grammar is analogical, I mean that Apollonius is concerned to show that there are general rules in grammar and that all apparent violations of these rules can be explained as the result of regular and codifiable corruptions. This view of the irregular as a traceable corruption of the regular belongs to the method of 'pathology', which detailed the changes (*pathē*) by which original forms became corrupted to yield the forms encountered in the language and its dialects. By this method of tracing corruptions, the apparent exceptions to linguistic rules are themselves made to prove the rules.

The rules themselves were found by Apollonius using logical, philosophical criteria or the master rule that 'the larger group of examples is the yardstick against which the smaller is judged' (*de Pronominibus* (*Pron.*) 72.6.)[28] Apollonius would observe that in most cases a certain regularity obtained, he would declare this the rule governing all such phenomena and would also try to explain this rule logically or naturally, then he would try to find a reason for each exception to his rule. A good example is his discussion

[27] *τὰ τοῦ λόγου ἐγγινόμενα μετά τινος φυσικῆς παρακολουθήσεως ἀποστήσει τὸ οὐ δέον τῆς συντάξεως.*

[28] On this rule, see Thierfelder, [461], 28 ff.

of verbal rection.[29] The vast majority of the actions arising from nominatives affect an accusative, and an acting subject and a passive object subsist on the two case-forms. Thus, according to the Apollonian rule that the more common phenomenon is the rule for the less common, verbs whose action expresses a state requiring an accusative expression (i.e. which govern an accusative) and which can also be expressed in the passive voice are the standard for the transitive verbs in general: they are the first to be explained by Apollonius, and other verbal constructions are explained as variants of these. The nature of the variations or derivations properly expressed in the genitive and accusative cases respectively determines the order of their treatment (remember that all linguistic phenomena obey a given order). The state expressed in the accusative is the passive state which is most 'active', and which is expressed by the most purely active *verba sentiendi*, verbs of vision. Verbs of sensation which govern the genitive might seem to violate the rule that transitive verbs normally govern the accusative, but their construction can be explained as a logical variant. For, in the operation of these senses, the body is passively acted upon by external objects by which it cannot help but be affected (for example we can close our eyes and prevent ourselves from seeing, but we can hardly prevent ourselves from hearing, much less from feeling or tasting). We can see that Apollonius' method is twofold: it establishes the most common construction as a standard, judging other constructions as variations derived from the standard; and it appeals to semantic properties of the verbs in question to explain their variation from the standard construction – the verbs have additional semantic properties when compared with the standardly constructed verbs, and these semantic properties are taken to entail a different syntax, as they should, given that (as we shall see below) syntax is considered under the heading of word-meaning, rather than word-form. Evidently, the fulfilment of Apollonius' promise not just to reveal irregularities but to show what causes them may require an appeal to 'natural', 'philosophical' or 'logical' principles. Next, the construction with the genitive is said by Apollonius to be the most closely related to passivity, as is shown by the standard passive structure, whose agent is expressed in the genitive with the preposition *hupo* ('by'). The activity of the senses, however, forbids their expression by a purely passive construction; thus as a compromise an active verb is used governing a genitive object. Another apparent exception to the rule, the fact that *eran* ('desire') takes a genitive object, while *philein* ('love') governs an accusative, is shown to be justified in a similar manner. *Eran* is more intense than the rational *philein* and implies that the subject is 'additionally affected' by the

[29] See Blank [457], esp. 244 ff.

object of desire (*Synt.* 491.1 = IV.71). All of the verbal constructions of the genitive are ultimately based on that case's expression of passivity. Transitive actions, on the other hand, which do not fit into the above classes are none the less derived ultimately from the actions expressed with an accusative, but they must be expressed with datives. This group includes actions expressed by verbs taking an indirect object (422.6 ff. = III.177). These verbs, that is, govern an accusative as well as a dative, and the dative is said to 'contain' the accusative (426.6–12 = III.183). Similarly, verbs of serving or following which govern a dative do so because their actions 'contain' the notion of servitude. Reciprocal actions demand an oblique case for their expression, since they are transitive, but since the two parties act and suffer equally, neither the accusative nor the genitive will do, and only the dative remains.

Another example of this method is Apollonius' discussion[30] of the 'spatial adverbs' *pou, pose/pothi, pothen* ('where/whither/whence') (*de Adverbiorum Constructione* (*Adv. Constr.*) 201.1–8):[31]

> The spatial adverbs have three distinct meanings: the meaning in a place, that to a place and that from a place. And it is clear that those meaning in a place are such as to come first, for those meaning from a place presuppose that something was earlier in a place, and further to make a change from a place presupposes going to a place. And this is also already clear from the word-forms themselves. For *pou* means in a place, from which comes the spatial derivate for to a place, *pose* and also *pothi*, and from a place, *pothen*.

Here the order of the spatial relations is determined by a logical reflection on the nature of local motion and supported by an appeal to the fact that the words *pose, pothi, pothen* themselves are derived from *pou*.

The connection of syntactic phenomena with semantic ones, as well as the derivation of altered constructions and word-forms in tandem with relations between original meanings and variations in meaning subordinate to the original one, suggests a Stoic inspiration for Apollonius' method. A further link between Apollonius and the Stoics can be seen in the organisation of the Apollonian works on the various parts of speech. Each treatise, that is, falls into two basic parts which treat the meaning (*ennoia*) and the sound-structure (*schēma tēs phōnēs*) respectively (for example *de Adverbiis* (*Adv.*) 119.1 ff.); the comparison to the Stoic division of the 'logical part' of philosophy into the part about expressions and that about what they signify is apparent. Apollonius treats the sense first, beginning with a

[30] *Ibid.*, 246 f.

[31] This name is conventionally given to that passage transmitted as part of the book *On Adverbs*, which seems rather to have originated as part of the treatment of adverbs in *On Syntax*.

discussion of the name of the part of speech, if there is disagreement, and continuing with its definition (for example *Pron.* 3.9 and 9.11), both topics belonging to the treatment of sense, since the name must suit the *ousia* whose *logos* is the definition (for example *de Coniunctionibus* (*Coni.*) 215.14). After the names and definitions, Apollonius distinguishes the *genera* of the part of speech, a distinction again based on the sense of the word (for instance *Coni.* 219.12). A discussion of syntax continues the section on *ennoia*, and the last topic here is the treatment of various words correctly or incorrectly assigned by others to this part of speech (cf. *Pron.* 67.6). The discussion of word-forms and their derivations or corruptions follows the section on sense.

Finally, the ordering principle lying behind Apollonius' syntax is basically Stoic in origin. It is the logical order of the thing which is said that determines the admissible order of the word-forms making up a sentence:

> For already even the so-called first, undivided matter of the elements of the alphabet (=*phōnē*) demonstrated this long before, in so far as it did not make combinations of elements in just any manner, but only in the construction which was according to the rule of necessity, whence they virtually took their name (=*stoicheia*); and the syllable, going beyond the element, has accepted this same thing, since the constructions resulting from syllables and filled-out according to necessity's law complete the word.
>
> And it clearly follows from this that the words too, since they are part of the sentence which is syntactically complete, accept the regularity of syntax; for the intelligible item which arises beside and from each word is in a certain sense an element of the sentence, and just as the elements in their combinations complete syllables, so too does the syntax of the intelligibles complete sentences in a certain sense, through the combination of the words. Again, as the word comes from the syllables, so does the complete sentence come from the regularity of the intelligibles. (*Synt.* 2.3–3.2=1.2)

It is not so much the words (*lexeis*) which are analogous to the elements (i.e. letters), but the intelligible items subsistent on the words. The syntax or construction of these intelligibles is effected by the combination of the words on which they subsist. Thus the words are the counters by means of which the intelligibles are joined. Ultimately, as incomplete, non-semantic syllables join together to make the semantic unit of the *lexis*, so the incomplete *noēta* ('intelligibles') subsistent on *lexeis* join together to make regularity (*katallēlotēs*), from which comes the complete semantic unit, the complete sentence. For example, it is the logical inconsistency of the intelligible plural subsistent on the noun *paidia* ('children': neuter plural) and the intelligible singular subsistent on the verb *graphei* ('writes': singular) which makes it 'irregular' to combine that noun and verb.[32]

Apollonius assumes that this underlying, intelligible level of meaning remains unchanged when words or word-forms are substituted (for example *Coni.* 224.11, *Adv.* 136.32). This assumption allows Apollonius to apply the method of pathology to syntax in the first place, for although the words may be different, the meaning will be the same, and the clash between words and meaning is Apollonius' clue to syntactic irregularity. In examining sentence structures, Apollonius will often consider the structure at hand as a translated substitute (*metalēpsis*) for some other construction, as we saw in the discussion of the rection of transitive verbs.[33] Underlying this method is the assumption that each underlying meaning is originally or properly represented by one word or construction. The comparison of a construction to the construction from which it was 'translated' thus constitutes a sort of normalisation of the surface structure of the sentence. This normalisation is a technique adapted from Stoic logic: in logical analysis, normalisation of the sentence's surface structure enables the Stoic to read off the logical structure from the expression. 'Substitutions' occur at all levels of the linguistic system: thus another word may be used for the 'proper' word, another construction instead of the 'proper' construction, one class of relations (for instance datives, as above) instead of the 'proper' class. Apollonius even uses this method in situations directly relevant to logical analysis, for example when he says that one conjunction is used instead of the conjunction which would actually express the logical relation intended by Homer in a particular passage, and that one should punctuate the passage in accordance with this intended logical relation, as though the correct conjunction had been used.[34] Apollonius also notes that the verb 'follows' is a 'translation' (*metalēpsis*) of 'if', since 'it follows from its being day that it is light' means the same as 'if it is day, then it is light' (*Coni.* 220.7 ff.). This method of 'translation' in linguistic analysis, further, is expressly connected to the Stoic thesis that language developed away from an original one-to-one correspondence of things-to-be-said and expressions. For Apollonius gives numerous examples of 'derived' forms (*paragōga*) which are said to be 'translations' of original or simple forms (*prōtotupa*). Thus, the participle arises from the verb, for example 'while writing I was distressed'

[32] In fact, neuter plural nouns normally take singular verbs in Greek, a construction they owe to their derivation from collectives.

[33] For descriptive accounts of *metalēpsis*, see Thierfelder [461], 42 ff., and W. Hörschelmann, 'Kritische Bemerkungen zu Apollonios Dyskolos *de pronomine*', *Rheinisches Museum* 35 (1880), 271–89.

[34] Blank [456], 64f. For the substitution of conjunctions see also Chrysippus in D.L. VII.71.

from 'I was writing and I was distressed' (*Synt.* 290.3, 15, 25, etc. = III.123 f.), while the subjunctive arises from the indicative (*Synt.* 272.2 = III.6).

Thus, we can see how the Stoic philosophical origins of grammatical thought continue to form the basis even of the grammatical work considered most 'technical' by the ancients. The understanding of the supposed analogy/anomaly controversy requires seeing the debate in philosophical, in particular, epistemological terms, according to which the facts then allow themselves to be incorporated into a well-attested wider debate between empiricists and rationalists. In the same way, it is important for the understanding of grammarians such as Apollonius Dyscolus to see them not as the faltering initial steps in the development of linguistic science from then until now. Apollonius wanted to demonstrate the coherence of the Greek language as a system rooted in the correspondence of thought and meaning. We shall understand Apollonius' way with this system only by seeing the Stoic logic at its origins and then going on to study how he extended and modified the Stoic theory as he worked on the details of the language. Certainly, not everything in Apollonius can be projected back on to the Stoics, but his basic methods and habits cannot be explained without them.

9

Usage and abusage: Galen on language*

R. J. HANKINSON

Galen of Pergamon in Asia Minor came from a wealthy background and he was, as he never tires of telling us, the beneficiary of a fine liberal upbringing.[1] One might be pardoned for thinking that this alone was responsible, as it so frequently is, for the excessive pedantry that characterises his works. But Galen's pedantry, if such it is, is of a peculiar nature; and it is part and parcel of a set of philosophical views about the nature of the relationship between language and thought, and about the proper application of terminology in science. It is these views that I intend to examine in this essay.

* Note on citations: all the ancient texts are referred to in the most generally acceptable standard ways; in the case of texts referred to for the first time, I cite author and full title, followed by a standard abbreviation for the title to be used in later references (which may not cite the author's name). Presocratics are cited by the way of the 6th (1951) edition of Diels–Kranz; the Stoics via von Arnim's *Stoicorum Veterum Fragmenta* (SVF). In many cases I give additional references to the ancient sources from which they are culled. Galen presents the greatest difficulties: the only passably complete edition (*Galeni Opera Omnia*, ed. C. G. Kühn (Leipzig, 1821–33)) is hopelessly inadequate and out of date; but it remains our only modern edition of vast tracts of Galen. I generally cite all of the texts of Galen that are contained in Kühn by way of Kühn, even where better, later editions are available, as they invariably reproduce the Kühn pagination. However, at the first mention of a text (where I also introduce standard abbreviations), I will refer the reader to better texts if any are available. I hope that this will prove neither infuriatingly incomplete and vague nor needlessly cumbersome.

[1] His father was a wealthy architect in the city (see *On the Order of his own Books* (*Ord. Lib. Prop.*) XIX.40 Kühn; *Ord. Lib. Prop.* is edited in I. Müller, *Galeni Scripta Minora*, vol. 2, Leipzig, 1891), at that time (A.D. 129) the greatest of Greek Asia Minor: see *On the Diagnosis and Cure of the Passions of the Soul* (*Aff. Dig.*) V.40–4 Kühn (*Aff. Dig*) is edited in J. Marquardt, *Galeni Scripta Minora*, vol. 1 (Leipzig, 1884), and by W. De Boer, in *Corpus Medicorum Graecorum* (CMG) (Berlin, 1937), V.4.1.1); cf. *On the Therapeutic Method* (*MM*) X.561, 609 Kühn.

I Is language natural?

In one sense that is a silly question, and the answer straightforward: of course it is. Human beings all have the capacity to learn language and to employ it creatively, and that is one of the things that makes us human. However, that question is susceptible of less fatuous interpretations: how far is our language capacity innate, programmed into us, and how far is language acquisition an empirical matter? Such questions have exercised human beings at least since the time of the legendary king Psammetichus (at any rate if we are to believe Herodotus).[2] And they have been a perennial topic for debate throughout the history of philosophy.[3] Such questions are a sub-class of the general dispute between empiricism and innatism as explanations for human learning, a dispute which also has ancient roots.[4]

But it is not these with which I shall be most concerned in this section. Rather I shall deal with the problem of whether words, significant articulate sounds, have their significance purely by convention, or whether there is a natural component to their signification. This question is closely related to the issue of etymology, and its significance, and I shall treat the latter first.

The Greeks were extremely, almost obsessively, interested in etymologies. This concern first appears in the Presocratics, notably Heraclitus;[5] was of abiding interest to the luminaries of the sophistic movement;[6] and its most celebrated, extended and lunatic efflorescence occurs in Plato's *Cratylus* (*Crat.*). In that dialogue, Hermogenes has been in dispute with Cratylus about the significance of names: Hermogenes holds that they are significant only by convention, Cratylus that their significance is entirely natural. Socrates, as a mediator, proceeds to argue against Hermogenes by offering a

[2] Herodotus records that the king, determined to find out which was the oldest language in the world, had two infants brought up out of all contact with human speech, in order to discover what was the first articulate sound they uttered: it turned out to be *bekos*, the Phrygian for bread; hence the king concluded that Phrygian was the ur-language (Herodotus II.2–5); the king's experiment at least presupposes some beliefs about the origin of language.

[3] From the Locke–Leibniz dispute on the matter of innate ideas, down to the current Chomskian debates.

[4] Galen himself, influenced by Hippocrates' doctrine that 'nature is sufficient in everything for everything' (*On Nutrition*, 15), inclined to innatism. This tendency would receive further confirmation if indeed the papyrus fragment of a commentary upon this very sentence derives from Galen's lost commentary on that work, as is claimed by Daniela Manetti in her presentation of the fragment in [17].

[5] See 22 B48, 51 D–K, on the double meaning of *bios*; and 32 B52 D–K, with a probable etymological play on *aiōn*. [6] See n. 8 below.

series of more or less wild 'natural' etymologies of words. However, while the actual etymologies offered may seem to sober modern consideration to be less than plausible (as indeed Socrates in the dialogue more or less admits), the underlying theory is of some interest. Plato's Socrates holds that there can be a natural fitness of certain types of noun[7] to their referents; in some cases, historical distortion has obscured this fitness (this is particularly true in the case of proper names, which are inherited in the Greek: thus a hero's pusillanimous son may inherit a heroic name). Effectively the names are held to function as disguised descriptions: thus *ho anthrōpos* (man) turns out really to mean *ho anathrōn ha opōpen* ('the one who looks up at what he sees'), a reference to the unique erect posture of the human (*Crat.* 399b). A further 'etymology' attempts, in effect, to demonstrate the link between the heroic and the erotic.

Whatever one thinks of such an enterprise, one thing is at least clear: even if these nouns are shown to be in some sense natural (in that they derive from antecedent descriptions), it is not necessarily the case that they are natural in any stronger sense: for the descriptive terms upon which they rest may themselves be applied as a matter of merest convention. As a matter of fact, the *Cratylus* contains arguments to the effect that certain phonemes, and indeed the letters of which they are made up, have natural values; but it is also argued (434b ff.) that in some cases the significance of the words is opposed to the natural semantic significance of their component letters (the example is *sklēros*, 'hard', where the 'l' is alleged to be a soft letter: 'perhaps it has got in by accident', Socrates' Cratylus rather desperately conjectures).

The *Cratylus* was not written in an intellectual vacuum: there is ample evidence of a fifth-century debate on the correctness of naming;[8] Democritus for one vigorously propounded conventionalism, and supported it by pointing to the fact that different peoples have quite distinct names for the same things (68 B26 D–K). And the debate continued into the fourth century and beyond. Aristotle took the Hermogenic line in *de Interpretatione* (*Int.*): 'a noun is an utterance made significant by convention' (*Int.*2.16a19); and he argues that most decompositional analyses of simple words are simply mistaken.[9] However, the most influential of the later

[7] I translate the Greek term *onoma* thus: its basic meaning is 'name', and that basic meaning infects later discussion of it; but in grammatical contexts it is contrasted with *rhēma*, which means 'verb' or 'predicate': cf. Aristotle, *de Interpretatione* 2–3.16a20–b26.

[8] Protagoras and Prodicus offered instruction in it: see Plato, *Crat.* 391c; *Euthydemus* 277b; for the sophists in general, see *Crat.* 391b; see Guthrie [3], 204–19.

[9] See on this my [292].

schools, the Epicureans and the Stoics, both adopted positions of naturalism, each in its own way extreme.

The Epicureans, in this regard at least repudiating their Democritean ancestry, held a very powerful naturalist account of the genesis of names, expressed most concisely in the *Letter to Herodotus* (*Hdtm.*) 75–6 (cf. Lucretius v.1028–90):

> Hence names as well were not originally due to convention, but in their different races men's actual natures underwent particular affections, and received particular impressions, and as a result emitted particular cries. The air thus emitted was moulded by their individual affections and impressions, differently according to the races' differing environments. Later, entire races adopted their own special names, to make communication briefer and less ambiguous.

Human beings are simply driven by their direct perceptual access to the world to utter certain sorts of sound under particular determinate circumstances: and those sounds form the basis for the development of language. Epicurus does not hold that *all* language is entirely naturally derived in this way; that would be too obviously absurd (particularly as he creates neologisms himself). But naturalism is the basis; and particularly noteworthy is the ingenious solution to the difficulty created for naturalist accounts by the evident divergences between languages: such differences can be explained on the basis of environmental distinctions. As Tony Long and David Sedley point out in their invaluable collection *The Hellenistic Philosophers*,[10] 'before Epicurus the doctrine that "names are natural" had meant not that they arose without contrivance, but that they somehow mirror the nature of their *nominata* ... On Epicurus' theory both views are combined.' Epicurus can thus rely on a naturalism about the original processes that lead to primitive language, but also allow a degree of conventionalism in its subsequent development.

The Stoics were less genetically naturalistic than the Epicureans; but they still adopt a natural rather than a conventional account of significance. Thus:

> The Stoics believe [that names come to be] by nature, the primary sounds being imitations of the things of which the names are said.
>
> (Origen, *Against Celsus* I.24 = SVF II.146)

And the Stoics provided etymologies. Chrysippus, the most celebrated and prolific of the early Stoics, wrote (according to Diogenes Laertius) two works

[10] [308], 100–1.

on etymology, in seven and four volumes respectively (D.L. VII.200);[11] and we know from fragments that survive in Galen's own work just how radically and seriously Chrysippus adopted the view reported by Origen. The following is alleged to be a direct quotation from Chrysippus' *On the Soul*:[12]

> We also say *egō* (I) in this way, pointing to ourselves at that place where thought appears to be, the gesture being carried there naturally and appropriately; and apart from such a gesture of the hand, we nod towards ourselves as we say *egō*; indeed the very word *egō* is of this description, and its pronunciation is accompanied by the gesture described. For as we pronounce *egō*, at the first syllable we drop the lower lip in a way that points to ourselves, and in conformity with the movement of the chin, the nod towards the chest, and such gesturing, the next syllable is juxtaposed. (Galen, *On the Doctrines of Hippocrates and Plato* (*PHP*) V.215 Kühn, tr. De Lacy[13])

All this occurs in the context of Chrysippus' 'proof' that the rational soul is located in the heart: the fact that when pronouncing the word *egō* the jaw points towards the chest (and hence the heart) is supposed to be evidence for that claim. Whatever one thinks of that (Galen savages the argument), the extent of Chrysippus' naturalism is clearly exhibited in this passage.

Galen has no time for that sort of thing; such arguments are (in his classification) unscientific. At best they are rhetorical; at worst merely sophistical:

> Chrysippus sometimes calls on non-experts as witnesses to the premisses that he postulates; sometimes he calls on poets, or etymology, that fine friend, or something else of that sort, things that prove nothing but spend and waste our time to no purpose . . . Indeed I have shown in another work *On the Correctness of Names*[14] that etymology is an impostor.
> (*PHP* V.213–14 Kühn)

[11] 'Volumes' in the ancient world means 'rolls of papyrus'; each roll would have been the rough equivalent of about thirty of our printed pages. A volume or a book, then, is more like a chapter, and with this in mind the bulk of Chrysippus' alleged output of more than 705 books (Diogenes Laertius (D.L.) VII.180) becomes slightly less forbidding; it is none the less a considerable achievement. None apart from a badly mutilated papyrus of his *Logical Investigations* survives.

[12] For the fragments of Chrysippus' *de Anima* preserved in Galen, arranged with some attempt to determine their original order, see SVF II.911.

[13] *Galen on the Doctrines of Hippocrates and Plato: Edition, Translation and Commentary* by Phillip De Lacy: *CMG* V.4.1.2 (three vols.). The first two volumes contain an invaluable introduction, text and translation of this key work; the third volume a concise but useful commentary and full indexes; I need hardly stress how much I am indebted to De Lacy's scholarship and learning.

[14] This work is no longer extant; it is mentioned in XIX.61 Kühn, and at *PHP* V.218 Kühn.

Galen, indeed, makes two claims: first that Chrysippus gets the etymologies wrong (Galen was interested, in a dilettante sort of way, in philology); but secondly that even when the etymologies are correct, that need tell us nothing at all about the actual facts of the matter. Such things tell as often against the truth as they do in favour of it; etymology, in short, even when reliably practised, is of no help in science (see *PHP* v.214 Kühn). So Galen's rejection of the Chrysippean position involves two components. First of all there is the refutation of the doctrine of natural signification; and secondly there is the repudiation of etymology.

But whatever one's views about the origin and development of language, language clearly matters to the theory of science. Even if you are quite convinced that all names are significant only by convention, none the less it is vital to determine just what they signify; and indeed in some cases to prescribe a revision for their usage. And, as we shall see, Galen is sensitive to this fact.

2 Galen on the correctness of names

At first sight, however, one might not imagine that that was the case. Galen repeatedly remarks that it does not matter what you call things as long as you do so consistently; but he also stresses that failure to stick to the conventions adopted, and failure properly to distinguish between correct and incorrect applications of names according to those conventions, is a source of continual error.[15] The important thing, then, is not the actual word itself ('you can call it Dion or Theon if you want to', Galen remarks on numerous occasions),[16] but the consistency and rigour with which it is applied to one and only one thing. He strongly denounces what he considers to be merely terminological disputes, as being fit subject-matter for logicians, rhetoricians and grammarians, but not for practising doctors and natural scientists,[17] whose sole concern should be with substantial issues;

[15] *MM* x.43–4, 61, 62, 139 Kühn; *On the Differences of Pulses* (*Diff. Puls.*) viii.493–7, 657–74; 641–3 Kühn; *de Plenitudine* (*Plen.*) vii.521 Kuhn; *On Unnatural Swellings* (*Tum. Pr. Nat.*) vii.750 ff. Kuhn; *On Respiratory Difficulties* (*Diff. Resp.*) vii.758–60 Kühn. See also *On Antecedent Causes* (*CP*) vi.47–55 (= *CMG* Supp. ii, 13.12–14.33); and see notes in my edition, translation and commentary on that text, forthcoming from Cambridge.

[16] 'Dion' and 'Theon' are the standard dummy-names in later Greek philosophy replacing Aristotle's favoured 'Socrates' and 'Coriscus': see, for example, Sextus Empiricus, *Adversus Mathematicos* (*M*) viii.12; D.L. vii.73–9; SVF ii.397; for Galen's own use of them, see, for example, *MM* x.70, 81 Kühn; (*Diff. Puls.*) viii.496 Kühn. As Jonathan Barnes remarks in his [454], 'Time and again ... Galen insists that he does not insist in the matter of names ... Indeed his insistence becomes as tiresome as the pedantry he rejects'; see *MM* x.43–5, 50, 54–9, 139, 155: I discuss these passages in my [439].

[17] See, for example, *On Critical Days* (*Di. Dec.*) ix.789 Kühn; *MM* x.630 Kühn.

and a constant refrain is that his opponents confuse substantial argument with mere trivial linguistic quibbling:

> they [i.e. substantial issues] are important for human preservation, and mistakes in them can be fatal; but whether we use names properly or not, our patients neither benefit nor suffer.
> (*On the Therapeutic Method* (*MM*) x.772)

The important thing is to ensure that names are consistently applied to similar types of thing; indeed

> even if one commits solecisms in naming, this does not damage the actual knowledge of the matter; the most important thing in exposition is to make absolutely clear what thing the name is being applied to. (*MM* x.43 Kühn)

Thus, in Galen's view, it doesn't matter whether you use the word 'disease' to describe the actual damage to some vital function, or whether rather you reserve that term for the underlying causes of the damage (*MM* x.50 Kühn), as long as you are aware of the distinction between the damage and its cause. However, Galen notes that

> this was a matter of dispute from the earliest times; and even now everyone is in disagreement: not only doctors, but philosophers too, some of them applying the term 'disease' to the damage to the activities, others to the dispositions which bring them about. There is nothing surprising about people disagreeing in such obscure matters; but not to diagnose it as a sophistic dispute about terminology is worthy of censure. (*MM* x.79 Kühn)

And a page or so further on, he remarks:

> Not even someone who calls it [sc. the disposition responsible for the impairment of an activity] 'Dion' or 'Theon' will harm the patient by so doing, provided that he applies the right cures. And even if one leaves it entirely nameless, but still administers what is necessary to the patient . . . he will bring about a cure in the best possible way. However, anyone who wishes to teach another what he knows will need at any rate to use some names for things, and will have clarity as his aim in their usage. The best teacher's concern will be to assign names in such a way that the patient can learn in the clearest possible way. And since we are currently engaged in such an activity, it is essential that we assign names to things in some way: that we do so clearly is now our concern. (*MM* x.81)[18]

So, provided we achieve clarity, it doesn't matter how outlandishly we refer to things. But although Galen is officially at least tolerant of barbarism and neologism, generally he champions what he takes to be the ordinary Greek usage:

[18] On this and other passages quoted from *MM*, see my [439] *ad loc.*

we can easily explain what the Greeks mean by the word 'cause'; indeed this is such a trifling matter that no-one brought up as a Greek speaker will be ignorant of its meaning.
(*On Antecedent Causes* (*CP*) VI.55 = *CMG* Supp. II, 14.27–33)

And he will on occasion inveigh against what he takes to be an improper mode of description: take the case of the word *pathos* ('affection'). In its proper, ancient usage, Galen says, it was applied to a change occurring in a body:

However, the more recent ones (I've no idea what they are thinking of) apply the term only to abnormal change. So the term 'affection' was used by the ancients particularly of any kind of change motivated from without; but now, incorrectly, they even call those dispositions that result from affections 'affections'. (*MM* X.89 Kühn)

The word for 'incorrectly' is *katachrōmenoi*: in a sense it is surprising to see Galen making much of an issue out of this, given the unimportance (on his account) of what name you apply to which thing (indeed, elsewhere Galen will occasionally even recommend a catachrestic usage).[19] Why can't the *arrivistes* call such things *pathē* if they feel like it? But this disapproval is not an isolated or anomalous phenomenon. After all, he did write *On the Correctness of Names*; and elsewhere he sometimes legislates linguistic correctness: at *MM* X.602–4, he forbids the application of the term 'ephemeral' to a certain type of fever, on the grounds that it does not necessarily last for twenty-four hours; as he puts it, 'the word *ephēmeros* does not belong to the essence of this sort of fever'. Why should he mind what the fever is called, given his official attitude to naming conventions? There are, I think, two answers to that question; the first ties in with the passage of *MM* we were discussing a moment ago; the second will form a natural bridge to the second part of this paper.

Galen's foremost concern in nomenclature is, as we have seen, clarity of exposition; indeed, were it not for the demands of exposition, naming would be of no concern at all. Galen opens his treatise *On the Differences of Pulses* with the following heartfelt words:

I wish I could learn and teach things without making use of names, so we might avoid the useless fuss over language. (*Diff. Puls.* VIII.493: irritations over language are a constant refrain throughout this work)

But such a utopian ideal is impossible of realisation; in order to communi-

[19] For example in his *Synopsis on the Pulses* IX.457 Kühn (if the work is genuine); cf. *Outline of Empiricism* 7, p. 63 Deichgräber; Galen's *Outline of Empiricism* (*Subfiguratio Empirica*) survives only in a medieval Latin translation (as does *On Antecedent Causes*); it is printed as fragment 10b of Deichgräber [432].

cate we must employ language. Indeed, Galen perhaps even recognises that language is essential for introspective concept formation:

> we use names and linguistic communication generally in order to express the thoughts in our minds that we have gained from an examination of the nature of things. (*PHP* v.724–5)

And one of the factors that bedevils the quest for clarity is the prevalent human tendency to take names as being in some sense disguised descriptions. We are, by psychological bent, Cratyleans; and we are inclined to think that, because a name for an ailment is taken from, or is etymologically connected with, some part of the body (for example), that ailment is necessarily linked with that particular part. This is one aspect of what Galen describes as 'the irregularity of naming' (*MM* x.81–4 Kühn); sometimes the common name for a disease is taken from the part affected, sometimes from the symptoms, sometimes (as in the case of heart-burn) from both, sometimes from the alleged cause, sometimes by analogy with other things ('elephantiasis, satyriasis and priapism'). Even when names are genuinely indicative of features peculiar to the ailment, some names refer to proper differentiae of the disease, while others merely pick out supervenient symptoms; and in some cases quite distinct names are given to the same condition, deriving from different considerations. Galen's discussion of the irregularities of naming is lengthy; but it is pointed, and he at least claims that it is not as lengthy as it might have been:

> there are many other cases of this type: but if I were to run over all of them, I would risk appearing to be concerned about precisely those things I said ought to be passed over, since it is essential for anyone who wants to discover the truth in this matter to try in every way to eschew any additional belief on the basis of the names, and to go straight for the actual substance of things. (*MM* x.84 Kühn)

'Additional belief' translates *prosdoxazomenon*, an important technical term in Epicurean epistemology (*Hdtm.* 50; cf. Lucretius iv.465, 816); for the Epicureans it is *prosdoxazomena* that account for the phenomenon of false belief, going beyond what is immediately given in sensation (which is, notoriously, for the Epicureans invariably veridical). Galen's point is not one in epistemology: but for all that it is exactly parallel to the Epicurean notion. We go wrong, Galen thinks, when we go beyond what we should legitimately rest with in the matter of names, by treating them in effect as though they were descriptions. What he has in mind are arguments such as the following: 'it is impossible for men to suffer from hysteria, since "hysteria" means "connected with the womb" and men have no wombs; hence they cannot be hysterical'. That is not Galen's example;[20] but arguments of that sort certainly flourished in the nineteenth century; and they are plainly fallacious, and inimical to science. And if that particular case seems obviously silly and jejune, it is worth reflecting for a moment on the fact that less obvious, more subtle and deeply hidden forms of the same fallacy continue to infect almost every area of informal argument.

Given all of that, it is clearly better to insist on names which cannot possibly lend themselves to such fallacious purposes. And that provides the first justification for making a fuss, in at least some cases, over what you should properly call things; and it is not surprising that Galen wrote *On the Correctness of Names*.[21]

The second reason for making an issue about naming, at least under certain circumstances, is that properly names should be applied one–one to appropriate classes of things. Galen's conception of the metaphysical structure of the world is a strongly realist one: the world cuts up into properly defined and organised classes; taxonomy is not a creative activity, involving the free and arbitrary creation of classes, but is rather a matter of determining just where as a matter of independent fact the furniture of the world divides. Indeed, the procedure of making the appropriate divisions and arriving by means of that process at definitions of classes is in Galen's opinion one of the central tasks of the scientist, and also the one where the inexperienced and logically inept are most likely to go wrong;[22] Galen talks of

> the many doctors who try either to demonstrate something before having practised in the logical methods, and fall into fallacy, or to divide something into species and differentiae, and then for these reasons, like bad cooks, fail to cut at the joints, but smash them up, crush them, and tear them apart. (*MM* x.123 Kühn)

The metaphor of 'cutting at the joints' is owed to Plato (*Phaedrus* 265e), but it is an apposite one: the structure of the entire world resembles that of an animal just in that there are clear and definite real breaks in its continuity, just as there are clear and definite real structural breaks in the make-up of animals – they have properly defined organs. Galen defines an organ as 'any

[20] For Galenic examples, see *MM* x.81–4.

[21] See above, n. 14. Galen also wrote a treatise *On Medical Terminology*, which survives in an Arabic version, which was edited with a German translation by M. Meyerhof and J. Schacht, in their [453].

[22] See, for example, his *Therapeutics to Glaucon* xi.3–4 Kühn. On the importance and difficulty of constructing proper divisions, see *MM* x.20–7 Kühn; and see my [292], n. 16, *ad loc.*

part of an animal's body which performs a complete activity (*energeia*)'[23] (*MM* x.47 Kühn); thus organs are individuated on the basis of functions; and for Galen what demarcates one natural kind from another is primarily a causal issue. But that is perhaps to trespass on the ground of the next section.

Galen discusses the topic of division, and its Platonic antecedents, in some detail at *PHP* v.752–73;[24] and he refers to the passage of the *Phaedrus* in which Plato invokes the butchering metaphor at v.754. At v.763, Galen remarks that

> divisions may err in two ways, either by not dividing enough, or by making a greater number of divisions than is appropriate to the matter being divided.

And he goes on to claim a Hippocratic authority for this assertion. However, what matters for us is not the authority on which this claim is based, but its implications for the philosophical account of naming. For it entails that, among other things, ordinary language may fail to provide an accurate terminology for classification; it may be either too fine-grained, or too coarse-grained properly to represent the architecture of reality. And in those cases, ordinary language must be supplemented or clarified.

Indeed, it is interesting to note that in his discussion of linguistic ambiguity, *On Linguistic Sophisms* (*Soph.*),[25] Galen adopts precisely this method of division in order exhaustively to classify the ways in which an utterance may be ambiguous, and as such form the raw material for sophistic argumentation.[26] Actually, his aim is broader than that. In effect, *Soph.* is a defence of the Aristotelian account of the *Sophistici Elenchi* (sometimes considered as book 9 of the *Topics*); but in order to conduct this defence successfully, Galen writes:

> since the business before us is to show that linguistic fallacies arise in the same number of ways as Aristotle said in the case of ambiguities, it is clear that we must show two things: (1) that all linguistic fallacies are due to ambiguity, and (2) that there are exactly that number of fallacies due to ambiguity [sc. as Aristotle said]. (*Soph.* xiv.585–6 Kühn = Edlow 92.8–11)

[23] On the notion of an *energeia* in Galen, see the essay '"Use" and "Activity"' in Furley and Wilkie [441], 58–69.

[24] Indeed the whole of the ninth book of *PHP*, v.720–805 Kühn, is devoted to the topic of 'how properly to distinguish between things that are very similar to one another': v.720.

[25] *Soph.* is an early work, dealing with ambiguities in language; an English version with a brief commentary appeared in 1977: Edlow [452]; Catherine Atherton is preparing a new English translation and commentary for the Clarendon Later Ancient Philosophy series.

[26] See n. 27 below.

And the way of doing that consists in showing first what the purpose of language is (it is to signify, on Galen's account: *Soph.* XIV.587–8 Kühn = Edlow XIV.94.16–18); which entails that excellence in language consists simply in signifying well (XIV.587–9 = Edlow 94.11, 16–18, 96.9 ff.). Galen is self-consciously relying on the Aristotelian account of function and excellence, most famously set out in the first book of the *Nicomachean Ethics* (*EN*): if the function of some species *S* is to *F*, then excellence for any member of *S qua S*-member is simply to be capable of *F*-ing well. It follows that badness in language is either (1) a failure to signify at all; or (2) a failure to signify well (XIV.587 = Edlow 94.10–11). However, (1) is properly to be discounted, on the grounds that failure to signify at all debars the utterance from being considered properly as a language at all, just as a man who can't play the flute at all isn't a bad flautist but rather simply *isn't* a flautist (XIV.587 = Edlow 94.13–14). In summary of these doctrines, Galen writes:

> in the case of each thing, its excellence (*aretē*) consists in that in which its essence is; the essence of language is signification, and when this has been destroyed there is no more language. Consequently its excellence consists in this. (XIV.587–8 = Edlow 94.16–18)

Anything else, such as euphoniousness and calligraphy, is merely ornamental window-dressing:

> even if these things seem good to some people, they are not so in virtue of the thing itself, but are as if a sword had an ivory handle, or an eye were wearing mascara. (XIV.587 = Edlow 94.3–5)

Whether Galen is successful in showing, *contra* Empson, that there are only six types of ambiguity need not detain us.[27] However, what is important is the power of his claim that only clarity and freedom from ambiguity are genuine linguistic virtues; anything else is merely incidental. Of the four excellences of language distinguished by Theophrastus: good Greek, clarity, appropriateness and ornamentation,[28] only clarity, or *saphēneia*, is to count (cf. Aristotle, *Rhetoric* III, 2.1404b1–3); Galen specifies that unclarity, *asapheia*, is the linguistic vice *par excellence*: *Soph.* XIV.588–9 = Edlow 96.6–13, cf. 96.7. Consequently, from the point of view of general linguistic excellence, nothing matters except the ability of the sentences in that language to convey transparently and without ambiguity their meaning; and for that, it is necessary only that the words be employed consistently

[27] His attempt takes the form of trying to show that there are only two possible genera of ambiguity, lexical and syntactic, and that each genus has three species, actual, potential and apparent (see Edlow, 76 ff., for an analysis of Galen's argument here); this analysis self-consciously involves the making of divisions.

[28] For the report of Theophrastus, see Cicero, *Orator* 79.

and in a referentially transparent manner. We need to know the referents of the words; and the significance of the operations performed upon them. Everything else is superfluous. Of course, how we can come to know the referents of referring expressions in a language, and, crucially, how we can know that the referring expressions genuinely pick out a properly and naturally demarcated class are another matter; and it will be the subject of the next section. But for Galen, as for Wittgenstein, a great many of the problems of philosophy are pseudo-problems, brought about by carelessness in language use, and lack of attention to definition:

> in order that nothing I say may be misunderstood and that precision and clarity be everywhere present, it is essential that the meaning of every term be accurately defined. Indeed, some of the questions that were earlier deferred are solved by this means ... [for example] whether desire, anger and the like are to be called activities (*energeiai*) or affections (*pathē*). (*PHP* v.506)

Of course, not all ambiguities occur in the referential terms; in the course of a brilliant and incisive stretch of destructive argument against Stoic psychology at *PHP* v.241–61 Kühn, Galen claims that part of the Stoic argument rests on a disguised ambiguity in the preposition *apo* ('out of'): it can mean either 'from the place where' or 'as a (causal) consequence of'; this ambiguity underlies and vitiates the entire argument.[29] But the basic point remains: all fallacies that are not merely invalidities of argumentative form are to be diagnosed as being caused by misuse of language in the course of the argument.

Let us turn now to a more detailed examination of a concrete Galenic case-study of the analysis of concepts. In his treatise *Thrasybulus, or Whether Health is the Province of Medicine or Gymnastics* (*Thras.* v.806–98 Kühn),[30] Galen sets himself the task of determining (as the sub-title might suggest) what professional discipline or *technē*[31] the study of health really belongs to; and this involves determining the precise conception (*ennoia*) that is appropriate to each of the crucial terms, medicine, gymnastics and health (*Thras.* v.807). This involves asking the question

[29] I analyse it more carefully in my [450] and [451].

[30] *Thras.* is edited by G. Helmreich in his [437], 33–100.

[31] The Greek term *technē* is notoriously difficult to translate in these contexts; essentially it is an organised body of knowledge capable of being transmitted, which is conducive to some useful end (that at least is what the Stoics thought: see Sextus, *PH* III.188, 241, 251; *M* I.75, II.10; SVF I.73; II.93–7. Galen stresses the condition of usefulness: see *Protrepticus* I.20 Kühn, where it is a failure to meet this condition that excludes such skills as funambulism and the ability to whirl at high speed without falling over from the canon of *technai*.

> whether health is proper to medicine or to gymnastics; and so when we have said what is signified by these three names, medicine, gymnastics and health, we will need to give an account of a fourth in addition to them, namely what 'proper' means, and what criterion of differentiation we have for this. (v.808)

The issue turns, for Galen, on whether medicine properly comprehends not merely the curing of illness but the preservation of health as well (v.810–11). Galen proceeds to offer provisional definitions of the relative spheres of medicine and of gymnastics: the former, you might say, aims at health, and the latter at good condition (*euexia*; v.811). But such an account would be too hasty; for medicine aims at the *production* of health, not at its preservation or safeguarding (v.811–13), and similarly with gymnastics and *euexia*. But surely if that is right, then there must be two further *technai* which deal with the safeguarding and preservation of health and *euexia* (v.813)? But what if *euexia* is itself a complex concept, involving two quite distinct forms of good condition, one for normal people and the other for athletes: do we not then have six distinct *technai* (v.813–14)? Furthermore, in determining whether medicine has anything to do with the preservation of health, rather than with its production, perhaps we should differentiate between people in robust good health, and those who have recently recovered from some malady, allowing that in the latter case medicine may have a role to play (v.814–15). But Galen then makes a fresh start from the claim that medicine is a knowledge of what is healthy and what is not (v.817), on the general grounds that one branch of knowledge comprehends opposites, and shows how this leads to different results; and he finally shows how, by employing slightly different criteria, one can make the number of *technai* involved seven, or even nine (v.819–21). But such a proliferation is absurd; and Galen begins afresh once more, attempting to show that, appearances to the contrary, health (whether a fragile temporary state or a full-blooded natural condition or *hexis*) and *euexia* (whether of the ordinary person or the athlete) are not separate types of thing, and consequently subject to separate *technai* (v.821–7).

The conditions for identity of health and *euexia* are spelled out at v.824; they are the same if they have the same causes, and secondly if they have the same essence (these conditions are, I take it, severally necessary and jointly sufficient). However, health is not merely a synonym for *euexia*: the latter consists in having a good (*eu*) natural constitution (*hexis*), as the name suggests (here Galen does not, apparently, think etymology a fool's guide); and a *hexis* is a persistent disposition, one that it is hard to break down, and is not (as health can be) merely temporary. The upshot of all this is that *euexia* is a type of persistent good health (v.824–5), and as such differs from it in degree only (as Galen later remarks, differences in degree in subject-matter cannot constitute the basis for a genuine differentiation of *technai*: v.841–2). But every *technē* aims at the good, the complete good, of its single subject-matter (in the Greek jargon it has that good as its target, or *skopos*; and achieving that good is the *telos*, or end, of the activity);[32] the subject-matter in question is the body; that subject-matter is not diverse but unitary; hence there is one *technē* associated with it (v.826–8; cf. 830–2), which aims not at a temporary condition, but at the final good of the subject-matter, namely persistent good condition. Indeed, Galen later sets out to demonstrate that there can be only one *technē* concerned with creation and preservation of the same condition (v.834–5). Against those who would object that there must be further *technai* concerned with the body, namely those that produce strength and beauty and other apparently different and separate properties, Galen replies that such properties are not really distinct from the general property of goodness in a body, but are related to it, either as component parts, or as causes, or 'as so to speak the fruit of it' (v.829; cf. 832–3). Thus it is, ultimately, the causal structure of reality that determines the identity-conditions for single, complete *technai*. This point is reinforced in what follows: it is no good concentrating on what turn out on investigation merely to be subsidiary activities of things (*energeiai kata meros*), and postulating separate *technai* to take care of each of them (v.843–6). Thus what makes a *technē* the unified enterprise it is is its concern with one particular aim, or *skopos* (v.848); and the unity of the *skopos* is secured by the causal unity of the objects of that aim.

I have detailed this argument at length, because of its intrinsic interest, and because of the insight it allows into the complexity and subtlety of Galen's account of how we are to determine whether a particular study is unitary or not; and because of its importance for an understanding of how, for Galen, language relates to facts. Language provides the starting-points for the enquiries, the common conceptions that are related to particular terms (what it is, roughly, that they are commonly taken to refer to); but in the course of the argument one can deviate considerably from what ordinary language explicitly has to say, pushed by considerations of logic, consistency and the meaning of key theoretical terms (such as *technē*, *telos*, and *skopos*). For Galen, then, as for J. L. Austin, ordinary language is not the last word; but it is the first word.

[32] On the distinction between *telos* and *skopos* in Galen, see *CP* VI.57–9 = *CMG* Supp. II, 15.5–27; see my comments *ad loc.* in my forthcoming edition (n. 15 above).

3 Naming and natural kinds

Galen's philosophical interests in naming, and in the topic of the status and determination of natural kinds, are conditioned by his basic concern with therapy. Thus it is not surprising to find his views on the one contained in his great examination of the other, *MM*. In order to appreciate the nature of Galen's account, it will be necessary to glance briefly at his general account of the procedures of science.

Science, at least science properly conceived, for Galen is axiomatic. The models are Euclid's *Elements* and Aristotle's *Posterior Analytics*. Galen firmly denies that any genuine science can or should be tolerant of vaguenesses in its axiomatic structure; if medicine is stochastic, it is so only because of the inadequacies of its practitioners, and the difficulties involved in making precise measurements.[33]

If that is true, then there has to be some way in which the practitioner of science can come to a knowledge of those axioms in their secure logical perfection, if science is to be more than a chimerical enterprise. How is that to be done? Galen holds that there are two sorts of primary and self-evident truths: those that are evident to the senses, and those which are known by the intellect (*MM* X.36–8 Kühn); the empiricists deal only in the first kind; but the rationalist doctor, who wishes to exhibit the deep structure of reality, must avail himself of the second class as well. In a key passage on the methodology of science, Galen writes that the rational doctor should set out

> from starting-points (*archai*) agreed by everyone, and proceed from there to the discovery of the rest. None the less, most of them [sc. the rationalist doctors] fail to do this, but rather adopt disputed starting-points, and instead of first demonstrating them and then proceeding to discover the rest according to the same method, they lay down the law instead of demonstrating. (X.32)

One might think that Galen is here claiming that the actual axioms must be evident and agreed by everyone, a view that would make him one of history's most optimistic epistemologists. The word *archē*, however, is ambiguous; the 'starting-points' here are not the axioms, but items of data

[33] For Galen's views on how, why and where imprecisions enter the science of medicine, see *On the Preservation of Health* (*San. Tu.*) VI.360–1 Kühn (*San. Tu.* is edited by K. Koch in *CMG* V.4.2 (Berlin, 1923)); *MM* X.206, 664–5, 806–7 Kühn; *On Prognosis by way of Pulses* (*Praes. Puls.*) IX.216, 278–9 Kühn; *Plen.* VII.590–1; *On Crises* (*Cris.*) IX.664–5: all these texts stress the idea that it is at the level of practice (the assessment of quantities, the evaluation of conflicting indications, in diagnosis and prognosis) that indeterminacies enter science, not at the level of theoretical structure of the science itself (for a powerful assertion of the latter claim, see the possibly spurious *On the Best Sect* (*Opt. Sect.*) I.114 ff.).

from which we can advance to the axioms. Perhaps the axioms are, in Aristotle's sense, better-known in themselves (*Posterior Analytics* (*An. Post.*) I.2.71b33 ff.; cf. *EN* I.4.1095b2–4): but in order to arrive at them, we have to start from things better known to us. Speaking of geometry, Galen asserts that ultimately we

> arrive at the primary ones [i.e. truths], which derive their justification not from others, or from demonstration, but from themselves.
> (*MM* X.33 Kühn).

When the process of investigation is completed, we can directly intuit that they are self-guaranteeingly true. Now *these* may not be 'agreed by everyone': some of them may even be agreed by nobody. They are what the scientist infers to, taking as a basis the 'starting-points' which are totally distinct in kind.[34]

But what sort of data can be sufficiently secure to constitute indubitable knowledge, and consequently serve as a starting point on the road to demonstratively secure first principles? That question for Galen has implications both in epistemology and philosophy of language; and the two strands are intimately interwoven and hard to disentangle. I shall treat briefly of the epistemological stance first, and then attempt to show, in conclusion, how that stance is intimately bound up with the philosophical account of language whose broad outlines we have been sketching. Galen has little time for Pyrrhonism in epistemological matters: on several occasions he rejects out of hand what he dismissively labels 'rustic Pyrrhonism' (*Diff. Puls.* VIII.711; *de Dignoscendibus Pulsibus* (*Dig. Puls.*) VIII.780–6; *An in Arteriis Sanguis Contineatur* (*Art. Sang.*) IV.727; *de Praenotione ad Epigenem* (*Praen.*) XIV.628). Often this amounts to no more than the bare assertion that we can come to know *via* the senses, as well as the intellect.

However, there is on occasion more to it than just that. Galen calls the senses and the intellect 'natural criteria' (*PHP* V.722–3, 778; *de Optima Doctrina* (*Opt. Doct.*) I.48–9; cf. I.44–7) for judgement; at *PHP* V.725–6, he writes that if there were no natural criteria of this kind, then animals would be incapable of making the sort of judgements they must make in order to preserve themselves; and he holds further that if the criteria were systematically unreliable, then sciences that were based upon them would be

[34] There are parallels with what I take Galen to be describing here and the infuriatingly vague account of the philosopher's ascent to the unhypothesised first principle in Plato's *Republic* VI.509d–11e; crucially in the idea that the properly philosophical geometer treats the hypotheses *as hypotheses* and not as self-evident, only later showing how they have to be true by showing how they derive from the unhypothesised; on this, see Robinson [103].

unreliable as well; but they are not; so the natural criteria cannot be systematically unreliable. This constitutes, I think, a sketch for a profound and interesting attempt at naturalising epistemology. In this context it is worth noting his assimilation of Carneadean Academic epistemology (an epistemology based on the notion of the plausible, *to pithanon*, plus various criteria for testing and evaluating the initial plausibility of impressions)[35] to that of the Stoics[36] (*PHP* v.777–8 Kühn); while such an assimilation might at first sight seem to be a piece of desperate Middle Platonic syncretism, it is perhaps rather the result of a careful analysis of the idea of confirmation, and of the extent to which we can construct a coherence theory of truth based upon our sense-reports on the one hand, plus broadly logical considerations of consistency, similarity and coherence on the other (see *PHP* v.723; and *Opt. Doct.* 1.41–4, on the nature and meaning of *katalēpsis*).[37]

That these criteria are natural, and common to all animals to a certain degree, is of basic importance to Galen's picture. But it is no less important that they can be in a better or a worse condition; and they can benefit from training. Galen's emphasis on the importance of training is ubiquitous in his works. What is important is that he thinks it is of no less value in the case of our perceptual than it is in the case of our intellectual criteria: we must train our intellects in order to be able to make the proper use of dialectic; but equally we must train our senses in order to be able to discern minute differences and hidden similarities. The latter is basic to the scientific enterprise; in a crucial passage of *Dig. Puls.*, VIII.786–806, Galen describes how he discovered the minute trace of the arterial systole in the pulse; he did so partly because theoretical considerations led him to expect there would be one, and so he knew what he was looking for;[38] but he would not have been able to detect it even so had he not trained his faculty of touch to be able to pick out such minute disturbances. And crucially, once discovered, the systole is, in the terminology of Hellenistic philosophers, *enargōs phainomenon*: clearly evident.

[35] See Sextus Empiricus, *M* VII.166–89.

[36] For the Stoics' epistemology, in particular their doctrine of 'graspable apprehensions' (*phantasiai katalēptikai*), see *M* VII.227–62, esp. 248–60; and D.L. VII.54; see also Long and Sedley [308], 241–53. Crudely, the Stoics thought that there were certain kinds of appearance or apprehension which were self-guaranteeingly true, that were, that is, such as to be impossible to be false (although the precise interpretation of this view is a matter of continuing scholarly dispute). On the history of this notion in Hellenistic times, see Frede [392]. See also my [448].

[37] For a defence of this view, see my [448].

[38] If this seems unacceptably un-empiricist, it is worth reflecting on the discovery of the outer planets Neptune and Pluto on the basis of theoretical predictions (even if the discovery of the latter now seems to have been a lucky accident).

I now turn to some passages in which Galen emphasises the generality and naturalness of the criteria as well as the difficulties facing the proper scientific investigator. In the fifth chapter of the book I of *MM*, he writes:

> we derive the meaning of terms from ordinary Greek usage, as I have said in the treatise *On Demonstration*. However, discoveries, investigations and demonstrations of the actual substance of the matter are not drawn from the opinions of the masses, but from scientific assumptions, the manner of whose discovery was elaborated in that work. (*MM* x.42 Kühn)

Galen opens his *On the Diagnosis and Cure of the Errors of the Soul* (*Pecc. Dig.*)[39] with the following words:

> I start with the best starting-point (*archē*), as everyone agrees (even if their actions do not show it), that is, by explaining what the word 'error' means, in order that no ambiguity will remain in the argument as it proceeds, and by showing how all the Greeks generally use the term.
> (*Pecc. Dig.* v.58–9 Kühn)

In the second book of *MM*, Galen returns again to the starting-points of the therapeutic method:

> The goal of the enquiry now before us is to discover cures for every disease. What is the starting-point of the road that leads to this? Knowledge of disease, what kind of thing it is by nature . . . . It is necessary first to discover what the generic and common indication (*endeixis*) of disease is, and then to proceed from there to the specific ones. It is necessary that all diseases are called 'diseases' because they share in one and the same thing, in the same way as man, cow, dog, and each of the other animals.
> (*MM* x.127–8 Kühn)

Ordinary language will usually give us the right names for the classes we need to investigate, in default of accidental and easily discoverable homonymies. Galen discusses briefly the case of 'dog' (*kuōn*), as applied to a land-mammal and to a fish: *MM* x.128–30 Kühn: *kuōn* is homonymous; it picks out both dogs that bark and dog-fish (it also picks out the dog-star, cynic philosophers, the fetlock of a horse, and the *frenum praeputii*; but none of these further complications are relevant here).[40] None the less,

> there is some one unique similar thing in all four-footed animals that bark, namely their being barking quadrupeds. There is also some one unique

[39] *Pecc. Dig.* is edited in Marquardt [435] and in W. De Boer, *CMG* v.4.1.1 (Berlin, 1937).

[40] Galen refers to the ambiguity of *kuōn* at *Soph.* xiv.587 Kühn = Edlow 88.9, 96.10; Edlow (88*, 96*) only refers to the meanings 'dog', 'dog-star' and 'cynic philosopher'; this passage of *MM* indicates that Galen is far more likely to have had its two distinct biological referents in mind.

> similar thing in those wild and predatory sea-creatures which we also call by the name of 'dogs' (*kunes*), but not the same as in their terrestrial homonyms. Thus they do not have anything in common with the nature of dogs [sc. terrestrial dogs] than their designation. (x.128–9 Kühn)

Classification starts from the kinds picked out in ordinary language; we begin from the natural kinds thus demarcated, and only then proceed to discover the actual reasons in nature why the classes divide in the way they do. A ground-floor mistake is made, on Galen's view, by people who think you should first start by dividing into exhaustive and exclusive categories ('rational', 'irrational', 'wild', 'tame', and so forth: x.20–1, 23–6); rather you should begin by enumerating the species:

> if someone were to pass over the differentiae, as indeed they should, and answered 'horse, cow, dog, man, eagle, bee, ant, lion, and sheep', and went on to enumerate all the other animals according to species, clearly this person will have given the right answer to someone who wants to know how many types of animal there are. (x.21–2)

So Galen looks to ordinary language use, and frequently remarks that ordinary Greek speakers are in no doubt whatsoever as to the denotation of the terms they use (see also *MM* x.130–1; and see above, p. 173); anyone who can speak Greek knows what *nosēma* ('disease') means. That basic grasp of the denotation of natural-kind terms is the starting-point from which the scientist can begin to investigate the structure of the classes so denoted; and that denotation is, in some relatively uncontroversial sense, available to any competent speaker of a language. Galen describes the progress of the scientist as follows:

> it was there [i.e. in *On Demonstration*] that I demonstrated that the starting-points (*archai*) of all demonstration are those things which are plainly apparent to the senses and to the intellect, and how in any [sc. scientific] enquiry into the structure of something, it is essential that the names be replaced by definitions. (x.39)

To 'replace a name by a definition' is simply the process of discovering the differentiae of each natural kind, and plugging an account of the differentiae into the places in the argument formerly occupied just by the names; this procedure, properly carried out, will render lucid the causal structure of reality, since, properly determined, the differentiae pick out the causal features in virtue of which each kind differs from another. But the basic tools to enable us to grasp the basic facts about the world from which this analysis can take off are available, to a greater or lesser degree of development, to us all.

Indeed, they are available to other animals besides human beings. In a passage central to the understanding of Galen's epistemology, he asserts that not only do human beings have an intuitive grasp of such natural-kind term denotations, as well as the ability to distinguish between types and the tokens of those types (or as Galen puts it, between forms and individuals); even donkeys, by general consensus the stupidest animals of all, possess it. Children can recognise that different tokens of the letter *alpha* are tokens of the same type, whether they are written on wood, scratched in the earth, or graven in stone (x.132); equally, they recognise that 'horse' and 'camel' and so on are not names, but general sortal terms (cf. Aristotle, *Phys.* I, 1.184a21–b14).

But donkeys are capable of seeing an animal *qua* species (as when they flee camels instinctively), and can do so immediately (x.133–4); but they also recognise individuals as individuals: for they know who their drivers are. Even donkeys, then, can treat one and the same thing at one time *qua* general type, and at another *qua* individual:

> And it is far from being the case that we ought to praise the ancient philosophers for having discovered something great and wise, namely that something can be both the same and different, one and not one, and that it is essential to conceive things not only numerically but also formally, since ... this is something even donkeys can do naturally. (x.134–5)

All animals, in Galen's view, are equipped to recognise natural kinds (or as he would put it, forms or species); if they didn't they wouldn't be able to survive. That recognition is not inductive. Galen despises induction, the simple inferential move from collections of particulars to a general truth, as a means of scientific discovery (see *Thras.* v.812; *de Semine* (*Sem.*) IV.581; *de Simplicium Medicamentorum Temperamentis ac Facultatibus* (*SMT*) XI.469–71), although he will on occasion allow that such methods are suggestive of the truth (see *Soph.* XIV.583 Kühn = Edlow 90.10–16). Neither we, nor the animals, infer to the truth about natural kinds from repeated contact with instances of them (although such contact may be necessary for our knowledge to be created); we are simply caused to have these basic grasps of the world's structure as a result of our brute acquaintanceship with it. Inference, of course, has a place in science: but it comes in, for Galen, after we already know *what* the kinds are; it serves to show us *why* they are as they are.[41]

What has this to do with the philosophy of language? Simply this.

[41] All this owes a great deal to Aristotle, at least Aristotle properly interpreted: see particularly *Met.* I.1, and *Post. An.* II.19; see also *Post. An.* II.1, on definition and knowledge of causes. But I have no space to develop these themes.

Everyone knows what diseases are in the same way as the donkey knows what camels are: that is to say, they can discern them from other things. For human beings, this is associated with the ability to apply their ordinary-language names correctly too. What is relied upon here is a common conception, a *koinē ennoia* (*MM* x.40), of what it is to be sick. The common conception in the case of disease is, according to Galen, that of damage or impediment to a natural activity. This need not be explicit; not everyone perhaps can give the general account of what is as a matter of fact common to the various applications of the term; but none the less, it must be true that there *is* some such general explication available if the term is to function properly as a natural-kind term. Thus if *K* is a natural-kind term, and I am in a position correctly to predicate *K* of all its instances, there must be some objective basis in nature which underwrites that ability; but I need not be consciously aware of it, any more than the donkey needs to be able to know *why* its fear of camels is generally justified.

The scientist's task, then, is to determine what is as a matter of fact the explication that underwrites that application of *K*: that is, what it is for the name to be replaced with a definition in the course of demonstration (x.39). But the scientist, no less than the ordinary man in the street, starts from basic facts of ordinary-language classification, a classification whose general success is guaranteed by basic soteriological facts. We have to be able to get around in the world; part of that getting around is achieved through language; we couldn't do it if our language were systematically and generally misleading about the structure of things. Thus Galen's philosophy of language turns out to be part and parcel of his epistemological and metaphysical realism.

10

Augustine on the nature of speech

CHRISTOPHER KIRWAN

Signs

Augustine's reflections about language can be found in three treatises, *de Doctrina Christiana* (*Doct. Christ.*, A.D. 396–426) on interpreting the Bible, *de Magistro* (*Mag.*, A.D. 389), a dialogue with his son Adeodatus on how and whether teaching is possible, and *de Dialectica* (*Dial.*,? A.D. 387), a fragmentary schoolbook containing prolegomena to logic. The last of these, sometimes referred to as *Principium Dialecticae*, is of disputed authorship; if genuine – and there now seems no strong reason for doubting its authenticity[1] – it will probably be one of the works about which Augustine wrote:

> Of the other five textbooks [*disciplinae*, courses of study] which I also started ⟨at Milan⟩, on dialectic, rhetoric, geometry, arithmetic and philosophy, only the beginnings survived, and I lost even those, though I reckon that some people have them. (*Retractationes* (*Retract.*) 1.5)

The characterisation of language which we find in these three texts is neither original nor profound nor correct. Nevertheless it is appealing, it is bold, and it has had – partly through the wide currency of Augustine's writings – a lasting influence. Augustine's theory is that language is a system of signs:

> A word is a sign of any kind of thing [*verbum est uniuscuiusque rei signum*], which can be understood by a hearer, and is uttered [*prolatum*] by a speaker. A thing is whatever is sensed [*sentitur*] or understood or is hidden [*latet*]. A sign is what shows [*ostendit*] both itself to the senses [*sensui*] and something beyond itself to the mind. To speak is to give a sign by an articulate utterance [*voce*]. By articulate I mean one that can be comprised [*comprehendi*] of letters. (*Dial.* 5.7)

[1] See Jackson's introduction to [467].

> A sign is a thing causing [*faciens*] something else, beyond the impression [*speciem*] which it presents to the senses, to come into thought from it. (*Doct. Christ.* II.1.1)

> All teaching [*doctrina*] is of things [*res*] or signs, but things are learnt through signs. I mean [*appellari*] here *things* in the proper sense, which are not employed for signifying anything [*non ad significandum aliquid adhibentur*]: for example, a log, a stone, a sheep, and the like. I do not mean the log which, as we read, Moses threw into the salt water to remove its salinity [Ex. 15:25] or the stone that Jacob placed at his head [Gen. 28:11] or the sheep that Abraham sacrificed in place of his son [Gen. 22:13] – these are things in such a way as also to be signs of other things. But there are other signs, such as words, whose sole use is in signifying. For no one uses words except for the purpose of signifying something. From this it can be understood what I mean [*appellem*] by signs, viz. things that are employed for signifying something. Hence every sign is also a thing of a kind – for what is not any kind of thing is nothing at all – but not every thing is also a sign. Accordingly in this distinction between things and signs, when we speak of things let us so speak that even if some of them *can* be employed for signifying, that fact is not to stand in the way of the division by which we shall deal first with things and then separately with signs. We must bear in mind that in the case of things we are to consider what they are, not what else they also signify beyond themselves. (*Doct. Christ.* I.2.2)

> One who speaks [*loquitur*] gives forth [*foras dat*] a sign of his will by means of articulate sound. (*Mag.* I.2)

These texts invite us – more or less compellingly – to attribute to Augustine four key propositions:

(1) Speaking is giving signs.
(2) Words are signs given in speech.
(3) A sign is a thing employed for signifying something.
(4) Words are things whose sole employment is for signifying.

The texts leave it unclear so far whether in a passage of speech each separate word is a separate sign; they also leave it unclear whether in the employment of words for signifying the signifying is done *by* the words or only through them by those who speak them. Both these questions get answered in the second chapter of *de Magistro*:

> AUGUSTINE: Are we agreed then that words are signs?
> ADEODATUS: We are.
> AUG: How can a sign be a sign unless it signifies something?
> AD: It cannot.

AUG: How many words are there in this verse?

Si nihil ex tanta superis placet urbe relinqui

[If it please the gods that nothing should be left from this great city, Virgil *Aeneid* II.659]

AD: Eight.

AUG: Then there are eight signs.

AD: Yes. (*Mag.* II.3)

So we can add:

(5) Every word is a sign;
(6) every sign signifies something.

In asserting (5) Augustine joins an ancient debate: mainline Stoicism had agreed with him, whereas Aristotle had earlier held that certain words, such as 'every' (*de Interpretatione* 10.20a13), only consignify – contribute to the significance of a larger whole – and certain others, such as prepositions (*Poetics* 20.1456b38 ff.) do not signify at all.

Indicative and representative signs

The word 'signum' had two main senses in classical Latin, 'indication' and 'representation', both of them common. In the former sense Cicero can ask whether the gods give signs of future events (*de Divinatione* I.82–3); in the latter Lucretius speaks of 'brazen signs' – statues – by the city gates, whose right hands are worn from the touch of passers-by (*de Rerum Natura* I.318). Although I shall call these indicative and representative signs, the distinction is of two senses of the word for 'sign', not two kinds of sign: for many things are signs in both senses, as with those roadsigns which indicate an approaching feature by depicting it.

The thousand or so years of philosophy before Augustine had seen much theorising and debate about indicative signs,[2] for which the Greek word was '*sēmeion*'. '*Sēmeion*' and its cognates such as '*sēmantikē*' were not used in the other Latin sense 'representation' (nor, I think, was the Latin 'significare', unlike the English 'signify'). So it will not be surprising if Augustine's definition of 'signum', drawing on what he had learned in the 'secular schools' (*Doct. Christ.* IV.1.2), should likewise ignore the sense 'representation'. And that is what we find in the passages quoted above, where there is nothing about representing: a sign, he says in his definitions, causes something beyond itself to come into thought (*Doct. Christ.* II.1.1), and shows something beyond itself to the mind (*Dial.* 5.7). Let us call 'indication' the philosophical sense of the word. Indicative signs can be subdivided into

[2] See Sedley [333].

evidence, for example of Napoleon's being dead, and reminders, for example of Napoleon; I have not found this subdivision in Augustine, but it may underlie the garbled account in Sextus (*Outlines of Pyrrhonism* II.101–2, *adversus Mathematicos* (*M*) VIII.152–3) of 'indicative' (*endeiktika*) and 'commemorative' (*hupomnēstika*) signs.

The definitions of 'signum' that we have found in *de Dialectica* 5.7 and *de Doctrina Christiana* II.1.1 are actually wrong, for both of them ignore the existence of undetected signs. For example, a reddish discolouration of the hair called kwashiorkor is an indicative sign – evidence – of protein deficiency. If in some sufferer this sign goes unnoticed or, though noticed, the protein deficiency is not diagnosed from it, then the sign fails to 'cause' the deficiency to come into thought, and fails to 'show' it to anyone's mind. But it is a sign no less. I think that Augustine is not misled by the error he makes here; and I shall assume that when he speaks of 'signa' he normally means the word in its ordinary philosophical sense of 'indication'.

It is of prime importance to recognise, however, that Augustine's sign theory of speech does *not* employ the non-philosophical sense of the Latin word, 'representation'. The evidence for this has been deployed in the last few paragraphs, and seems to me decisive: the philosophical tradition which he inherited, being Greek, ignored that sense; and his own definitions are obviously intended to stand in the tradition. I do not need to deny, of course, that outside the theory of speech he may sometimes have intended the non-philosophical sense, as perhaps for example when he reminds his congregation that Christ's sign, the sign of the cross, is 'fixed' in the forehead of every baptised Christian (for example *Enarr. Ps.* 30 [Heb. Bib. 31].4.7).

There are powerful twin temptations to read Augustine's sign theory anachronistically as asserting that words are representative signs: first, that would be the right way – the obvious way – to understand such an assertion in modern English (or, I dare say, modern Latin), and secondly, the theory so understood has much more initial plausibility. Indeed the proposition that words represent is not only plausible but true, provided that it is qualified doubly: both so as not to apply to all words and groups of words, but only to referring expressions and certain kinds of sentence; and also so as not to carry the implication which in *my* use I intend 'represent' to carry, that what is represented is modelled or pictured – that is, the structures contained within the represented thing are matched by structures within its representation. But then we are in a dilemma. On the one hand the implication, if it *is* present, delivers a false theory, the 'picture theory' of language once held, and later convincingly demolished, by Wittgenstein. Whereas alternatively, once the implication and the claim to generality are dropped, what remains is too weak to be interesting: 'represent' applied to speakers or to words comes to say no more than 'mean', leaving, as we shall see and as all modern discussions of language acknowledge, the serious work still to be done in explaining what meaning is. In any case, whether interesting or not the representation theory is not Augustine's, and we can conclude that for him:

(7) 'Sign' means 'indication'.

What is signified?

In order to complete the outline statement of Augustine's theory we need now to ask what kinds of thing words signify. Augustine gives divergent answers. On the one hand, his general remarks about signs in the passage already quoted from *de Doctrina Christiana* suggest that words will regularly signify external objects – the same kind of thing as Moses' log specially signified (in that case, Augustine thinks, the cross of Christ); and this is confirmed in a later passage of the *de Magistro* (4.8) when we learn that the nouns (*nomina*) '*Romulus*', '*Roma*' and '*virtus*' signify respectively Romulus, Rome and virtue. On the other hand we have already found Augustine asserting that a speaker may give a sign of his *will* (*Mag.* I.2); just so

> banners and standards impart [*insinuant*] through the eyes the military leaders' will, and all these things are, as it were, a sort of visible word ... Words ⟨themselves⟩ have acquired complete dominance among men for signifying anything conceived in the mind that anyone may wish to communicate [*prodere*]. (*Doct. Christ* II.3.4)

This rival suggestion that words signify thoughts and wills, not external objects, is a natural corollary of the view that thoughts are *conveyed* by words. Locke was to make the connection:

> The Comfort, and Advantage of Society, not being to be had without Communication of Thoughts, it was necessary, that Man should find out some external sensible Signs, whereby those invisible *Ideas*, which his thoughts are made up of, might be made known to others. For this purpose, nothing was so fit, either for Plenty or Quickness, as those articulate Sounds, which with so much Ease and Variety, he found himself able to make. Thus we may conceive how *Words*, which were by Nature so well adapted to that purpose, come to be made use of by Men, as *the Signs of* their *Ideas*; not by any natural connexion, that there is between particular articulate Sounds and certain *Ideas*, for then there would be but one Language amongst all Men; but by a voluntary Imposition, whereby such a Word is made arbitrarily the Mark of such an *Idea*. The use then of Words, is to be sensible Marks of *Ideas*; and the *Ideas* they stand for, are their proper and immediate Signification.
> (*Essay* 3.2.1; cf. Hobbes, *Leviathan*, part 1, chapter 4)

We shall gradually discover that Augustine agrees with most of this. What is now relevant is that he agrees that words were instituted for bringing thoughts (*cogitationes*) to another's notice (*Enchiridion* (*Ench.*) 20.7, quoted on p. 198 below). Suppose that on some occasion you told me what you were thinking: then

> The sound of your syllables delivered [*perduxit*] your thought to my ear, and through my ear your thought [*cogitationem tuam*] descended into my heart. (*Tractatus in Johannem Evangelistam* (*Ev. Joh.*) VIII.37.4).

At one place Augustine even calls the transferred item a 'significatio', which is given by the speaker to his words and conveyed (*deportaret*) to the hearer through the hearer's ears (*de Quantitate Animae* (*Qu. An.*) 32.66).

There is thus an important unclarity at the core of Augustine's theory of language, which we can record as follows:

(8) Words convey thoughts, but it is unclear whether Augustine means that words signify the thoughts they convey or the things which are the subject-matter of those thoughts (or both).

We shall find that the former alternative more naturally fits groups of words, such as sentences, the latter single words, such as names.

Given signs

More needs now to be said about proposition (2), that words are signs given in speech.

Book I of *de Doctrina Christiana* has discussed the teaching of things; book II turns to the teaching of signs. Not all signs are to be considered, but only 'given signs'. Here is how these are differentiated:

> Among signs, some are natural, some given. The natural ones are those which, without a will or any kind of urge [*appetitu*] to signify, cause [*faciunt*] something else beyond themselves to be recognised [*cognosci*] from them. An example is smoke signifying fire, which it does [*facit*] without willing to signify; rather by observation of and attention to familiar phenomena [*rerum expertarum*] it is recognised that there is fire lurking, even if only smoke is apparent. The track of a passing animal belongs to this kind; and a face will signify the state of mind of someone who is angry or sad, even without any will on the part of the angry or sad person ... Given signs are those which living things give among themselves for demonstrating, so far as they are able, the impulses of their mind, or whatever it may be that they have sensed or understood. There is no reason [*causa*] for our signifying – that is, giving a sign – except to express [*depromendum*] and transmit to someone else's mind what is going on in the mind of him who gives the sign. (*Doct. Christ.* II.1.2–II.2.3)

This passage invites several criticisms, most but not all of which can readily enough be turned aside by a friendly interpretation. First, Augustine's labels 'natural' and 'given' are misleading in suggesting that he divides signs according to whether they originate from inanimate or animate things. The basis of his division is actually quite different, for a sign made by a living thing, as for example a footprint, even if made deliberately, as for example a campfire, will be natural in Augustine's sense if it is not intended as a sign of that of which it is a sign. Hence natural as opposed to artificial *origin* is not necessary for membership of Augustine's first class of signs. Conversely his given signs include less than the word 'given' suggests, and not only by excluding, as we have just seen, signs given but not meant to signify: they also exclude some things meant to signify, and so given *as* signs. For Augustine is simply wrong to assert that the only reason for anyone's giving a sign is to transmit the contents of his mind. I might shout as a sign of my presence, or walk along a chalked line as a sign of sobriety. Sundials and clocks give signs of the time without having minds to transmit the contents of. These cases do not fit under Augustine's definition of given signs. So the fact that a sign originates by being given, or even given as a sign, is not sufficient for membership of his second class.

Secondly, if we go by the letter of Augustine's definitions in *de Doctrina Christiana*, given signs do not need to be signs. For signs must succeed in 'causing' something further to come into thought (II.1.1, and compare the requirement on natural signs that they cause recognition), while given signs need only be meant to cause this. Even if we go, more reasonably, by the ordinary philosophical sense of 'signum' as 'indication', there is a gap between something's being meant to indicate and its doing so. Two conceptions of a given sign thus seem to contend in Augustine's text, that of an indication which is given and that of something which is given as an indication.

Thirdly, in defining a natural sign Augustine slides from the requirement that *there is no will* to signify to the weaker requirement that *it*, the sign, does not will to signify. The latter would allow a sign to be at the same time both natural and given. For example, if before leaving my burning bedroom I open the window in order to show neighbours by the issuing smoke that there is fire inside, then although the smoke does not will to signify fire, I do. Since I do, the smoke that issues from my window will apparently count for Augustine as a given sign – I give it to my neighbours for demonstrating something I have sensed – even though it also counts as a natural sign if it succeeds in the purpose I assign it of causing recognition of something beyond itself, without *its* willing to do so. By the same argument all words will be not only given but also natural signs whenever they succeed in the purposes which, as given signs, are allegedly assigned to them by their speakers. Here we should surely respond on Augustine's behalf by revising his definition of natural signs to exclude all signs intended as such.

Fourthly, Augustine makes a false – though only incidental – contrast ('rather', 'sed') between one thing's willing to signify another and one thing's causing recognition of another by 'attention to familiar phenomena', that is, by constituting inductive evidence. Given signs too are often inductive evidence: if I cough discreetly with the object of giving you a sign of my presence in a room where you think you are alone, your recognition of my sign depends no less on learned correlations and experience of causal connections than it would do if, intending no sign but rather bent on concealment, I let slip an inadvertent hiccup. It is possible that Augustine is influenced at this point by the fact that *verbal* signs are non-natural in a different sense, noticed by Locke in the passage quoted above: *viz.* that their *being signs* – their constituting evidence of the things they are signs of – arises through 'arbitrary' imposition (sustained, in the normal case, as a convention). But aside from the fact that not all given signs are arbitrary in Locke's sense (or conventional) – something noticed by Jackson[3] – even the arbitrary ones will be recognised only by people whose ability to recognise was learned in ordinary inductive ways.

In spite of all these difficulties, I think there emerges from this passage of *de Doctrina Christiana* a fairly definite account of the way in which, according to Augustine, words are signs. They are given signs in the sense that a speaker gives them to demonstrate or reveal some further thing beyond themselves. In order to be so given they do not, in fact, need to be signs in Augustine's official sense of causing the further thing to come into thought; but they do need to be given *as* signs in that official sense. Unclarity remains over the ordinary philosophical sense of 'sign', *viz.* 'indication'. Augustine's given signs *need* not be signs even in that sense; but they normally will be so (you do not normally give as an indication what is not an indication), and it is hard to suppose, in view of his confident use of the word, that he thought they would ever not be. As to what they are signs of, the description 'impulses of the mind, or whatever it may be that ⟨living things⟩ have sensed or understood' still leaves us in the dark whether Augustine means to specify mental contents, or admits external objects too among the things signified by words.

Finally, the fact that at least some of the things signified by given signs are mental – 'impulses of the mind' – can be used to show that Augustine thought that given signs, at least when they qualify as signs in the

[3] See Jackson [470], 97.

philosophical sense, qualify by falling under the sub-head of evidence rather than that of reminders (they are *endeiktika*, not *hupomnēstika*). He says that living things give signs for demonstrating the impulses of the mind 'so far as they are able'. Minds, he generally assumes, are inner and opaque, difficult things to expose; and he would surely have agreed with Locke that if exposure is to be achieved it is 'necessary ... to find out' devices for the purpose. If so, the role of those signs which someone gives of his mental impulses will be not to remind observers of them but to make them evident to observers. Given signs will be given as evidence – and, we are assuming Augustine infers, will therefore at least normally *be* evidence. Thus his account in *de Doctrina Christiana* seems to commit him to the view that all given signs are, or at least are meant as, evidence; and since, by (2) and (5), all words are given signs, he is committed to the view that all verbal signs are, or at least are meant as, evidence.

Sentences

We are now in a position to embark on an assessment of Augustine's theory. I shall start with the propositions numbered (1) and (2) above, that speaking is giving signs and that words are signs given in speech. I shall not yet hold Augustine to his strong claim (5) that *every* word is a sign, but shall first consider the more modest and more plausible view that words are signs at least when taken together in suitable groupings. We shall find that even the modest view is indefensible; and we shall then have to ask whether anything can be salvaged from this part of the theory.

The reason why it is more plausible to describe groups of words than individual words as signs is only partly that, as will later appear, some classes of individual words – for example prepositions – are recalcitrant. More importantly, we have seen that Augustine appears to be committed to the view that verbal signs are evidential; and what is signified by an evidential sign always can, and often must, be identified not as a thing (for example a passing animal) but as a purported fact (for example that an animal has passed). This is a perfectly general fact about evidence; and it has the consequence for a theory of speech that the best candidates for being evidential verbal signs are to be found among those groups of words – they are rarely single words – which constitute sentences: for example, a good candidate for being an evidential verbal sign of a recently passing animal would be the English sentence 'An animal has recently passed.' In this section, therefore, we are to test Augustine's theory as it applies to sentences.

It will be convenient to work with a single illustrative sentence, labelling it 'S':

S Your grandmother was in Brussels.

Augustine's theory does not demand any particular answer to the questions 'What is S a sign of?' and 'What does S signify?' In fact, there is no reason why he should not allow S to be a sign of anything whatever, because words are of arbitrary imposition; and even if we assume – as he invariably does – that our sentence is used in conversation between people who know and observe the conventions of the language to which it belongs, the answers to the questions may depend on who is addressing whom, which of the addressee's two grandmothers is referred to, and what time-period is referred to. (Actually I suspect that Augustine would give multiple answers to the second question, 'What does S signify?' but a single answer to the first question, 'What is S a sign of?': *viz.* 'S is a sign of *all* the things it ever signifies, or all the things it can signify'; for at *de Magistro* 4.10 he implies about the noun 'signum' that it is a sign of *all* signs. If so, signifying, for a word, is not the same thing as being a sign, despite proposition (6) above; rather, they are related as gardening is related to being a gardener, or drilling, for a drill, is related to being a drill: S's being a sign of X will be a disposition or capacity activated when S signifies X, just as being a drill is a disposition or capacity activated when the drill is drilling.) Let us further assume, then, that what S signifies does vary from one utterance of it to another, and let us reduce – with luck eliminate – the variability by specifying a context C in which speaker, grandmother and date have all been identified – let us say: me, the Queen and VE Day.

What, then, does Augustine's theory entail about an utterance of S in context C? We are confining indications to evidence; but because of the clash between the ordinary philosophical notion of a sign ('indication') and Augustine's special definition of given signs in *de Doctrina Christiana* ('something intended as an indication'), and because of the doubt recorded in proposition (8) above about signifying things outside the mind, there are two uncertainties generating four basic interpretations of how the sign theory applies to S:

(9) In C, S is intended by me as evidence that I believe that the Queen was in Brussels on VE Day.
(10) In C, S is intended by me as evidence that the Queen was in Brussels on VE Day.
(11) In C, S is evidence that I believe that the Queen was in Brussels on VE Day.
(12) In C, S is evidence that the Queen was in Brussels on VE Day.

For each of (9)–(12) it is possible to think of circumstances (consistent with C) which show it, and so the interpretation of the theory it applies, to be false. For example, against (9): I will not intend S as evidence that I believe that the Queen was in Brussels on VE Day if I utter it to the empty air, or expecting to be taken as romancing. Against (10): I will not intend S as evidence that she was there then if I know that my hearer already knows whether she was and is testing me. Against (11): S will not be evidence that I believe she was there then if I utter it on the stage or in my sleep. Against (12): S will not be evidence that she was there then if I am known to be a liar, or known to be misinformed about the period. And against all four there is this vital fact: S may occur 'embedded' in some longer linguistic unit which is not an assertion, or at any rate not an assertion of S; for example it may be followed by a further sentence, 'So says my guidebook, but it is unreliable', or appended to a prefix, 'It is not true that'. On the other hand if Augustine's theory proposed that in such cases S has a different signification from any of (9)–(12), it is hard to see what that would be. S with its context C was an example, meant as a basis for generalisation. These objections show that there is no way in which generalisation from S to all similar sentences can yield a true theory, on any of the four interpretations (9)–(12). We do not need, therefore, to consider whether the sign theory would work for dissimilar sentences, such as interrogatives.

What, if anything, can be salvaged? Discussing lying in the *Enchiridion* Augustine wrote:

> And undoubtedly, words were instituted among men not so that men should deceive one another by means of them but so that anyone might bring his thoughts [*cogitationes*] to another's notice by means of them. Therefore to use words for deceit, not for the purpose for which they were instituted, is a sin. (*Ench.* 22.7)

The claim made here is different from, and importantly narrower than, the claim made by the sign theory under any of interpretations (9)–(12). For in the *Enchiridion* passage Augustine does not assert that a speaker's words *are* evidence of his thoughts, let alone of purported facts, or even are intended by him as evidence of either of those things; rather, giving evidence of thoughts (bringing to notice) is what speech is *for*. The claim is still bold, surely too bold, since like most activities speech has multifarious purposes, some of which, such as promising, need not go through exposure of the speaker's mind (promising is also a counter-example to the weaker claim made at *de Magistro* 1.1 that 'in speech we aim at nothing but to teach', i.e. inform, or, he later adds, remind). Nevertheless, given a suitably wide sense of 'thought' the *Enchiridion* claim will cover a great part of the human activity of speech: think how often one could append to a sentence 'That's what I think/feel/want/want to know.' Now, the question may be raised about this central purpose: how does speech manage to achieve it? And that question is so abstruse and difficult that it will not be surprising if examination of it obscures, and enquirers into it wrongly deny, the fact that not all speech even aims to achieve such a purpose. What the new question really asks is this: given that speakers often do have the central purpose, of 'demonstrating an impulse of their mind', 'giving forth a sign of their will' and the like, and given that the purpose is often achieved, by what means is it achieved? Perhaps the use of language begins to look like magic, but it cannot really be magic. What is the secret? Well, one requirement of successful mind-exposure by speech will be that the hearer of the speech should trust the speaker to have the mind-exposing intention which (in the kind of case we are considering) he does have; but that is not difficult to grasp – trust is natural. The other requirement is that the hearer should *understand* the speaker's utterance. What is needed, then, is an account of understanding speech.

This is not the place to attempt even a sketch of such an account, but a few remarks may help to relate it to Augustine's unsuccessful theory. Understanding an utterance – for example S in C – is indeed a case of recognising the utterance as a sign, but not as a sign of the speaker's belief – for example of my belief that the Queen was in Brussels on VE Day – let alone of the purported fact purportedly believed – that she was there then. Rather, the hearer understands S (i.e. the speaker's utterance of S) in C when he recognises S as a sign of a certain *intention* which the speaker must have had if there is anything to be understood; and the intention is what the speaker *meant* by S in C (in the case of S, what the speaker meant by it in C was that the Queen was in Brussels on VE Day). So the final stage in accounting for the hearer's understanding of S in C will be to analyse what it is in general for a speaker *u* to mean by a sentence *s* that *p*. But by this point we have evidently moved a long way from Augustine.

Words

So far we have examined the application of Augustine's sign theory only to sentences. Although in Latin it is comparatively easy to construct single-word sentences ('ambulavi' – 'I went for a walk', 'precabantur' – 'they used to pray', 'i' – 'go') nevertheless most Latin words, of course, cannot function as sentences on their own, and even those that can usually do not. Consequently proposition (5), that every word is a sign, needs different arguments in its defence from any we have yet considered.

To be sure, one might attempt to extend Augustine's theory about sentences by stages into a theory about single words. Suppose, for example, that Augustine accepts interpretation (10) of the significance of sentence S in context C, and suppose he is then asked what the predicate-component of S, 'was in Brussels', signifies in C. One way of answering would be to indicate the contribution made by 'was in Brussels' to the significance of S as a whole, as might be done like this: in C, *any* sentence 'A was in Brussels' is evidence that the speaker believes that *anything* B was in Brussels on VE Day, if and only if 'A' names B. By further stages the contributions made by the elements within 'was in Brussels' could then be isolated similarly. This kind of explanation (characteristic of modern truth-theories of meaning) takes sentences as the minimum units of significance: parts of sentences do not signify anything but only contribute, in a rule-governed way, to the significance of the sentence in which they are parts (some parts of sentences must, however, *name*).

There is a hint of this procedure in the first answer which Adeodatus gives in *de Magistro* to Augustine's question about the line he has quoted from Virgil, 'If it please the gods that nothing should be left from this great city'. The question is, 'What does each word in the line signify?', and about the first word 'if' ('si') Adeodatus says: 'It seems to me that 'if' signifies doubt; and where is doubt if not in the mind?' (*Mag.* 2.3). Perhaps the suggestion is: the line as a whole is evidence of its speaker's doubt whether a certain purported fact obtains; and the contribution of 'if' is to make the line evidence of *doubt* whether it obtains rather than, say, belief that it does. However, the suggestion is not pursued, and Adeodatus' next answer, though reverting eventually to something similar, at first proceeds differently.

The second word in Virgil's line is 'nihil' – 'nothing'. Adeodatus says: 'What can "nothing" signify except what is not?' (*ibid.*). At once he and Augustine find themselves in trouble: signifying what is not is signifying nothing; but if 'nothing' signifies nothing, according to propositions (5) and (6) it is not a word.

Adeodatus seems to have been attracted to this troublesome second answer by some such principle as the following: when a word is put for the two occurrences of 'A' in the formula '"A" signifies A', the result will always come out true provided that it is capable of truth. The proviso is important, and doubtless explains why Adeodatus did not apply the principle to 'if'; for '"If" signifies if' is not capable of truth – it is not a complete sentence. The cases for which the proviso *is* fulfilled are, roughly speaking, the cases in which 'A' is replaced by a name. So the principle can be reformulated as *'"A" signifies A' is the right formula for the significance of names.*

It is clear that in return for now assessing Augustine on his full statement that every word is a sign we shall have to abate the charge that by signs he means evidence. And it is only reasonable to do so, despite the fact that a word such as 'Brussels' in sentence S could be supposed to offer evidence for a mental state, *viz.* that the speaker is thinking of Brussels, has Brussels in mind. Adeodatus' formula would exclude this reading, because it requires the word to be evidence not of a mental state at all, but of Brussels; and what could that mean – evidence that Brussels exists, evidence that it is present? The suggestions are absurd. On the other hand reminding, which is also a feasible way of being an indicative sign, is precisely the relation needed for constructing a legitimate application of Adeodatus' formula to words like 'Brussels'. Among the many descriptions that come to mind of the relation between 'Brussels' and Brussels some are unhelpful ('means', 'names', 'denotes', 'designates'), some wrong ('stands for' in the sense 'takes the place of', 'represents' in the sense 'depicts'); one that is both right and helpful is 'refers to', where what it means to say that 'Brussels' refers to Brussels (for example in sentence S in context C) is

'Brussels' is intended to bring to mind Brussels.

It is not possible, as Augustine saw, to bring to a person's mind by naming it something which was never in his mind before ('perception of the signification [of words] ... occurs not by hearing the vocal sounds [*vocum*] uttered, but by recognition [*cognitione*] of the things signified', *Mag.* 11.36). The bringing to mind that is intended by utterance of a word such as 'Brussels' is therefore bringing back to mind, reminding, and the truth that 'Brussels' refers to Brussels can readily be understood as identical with the corresponding application of Adeodatus' Principle, that is, as identical with the proposition that 'Brussels' signifies Brussels.

In *de Dialectica* and *de Magistro* Augustine argues that this application can be extended to all single words. The argument is from two premises:

(13) Adeodatus' Principle can be extended to all names;
(14) all words are names;
therefore Adeodatus' Principle can be extended to all words.

But we shall have to conclude that (13) is false and (14), though true in a way, would not support the argument.

Names

What is a name? Augustine seems to have accepted a criterion which, owing its origin (so far as we know) to Plato's *Sophist* (262a), had been developed over the succeeding 700 years in the hazy tradition of ancient grammar (from which little survives complete before the Latin grammar of Priscian, from the early sixth century A.D.). In this classification names, *nomina*, comprised all that we call nouns, including adjectives, and often also pronouns. Among the examples of names cited by Augustine are (put into English) 'Romulus', 'Rome', 'virtue', 'silver', 'river' and 'great'. I have already mentioned the first three; they and also 'silver' fit Adeodatus' Principle neatly, since each is (in correct usage) a referring expression and each refers (in a context of correct usage) to one of the things so named, 'Romulus' to Romulus, and so on. Difficulties begin with the common noun 'river' ('fluvius', *Mag.* 4.8). Augustine never suggests that 'river' and its like are signs of the *class* of rivers and their like (the 'extension' of the name): as we have seen, the word is a sign of *rivers*, all of them. Thus the application of Adeodatus' Principle to 'river' will presumably yield: in any context of correct usage, 'river' signifies some (one) river. Given our understanding of 'signifies' as 'refers', this application is always wrong for English, which requires combination with some other word, minimally 'the', if a common noun is to refer to some member of its extension; Latin, however, lacking articles, could use 'fluvius' thus on its own. Nevertheless even in Latin a common noun can also appear in combinations where it does not refer to a member of its extension: for example, in the phrases 'nullus fluvius' – 'no river' or 'omnis fluvius' – 'every river' there is no river which the word 'fluvius' – or indeed the phrase as a whole – serves to bring to mind (which river would it be – the Danube?). The same is true of predicative combinations, as in 'the Danube is a river'. These cases call for a distinction among names which grammar may be able to do without but a theory of signs cannot: perhaps the distinction between singular terms and universal terms that underlies Aristotle's syllogistic logic, or the distinction between subjects and predicates that underlies Frege's quantificational logic. By building on such a distinction we may then also be able to explain names like 'nihil' – 'nothing' and 'nemo' – 'nobody', the initial troublemakers for Adeodatus' Principle in *de Magistro* and a source of philosophical teasing ever since Homer's story of Cyclops (*Odyssey* IX.366, 408).

Augustine fails, then – and in the case of 'nihil' hardly tries – to show that Adeodatus' Principle is satisfied by all names in his generous acceptation of the word 'name'. In the 1940s Gilbert Ryle detected and castigated in Carnap what he called the 'Fido'–Fido principle, that 'signify' in its modern sense of 'mean' states a relation which holds from every expression to 'some extra-linguistic correlate to the expression, like the dog that answers to the name "Fido"'.[4] So far as that principle applies to names its recorded history begins, I fear, with Augustine.

A passage from *de Dialectica* on the vices of *obscuritas* and *ambiguitas* will serve both to confirm the failure of proposition (13) and to introduce our examination of proposition (14):

[4] Ryle [527], 226.

> Let us suppose that ⟨a teacher in class⟩ has said 'Great' ['magnus'] and then stopped. Notice what uncertainties result from hearing that name. Perhaps he is going on to say. 'What part of speech is it?', or perhaps, 'What [metrical] foot?', or perhaps he is going on to ask a question in history, 'Great Pompey fought how many wars?', or to make a remark in literary criticism, 'Great, almost unique, is Virgil's contribution to poetry', or to deliver a rebuke to a lazy pupil with, 'Great idler that you are'. You can see, I expect, that when the fog of obscurity has been dispelled, the word said above stands out like a junction of many roads. For that single thing that was said, Great, is both a name and also a trochaic foot and also Pompey and also Virgil and also an idler; and numberless other things not mentioned, that are capable of being understood through utterance of the word. (*Dial.* 8.15)

'Great', being an adjective, already counts as a name by Augustine's relaxed criterion, and therefore is supposed by him to be a sign of all great things just as, I remarked earlier, 'sign' is supposed to be a sign of all signs (and 'river' of all rivers). The new point that needs to be noticed is that also among the things 'capable of being understood through utterance of the word' is, according to Augustine, the word itself, which is 'a name and a trochaic foot'. If a modern pupil wrote 'Great is a name', giving the Augustinian answer to Augustine's first question, 'What part of speech is it?', he would be taught to enclose 'Great' in its own further quotation marks in order to indicate that the word was being mentioned (a convention I have myself scrupulously observed in this article; there was no comparable device in ancient writing). Some twentieth-century philosophers hold that *mention* of a word excludes *use* of it. But Augustine's reasonable view is that what we would call quotation-mark utterances mention a word *by* using it. Thus the word occurs in such utterances; and what it signifies in them is itself.

This doctrine conflicts with the requirement in Augustine's definitions of 'sign' that signs 'show something *beyond* themselves' (*Dial.* 5.7, p. 188 above; see also *Doct. Christ.* II.1.1, p. 189 above). Nevertheless he labours the doctrine in both *de Dialectica* and *de Magistro*. It is not quite clear why so much effort is spent on it. There is some evidence that Stoics had used it as a basis on which to defend the paradox that all words are ambiguous (attributed by Augustine to 'the dialecticians', and endorsed by him, *Dial.* 9.15, see also *Mag.* 8.22). In the early chapters of *de Magistro* we find it playing a part in a series of curious arguments in defence of proposition (14).

Augustine has begun by denying (14): in the lines from Virgil '"If" ["si"] ... and "from" ["ex"] ... are words yet not names; and many such are found' (*Mag.* 4.9). But later he undertakes to show otherwise:

> AUGUSTINE: Utter a few conjunctions for me, any you like.
> ADEODATUS: 'And', 'too', 'but', 'also' [the Latin is 'et que at atque'].

> AUG: Don't you think that all these you have said are names?
> AD: Not at all.
> AUG: But at least you think that I spoke correctly to you in saying 'All these you have said.'
> AD: Quite correctly; and now I understand to my surprise that you have shown that I did utter names; for otherwise one could not rightly say of these, 'All these'. (*Mag.* 5.13)

'These' ('haec') is a pronoun referring to 'and','too', etc.; and in the preceding lines pronouns (*pronomina*) have been classified among names (*nomina*). At first sight, therefore, Augustine's case appears to be the preposterous one that 'and', 'too', etc. must be names because it is possible to refer to them by name. The real case is deeper, and emerges from details of the preceding passage:

> AUG: I believe you have accepted and will agree that a so-called pronoun, which does the work of the name itself [*pro ipso nomine valeat*], nevertheless denotes [*notet*] a thing with less full signification than the name does. This is how your grammar teacher defined it, I think: a pronoun is a part of speech which, put in place of the name itself [*pro ipso posita nomine*], signifies the same as it, although less fully. (*Mag.* 5.13)

So the reasoning is:

(15) what pronouns are put in place of are names;
(16) in the exchange quoted, 'these' was put in place of 'and', 'too', etc.;
therefore 'and', 'too', etc. are names.

Such conjunctions, he is arguing, are names because it is possible to use *themselves* to refer to them.

There follows a sound demonstration that at 2 Cor. 1:19 Paul must be understood as using 'is' ('est', Greek '*nai*' meaning 'yes') as a name – one *not* referring to itself – when he says of Christ that 'Is was in him [*est in illo erat*]' (*Mag.* 5.14). In case it is thought that Paul lacked linguistic finesse, another argument can be drawn from translatability: anyone who says that the Latin 'qui' ('who') means the same as the Greek '*tis*' is using 'qui' and '*tis*' as names; but he is correct to say so; therefore they are names (*Mag.* 5.15). The most eminent professors of logic (*disputationum*) teach that every complete sentence contains a name and a verb. Suppose then that I say of a dimly perceived object, 'Because it is a man it is an animal', while you prefer the more cautious, 'If it is a man it is an animal': where are the names in your comment to me, '"If" is satisfactory, "because" is not? (*Mag.* 5.16).

Every word, we are thus invited to conclude, can be used to refer to itself, and when so used it is a name. Here Augustine is surely right; and what is more, the kind of name in question is a referring expression, the kind for which Adeodatus' Principle holds good. We modern pedants would write such applications of the Principle with nested quotation-marks: '"the word 'because'" signifies the word "because"' or, more briefly but confusingly, '"'because'" signifies "because"'. But no notational purism will refute Augustine's intuition that the word 'because' is *used* to refer in these claims; and in that use it is a name satisfying the Principle.[5]

Every word, therefore, *is* a sign, in the sense that every word is capable of being used with the intention of bringing something – itself – to mind. Unfortunately, as is obvious, this result is less than Augustine's sign-theory needs. *De Doctrina Christiana* asserts that 'no one uses words except for the purpose of signifying something' (1.2.2, proposition (4)); but of words like 'because' the arguments in *de Magistro* show at best that they are exceptionally so used. Wittgenstein wrote:

> Augustine, in describing his learning of language, says that he was taught to speak by learning the names of things. It is clear that whoever says this has in mind the way in which a child learns such words as 'man', 'sugar', 'table' etc. He does not primarily think of such words as 'today', 'not', 'but', 'perhaps'. (*Brown Book* 1)

In his later *Philosophical Investigations* Wittgenstein quoted the relevant passage (*Conf.* 1.8.13), repeated the same criticism, asked us to 'imagine a language for which the description given by Augustine is right', and concluded that 'Augustine, we might say, does describe a system of communication [*Verständigung*]; only not everything that we call language is this system' (*Philosophical Investigations* 1.3). The criticism is essentially right: for although *de Dialectica* and *de Magistro* do show Augustine 'thinking of such words as "not"', nevertheless when he thinks hard about them he comes out with the judgement that they are names. Not everything that we call language is like that.

Learning to speak

Wittgenstein also wrote:

> Augustine describes the learning of human language as if the child came into a strange country and did not understand the language of the country; that is, as if it already had a language, only not this one. Or again: as if the child could already *think*, only not yet speak. And 'think' would here mean something like 'talk to itself'. (*Philosophical Investigations* 1.32)

As Baker and Hacker note,[6] the evidence for this attribution seems to come

[5] But see Geach [501] for caveats.
[6] Baker and Hacker [473], 60.

not from the few sentences of Augustine's *Confessions* (1.8.13) quoted at the beginning of the *Investigations* but from slightly earlier passages in which Augustine, using his own observations of babies, imagines himself in infancy frustrated by inability to express (*edere*), and not merely to satisfy, his desires (*Conf.* 1.6.8, 1.8.13). Wittgenstein connects possession of an earlier language – which in the infant would have to be a wordless language of thought – with the effectiveness of ostensive definition in teaching a new language: only if the learner is already a talker, at least a talker-to-himself, will he be able to gain understanding when a teacher says to him such things as, '"Purple" is the name of *that*'; for only then will he be equipped to know or guess the nature of his teacher's intention (does he mean colours?) when the teacher points and says 'that'. Hence a false picture of the infant mind could tempt philosophers into too crude an account of language acquisition.

Augustine's picture of the infant mind is certainly false, since it contains the inconsistent claims that adults 'have no means by any of their senses of entering into' a speechless baby's soul, and yet that he himself learned about babies' frustrations by his own observation of them (*Conf.* 1.6.8). Certainly, too, his attitude is that of someone who models infant mentality on the mentality of a speechless stroke-victim; but how far that is a false model only empirical psychologists are in a position to tell us. Whatever the psychologists' verdict may be, however, we can at least exculpate Augustine from the philosophical error imputed to him by Wittgenstein, of inferring from this model to an excessively crude account of language acquisition. Passages in *de Magistro* furnish, ironically, the best anticipation known to me of Wittgenstein's insights about ostensive definition. Augustine stresses how hard it is to explain signs except by means of other (given) signs; even explanation by gesture, as in pointing, is a use of such signs (*Mag.* 3.6, 10.34). If one seeks to explain a sign by manifesting what it is a sign of, for example 'walking' by walking, there will always be the possibility of misunderstanding:

> ADEODATUS: If someone ... were to ask me what walking is, and I were to attempt to teach him what he asked without a sign, by promptly walking, how am I to guard against his thinking that it is just the *amount* of walking I have done? If he thinks that, he will be mistaken; for he will judge that anyone who walks farther than I have, or less far, has not walked. And what I have said about this one word can be transferred to every word which I had agreed could be exhibited [*monstrari*] without a sign, apart from the two we have excepted. (*Mag.* 10.29)

The exceptions were 'speak' and 'teach'; but Augustine later includes them too.

Writing

A brief passage of Aristotle which Kretzmann has called the most influential text in the history of semantics contains this claim: 'Spoken sounds are symbols of affections in the soul, and written marks of spoken sounds' (*de Interpretatione* 1.16a3–4).[7] Aristotle goes on to describe spoken sounds as also signs, *sēmeia*, of such affections, but he does not say that written marks are signs of spoken sounds. In each of our three main texts we find Augustine in partial agreement with this. Without acknowledging any distinction between sign and symbol – in his ecclesiastical Latin 'Symbolum' designated the Creed – he nevertheless denies that there is a direct relation between written marks and mental states (or between written marks and external things); according to Augustine, what writing signifies is *speech*:

> Every word makes a sound. For when it is in writing, it is not a word but the sign of a word, the reason being that when letters are seen by a reader, what [*quid*] would be issued vocally is suggested to his mind. For written letters show to the eye something beyond themselves, and show to the mind vocal sounds [*voces*] beyond themselves. (*Dial.* 5.7)

> AUGUSTINE: What happens when we find words written? Are they words? Are they not more truly understood as signs of words, a word being what is uttered in an articulate vocal sound with some signification? . . . Thus it is that when a word is written, a sign is made to the eyes by which something comes into the mind which pertains to the ears. (*Mag.* 4.8)

> But because words strike the air and pass, lasting no longer than their sound, signs of words have been devised through their letters [i.e. phonetically]. In this way vocal sounds are shown to the eyes, not through themselves but through what are signs of them. (*Doct. Christ.* II.4.5)

The things called written words are not properly words at all, Augustine insists; nor are written letters properly letters – a 'letter', in Augustine's Latin usage, being something vocal, 'the smallest part of articulate vocal sound' (*Dial.* 5.7), i.e. a vowel or consonant.

It is not clear whether Augustine would have espoused this doctrine had Latin script not been, like its ancestors and descendants, phonetic. At any rate, it is correct to describe phonetic writing as *modelling* spoken words, whose internal sound structure gets represented by letters (in our sense of 'letter'); and accordingly written Latin words are signs, *signa*, of spoken Latin words in the accredited sense 'representations'. Whether or not encouraged by this – irrelevant – fact, Augustine makes written words signs

[7] Kretzman [258], 3.

of spoken words in his own official sense of 'sign': they indicate them – writing 'suggests to the reader's mind what would be issued vocally'.

The doctrine fits some kinds of writing well enough, for example the text of a play or the libretto of a song. The latter in particular can sensibly be regarded as giving an indication of vocal sounds, an indication not exactly in the sense of evidence, or yet reminder, but in the sense of instructions for making sounds. Musical notation is similar, the prime function of a score being to give instructions for the production of – usually non-vocal – sounds. And a sacred text, for example a scroll of the Jewish Torah, could well be thought of in the same way, as intended to guide the performance of liturgical readers.

And if not vocal performance, then sub-vocal: for the kind of inner vocalisation we shall find Augustine examining in the next section – what Evelyn Waugh called 'pronouncing ⟨words⟩ in the mind' – is often the effect of silent reading, when one reads *to* oneself. Perhaps Augustine would be content with the view that writing is a sign of vocal *or* sub-vocal pronouncing.

Yet even musical scores *can* be used differently, by those with the skill to 'read' them. Such people are able to learn how the music goes simply by following the notes with their eyes; they may or may not hear the music with the mind's ear, but they do not need to play or sing it, even sub-vocally, in order for their understanding to be activated. With written words this same non-vocalising skill, now common, may also once have been rare, its exercise secondary to the use of texts for reading aloud or at best reading *to* oneself; and in such conditions there would be some justification for defining writing as an 'indication' of what to say (the sole reference to writing in Homer describes a missive as 'sinister signs', *Iliad* VI.168–9). Yet long before Augustine people must often have read without pronouncing; and even if in provincial Africa the custom was to speak or mouth the words (the young Augustine in Milan was startled to find that Ambrose read silently, *Conf.* VI.3.3), it cannot still have been reasonable in his time to conceive the writer's normal purpose as provision of a 'score' for vocal or sub-vocal performance. I think we have to rate Augustine's doctrine of written signs superannuated.

Inner words

According to Christian orthodoxy God's word is his deed; that is, God effects his will by speaking it (*Gen. Lit.* I.3.8), as in 'Let there be light' (Gen. 1:3). Since God has no body, divine speech is not vocal: it is what Augustine called an inner word ('verbum quod intus lucet', *Trin.* XV.11.20). God speaks in the same way to human beings, who hear his word internally (*Serm.* CLXXX.7.7). He uses no 'tongue', i.e. language, neither Hebrew nor

Greek nor Latin. The word of God that a man may hear is like the word of a man who has not yet uttered it:

> Observe your own heart. When you conceive a word ⟨that you wish⟩ to speak – I shall describe, if I can, what we observe in ourselves, not how we come to grasp it – when you conceive a word ⟨that you wish⟩ to produce, there is some thing which you wish to say and the very conception of that in your heart is a word: not yet uttered, but already born in your heart and waiting to be uttered. You take note who it is to be uttered to, who you are talking to: if he is Latin, you search for a Latin vocal sound [*vocem*]; if he is Greek you think of Greek words; if Punic, you see whether you know any Punic. Matching the differences in your audience you employ different languages in order to produce the word you have conceived; but what you had conceived in your heart was confined to no language.
> (*Ev. Joh.* III.14.7)

Similarly:

> A thought that is formed from a thing that we know is a word that we say in the heart. It is neither Greek nor Latin nor any other language, but when we need to bring it to the notice [*notitia*] of those to whom we speak, a sign is picked with which to signify it. (*de Trinitate* (*Trin.*) XV.10.19)

Inner words occur not only when we are preparing to speak; for any kind of notion (*notitia*) is a word:

> In one way we call a word what occupies a stretch of time by its syllables, whether it is pronounced or thought, in another everything of which we have a notion [*omne notum*] is called a word impressed on the mind, so long as it can be produced from the memory and defined, even if the thing itself displeases us; in another when what is conceived in the mind pleases us.
> (*Trin.* IX.10.15)

The purpose of the passage surrounding this quotation is to distinguish loved from hated notions, but that purpose is here overlaid by the more important distinction between thoughts (or perhaps knowledge or concepts) that are verbalisable and those that have been verbalised. The latter appear again in *de Quantitate Animae*:

> AUGUSTINE: Now before the word ⟨'sun'⟩ itself is uttered from your mouth suppose that, wishing to pronounce it, you hold yourself in silence for a time. Does not something stay in your thought which someone else is about to hear vocally expressed? ... Does it not seem to you that the name itself as it were received from you the signification it was to convey to me through my ears? ... The sound is a body, but the signification is, so to speak, the soul of the sound. (*Qu. An.* 32.65–6)

The complex details of these passages, since they come from different works and dates, need not be assumed to be all consistent with one another. A general picture emerges, however, according to which at least two kinds of thoughts *are* words: the thoughts which a thinker has already formulated in words, saying the words to himself perhaps in rehearsal before speaking or writing; and the thoughts in no language which, allegedly, he is able to draw on in these processes of silent and vocal formulation.

Augustine's construction of this doctrine is typical of his philosophical method. He starts from a familiar phenomenon that 'we observe in ourselves', the rehearsal of phrases and sentences in advance of speech or writing. He uses the phenomenon to elucidate a theological obscurity, the notion of the word of God. In doing so he moves beyond the evidence into a theory, that all thought is inner speech; and the theory is one which he can support both from the Bible (for example 'The fool hath said in his heart, There is no God', Ps. 13 (Heb. Bib. 14):1) and from Platonism (for example Plato, *Sophist* 263e). Finally, he leaves his own stamp on the theory, again for theological reasons, when he insists that the words in which thoughts are 'formed from a thing that we know' are not in any language.

Without commenting generally on this theory I shall end by looking at its relation to an earlier episode in the history of philosophy of language, the Stoic doctrine of *lekta*, sayables.[8]

Cicero's and Seneca's allusions to the doctrine of *lekta* had refrained from the neologism 'dicibile', which would have been the most direct Latinisation of the Stoics' Greek. 'Dicibile' got invented at some time between Seneca and Augustine, to be used by Augustine in a single passage of *de Dialectica*:

> Whatever is perceived [*sentit*] from a word by the mind, not the ears, and is kept shut up in the mind itself, is called a sayable [*dicibile*]. When a word is uttered [*procedit*] not for its own sake but for the sake of signifying something else, it is called a saying [*dictio*]. The thing [*res*] itself, which is not a word nor the conception of a word in the mind, whether or not it has a word by which it can be signified, is called merely a thing in the proper sense of that name. So these four must be kept distinct: word, sayable, saying, thing. 'Word' [literally, What I have said: word] both is a word and signifies a word. 'Sayable' is a word; however it signifies not a word but what is understood in a word and retained [*continetur*] in the mind. 'Saying' is a word but signifies both together of the things signified by the first two, that is, both a word itself and what occurs in the mind by means of a word. 'Thing' is a word which signifies whatever remains beyond the three that have been mentioned [literally, said] ... But when they [sc. some words said by a teacher] are perceived in advance of vocal sound [*ante vocem*] they will be sayables; when for the purpose I have mentioned they are expressed in vocal sound, they become sayings. (*Dial.* 5.8)

[8] For a fuller treatment of the doctrine of *lekta*, see Michael Frede in ch. 6 above.

According to this passage a *dicibile* is:

(a) perceived from a word by the mind, not the ears, and kept shut up in the mind;
(b) a conception of a word in the mind;
(c) not a word but what is understood in a word and retained in the mind;
(d) what occurs in the mind by means of a word;
(e) a word perceived in advance of vocal sound.

It is hard to fit all these into a coherent account. (e) describes inner words in the sense Augustine was later to use for explaining how God speaks to men, while (b) suggests inner words in Augustine's extended sense, i.e. thoughts in general. (a) and (d) refer us to items that are given a place in a hearer's mind as a result of his exposure to speech: these also, in view of the sign-theory of speech, might be identified as thoughts, in particular the speaker's thoughts which he intends to convey. Alternatively, (a) and (d) could be interpreted so as to conform with (c), which appears to identify the *dicibile* with the meaning of a speaker – his intention to convey thoughts (or facts), rather than the thoughts conveyed.

Such uncertainty would not be surprising if Augustine were inheriting, doubtless in a changed and enfeebled state, the tradition of Stoic doctrine about *lekta*. According to the Stoics words are corporeal but *lekta* are incorporeal things 'signified' by them (Sextus, *M* VIII.11–12). Thoughts too are corporeal, they believed; and *lekta* 'accord with' a certain kind of thought, the 'rational *phantasia*' (*M* VIII.70). A central function of *lekta* is to be true or false, 'complete' ones being those whose 'utterance is finished, for example "Socrates writes"' (Diogenes Laertius, *Lives of the Philosophers* VII.63), which therefore correspond to sentences rather than individual words; while the incomplete ones, we also learn, correspond to predicates. It appears therefore that the Stoics, or some of them, felt they had identified a need for incorporeal entities corresponding to sentences and predicates which was *not* matched by any need for incorporeal entities corresponding to names. Here is an emphasis on difference of function among words and word-groups which we have found Augustine playing down in his doctrine that all single words are names, and which he seems to ignore altogether in what he says about *dicibilia*. Like Locke in the passage quoted on p. 192 above but unlike the Stoics, Augustine was tempted to assume that whatever corresponds to a sentence, in the mind or in the world, must be formed of parts – be they 'inner words' or ideas – which correspond to the parts – words – forming the sentence. This beguiling error is the picture theory of language, which I have already mentioned in connection with the non-Greek meaning of 'signum', 'representation'. It was to impede the philosophy of language for many centuries after Augustine.

11

The verb 'to be' in Greek philosophy: some remarks

LESLEY BROWN

I Introduction

Those who read Greek philosophy soon learn that the concept of being, and the verb 'to be', play a central part in the thought of many thinkers. Parmenides (on whom more below) inaugurated metaphysics by his insistence on a choice between two ways of enquiry, 'it is' and 'it is not', and by the momentous consequences he drew concerning the nature of being. Protagoras, according to Plato, *Theaetetus* 152a, propounded the thesis that man is the measure of all things, of things that are, that they are, of things that are not, that they are not. Plato characterised his Forms or Ideas, the objects of knowledge and of philosophic enquiry, as 'the being that really is' (*Phaedrus* 247c7), and as 'the being which has the denomination of "what is"' (*Phaedo* 93d8–9). He drew a famous contrast (discussed below in section III) between the Form which *is purely and fully*, and the many sensibles which *are and are not*. Aristotle chose the terms 'being' (*ousia*) and 'what it is' (*ho esti*) as designations for his key concept, substance; his theory of categories is founded on the claim that 'is' and 'being' vary in sense with the different categories (for example *Metaphysics* 1017a20–4, 1028a10–13); and he propounded a famous definition of truth as 'saying that what is is and that what is not is not' (*Met.* 1011b27).

As we read these statements we must ask ourselves how to understand the key terms involved, whether nouns such as *ousia*, participial phrases such as *to on* ('that which is') or *to ontōs on* ('that which really is'), or various other forms of the Greek verb *einai* from which these are derived. Both when the writer is self-conscious in his employment of a key term (as when Aristotle draws attention to different uses or meanings of 'is') and when the term plays a central but unquestioned role (as in Parmenides), the reader trying to understand the text will be aware of a variety of possible interpretations, and is likely to invoke the aid of distinctions current in contemporary philosophy in the task of interpretation. Many interpreters preface their discussions with a list of different senses or uses of 'is', a list which is the legacy of much philosophical analysis. And since, for the first two-thirds of this century, the influence of Frege and Russell, and of their formal logic, in particular the apparatus of first-order predicate calculus, held sway over interpreters of ancient philosophy, I start with a discussion of their legacy.

It is, or used to be, an accepted commonplace that the English verb 'to be', along with most of its Indo-European counterparts and in particular with *einai* in ancient Greek, has a number of distinct uses. As Charles Kahn reminded readers in his well-known essay 'The Greek Verb "to be" and the Concept of Being', John Stuart Mill complained of the fog which arose from overlooking the double meaning of the word 'to be' (when it signifies *to exist*, and when it signifies to *be* a man . . . to *be* seen . . . to *be* a non-entity), 'a fog which diffused itself at an early period over the whole surface of metaphysics' (Kahn [28], 247, quoting Mill's *Logic* I.iv.i). Kahn refers to Mill's distinction (between the 'is' which means 'exists' and the 'is' of 'is . . .') as the 'traditional dichotomy'; he points out that it conflates two different distinctions, one syntactic, the other semantic. The syntactic (or grammatical) distinction is between uses of 'be' which are absolute (or complete), as in Hamlet's question 'To be or not to be?', and those which are predicative (or incomplete), where 'is' is followed by a predicate or by some other completion (for example 'is a man', 'is seen', 'is in heaven'). In Kahn's view, applications of this dichotomy to ancient Greek have been flawed, because of this conflation. Kahn accepts that some uses of *esti* ('is') are complete, some incomplete (the syntactic point), but insists that a complete or absolute use of *esti* does not always mean 'exist', but can also mean 'is true', 'is the case' or 'is real'. Further, the incomplete or predicative uses of *esti* can have a variety of nuances, such as durative ('is' meaning 'endures in time'), or locative-existential ('is' meaning 'is spatially located'), so that they may go beyond the mere copula in meaning. (The copula, in traditional theory, is the verb whose sole function is to join subject to predicate and which has no 'further meaning of its own'.)

Thus Kahn identifies two assumptions involved in the 'traditional dichotomy': it assumes first that all absolute uses of 'is' bear the meaning 'exists' and secondly that predicative uses lack meaning and serve merely to join subject to predicate. He insists that both these assumptions are false of ancient Greek *esti*, and that questions of syntactically different uses should be kept apart from issues about meaning.[1]

[1] Like all who work on the verb 'to be' in Greek philosophy I am deeply indebted to the many writings of Charles Kahn. Kahn [153] lists his publications on the topic, and he reviews them in the opening article of [30]. This collection assembles articles which, in different ways, question the applicability of modern distinctions in the verb 'to be' to ancient Greek philosophical thought.

Kahn's writings on the use of *esti* in Greek philosophy are of great importance, and in this paper I try to explore some key passages which rely on the verb 'to be' with the help of his observations. Indeed, I press Kahn's doubts further, questioning what he did not dispute, the syntactic distinction: that is, I urge a more careful scrutiny of the distinction and of the relation between the syntactically different uses. First a word about terminology: while Kahn labels the constructions 'absolute' and 'predicative', I shall call them 'complete' and 'incomplete', following recent practice (for example that of Owen in [18]), but reserving judgement on whether so sharp a distinction as the pair of terms suggests can be drawn.

So far we have considered the distinction of complete from incomplete uses of the verb 'to be', where the complete 'is' is thought of as the 'is' meaning 'exists'. A further aspect of the early twentieth-century legacy concerning the verb 'to be' is the doctrine of the 'is' of identity. Russell, pursuing Mill's theme, insisted on a further distinction within the incomplete use, dividing the 'is' which relates subject to predicate from the 'is' which expresses identity. Like Mill he accompanied this dogma with a complaint: 'It is a disgrace to the human race that it has chosen to employ the same word 'is' for the two entirely different ideas – a disgrace which a symbolic language of course remedies' (Russell [526], 172). Like the traditional dichotomy, this further subdivision of the incomplete 'is' has become – thanks more to Frege than to Russell – part of our philosophical bread and butter, enshrined in logic textbooks and in the formal apparatus of the predicate calculus, where the 'is' of identity is represented as a dyadic relation (as in a=b) while the predicative 'is', as in 'John is angry', disappears in the formalisation Fa. It is worth noting that, unlike the 'traditional dichotomy', which was recognised by grammar books and dictionaries, the subdivision of the incomplete use into the 'is' of identity and the 'is' of predication has remained a preoccupation of philosophers. Linguists have not been greatly concerned to mark off these two uses, and perhaps they were right. The reason for representing sentences containing the alleged 'is' of identity differently from those containing the mere copula or 'is' of predication is a recognition that arguments of the form:

a is b
a is c
therefore b is c

may be valid or not, and, the theory goes, they are valid when the 'is' is one of identity, and not when it isn't. The question whether, and if so where, Plato, Aristotle or some other writer explicitly distinguished the 'is' of identity from the 'is' of predication is beyond the scope of this paper. The distinction has been discerned in Plato's *Sophist* at 256ab, but it may be nearer the mark to say that there Plato notes a distinction between sentences which express identity and those which express predication (participation), rather than a distinction between uses of 'is' in such sentences.[2] Indeed this seems to be the correct account of the matter: it is preferable to say that among sentences of the form 'a is b', some do and others don't express identity, rather than to say that some contain the 'is' of identity, others the 'is' of predication. This proposal avoids the suggestion that we could identify an 'is' of identity independently of knowing whether the sentence in which it is embedded is an identity sentence.[3]

The existence of at least these three distinct uses of 'is' was taken for granted by commentators and assumed to apply, by and large, to ancient Greek, though with some salient differences. These include the fact that Greek can and regularly does omit *esti* in the present tense, though not in other tenses, and that the complete 'is' is still very much a going concern, though more or less defunct in modern English. The fact that the *esti* of the copula can be omitted means that a predicative use of *esti* can convey a nuance over and above that of the mere copula (for instance connoting what really is F rather than merely appearing F, or what is enduringly F). And the fact that current English has more or less abandoned the use of the complete 'is' to mean 'exist' (as in Hamlet's 'To be or not to be), while in Greek it is very much a going concern, may lead us to question whether the complete *esti* really shares the features of the 'is' which means (or used to mean) 'exist'.

Armed with these distinctions, interpreters have turned their critical gaze on the ancient texts. For those who assumed that the same uses of 'is' are to be found in ancient Greek *esti* there were obvious questions to ask:

> Which, if any, ancient writer among the Greek philosophers first drew explicit attention to the distinction between uses?
> Prior to their coming to explicit philosophical consciousness, were the distinctions implicitly observed, though not explicitly noted, or did a failure to observe the distinctions cause some philosophers to produce invalid arguments and confused theories?

A myriad different combinations of answers have been given to these questions. It has been thought that Parmenides, and Plato up to a certain point in his career, confused the complete 'is' of existence with the

[2] Among those who interpret *Sophist* 256ab as drawing a distinction between two uses of incomplete *esti* ('is'), that of identity and that of predication, are Ackrill [187], 211–13, and Vlastos [213], esp. n. 46. *Contra*, see Bostock [190], 90 f. with refs. Lewis [154] contains an excellent discussion.

[3] Recent expressions of scepticism about the alleged 'is' of identity include Kahn [29], 372 n. 1 and Sommers [535].

predicative 'is', resulting in the curious theories of being which each espoused; that Plato in his later dialogue the *Sophist* recognised Parmenides' error (perhaps shared by his earlier self) and pointed out the different uses of 'is' – on some accounts (for example Ackrill [187], 211–13) he distinguished all three uses (complete/existential and the two subdivisions of the incomplete, the predicative 'is' and the 'is' of identity), on others (for example Vlastos [213], 288 n. 44) only the latter distinction. Some have thought that Plato never drew explicit attention to the distinction between the complete and the incomplete 'is', but was never in danger of confusing them, thanks to his knowledge of the language in which the distinction was so firmly entrenched. (This last, the view of Vlastos, I shall return to in section III.) If the distinction between the complete/existential use and the incomplete was not articulated by Plato, then, it was held, at least it can be credited to Aristotle, whose penchant for distinguishing the number of ways in which things are said led him to make many different claims about the multivocity of *esti*, one of which – his distinction between 'to be something' (*einai ti*) and 'to be *simpliciter*' (*einai haplōs*) – looks to be the very distinction we are after.

In section VI I discuss the passages where Aristotle draws this distinction, and suggest that things are by no means as simple as they look. Aristotle does not see the two uses as so sharply distinct and unrelated as the passages suggest at first sight, and he is not to be interpreted as straightforwardly distinguishing the existential from the predicative use of 'is'. But first, a look at Parmenides (section II), to set the scene, and at Plato, who has both been accused of falling into fallacy by failing to distinguish the complete from the incomplete 'is', and been credited (by some) with drawing that same distinction in his later dialogue the *Sophist* (sections, III, IV, V). I argue that no straight answer can be given to the two questions, for the conceptual scheme for *einai* (to be) within which the writers are operating does not normally allow us to say either that they fall into fallacy by ignoring the distinction between the existential and the predicative *esti* (for example) or that they deftly avoid fallacy by eschewing illicit moves from one use to another.

II Parmenides

Writing in verse some time in the fifth century B.C., Parmenides of Elea invented a philosophical method, the delineation of the only possible 'way of enquiry', and derived a set of startling metaphysical conclusions: that being (or what is) is ungenerated, imperishable, continuous, unchanging. His philosophical predecessors had investigated and speculated upon the origin and nature of the cosmos. Parmenides questioned the assumptions of such a project, by probing the preconditions of enquiry. The goddess who in Parmenides' poem promises insight into truth and mortal opinion announces that any enquiry must follow one of two ways: 'it is and that it is impossible for it not to be' or 'it is not and it is needful that it not be'. Here are the goddess's words:

> Come now, and I will tell you (and you must carry my account away with you when you have heard it) the only ways of inquiry that are to be thought of. The one, that it is and that it is impossible for it not to be, is the path of Persuasion, for she attends on Truth; the other, that it is not and that it is needful that it not be, that I declare to you is an altogether indiscernible track: for you could not know what is not – that cannot be done – nor indicate it. (Fr. 2)
>
> What is there to be said and thought must needs be: for it is there for being but nothing is not. (Fr. 6)
>
> For never shall this be forcibly maintained, that things that are not are, but you must hold back your thought from this way of enquiry. (Fr. 7)
>
> There still remains just one account of a way, that it is. On this way there are very many signs, that being uncreated and imperishable it is, whole, of a single kind and unshaken and perfect. It never was nor will be, since it is now, all together, one, continuous. For what birth will you seek for it? How and whence did it grow? I shall not allow you to say nor to think from not being: for it is not to be said or thought that it is not. (Fr. 8, lines 1–9)
>
> How could it come to be? For if it came into being, it is not: nor is it if it is ever going to be in the future. Thus coming to be is extinguished and perishing unheard of.
>
> But changeless within the limits of great bonds it exists without beginning or ceasing.
> (Fr. 8, lines 19–21 and 26–7) (Translations from Kirk, Raven and Schofield [43])

How should we understand the way of enquiry designated 'it is', *esti*? No subject of the verb is given: let us accept without further ado the prevailing view that Parmenides is talking about *whatever can be enquired into*; so that his initial point is this: concerning whatever can be enquired into (let it be O, for the object of enquiry), either O is and must be, or O is not and cannot be. What is meant by the claim that O is? The use of *esti* is complete; it has no completion and is most naturally interpreted as 'it exists'. That this is what the claim in fr. 2 means is suggested by the end of that fragment 'you could not know what is not nor indicate it'. If this is right, Parmenides is the first in a long line of thinkers to insist that only what exists can be known or and thought must needs be'. And as Kahn himself allows, the development referred to or spoken of or thought about (adding fr. 6). Though highly plausible, the claim is a source of paradox, for do we not think and talk about things which don't exist, mythical creatures, for example, and future events, fictional characters, Santa Claus and so forth? And if it is hard to see how 'Santa Claus brings children presents' can be meaningful if there is no such personage, it is yet odder to express that with the claim 'Santa Claus does not exist.' How can the subject term of that sentence, the name 'Santa Claus', be meaningful if, as the rest of the sentence claims, no such person exists? Can it even be a name, if it names no one and nothing? In insisting that what can be thought of or spoken about must exist, Parmenides (on this interpretation) discovered a paradox in the sense of a thesis that seems at once necessarily true but falsified by everyday experience. We do talk about what doesn't exist, however impossible that seems in theory. And the conclusions he drew from this opening move are far more startling. But first we must look at an alternative interpretation of the opening move.

Kahn emphasises the poem's references to truth as the goal of enquiry, for example in fr. 2, and proposes that the poem's controlling thought is that what is enquired into should be something that can be known, and in turn that what is known must be true. Parmenides' path 'it is', then, becomes 'it is true' rather than 'it exists'. As we saw in section I above, in criticising the application of the 'traditional dichotomy' to ancient Greek, Kahn pointed out that a complete *esti* does not always mean 'exists' but may mean 'is true', as when Herodotus uses *ton eonta logon* (literally, the story that is) to mean 'the true story' (Herodotus 1.95.1, 1.116.5). The new proposal is that the traditional interpretation of Parmenides' *esti* as 'it exists' should be supplanted by the interpretation 'it is true', at least at the beginning of the poem's argument, when Parmenides links enquiry with knowledge and with 'it is'. For the thought that what is known must be true is indeed an unassailable starting-point, while the claim that what is known or referred to or thought about must exist is more questionable. But while this proposal emphasises the connection between knowledge and truth in favour of *esti* as 'is true', support for *esti* as 'exists' derives from fr. 6, 'what is there to be said and thought must needs be'. And as Kahn himself allows, the development of thought in the poem seems to require the sense 'exists' for *esti* at a later stage, even if it was not the key notion in the opening move. So let us follow that development.

As fr. 8 reveals, the object of enquiry, that which is, is declared to be uncreated and imperishable. Why? If this is to follow from the impossibility of the way 'it is not', then that must mean 'it does not exist' rather than 'it is not true' or 'it is not the case'. If to create something is to bring it about that something which at one time does not exist does exist at a later time, then that is ruled unintelligible if we are prohibited from thinking or uttering 'does not exist'. So even if, as Kahn suggests, the guiding thought at the outset is the insistence on 'it is true', by fr. 8 the forbidden 'it is not' must be 'it does not exist'. Then come some further claims about the nature of what is, and by lines 26–8 of fr. 8 we find the claim that what is is changeless. Why? One response goes as follows: when a thing changes, it goes from being F to not being F, or from not being F to being F. Perhaps the ban on 'it is not' has now been illicitly extended to include a ban on 'it is not F'. If so, Parmenides has committed an unwarranted move from the complete 'is not' (i.e. does not exist) to the incomplete 'is not ...'. For while the former is certainly problematic, mere not being ... (for example not being green, or not being cold) could hardly be a proper object of philosophical suspicion. Mill's complaint of a fog which at an early period arose from overlooking the distinction between the 'is' of existence and the predicative 'is' may well derive in part from such a reading of Parmenides.

We can defend Parmenides against this accusation (of confusing not being (for example) green with not existing) by supplying him with the following principle (as in Barnes [40], 216): every change requires a generation or a destruction. When a green apple turns red, green perishes and red is created, or perhaps the complex object – the green apple – is destroyed and a new one – the red apple – is created. If generation is ruled out, because of the impossibility of 'it is not', then change which requires generation is also ruled out. On this reading Parmenides need forbid only 'is not' (complete), and not also 'is not F'. Read this way, no confusion between the complete 'is not' and the incomplete 'is not ...' is to be imputed to Parmenides. But for all that, as I argue in section V below, Plato in the *Sophist* presents the great man's thought in such a way as to suggest that Parmenides *did* include a ban on 'is not F' within his dismissal of 'is not'.

Though it does not try to adjudicate between interpretations, this brief foray into the much-dissected thought of Parmenides provides some insight into the importance of the topics of being and not being, of 'is' and 'is not', for Greek philosophy. For the arguments which decreed that what can be known or enquired into, in other words what is, must be free from creation, destruction and change set an agenda which later thinkers had to take account of. As we have seen, Parmenides' words have been interpreted in many different ways: some critics insist that but a single, univocal *esti*, the syntactically complete 'is' meaning 'exists', is needed to convey Parmenides' meaning, while Kahn's more nuanced reading suggests that first 'it is true', then 'it exists' (these are both complete uses), and finally the incomplete 'it is

. . .' are needed to capture the full sense of Parmenides' thought.[4] And as we shall see in the next section, the very same possibilities of interpretation offer themselves in a famous argument of Plato's about the connection between knowledge and what is, an argument in which the influence of Parmenides is unmistakable.

III Plato in a muddle?

In one of his most famous discussions of the Forms, Plato slips in an alarming way between theses employing what look to be complete uses of the verb 'to be', and others where a complement is present. The goal of *Republic* v.475–80 is to show that knowledge differs from opinion, and that it is therefore those who have knowledge, *viz.* philosophers, who should rule. In the course of the argument he seems to argue not only that knowledge and opinion differ but also that their objects differ, for the object of knowledge is that which is, while the object of opinion is that which is and is not, also described as being 'between that which purely is and that which in no way is' (*Republic* 477a). Plato identifies the object of knowledge with the Forms, with the just itself, the beautiful itself, and so on, and the object of opinion with 'the many beautiful, the many just, etc. things'. What he means by the 'many beautifuls' I discuss briefly below; the Forms, such as the just itself, the beautiful itself, are for Plato immaterial and unchanging entities, perhaps properties, which exist independently of and prior to minds and material objects. They play an explanatory role in the nature of things, serve as the objects of knowledge and as guarantors of ethical objectivity. The argument is complex, much ink has been spilled over its interpretation, and I cannot do full justice to it here. It begins with the following exchanges, in which Socrates starts by asking Glaucon to reply on behalf of the opponent who tries to resist Socrates' claims about knowledge and opinion.

> S. Tell me this: does one who knows know something, or nothing? You answer me on his behalf.
> G. I answer that one who knows knows something.
> S. Does he know what is, or what is not?
> G. What is. For how could something that is not be known?

[4] Kirk, Raven and Schofield [43], 246 suggest that Parmenides' use of *estin* is 'simultaneously existential and predicative, but not therefore confused' and argue in favour of this that for Parmenides 'non-existence is being nothing at all, i.e. having no attributes; and . . . to exist is in effect to be something or other'. The substance of this account seems to me quite correct and, as I argue in section IV, it can be said to apply also to Plato's understanding of the complete *esti* and its negation. But I urge caution in the use of expressions such as 'simultaneously existential and predicative' and 'for Parmenides non-existence is . . .' as if it were unproblematic to use these terms in elucidating Parmenides' thought.

S. Then we are sure of the following, however we may look at it, that what fully is is fully knowable and what is not in any way is totally unknowable.
G. Absolutely.
S. Fine. Now if there is something such that it both is and is not, would it not lie between that which purely is and that which in no way is?
G. Yes.
S. Then knowledge is matched with what is, ignorance necessarily with what is not, and we need to search for something between knowledge and ignorance to be matched with this thing which is between ⟨what is and what is not⟩, if indeed there is such a thing. (*Republic* 476e6–477b1)

Thus the argument begins with the claim that *one who knows knows something; indeed, something which is; for what is not could not be known*. Here, it appears, we have what Aristotle would call an example of 'to be *simpliciter*', a complete use which we are inclined to translate as 'exist': one who knows knows something, a thing which exists; for how could something non-existent be known? But an alternative suggests itself. As already noted, a complete *esti* is sometimes best translated 'is true'. Bearing this in mind, we must ask whether we shouldn't import this translation into Plato's original premise, *one who knows knows something that is, for how can what is not be known?* This too gives Plato an acceptable starting-point; what is known must be true, for what is not true cannot be an object of knowledge. As we saw, this was one favoured candidate for the interpretation of Parmenides' leading thought that what can be enquired into and known must be.

So, just as with Parmenides, we seem to be faced with a choice between two interpretations of the opening premise of Plato's argument, each involving a complete use of *esti*, a choice, that is, between *one who knows knows what exists*, and *one who knows knows something true*. The sequel, we can only hope, will make clear how we should choose. But we are in for a shock. Plato claims that we shall find the object of opinion when we find something that is and is not (*Republic* 478d5). Does this mean something which both exists and does not exist? Heaven forbid. The idea of finding something which is both true and not true is perhaps somewhat less problematic. One might think of a sense in which a single proposition could be partly true, partly false. Alternatively, one might interpret the suggestion that the object of opinion is what is and is not (call this claim O) so that it applied not to propositions taken singly but to the class of opinions, in other words, as making the correct point that opinion is both true and false (i.e. some opinions are true, some false) while knowledge is only true, never false.

But when Plato reveals his hand, his point is this: the objects of opinion are the many just, the many beautiful, etc. things, and, Plato goes on to say, each of the many just things is also unjust, each of the many beautiful things also ugly, and in general each of the many Fs no more is what it is said to be than it is not that (479b).

First we must ask how we should understand the expression 'the many beautifuls' and the associated claim that each of them is also ugly (and therefore not beautiful). It is natural to suppose that Plato means the many sensible instances of beauty – this woman, that statue – and is claiming that each instance, while beautiful in one setting or respect or comparison, is ugly in a different respect, a different setting or in comparison with a more beautiful thing. Alternatively, on a more subtle interpretation, the many beautifuls are the many sensible properties (such as being brightly coloured) which people wrongly identify with beauty.[5] And the claim that each of these is both beautiful and ugly will amount to this: each of the 'many beautifuls', such as being brightly coloured, will be both ⟨what makes some things⟩ beautiful and ⟨what makes other things⟩ ugly. Either way the claim is that each of the many Fs both is F and is not F, and here Plato no longer uses the complete 'is', despite saying that to find the object of opinion we were to search for that which is and is not, in contrast to that which purely is, the object of knowledge. So in developing his claim that the object of opinion is that which is and is not (claim O), Plato insists that each of the many Fs is and is not F. This seems to rule out the promising interpretation of O mooted above: opinions are and are not true (i.e. some are true, some false). It is ruled out on two counts, first, because Plato moves to the claim that the objects of opinion are and are not F – an incomplete use of *esti* – and secondly, because he now insists that *each* of the many beautifuls is and is not beautiful, while the promising interpretation required O to mean that some opinions are (true) while others are not (i.e. are false).[6]

The puzzle, of course, is this: how are these two claims related?

(1) Each of the many Fs is and is not F.
(2) Each of the many Fs is and is not.

[5] Fine [150] in her discussion of this argument defends this second interpretation of 'the many beautifuls'. She argues for a veridical 'is' (i.e. 'is true') in the interpretation of the opening premise (knowledge is of what is true) and of claim O (that opinion is of what is and what is not). Though she accepts that in the crucial claim 'the many Fs are and are not F' Plato has moved to a predicative (incomplete) 'is', she believes that this can be dovetailed with the veridical use which, in her view, predominates in the argument. See also Fine [151].

[6] Fine [151] has an account which aims to circumvent this difficulty (91–3). She argues for a 'convincing link' between the claim that beliefs (opinions, in my version) are both true and false (while knowledge is always true) and the claim that each of the many Fs are both F and not-F.

Or again, what is the relation between

(3) The Form F is fully and purely F.
(4) The Form F fully and purely is?

On the face of it, if we take the uses of 'is' in (2) and (4) to be complete, (2) and (4) say something quite different from (1) and (3) respectively, and (2) at least seems ridiculous: how could the many Fs both exist and not exist? This looks to be just the sort of confusion of which Mill complained in his remark about the fog (caused by the neglect of the distinction in meanings of 'to be') which diffused itself at an early period over the whole surface of metaphysics (see section I above). Various possibilities suggest themselves:

(a) Plato intends (2) to be an inference from (1), and is (presumably) unaware of the equivocation on 'is' which renders the inference invalid; likewise with (4) and (3). Those who think a fallacy is involved here are unlikely to hold that Plato was aware of it, for, though conscious fallacy is occasionally to be found in Plato, he is hardly likely to have employed it in the service of his theory of Forms.[7]

(b) There is no fallacy because there is no inference: (2) is not, for Plato, inferred from (1), but is an elliptical expression of (1), and does not, despite appearances, contain a complete use of the verb 'to be'; again, the same goes for (4)'s relation to (3).

These two views, (a) and (b), share the feature that they both assume that Mill's traditional dichotomy between the complete 'is' which means 'exist' and the incomplete 'is' can be applied to 'is' in ancient Greek; they differ over whether Plato's position involves (a) a fallacious inference from the incomplete to the complete use, or (b) no fallacy because no inference; on (b) Plato is seen as steering well clear of the complete/existential use at all points. For the adherents of the traditional dichotomy, (b) is the more attractive option, and it has been stoutly defended.

One such defender is Annas in her account of the *Republic* v argument (Annas [146], ch. 8). Another is Vlastos ([152]; see also [156]), though his claims are not made with particular reference to the argument at *Republic* v, but in general elucidation of Plato's striking descriptions of the Forms as 'more real' (*mallon onta*, using the participle 'being', *Republic* 515d), 'really real' (literally, 'beingly being', *Republic* 597d), and so forth. Why does Plato say that Forms are really real but sensibles not really real? He cannot mean that sensibles do not really exist. Vlastos reminds us that the English expression 'are not real' has two distinct uses: to say that unicorns are not

[7] *Euthydemus* 283c–d contains a deliberately fallacious argument which is often held to depend upon equivocation between existential and predicative *esti*. But I argue in Brown [191], 57 that this is not the correct account of that fallacy.

real is to deny that they exist, but to say that these flowers are not real is to presuppose that they do exist but deny they are genuine flowers. In effect, Vlastos distinguishes and applies to Greek *esti* ('is') a complete, one-place use from an incomplete, two-place use of 'is real', in line with the distinction between the 'is' of existence and that of predication ([152], 47). He insists that Plato's designations of the Forms as really real and his denigration of particulars as 'not really real' must be understood in terms of 'real' as in 'real flowers', not in terms of the 'real' which means 'existent'. (Note that the Greek word for 'real' throughout – *on* – is simply the participle of the verb 'to be'.) For though Plato nowhere explicitly states or discusses the difference between the 'is' of existence and that of predication, he none the less, claims Vlastos, observes the difference in his writings. For Vlastos is convinced that there is just such a distinction in the Greek verb *einai*; even a Greek child would, without being aware of it, have had a knowledge of the difference between the 'is' in 'Troy is famous' and 'Troy is' (or rather, their Greek equivalents).

None will dispute that to understand Plato's views about Forms we must start by recognising that the Form, for example the beautiful, is purely and unqualifiedly beautiful, in contrast to the many sensible beautifuls which are beautiful only in some qualified way. In understanding the superior being of the Forms, we must start from the incomplete 'is', the way in which the Form F is F. My disagreement with Vlastos is not on that point, but over his claim that this use of 'is' must be, and was by Plato and every Greek speaker, kept clearly distinct from the complete, and by implication existential, 'is' to be found in 'Troy is'.

I shall label (b) the ellipse interpretation. Its defenders argue that (2) and (4) must be elliptical, for, if taken at face value as containing a complete 'is', this would mean 'exist', which cannot be what Plato intended. For that would have committed him to a theory of degrees of existence, which is absurd, and to holding that the many sensibles both do and don't exist, and are between existence and non-existence.

I agree that the above sound absurd when phrased using the English 'exist'. But we do not have to infer that since 'is' in (2) and (4) cannot mean 'exist', these must be ellipses of (1) and (3) respectively (as Vlastos [152], 48, [156], 63 with n. 21 and Annas [146], 198 argue). Rather, I suggest, they should be taken at face value as containing complete uses of 'is', but ones which are closely related to the predicative, incomplete, 'is' in a way I now outline.

IV A suggested analogy

Drawing on an earlier proposal (Brown [191]), I want to suggest that in ancient Greek a complete use of 'is', as in 'The Gods are' or 'The form

F fully is', is closely related to the incomplete 'is'. The connection is akin to that between the incomplete and complete uses (in English and other languages, including Greek) of verbs such as 'teach' and 'eat'. One can say 'Jane teaches' or 'John is eating' as well as 'Jane teaches French' or 'John is eating grapes.'[8] The former, complete uses are related to the incomplete in the following ways: 'John is eating grapes' entails 'John is eating', which in turn is equivalent to 'John is eating something.' One who hears 'John is eating' can properly ask 'eating what?'. Despite this, it would be wrong to say that 'John is eating' is elliptical. In like vein I have proposed that the complete 'is' in Greek allows further completion: to any assertion that such-and-such is, it can properly be asked 'is what?'. This is why it is misleading to link the complete 'is' too closely to 'exist': for the follow-up question 'exists what?' is not permissible.[9]

While this proposal allows us to classify some uses as complete, others as incomplete, it envisages a continuous spectrum of uses with no sharp boundary between the complete and the incomplete, and *a fortiori* no boundary to which a semantic distinction could correspond. The evidence suggests just such a spectrum of uses. Consider the following selection of literal translations of typical Greek sentences containing 'to be':

(a) Socrates is snub-nosed.
(b) Socrates is a poet.
(c) Socrates is in the *agora*.
(d) They are silently (adverb used adjectivally, see Kahn [29], 151).
(e) It is in every way, in some way, purely, etc. (as said by Plato, for example of Forms).
(f) The gods are for ever.
(g) Socrates is no longer.
(h) The gods are.

How do we distinguish syntactically incomplete from complete? If we insist that the presence of any completion makes the 'is' incomplete, then only (h), 'The gods are', counts as a complete use. (For a non-philosophical occurrence of this, see Menander, *Dyskolos* 639, where, on seeing Knemon, who had insulted him, fallen into a well, the cook exclaims 'the gods do exist' (sc. and have punished him).) But uses with temporal adverbs, such as (f) and (g), are also taken to be complete or absolute, rather than incomplete or predicative (see, for example, Kahn [29], 240), in part no doubt because we would paraphrase them with 'exist', (a), (b) and (c), where 'is' is the nominal or locative copula, are the typical examples of an incomplete use. But (d) and (e), with adverbial completions, are hard to classify and may be called

[8] In suggesting the analogy between 'be' and verbs such as 'teach' and 'eat' I should like to repeat the acknowledgement to Michael Woods made in my [191].

[9] Note that this was not so in Latin, where *existere* could be a copula.

borderline cases. In (d) the adverb functions as an adjective, so it may be classed with (a), perhaps, but (e) is particularly problematic, and involves the very use we find in philosophically important passages in Plato. Should it be classed with (f) and (g) as complete? Or should we suppose that 'it is in some way' is equivalent to the predicative 'it is something', or 'for some F, it is F'? This attractive suggestion runs into difficulty when we try to apply it to the locution Plato occasionally uses: 'it is in every way'. This can hardly mean 'For all F, it is F' since this could not sensibly be asserted of anything. The examples in (e) show most clearly the difficulty of trying to pigeonhole uses of *esti* in Greek as either complete or incomplete. They are, as it were, on the point where one use shades into the other, and we would be wrong, because imposing our own categories, to suppose that there must be an answer which categorises them firmly as either complete or incomplete, either one-place or two-place. Many critics insist that any use must be categorisable as complete or incomplete, and, if complete as meaning either 'is true' or 'exists', but just because a clear answer can sometimes be given, it doesn't follow that it always can. I suggest, then, that there is a certain seamlessness, or continuity, between uses of *esti* which the dichotomy 'complete/incomplete' masks. I suggest there is no point at which a Greek speaker would detect a quantum leap from one *esti* to another. Further, that even where uses can be safely classed as either incomplete (as in the first three) or as complete (as in the last), these are thought of as connected in very much the way 'Fred teaches Greek' connects with 'Fred teaches.'

A further feature of my proposal concerns the question of ellipsis. On my view the argument in *Republic* v moves from (1) to (2) and from (3) to (4), while on the ellipse view (2) and (4) are merely elliptical restatements of (1) and (3) respectively. Is there a way of deciding between these interpretations? Where I suggest that the claim that the Form F fully is is derived from, but is not identical with, the claim that the Form F is fully F, the other view sees it as simply an elliptical restatement of the latter. Vlastos argues that if it is not an ellipse, it must mean that the Form F fully exists. Since Plato was quite clear about the difference between these two claims, he must have intended one rather than the other, and the one he intended was the elliptical reading. But I suggest that he was not quite clear about the distinction between the two, for the reason that the linguistic and conceptual scheme within which he spoke, thought and wrote did not contain the distinction Vlastos alleges.

Now it is certainly true that in some cases an apparently complete use of 'is' must be supplied with an elided complement. In fact this is far less frequent in ancient Greek than in modern English, which has: 'John was angry and Jane was as well' (sc. was *angry* as well); 'Is she ready?' 'No, she isn't' (sc. ready). But while Greek does not have these frequent ellipses of the complement, ellipse is to be found in certain contexts, notably where there is a contrast between what is really such-and-such and what only appears to be such (for an example see *Sophist* 233c6–8). In many cases Vlastos is certainly right in his contention that when Plato contrasts the Form which really is with the sensibles which are and are not, or which only appear to be, a complement F has been elided and must be supplied. He instances Plato's odd description of constitutions which, being less than the best, are 'not genuine or really real' (*oud' ontōs ousas* (*Statesman* (*Plt.*) 293e)): each epithet, 'not genuine' and 'not really real', requires completion – they are not genuine constitutions.

But in other cases the matter is not so clear-cut. I illustrate this from Plato's discussion of representative art (*mimētikē technē*) in *Republic* X, where his aim is to show that the products of the artist (painter or poet) are two removes from reality. He makes the strange claim that everyday objects such as the beds a carpenter makes are already at one remove from reality (for only the Form of bed is truly real). At 597a4–5 Plato says that the carpenter, since he doesn't make what is, doesn't make the real (*ei mē ho esti poiei, ouk an to on poioi*). Now here there certainly is an ellipse. We must supply ⟨bed⟩ from the earlier lines; what the carpenter makes is not the real bed, because it is not 'the bed itself', the Form of bed. But though what the carpenter makes is not the real bed, it is still something, indeed still a bed of sorts. So in this case when we find the claim that what the carpenter makes is not real, not what is, we must regard it as elliptical and supply ⟨bed⟩.

However, this notion of producing a semblance, not the real thing, has just been introduced (596de) via a different example, the example of producing things such as the sun, trees, animals, etc. with a mirror. What you produce thus are things which appear, *phainomena*, but are not in reality (*ou mentoi onta tēi alētheiai*). Can we say with equal certainty that here too we have an ellipse? That Plato's point is that what you see in a mirror appears to be but is not a tree? Might his point not be this: what you see in a mirror is something which only appears but is not (or, as we should say, does not exist)? Vlastos would argue that 'appears but is not' *either* is elliptical for 'appears F but is not F' *or* is complete and means 'appears but does not exist', and that Plato must have been quite clear about the difference between these two claims. But I suggest that this makes matters too clear-cut. In the one case – that of the carpenter's bed and the painter's bed, which appear to be but are not real beds – the elliptical reading is demanded; in the other the decision is not so clear. It may well be that, if pressed, Plato would have said that likewise the tree produced by holding a mirror in sunlight is indeed not a real tree but is still something, *viz.* an image, i.e. that he would accept the ellipse reading of 'they appear but are not in reality'. But it is far less obvious in this case than in the case of the carpenter's bed, and my point is the following: that Plato chose to introduce us to the idea that the carpenter's bed is not real, not one that is, by using the example of trees, etc. in a mirror which appear but are not in reality suggests that he did not observe so sharp a distinction between the two-place and the one-place 'is' as Vlastos maintains.

The evidence of the *Republic* and other middle dialogues, then, which has perforce been sketchily and dogmatically presented above, suggests the picture for which I've argued. In arguing for the superior status of the Forms, Plato employs both incomplete and complete uses of the verb 'to be', saying (or at least implying, as at *Symposium* (*Symp.*) 211a) that both *the Form, beautiful, is purely and fully beautiful* and *the Form purely and fully is*. We need say neither that Plato moves illicitly from a predicative to an existential 'is' (view a) nor that the apparently complete uses are merely elliptical restatements of the incomplete (view b). Rather, the claim that the Form F purely and fully is is derived from, but is not a mere elliptical restatement of, the claim that the Form F is purely and fully F. Complete being is intimately related to, and derived from, incomplete being – being such and such – without merely reducing to it.

V The *Sophist*

In discussing some famous arguments in the *Republic* I have argued for a certain understanding of how Plato saw the relation between such statements as 'The Form F is fully F' and 'The Form F fully is', an understanding which obviates some of the traditional questions about whether Plato illicitly infers an existential from a predicative 'is'. I have not yet discussed what, on the model I suggest, would be the relation between negative uses of 'is', complete and incomplete. To do so I turn to the *Sophist*.

The *Sophist* is one of Plato's late, so-called critical dialogues; written after the central dialogues such as the *Republic*, it explicitly promises to face a problem about not being bequeathed by Parmenides, the ban on saying that what is not is, or that what is is not (see fr. 7, quoted in section II above). The chief speaker in the dialogue, a stranger from Elea (Parmenides' own city), raises a variety of problems about not being (236–41), before promising to solve them by tackling Parmenides head on (241d). Here was Plato's chance to make explicit any distinctions embedded in the verb 'to be', and to analyse and expose any errors, in Parmenides or in his own earlier writings, which depended on confusing different uses of the verb. As noted in section I, many scholars have read this dialogue as drawing one or more of the 'traditional' distinctions.

But though much painstaking analysis fills the central part of the *Sophist*, the results disappoint those who hope to find a clear disambiguation of uses of *esti* which would expose earlier confusions. I cannot offer here a full account of what I take to be the results of the *Sophist*, far less a defence of such an account, but confine myself to a few points. To the question whether the dialogue distinguishes an 'is' of identity from an 'is' of predication, I have indicated my answer: that it does not, but it does draw an important distinction between identity-sentences and predications (see section I and n. 2 above). Here I focus on the question whether and if so how it distinguishes complete from incomplete uses. I shall suggest that Plato developed a better theory about the negative 'is not' than his argumentation in the *Republic* suggests, while continuing to treat the relation between the complete use (X is) and the incomplete (X is F) in the way I have described in section IV, that is, by analogy with the relation between 'X teaches' and 'X teaches singing'.

Recall that in discussing the argument in *Republic* v I suggested that Plato moves from

(1) The many Fs are and are not F   to
(2) The many Fs are and are not.

While the positive half of this inference is unproblematic, the negative part is very odd. How is it supported? Here we face the question of the relation between the two negations, 'X is not F' and 'X is not.' Recalling the analogy I discussed in section IV, we should expect the following schema, which I label H (for Healthy).

X is F $\rightarrow$ X is
X is not $\rightarrow$ X is not F, X is not G, etc. (i.e. for all F, X is not F)

But in the argument from the *Republic*, in arguing from (1) to (2) above, Plato seems to operate with a different schema, Schema U (for Unhealthy):

X is F $\rightarrow$ X is (this line is the same on each schema)
X is not F $\rightarrow$ X is not.

The difference lies in the second line, where the second schema allows the inference from 'X is not F' to 'X is not.' To the modern eye, this is unsound, just as it would be unsound to argue from 'Fred doesn't teach singing' to 'Fred doesn't teach.' Dancy [301] suggests that, if the unhealthy schema is operative, the complete 'X is not' may be understood as 'there is some mode of being which X lacks'. We seem to find this move from 'X is not F' to 'X is not' at a point in the early, paradox-mongering section of the *Sophist*. One of the puzzles concerns the definition of an image. It is argued that since an image is not really that which it is an image of (i.e. since an image of an F is not really F), it both is in a way (since it is an image) and is not really (since it is not really F) (240b). As with the similar argument in *Republic* v, we want to know whether 'X is in a way and is not really' is merely an elliptical restatement of 'X is an image but is not really an F', or an inference from it. And again, if we have an inference here, it is the negative half which causes trouble: why should 'X is not really an F' entail 'X is not really'? Schema U seems to be operating here, and it presented Plato with a problem which necessitated a rethink. In the *Republic*, the contrast between Forms and sensibles was to lie in the fact that Forms simply are, while sensibles are and are not. But as Plato will insist in the *Sophist*, everything, Forms included, would turn out to 'be and not be', for 'in the case of each of the Forms, there is much that it is and an indefinite number of things it is not' (*Sophist* 256e). So if he continues to infer 'X is not' from 'X is not F', then it must be said of Forms too that they are and are not (see Dancy [301], 52).

In the constructive section of the *Sophist*, Plato responds by a new proposal about 'is not'. Since it is true of a Form as much as of anything else that 'it is many things and is not an indefinite number of things', this cannot be allowed to impute unvarnished not being to a Form, or indeed to anything. So Plato distinguishes in the *Sophist* what he calls the contrary of being (*to mēdamōs on*, that which is not in any way) from the mere negation of being (*to mē on*), and insists that the latter must always be understood as not being something. He rejects outright *that which is not in any way* as a notion having no application whatsoever (*Sophist* 258e–259a). The only use of 'is not' which he allows is a use in which it has a completion (X is not F).[10] Hence Plato sets his face against schema U, which led him into difficulties once he realised that Forms too 'are ... and are not ...'. We can perhaps say that he accepted schema H instead, for the rejection of plain not being (the so-called contrary of being) rests on its equivalence with 'not being anything at all', in other words 'for all F, is not F'. Because he regards the complete 'is not' as equivalent to 'is not anything at all', he disallows such a complete 'is not'. Some remarks on this:

(1) This move seems to concede to Parmenides the unthinkability of 'is not' in its complete use, so the attack on 'father Parmenides' is not as

[10] There is a troublesome problem which need not detain us here: much of the time in the *Sophist* Plato explicates 'Kind K is not F' as 'Kind K is different from F', i.e. as a denial of identity, rather than as the negative predication we should expect. If he does offer to analyse 'Kind K is not F' where this is a negative predication – and whether and if so how he does is a highly controversial matter – the analysis is still somehow in terms of 'is different from'. For present purposes it is enough to note that the only uses of 'is not' he allows are those which have some completion – whether they are, as we should put it, negative predications or negative identities.

comprehensive as we might have expected. Plato insists on a role for 'is not', but only when it is completed in some way or other. But the Eleatic stranger, the main speaker in the *Sophist*, none the less presents this as a rebuttal of Parmenides, from which we may perhaps infer that Plato regarded it as an important point against Parmenides to establish the difference between 'is not' and 'is not . . .', and to legitimise the second while conceding the unintelligibility of the first. So Plato, apparently, did hold Parmenides guilty of confusing the complete with the incomplete 'is not' (see section II above).

(2) Plato's refusal to countenance a use of the complete 'is not' tells against a suggestion that may lie behind the remark of Vlastos (quoted in section IV). Vlastos insisted that any Greek child (and *a fortiori* Plato) would have known the difference between the *is* in 'Troy is famous' and in 'Troy is', suggesting (though not asserting) that a Greek child would know that the first was true while the second was false. But though this might seem obvious to us, Plato could not have agreed, for he firmly resisted a role for the complete 'is not'. A locution such as 'Troy is not' is outlawed by the arguments of the *Sophist* unless it can be supplied with a completion.

(3) Equally important, Plato never queries the positive claim, common to both schemata, that 'X is F' entails 'X is.' Another of the early paradoxes depends on this assumption. It goes as follows:

> What can be said about what is not? Whatever we try to say about it involves somehow attributing being to it. Even if we conclude that what is not is unthinkable, unsayable, indefinable, etc., we appear to be contradicting ourselves, for in saying that it is unthinkable, are we not saying that it is? (Paraphrase of *Sophist* 238e)

An obvious way out of this paradox is offered by the traditional dichotomy, in the light of which someone could urge that the 'is' in 'is unthinkable' is distinct from the (existential) 'is'. But Plato does not offer this (to us) obvious solution to the puzzle. Whereas other false moves underlying the early paradoxes are exposed and corrected, Plato nowhere queries the entailment between 'X is F' and 'X is', even where this has led to paradox. Indeed the remainder of the discussion in the *Sophist* suggests that Plato accepted the entailment between 'X is F' and 'X is', even though this led to paradox. How Aristotle tackled the same problem we shall see in section VI.

We are now ready to consider a famous passage in the *Sophist* where Plato does appear to draw the distinction between a syntactically complete and an incomplete use of *esti*. The point is not made as part of a general solution to the problems involved in being and not being, but for a more limited purpose, to prove the distinctness of two of his 'very great kinds', *being* and *different*. (Kinds in the *Sophist* are the descendants of Forms in the middle dialogues.) To effect this proof he contrasts 'is' with 'different' by pointing out that 'of things that are, some are said to be themselves by themselves (*auta kath' hauta*), while others are said to be in relation to other things (*pros alla*). What is different, on the other hand, is always said in relation to something different' (255cd). The point seems to be that 'is different' always requires completion (different from such-and-such), while 'is' sometimes has such a completion, but sometimes stands on its own, requiring no completion. (You can say 'Justice is' as well as 'Justice is a virtue', but you cannot say 'Justice is different', only 'Justice is different from such-and-such.') If this is the correct interpretation,[11] it shows that Plato was prepared to exploit the availability of both syntactic forms of 'is' for the purposes of this argument. But he makes no further use of this distinction, in a dialogue whose concerns might seem to demand it, and this confirms the view for which I have been arguing, that though distinct, the uses were felt to be so closely connected that nothing important in the philosophy of being hung upon the distinction.

To sum up the results of this too brief discussion of the *Sophist*: in a dialogue in which Plato promises to challenge Parmenides, he does so by insisting on the legitimacy of the expression 'is not . . .' while refusing to allow the expression 'is not in any way', his understanding of the complete 'is not'. Thus he accepts Parmenides' strictures against the complete 'is not' while chiding him for not allowing *any* use of 'is not'; from which we may infer that Plato thought Parmenides erred in not distinguishing the complete from the incomplete 'is not'. But Plato does not go so far as to insist on finding a role for the complete 'is not'. If, as I have tentatively suggested, he had erred in *Republic* v by allowing the inference from 'X is not F' to 'X is not',

[11] Another highly disputed issue. Owen [207] and Frede [192] take a different view, arguing that two *incomplete* uses of *esti* are distinguished under the labels *auto kath'hauto* and *pros allo*, and not, as on the view here defended, a complete and an incomplete use. However, Owen also holds, and here I agree, that though Plato distinguishes different tasks of the verb 'to be', *being* remains for him a unitary concept.

Note that the distinction at 255c10–11 is drawn in terms of how things that are are said to be, in other words, between uses of 'is'. The claim is then made that the Form Being shares in both the *auto kath'hauto* and the *pros ti*, and there may be a temptation to interpret this as a metaphysical claim that being can be both relative and absolute. However, claims about Forms (i.e. Kinds) in this section of the *Sophist* are cashed in terms of the cognate predicates, so the new formulation at d4–5 does not go beyond the point made at 255c10–11.

he here shows that such a move is illegitimate; in other words, he can be read as operating with what I called the Healthy Schema. He continues to assume that it is legitimate to infer 'X is' from 'X is F', despite the paradox this can entail, and though he does draw attention in the famous passage at 255cd to a distinction between complete and incomplete uses of 'is', the close connection between them meant that he could not exploit the distinction in the way those who accept the 'traditional dichotomy' would expect.

VI Aristotle

In discussing Plato, we have seen good reason to doubt the claim that any Greek speaker implicitly recognised a difference between the complete and the incomplete 'is', to doubt indeed that any clear semantic distinction existed. Though a syntactic distinction between complete and incomplete is undeniable, and may have been noted and used by Plato for a specific purpose at *Sophist* 255cd, it is a distinction where the extremes are clear but the boundary indistinct, and one which offered no help in solving problems of being or of not being.

What of Aristotle's testimony? Does he not expose the distinction, and the fallacy of inferring 'Troy is' from 'Troy is famous'? The distinction that he labels that between 'to be something' and 'to be *haplōs*' – to be *simpliciter* – certainly looks very like what Kahn labelled the traditional dichotomy. Here are some texts:

> (i) *Posterior Analytics* II.1.89b32–5
> (Among the things we seek by enquiry are)
> whether a centaur or a god is or is not – I mean whether one is or is not *simpliciter* and not whether one is white or not. And knowing that it is, we seek what it is, for example so what is a god? or what is a man?
>
> (ii) *Sophistici Elenchi* v.167a1–2
> (Discussing a certain kind of fallacious inference)
> for instance, if what is not is thought about, it does not follow that what is not is. For it is not the same thing to be something and to be *simpliciter*.
>
> (iii) *Sophistici Elenchi* v.180a36–8
> To be something and to be are not the same (for then if what is not is something, it also is *simpliciter*).

Is not Aristotle here drawing attention to the very two uses Mill discusses, the traditional dichotomy between complete (is *simpliciter*) and incomplete use (is something), and assigning the meaning 'exist' to the former? To ask whether a centaur is (passage (i)) is surely to ask whether one exists. But this meaning – is Aristotle not insisting? – is not to be found in the use 'is something', and one falls into fallacy (he tells us in passages (ii) and (iii)) if one tries to infer 'X is' from 'X is something.' Here the point is illustrated by the example of inferring that what is not is from the truth that what is not is thought about. It doesn't matter whether 'what is not' designates some abstract concept or something that is not, such as my first grandchild. In neither case does being thought about entail being.[12] Elsewhere he uses the example of inferring 'Homer is' from 'Homer is a poet' (*de Interpretatione* 21a25–33), though the distinction is there labelled differently. The point is that 'Homer is' implies the falsehood that Homer is alive, so it cannot be validly inferred from 'Homer is a poet.'

At first glance it certainly looks as if Aristotle is pointing out the difference between 'X exists' and 'X is F', warning of the dangers of inferring the former from the latter, and thereby giving in a nutshell the answer Plato should have given in the *Sophist* to the problem of what is not as discussed in the previous section. Aristotle here appears to have given an easy answer to the problem that in saying 'what is not is unthinkable', you are committed to 'what is not is'. The reply seems to be this: in saying that what is not is F you are not saying that what is not is *simpliciter*, that it exists. So you are not after all contradicting yourself: end of problem.

But a closer look at Aristotle's argumentation shows that his distinction is not Mill's:

(1) When discussing the fallacious inference in (ii) and (iii) he classifies it as (what has come to be known as) a fallacy *secundum quid*, the fallacy of moving from a qualified to an unqualified assertion, as when one moves from 'The Indian is white in the tooth' to 'The Indian is white', or from 'He swears truly that he will perjure himself' to 'He swears truly.' In each case the fallacy lies in taking a qualified (*pros ti*) use to license an unqualified use. But there is no suggestion that 'is white' in the two occurrences differ semantically, rather that being white in the tooth is not a way of being white *kuriōs*, in the proper manner (167a17). Similarly being thought about is not a proper way of being. In general, Aristotle believes (I think) that the inference from 'X is F' to 'X is' is a perfectly safe one (just like that from 'Jane teaches French' to 'Jane teaches'), but that for some values of F (being thought about, being dead) the inference is unsafe, but the blame, as it were, lies on the particular value of F, not on a move from one meaning of 'is' to another. The point is a crucial one.

(2) In passage (i), Aristotle distinguishes the questions *whether it is* and *what it is*. A few chapters later (II,7.92b5–8) he insists that it is necessary to know that a thing is in order to know what it is; the answer to the question

[12] A fascinating discussion of medieval solutions to the problem posed by 'being thought about' may be found in 'The Chimaera's Diary' by S. Ebbesen in [30].

whether it is must be 'yes' before one can know what it is. (Compare: in order to know what John is eating, one must know that John is eating.) Where the answer to the question whether it is is 'no', as with a centaur or a goatstag, one cannot say what it is; one can only say what the name signifies. This suggests that Aristotle saw a close connection between the statement 'X is' and the statement 'X is . . .', at least where the latter tells you what X is (which of course 'What is not is thought about' does not). Unless X is, you can't say what X is: again the connection between the complete and incomplete uses shines out.

(3) The distinction between being something and being *simpliciter* is by no means the only or the most important distinction Aristotle draws between the ways in which 'is' or being is said. In his philosophical dictionary, *Metaphysics* v.7, he distinguishes four kinds of 'is': to be accidentally, to be essentially, 'is' in the sense 'is true' (or perhaps 'is truly'), and 'is' meaning 'is potentially'. The 'is something'/'is *simpliciter*' distinction is not on parade. Elsewhere he goes to great lengths to explain that 'is' is 'said in as many ways' as the categories, depending on whether a substance, a quality, a quantity, etc. is (see, for example, *Met.* IV.2; see also VIII.2.) Now this might appear to be a further subdivision of the complete/existential 'is', but Aristotle doesn't stick to a single way of making his point. He uses both complete and incomplete 'is', and sometimes it is hard to tell which use he is analysing. For instance, his point about ice, defined by its composition, may be either of the following:

> for ice to be is for it to be compacted in such a way

or

> to be ice is to be compacted in such and such a way (*Met.* 1042b27–8).

It is hard to tell, and the truth is that it doesn't matter; it is wrong to think that we must decide whether Aristotle was analysing existential or predicative uses in his remarks on how 'is' differs with (and sometimes within) the categories. While modern logic has focused on the difference between the 'is' meaning 'exists' and the predicative 'is', Aristotle placed far more emphasis on what he took to be the different uses or senses connected with the different categories.

What these points show, I suggest, is the following: though Aristotle does distinguish 'is something' from 'is *simpliciter*', his treatment of the distinction does not suggest that he saw here a semantic distinction, or even a syntactic distinction of general importance. The move from 'is F' to 'is' *simpliciter* is disallowed only where the predicate 'F' is for some reason

[15] M. Frede, *Essays in Ancient Philosophy* (Oxford/Minneapolis, 1987)
[16] E. N. Lee, A. P. D. Mourelatos and R. M. Rorty (edd.), *Exegesis and Argument* (Assen, 1973)
[17] D. Manetti *et al.*, *Studi su papiri Greci di logica e medicina* (Florence, 1985)
[18] G. E. L. Owen, *Logic, Science and Dialectic: Collected Papers in Greek Philosophy* (London/Ithaca, 1986)
[19] M. Schofield and M. C. Nussbaum (edd.), *Language and Logos* (Cambridge, 1982).

The following books and articles are concerned with more than one period of ancient thought:

[20] W. Ax, *Laut, Stimme und Sprache: Studien zu drei Grundbegriffen der antiken Sprachtheorie*, *Hypomnemata* 84 (Göttingen, 1986)
[21] J. Corcoran (ed.), *Ancient Logic and its Modern Interpretations* (Dordrecht, 1974)
[22] N. Denyer, *Language, Thought and Falsehood in Ancient Greek Philosophy* (London, 1991)
[23] D. Di Cesare, *La semantica nella filosofia Greca* (Rome, 1980)
[24] M. Frede, 'An Empiricist View of Knowledge: Memorism', in [13], 225–50
[25] P. M. Gentinetta, *Zur Sprachbetrachtung bei den Sophisten und in der stoischhellenistischen Zeit* (Winterthur, 1961)
[26] A. Graeser, 'On Language, Thought and Reality in Ancient Greek Philosophy', *Dialectica* 41 (1977), 360–88
[27] R. Haller, 'Untersuchungen zur Bedeutungsproblem in der antiken und mittelalterlichen Philosophie', *Archiv für Begriffsgeschichte* 7 (1962), 57–119
[28] C. H. Kahn, 'The Greek Verb "to be" and the Concept of Being', *Foundations of Language* 2 (1966), 245–65
[29] C. H. Kahn, *The Verb 'be' in Ancient Greek* (Dordrecht, 1973)
[30] S. Knuuttila and J. Hintikka (edd.), *The Logic of Being* (Dordrecht, 1986)
[31] M. Matthen, 'Greek Ontology and the "Is" of Truth', *Phronesis* 28 (1983), 113–85
[32] G. Nuchelmans, *Theories of the Proposition: Ancient and Medieval Conceptions of the Bearers of Truth and Falsity* (Amsterdam, 1973)
[33] J. Pinborg, 'Historiography of Linguistics: Classical Antiquity: Greece', in *Current Trends in Linguistics* 13 (The Hague, 1975), 69–126
[34] R. H. Robins, *Ancient and Medieval Grammatical Theory in Europe* (London, 1951)
[35] R. Robinson, *Essays in Greek Philosophy* (Oxford, 1969)
[36] D. J. Taylor, 'Rethinking the History of Language Science in Classical Antiquity', *Historiographica Linguistica* 13 (1986), 175–90.

The Presocratics

Texts and translations

The writings of the Presocratic philosophers survive only in fragments cited by later writers. The standard collection of these fragments, together with later ancient reports of presocratic philosophy is

[37] H. Diels and W. Kranz, *Die Fragmente der Vorsokratiker*, 10th edn (Berlin 1960).

Translations of all the fragments within their doxographical context are provided in

[38] J. Barnes, *Early Greek Philosophy* (Harmondsworth, 1987).

See also

[39] J. Mansfeld, *Die Vorsokratiker* (Stuttgart, 1987).

The following provide general accounts of the Presocratics:

[40] J. Barnes, *The Presocratics*, 2 vols. (London, 1979); revised in one volume (London, 1982)

[41] H. Fränkel, *Early Greek Poetry and Philosophy*, tr. M. Hadas and J. Willis (Oxford, 1975)

[42] E. Hussey, *The Presocratics* (London, 1972)

[43] G. S. Kirk, J. E. Raven and M. Schofield, *The Presocratic Philosophers*, 2nd edn (Cambridge, 1983).

Two collections of articles on Presocratic philosophy are

[44] D. J. Furley and R. E. Allen (edd.), *Studies in Presocratic Philosophy*, 2 vols. (London, 1970, 1975)

[45] A. P. D. Mourelatos (ed.), *The Presocratics* (Garden City, 1974).

See also

[46] H. Fränkel, *Wege und Formen frühgriechischen Denkens*, 2nd edn (Munich, 1960).

For the linguistic interests of thinkers before Plato, see

[47] W. Burkert, 'La Genèse des choses et des mots', *Les Etudes philosophiques* (1970), 443–55

[48] J. C. Classen, 'The Study of Language among Socrates' Contemporaries', *Proceedings of the African Classical Association* 2 (1959), 33–49

[49] H. Diels, 'Die Anfänge der Philologie bei den griechen' *Neue Jahrbuch für Philologie* 25 (1910), 1–25

[50] D. Fehling, 'Zwei Untersuchungen zur griechischen Sprachphilosophie', *Rheinisches Museum* 108 (1965), 212–29

[51] M. Kraus, *Name und Sache: Ein Problem im frühgriechischen Denken* (Amsterdam, 1987)

[52] K. Robb (ed.), *Language and Thought in Early Greek Philosophy* (La Salle, 1983)

Heraclitus

[53] E. Hussey, 'Epistemology and Meaning in Heraclitus', in [19], 33–60

Parmenides

For a critical text of the fragments, see

[54] A. H. Coxon, *The Fragments of Parmenides, Phronesis* supplementary volume III (Assen/Maastricht, 1986)

as well as

[55] L. Tarán, *Parmenides* (Princeton, 1965)

and

[56] P. Aubenque (ed.), *Etudes sur Parmenide*, 2 vols. (Paris, 1987), of which the first volume contains a critical text by Denis O'Brien together with translations in French and English.

See also

[57] D. Gallop, *Parmenides of Elea: fragments* (Toronto, 1984).

Studies of Parmenides include

[58] S. Austin, *Parmenides, Being, Bounds and Logic* (New Haven, 1985)

[59] A. P. D. Mourelatos, *The Route of Parmenides* (New Haven, 1970)

[60] L. Woodbury, 'Parmenides on Names', *Harvard Studies in Classical Philology* 63 (1958), 145–60, and in [8].

Discussions of how *einai* should be construed in Parmenides include

[61] M. Furth, 'Elements of Eleatic Ontology', *Journal of the History of Philosophy* 6 (1986), 111–32, and in [45], 241–70.

[62] B. Jones, 'Parmenides' "The Way of Truth"', *Journal of the History of Philosophy* 11 (1973), 287–98

[63] C. H. Kahn, 'The Thesis of Parmenides', *Review of Metaphysics* 22 (1968–9), 700–24

[64] C. H. Kahn, 'More on Parmenides', *Review of Metaphysics* 23 (1969–70), 333–40.

Democritus

[65] R. Philippson, 'Platons Kratylos und Demokrit', *Philologische Wochenschrift* 49 (1929), 923–7

The sophists

A general introduction can be found in

[66] G. B. Kerferd, *The Sophistic Movement* (Cambridge, 1981)

[67] J. De Romilly, *Les Grands Sophistes dans l'Athènes de Périclès* (Paris, 1988), which is translated by Janet Lloyd as

[68] J. De Romilly, *The Great Sophists in Periclean Athens* (Oxford, 1992).

[69] C. J. Classen (ed.), *Sophistik, Wege der Forschung* 187 (Darmstadt, 1976) contains a series of essays on the sophists.

Gorgias

[70] A. P. D. Mourelatos, 'Gorgias on the Function of Language', *Philosophical Topics* 15 (1987), 135–70

Prodicus

As well as ch. 7 of [66] and pp. 136–40 of [78], see

[71] H. Mayer, *Prodikos von Keos und die Anfänge der Synonymik bei den Griechen* (Paderborn, 1913).

For Prodicus' claim that contradiction is impossible, see

[72] G. Binder and L. Liesenborghs, 'Eine Zuweisung der Sentenz *ouk estin antilegein* an Prodikos von Keos', in [69], 452–62
as well as ch. 3 of [22].

The *Dissoi Logoi*, a set of opposed arguments, contains a section on truth and falsehood. See

[73] T. M. Robinson, *Contrasting Arguments* (Salem, 1984).

Socrates

Our major source of evidence for Socrates' views and his approach to philosophy is the early dialogues of Plato. Translations of these can be found in

[74] T. J. Saunders (ed.), *Early Socratic Dialogues* (Harmondsworth, 1987).

Two translations of individual dialogues, together with commentaries, are

[75] R. E. Allen, *Plato's Euthyphro and the Earlier Theory of Forms* (London, 1970)

[76] P. Woodruff, *Plato's Hippias Major* (Oxford, 1982).

Two dialogues which are probably slightly later than the very early ones but in which recognisably 'Socratic' views are presented are the *Protagoras* and the *Gorgias*. A commentary on the Greek text of the latter is

[77] E. R. Dodds, *Plato's Gorgias* (Oxford, 1959).

Commentaries on the dialogues in translation are

[78] C. C. W. Taylor, *Plato: Protagoras* (Oxford, 1977)

[79] T. H. Irwin, *Plato, Gorgias* (Oxford, 1979).

Introductions to Socratic thought are

[80] N. Gulley, *The Philosophy of Socrates* (London, 1968)

[81] G. Santas, *Socrates* (London, 1979)

[82] G. Vlastos, *Socrates: Ironist and Moral Philosopher* (Cambridge, 1991).

Two collections of essays on Socratic thought are

[83] G. Vlastos (ed.), *The Philosophy of Socrates* (Garden City, 1971)

[84] H. H. Benson (ed.), *Essays on the Philosophy of Socrates* (New York/ Oxford, 1992).

There is no Socratic theory of language as such – but his general concern for eliciting definitions has implications for the understanding of language. For this, see

[85] H. H. Benson, 'The Priority of Definition and the Socratic Elenchus', *Oxford Studies in Ancient Philosophy* VIII (1990), 18–65

[86] H. H. Benson (ed.), 'Misunderstanding the 'What-is-F-ness' Question', *Archiv für Geschichte der Philosophie* 72 (1990), 125–42, and in [84], 123–36

[87] J. Beversluis, 'Socratic Definition', *American Philosophical Quarterly* 11 (1974), 331–6
[88] J. Beversluis, 'Does Socrates Commit the Socratic Fallacy?', *American Philosophical Quarterly* (1987), 211–23 and in [84], 107–22
[89] P. T. Geach, 'Plato's *Euthyphro*', *Monist* (1966), 369–82 and in [502], 31–43
[90] R. M. Gordon, 'Socratic Definitions and Moral Neutrality', *Journal of Philosophy* 61 (1964), 433–50
[91] G. Nakhnikian, 'Elenctic Definitions', in [83], 125–57
[92] A. Nehamas, 'Confusing Universals and Particulars in Plato's Early Dialogues', *Review of Metaphysics* (1975), 287–306
[93] T. Penner, 'The Unity of Virtue', *Philosophical Review* (1973), and in [84], 162–84
[94] G. Santas, 'The Socratic Fallacy', *Journal of the History of Philosophy* (1972), 127–41
[95] G. Vlastos, 'What did Socrates Understand by his "What is *F*?" Question?', in his [113], 410–17
as well as ch. IV of [81] and ch. III of [101].

Plato

Translations of all the dialogues, by various hands, can be found in

[96] E. Hamilton and H. Cairns (edd.), *The Collected Dialogues of Plato* (Princeton, 1961).

Introductions

[97] I. M. Crombie, *An Examination of Plato's Doctrines* 2 vols. (London, 1962, 1963)
[98] J. C. B. Gosling, *Plato* (London, 1973)
[99] R. Kraut, 'Introduction to the Study of Plato', in [108], 1–50
[100] C. J. Rowe, *Plato* (Brighton, 1984).

The following are wide-ranging studies of various aspects of Plato's thought:

[101] T. H. Irwin, *Plato's Moral Theory* (Oxford, 1977)
[102] J. Moline, *Plato's Theory of Understanding* (Wisconsin/London, 1981)
[103] R. Robinson, *Plato's Earlier Dialectic* (Oxford, 1953)
[104] K. M. Sayre, *Plato's Analytical Method* (Chicago/London, 1969)
[105] N. P. White, *Plato on Knowledge and Reality* (Indianapolis, 1976).

The following contain articles on Plato:

[106] R. E. Allen (ed.), *Studies in Plato's Metaphysics* (London, 1965)
[107] J. P. Anton and A. Preus (ed.), *Essays in Ancient Greek Philosophy*, III, *Plato* (New York, 1989)
[108] R. Kraut (ed.), *The Cambridge Companion to Plato* (Cambridge, 1992)
[109] J. Moravcsik (ed.), *Patterns in Plato's Thought* (Dordrecht, 1973)
[110] D. J. O'Meara (ed.), *Platonic Investigations* (Washington, D.C., 1985)
[111] G. Vlastos (ed.), *Plato*, I, *Metaphysics and Epistemology* (Garden City, 1971)

[112] G. Vlastos (ed.), *Plato*, II, *Ethics, Politics and Philosophy of Art and Religion* (Garden City, 1971)
[113] G. Vlastos, *Platonic Studies*, 2nd edn (Princeton, 1981).

The relative dating of the dialogues is discussed in
[114] G. E. L. Owen, 'The Place of the *Timaeus* in Plato's Dialogues', *Classical Quarterly* (1953), 79–95, in [106], 313–38 and in [18], 65–84
[115] H. Cherniss, 'The Relation of the *Timaeus* to Plato's Later Dialogues', *American Journal of Philology* (1957), 225–66, in [106], 339–78 and in his [12], 298–339.

For the date of the *Cratylus*, see
[116] J. V. Luce, 'The Date of the *Cratylus*', *American Journal of Philology* 85 (1964), 136–54
and [169]

The following are discussions of various topics in Plato's treatment of language:
[117] D. Gallop, 'Plato and the Alphabet', *Philosophical Review* 72 (1963), 364–76
[118] P. B. Levinson, 'Language, Plato and Logic', in [8], 259–84
[119] T. G. Rosenmeyer, 'Plato and Mass Words', *Transactions of the American Philological Association* 88 (1957), 88–102
[120] G. Ryle, 'Letters and Syllables in Plato', *Philosophical Review* 69 (1960), 431–51, and in [528], 54–71.

The theory of Forms

As well as ch. 9 of [146] and ch. x of [144], see
[121] R. E. Allen, 'Participation and Predication in Plato's Middle Dialogues', *Philosophical Review* 69 (1960), 147–64 and in [106], 43–60
[122] G. Fine, 'Separation', *Oxford Studies in Ancient Philosophy* 2 (1984), 31–87
[123] A. Nehamas, 'Participation and Predication in Plato's Later Thought', *Review of Metaphysics* 36 (1982), 343–74
[124] C. Stough, 'Forms and Explanation in Plato', *Phronesis* 21 (1976), 1–30
[125] R. Turnbull, 'Knowledge and the Forms in the Later Platonic Dialogues', *Proceedings and Addresses of the American Philosophical Association* 51 (1978), 735–58
[126] A. Wedberg, 'The Theory of Ideas', in [111], 28–52.

The claim that Forms can be predicated of themselves is discussed in
[127] J. S. Clegg, 'Self-predication and Linguistic Reference in Plato's Theory of the Forms', *Phronesis* 18 (1973), 26–43
[128] J. Malcolm, 'Semantics and Self-predication in Plato', *Phronesis* 26 (1981), 286–94
[129] J. Malcolm, *Plato and the Self-predication of Forms* (Oxford, 1991)
[130] A. Nehamas, 'Self-predication and Plato's Theory of Forms', *American Philosophical Quarterly* 16 (1979), 93–103

[131] A. Silverman, 'Synonymy and Self-predication', *Ancient Philosophy* 10 (1990), 193–202
[132] G. Vlastos, 'Self-predication and Self-participation in Plato's Later Period', *Philosophical Review* 78 (1969), 74–8, and in [113], 335–41
[133] G. Vlastos, 'A Note on "Pauline predications" in Plato', *Phronesis* (1974), 95–101
[134] G. Vlastos, 'On a Proposed Redefinition of "Self-predication" in Plato', *Phronesis* 26 (1981), 76–9 (which is a criticism of [130]).

For Aristotle's criticisms of the theory, see
[135] R. Barford, 'A Proof from the *Peri Ideōn* Revisited', *Phronesis* 21 (1976), 198–219
[136] G. Fine, 'The One Over Many', *Philosophical Review* 89 (1980), 197–240
[137] G. Fine, 'Aristotle and the More Accurate Arguments', in [19], 155–78
[138] J. Kung, 'Aristotle on Thises, Suches and the Third Man Argument', *Phronesis* 26 (1981), 207–47
[139] G. E. L. Owen, 'A Proof in the *Peri Ideōn*', *Journal of Hellenic Studies* 77 (1957), 301–11, in [106], 293–312 and in [18], 165–79
[140] C. J. Rowe, 'The Proof from Relatives in the *Peri Ideōn*: Further Reconsideration', *Phronesis* 24 (1979), 270–81.

A critical text of the *Peri Ideōn* by D. Harlfinger is contained in
[141] W. Leszl, *Il 'De Ideis' di Aristotele e la teoria Platonica delle Idee* (Florence, 1975).

For Plato's own criticisms of the theory, see the items listed under the *Parmenides* below.

Phaedo

A commentary on the Greek text of the *Phaedo* is:
[142] J. Burnet, *Plato's Phaedo* (Oxford, 1911).

A modern philosophical commentary on the *Phaedo* translated is
[143] D. Gallop, *Plato's Phaedo* (Oxford, 1975).

A recent philosophical introduction to the dialogue is
[144] D. Bostock, *Plato's Phaedo* (Oxford, 1986).

The Republic

A commentary on the Greek text is
[145] J. Adam, *The Republic of Plato*, 2 vols., 2nd edn with introduction by D. A. Rees (Cambridge, 1963)

Introductions to the *Republic* include
[146] J. Annas, *An Introduction to Plato's Republic* (Oxford, 1981)
[147] A. C. Cross and A. D. Woozley, *Plato's Republic: A Philosophical Commentary* (London, 1964)
[148] N. P. White, *A Companion to Plato's Republic* (Indianapolis, 1979).

In Book v of the *Republic*, Plato distinguishes belief (*doxa*) from knowledge (*epistēmē*), an argument which is discussed in ch. 11. Discussions of Plato's argument include ch. 4 of [22] and

[149] N. Cooper, 'Between Knowledge and Ignorance', *Phronesis* 31 (1986), 229–42
[150] G. Fine, 'Knowledge and Belief in *Republic* v', *Archiv für Geschichte der Philosophie* 60 (1978), 121–39
[151] G. Fine, 'Knowledge and Belief in *Republic* v–vii', in [13], 85–115.

For Plato's use of *einai*, see

[152] G. Vlastos, 'A Metaphysical Paradox', in [113], 43–57
[153] C. H. Kahn, 'Some Philosophical Uses of 'to be' in Plato', *Phronesis* 26 (1981), 105–34
[154] F. A. Lewis, 'Did Plato Discover the *estin* of Identity?', *California Studies in Classical Antiquity* 8 (1975), 113–43
[155] B. Mates, 'Identity and Predication in Plato', *Phronesis* 24 (1979), 211–29
[156] G. Vlastos, 'Degrees of Reality in Plato', in [113], 58–75

The Cratylus and names

[157] G. Anagnostopoulos, 'Plato's *Cratylus*: The Two Theories of the Correctness of Names', *Review of Metaphysics* 25 (1971–2), 691–736
[158] G. Anagnostopoulos, 'The Significance of Plato's *Cratylus*', *Review of Metaphysics* 27 (1973–4), 320–45
[159] J. Annas, 'Knowledge and Language: the *Theaetetus* and the *Cratylus*', in [19], 95–114
[160] T. W. Bestor, 'Plato's Semantics and Plato's *Cratylus*', *Phronesis* 25 (1980), 306–30
[161] B. Calvert, 'Forms and Flux in Plato's *Cratylus*', *Phronesis* 15 (1970), 26–34
[162] G. Fine, 'Plato on Naming', *Philosophical Quarterly* 27 (1977), 289–301
[163] J. Gold, 'The Ambiguity of "Name" in Plato's *Cratylus*', *Philosophical Studies* 34 (1978), 223–51
[164] C. H. Kahn, 'Language and Ontology in the *Cratylus*', in [16], 152–77
[165] R. J. Ketchum, 'Names, Forms and Conventionalism: *Cratylus* 383–95', *Phronesis* 24 (1979), 133–47
[166] N. Kretzmann, 'Plato on the Correctness of Names', *American Philosophical Quarterly* 8 (1971), 126–38
[167] K. Lorenz and J. Mittelstrass, 'On Rational Philosophy of Language: The Programme in Plato's *Cratylus* Reconsidered', *Mind* 75 (1966), 1–29
[168] J. V. Luce, 'The Theory of Ideas in the *Cratylus*', *Phronesis* 10 (1965), 21–36
[169] M. M. Mackenzie, 'Putting the *Cratylus* in its Place', *Classical Quarterly* 36 (1986), 124–50
[170] M. Richardson, 'True and False Names in the *Cratylus*', *Phronesis* 21 (1976), 135–45
[171] J. C. Rijlaarsdam, *Platon über die Sprache: eine Kommentar zum Kratylos* (Utrecht, 1978)

[172] R. Robinson, 'A Criticism of Plato's *Cratylus*', *Philosophical Review* 65 (1956), 324–41, and in [35], 100–17
[173] R. Robinson, 'The Theory of Names in Plato's *Cratylus*', *Revue internationale de philosophie* 9 (1955), 221–36, and in [35], 118–38
[174] M. Schofield, 'The Dénouement of the *Cratylus*', in [19], 61–81
[175] A. Silverman, 'Plato's *Cratylus*: The Naming of Nature and the Nature of Naming', *Oxford Studies in Ancient Philosophy* x (1992), 25–71
[176] R. H. Weingartner, 'Making Sense of the *Cratylus*', *Phronesis* 15 (1970), 5–25

Theaetetus

[177] J. H. McDowell, *Plato's Theaetetus* (Oxford, 1973)
provides a philosophical commentary on the dialogue in translation.
[178] F. M. Cornford, *Plato's Theory of Knowledge* (London, 1935)
contains a translation of both the *Theaetetus* and the *Sophist* with a running commentary.
Discussions of the whole dialogue include
[179] M. F. Burnyeat (ed.), *The Theaetetus of Plato* (Indianapolis, 1990), which contains a translation of the *Theaetetus*, together with a 250-page introduction.
[180] D. Bostock, *Plato's Theaetetus*, (Oxford, 1988)
provides another highly sophisticated treatment of the dialogue.
[181] M. F. Burnyeat, 'Plato on the Grammar of Perceiving', *Classical Quarterly* 70 (1976), 29–51
[182] G. Fine, 'Knowledge and *Logos* in the *Theaetetus*', *Philosophical Review* 88 (1979), 366–97
[183] J. H. McDowell, 'Identity Mistakes: Plato and the Logical Atomists', *Proceedings of the Aristotelian Society* 70 (1969–70), 181–96
[184] A. Nehamas, 'Epistēmē and Logos in Plato's Later Thought', in [107], 267–92
[185] G. Ryle, 'Logical Atomism in Plato's *Theaetetus*', *Phronesis* 35 (1990), 21–46

The Sophist

[186] J. L. Ackrill, '*Symplokē eidōn*', *Bulletin of the Institute of Classical Studies* 2 (1955) 31–5, and in [111], 201–9, and in [106], 199–206
[187] J. L. Ackrill, 'Plato and the Copula', *Journal of Hellenic Studies* 77 (1957), 1–6, and in [111], 210–22
[188] R. S. Bluck, *Plato's Sophist* (Manchester, 1975)
[189] R. S. Bluck, 'False Statement in the *Sophist*', *Journal of Hellenic Studies* 77 (1957), 181–6
[190] D. Bostock, 'Plato on "is not"', *Oxford Studies in Ancient Philosophy* 2 (1984), 89–120
[191] L. Brown, 'Being in the *Sophist*, a Syntactical Enquiry', *Oxford Studies in Ancient Philosophy* 4 (1986), 49–70
[192] M. Frede, *Prädikation und Existenzaussage*, *Hypomnemata* 18 (Göttingen, 1967)
[193] M. Frede, 'Plato's *Sophist* on False Statements', in [108], 397–424

[194] R. Hackforth, 'False Statement in the *Sophist*', *Classical Quarterly* 39 (1945), 56–8
[195] R. Heinaman, 'Communion of Forms', *Proceedings of the Aristotelian Society* 83 (1982–3), 175–90
[196] R. Heinaman, 'Being in the *Sophist*', *Archiv für Geschichte der Philosophie* 65 (1983), 1–17
[197] R. Heinaman, 'Self-predication in the *Sophist*', *Phronesis* 26 (1981), 55–66
[198] R. J. Ketchum, 'Participation and Predication in *Sophist* 251–60', *Phronesis* 23 (1978), 42–62
[199] D. Keyt, 'Plato on Falsity: *Sophist* 263B', in [16], 285–305
[200] J. P. Kostman, 'False Logos and Not-being in Plato's *Sophist*', in [109], 192–202
[201] E. N. Lee, 'Plato on Negation and Not-being in the *Sophist*', *Philosophical Review* 76 (1972), 267–304
[202] F. A. Lewis, 'Plato on "Not"', *California Studies in Classical Antiquity* 9 (1976), 89–115
[203] J. McDowell, 'Falsehood and Not-being in Plato's *Sophist*', in [19], 115–34
[204] J. Malcolm, 'Plato's Analysis of *to on* and *to mē on* in the *Sophist*', *Phronesis* 12 (1967), 130–46
[205] J. M. E. Moravcsik, 'Being and Meaning in the *Sophist*', *Acta Philosophica Fennica* 14 (1962), 23–64
[206] J. M. E. Moravcsik, '*Symplokē Eidōn* and the Genesis of *Logos*', *Archiv für Geschichte der Philosophie* 42 (1960), 117–29
[207] G. E. L. Owen, 'Plato on Not-being', in [111], 223–67 and in [18], 104–37
[208] F. J. Pelletier, *Parmenides, Plato and the Semantics of Not-being* (Chicago, 1990)
[209] A. L. Peck, 'Plato's *Sophist*: The *Symplokē tōn Eidōn*', *Phronesis* 7 (1962), 46–66
[210] L. M. de Rijk, *Plato's Sophist: A Philosophical Commentary* (Amsterdam, 1986)
[211] J. Roberts, 'The Problem about Being in the *Sophist*', *History of Philosophy Quarterly* 3 (1986), 229–43
[212] J. R. Trevaskis, 'The *Megista Genē* and the Vowel Analogy of Plato, *Sophist* 253', *Phronesis* 11 (1966), 99–116
[213] G. Vlastos, 'An Ambiguity in the Sophist', in [113], 270–322
[214] D. Wiggins, 'Sentence-meaning, Negation, and Plato's Problem of Non-being', in [111], 268–303

The Parmenides

[215] R. E. Allen, *Plato's Parmenides* (Oxford, 1983)
contains a translation of the dialogue, together with an analysis of its arguments.
[216] C. C. Meinwald, *Plato's Parmenides* (New York, 1991)
is a full-length discussion of the *Parmenides*.

[217] T. W. Bestor, 'Plato's Semantics and Plato's *Parmenides*', *Phronesis* 25 (1980), 38–75
[218] S. Marc Cohen, 'The Logic of the Third Man', *Philosophical Review* 80 (1971), 448–75
[219] P. T. Geach, 'The Third Man Again', *Philosophical Review* 65 (1956), 72–82
[220] C. C. Meinwald, 'Good-bye to the Third Man', in [108], 365–96
[221] J. Moravcsik, 'Forms and Dialectic in the Second Half of the *Parmenides*', in [19], 135–53
[222] S. Peterson, 'The Greatest Difficulty for Plato's Theory of Forms: The Unknowability Argument of *Parmenides* 133c–134c', *Archiv für Geschichte der Philosophie* 63 (1981), 1–16
[223] M. Schofield, 'The Antinomies of Plato's *Parmenides*', *Classical Quarterly* 27 (1977), 139–58
[224] W. Sellars, 'Vlastos and the Third Man', *Philosophical Review* 64 (1955), 405–37
[225] R. Sternfeld and H. Zyskind, *Meaning, Relation and Existence in Plato's Parmenides: The Logic of Relational Realism* (New York, 1987)
[226] C. Strang, 'Plato and the Third Man', *Proceedings of the Aristotelian Society* Suppl. Vol. 37 (1963), 147–64, and in [111], 184–200
[227] R. G. Turnbull, 'The Third Man Argument and the Text of the *Parmenides*', in [107], 203–26
[228] G. Vlastos, 'The Third Man Argument in the *Parmenides*', *Philosophical Review* 63 (1954), 319–49
[229] G. Vlastos, 'Plato's "Third Man" Argument (*Parm.* 131a1–b1): Text and Logic', *Philosophical Quarterly* 191 (1969), 289–301, and, with appendices, in [113], 342–65

Aristotle

A complete translation of Aristotle's surviving work is

[230] J. Barnes (ed.), *The Complete Works of Aristotle: The Revised Oxford Translation*, 2 vols. (Princeton, 1984).

A useful selection of Aristotelian texts is

[231] J. L. Ackrill (ed.), *A New Aristotle Reader* (Oxford, 1987).

Introductions

Two short introductions to Aristotle's thought are

[232] J. L. Ackrill, *Aristotle the Philosopher* (Oxford, 1981)
[233] J. Barnes, *Aristotle* (Oxford, 1982).

Longer introductions include

[234] I. Düring, *Aristoteles: Darstellung und Interpretation seines Denkens* (Heidelberg, 1966)
[235] J. D. G. Evans, *Aristotle* (Brighton, 1987)
[236] J. Lear, *Aristotle: The Desire to Understand* (Cambridge, 1988)
[237] G. E. R. Lloyd, *Aristotle: The Growth and Structure of his Thought* (Cambridge, 1968)
[238] W. D. Ross, *Aristotle* (London, 1923).

[239] T. H. Irwin, *Aristotle's First Principles* (Oxford, 1988)
provides a systematic account of Aristotle's thought and method.

For a discussion of Aristotle's treatment of language, see
[240] W. Belardi, *Il Linguaggio nella Filosofia di Aristotele* (Rome, 1975).

The following are anthologies of articles on various aspects of Aristotle's thought:
[241] J. Barnes, M. Schofield and R. Sorabji (edd.), *Articles on Aristotle*, vol. 1, *Science* (London, 1975)
[242] J. Barnes, M. Schofield and R. Sorabji (edd.), *Articles on Aristotle*, vol. 2, *Ethics and Politics* (London, 1977)
[243] J. Barnes, M. Schofield and R. Sorabji (edd.), *Articles on Aristotle*, vol. 3, *Metaphysics* (London, 1979)
[244] J. Barnes, M. Schofield and R. Sorabji (edd.), *Articles on Aristotle*, vol. 4, *Psychology and Aesthetics* (London, 1979)
[245] E. Berti (ed.), *Aristotle on Science: The Posterior Analytics* (Padua/New York, 1980)
[246] I. Düring and G. E. L. Owen (edd.), *Plato and Aristotle in the Mid-fourth Century* (Göteborg, 1960)
[247] J. M. E. Moravcsik (ed.), *Aristotle* (Garden City, 1967 and Oxford, 1968)
[248] D. J. O'Meara (ed.), *Studies in Aristotle* (Washington, 1981).

The following monographs are referred to in this book:
[249] F. Brentano, *Die Psychologie des Aristoteles* (Mainz, 1967), which is translated by R. George as
[250] F. Brentano, *The Psychology of Aristotle* (Berkeley/Los Angeles/London, 1977)
[251] D. Charles, *Aristotle's Philosophy of Action* (London, 1984)
[252] R. Sorabji, *Necessity, Cause and Blame* (London, 1980).

[253] J. L. Ackrill, *Aristotle's Categories and De Interpretatione* (Oxford, 1963) and
[254] J. Barnes, *Aristotle's Posterior Analytics* (Oxford, 1976)
contain translations and philosophical commentaries. (A new edition of [254] is in preparation.)

Semantic theory

[255] R. Bolton, 'Essentialism and Semantic Theory in Aristotle', *Philosophical Review* 85 (1976), 514–44
[256] D. De Moss and D. Devereux, 'Essence, Existence and Nominal Definition in Aristotle's *Posterior Analytics* II.8–10', *Phronesis* 33 (1988), 133–54.
[257] T. H. Irwin, 'Aristotle's Concept of Signification', in [19], 240–66
[258] N. Kretzmann, 'Aristotle on Spoken Sound Significant by Convention', in [21], 3–21
[259] R. Polansky and M. Kuczewski, 'Speech and Thought, Symbol and Likeness: Aristotle's *De Interpretatione* 16a3–9', *Ancient Philosophy* 0 (1900), 000–000

[260] P. Tselemanis, 'Theory of Meaning and Signification in Aristotle', in *Language and Reality*, ed. C. Voudouris (Athens, 1985), 194–9

See also

[261] M. Matthen, 'Aristotle's Semantics and a Puzzle concerning Change', *Canadian Journal of Philosophy* Suppl. 10 (1984)

[262] M. C. Nussbaum, 'Saving Aristotle's Appearances', in [19], 267–93.

Essentialism

[263] A. Code, 'Aristotle: Essence and Accident', in [505], 411–39

[264] S. Marc Cohen, 'Individual and Essence in Aristotle's *Metaphysics*', *Paideia* (1978), 75–85

[265] F. A. Lewis, 'What is Aristotle's Theory of Essence?', *Canadian Journal of Philosophy*, supplement 10 (1984), 89–131

[266] A.C. Lloyd, 'Necessity and Essence in the *Posterior Analytics*', in [245], 151–71

[267] N. P. White, 'Origins of Aristotle's Essentialism', *Review of Metaphysics* 26 (1972–3), 57–85

[268] M. J. Woods, 'Aristotle on the Identity of Substance and Essence', *Proceedings of the Aristotelian Society* 75 (1974–5), 167–80

Definitions

[269] J. L. Ackrill, 'Aristotle's Theory of Definition: Some Questions on *Post. An.* II.8–10', in [245], 359–84

[270] J. E. Hare, 'Aristotle and the Definition of Natural Things', *Phronesis* 24 (1979), 168–79

[271] R. Sorabji, 'Definitions: Why Necessary and in What Way?, in [245], 205–44

Predication

[272] R. E. Allen, 'Substance and Predication in Aristotle's *Categories*', in [16], 362–73

[273] V. Celluprica, 'Logica e semantica nella teoria Aristotelica della predicazione', *Phronesis* 32 (1987), 166–87

[274] A. Code, 'On the Origins of Some Aristotelian Theses about Predication', in [476], 101–31

[275] S. M. Cohen, '"Predicable of" in Aristotle's *Categories*', *Phronesis* 18 (1973), 69–70

[276] J. Duerlinger, 'Predication and Inherence in Aristotle's *Categories*', *Phronesis* 15 (1970), 179–203

[277] D. J. Hadgopoulos, 'The Definition of the "Predicables" in Aristotle', *Phronesis* 21 (1976), 59–63

[278] D. W. Hamlyn, 'Aristotle on Predication', *Phronesis* 6 (1961), 110–26

[279] F. A. Lewis, 'Form and Predication in Aristotle's *Metaphysics*', in [476], 59–83

[280] F. A. Lewis, *Substance and Predication in Aristotle* (Cambridge, 1991)

[281] M. Loux, 'Form, Species and Predication', *Mind* 88 (1979), 1–23

[282] J. M. E. Moravcsik, 'Aristotle on Predication', *Philosophical Review* 76 (1967), 80–96
[283] G. E. L. Owen, 'Inherence', *Phronesis* 10 (1965), 97–105, and in [18], 252–8
[284] H. Weidemann, 'In Defence of Aristotle's Theory of Predication', *Phronesis* 25 (1980), 76–87

Categories

[285] B. Jones, 'An Introduction to the First Five Chapters of Aristotle's *Categories*', *Phronesis* 20 (1975), 146–72
[286] M. Frede, 'Categories in Aristotle', in [15], 29–48 and [248], 1–24
[287] N. Garver, 'Notes for a Linguistic Reading of the *Categories*', in [21], 27–32
[288] R. Heinaman, 'Non-substantial Individuals in Aristotle's *Categories*', *Phronesis* 26 (1981), 295–307
[289] A. C. Lloyd, 'Aristotle's *Categories* Today', *Philosophical Quarterly* 16 (1966), 258–67
[290] J. M. E. Moravcsik, 'Aristotle's Theory of Categories', in [247], 125–45
[291] C. L. Stough, 'Language and Ontology in the *Categories*', *Journal of the History of Philosophy* 10 (1972), 261–72

Names and reference

[292] J. Hankinson, 'Improper Names', *Apeiron* 20 (1987), 219–25
[293] R. W. Jacobs, 'Aristotle and Non-referring Subjects', *Phronesis* 24 (1979), 282–300
[294] M. Wedin, 'Aristotle on the Existential Import of Singular Sentences', *Phronesis* 23 (1978), 179–96

See also

[295] W. Jacobs, 'The Existential Presuppositions of Aristotle's Logic', *Philosophical Studies* 37 (1980), 419–28.

Referential opacity

[296] F. J. Pelletier, 'Sameness and Referential Opacity in Aristotle', *Nous* 13 (1979), 283–311
[297] S. L. Peterson, 'Substitution in Technical Aristotelian Contexts', *Philosophical Studies* 47 (1985), 249–56
[298] L. Spellman, 'Referential Opacity in Aristotle', *History of Philosophy Quarterly* 7 (1990), 17–32
[299] C. J. F. Williams, 'Aristotle's Theory of Descriptions', *Philosophical Review* 94 (1985), 63–80

Einai

[300] G. E. L. Owen, 'Aristotle on the Snares of Ontology', in [10], 69–75 and in [18], 259–78
See also
[301] R. M. Dancy, 'Aristotle and Existence', *Synthèse* (1983), reprinted in [30].

Focal meaning and homonymy

[302] G. E. L. Owen, 'Logic and Metaphysics in Some Earlier Works of Aristotle', in [246], 163–90; [243], 13–32 and [18], 180–99

[303] M. Ferejohn, 'Aristotle on Focal Meaning and the Unity of Science', *Phronesis* 25 (1980), 117–28

[304] D. W. Hamlyn, 'Focal Meaning', *Proceedings of the Aristotelian Society* 78 (1977–8), 1–18

[305] T. H. Irwin, 'Homonymy in Aristotle', *Review of Metaphysics* 34 (1981), 523–44

Hellenistic Philosophy

A good brief introduction to Hellenistic philosophy can be found in:

[306] A. A. Long, *Hellenistic Philosophy*, 2nd edn (London/Berkeley/Los Angeles 1986).

[307] E. Zeller, *Stoics, Epicureans, and Skeptics*, tr. O. Reichel (London, 1880) remains a worthwhile account of the Hellenistic schools.

Most of the writings of the Hellenistic philosophers survive only in fragments – either as reported by writers whose work has survived in full or, especially in the case of Epicurus and later Epicureans, on invariably damaged rolls of papyrus. A recent collection of key fragments and testimonia is

[308] A. A. Long and D. Sedley, *The Hellenistic Philosophers*, 2 vols. (Cambridge, 1987),
of which the first volume contains the translations and commentary and the second the original texts.
A shorter collection of texts in translation is

[309] B. Inwood and L. P. Gerson (edd.), *Hellenistic Philosophy: Introductory Readings* (Indianapolis, 1988).

A general account of Hellenistic psychology is given by

[310] J. Annas, *Hellenistic Philosophy of Mind* (Berkeley/Los Angeles/Oxford, 1992).

The following contain articles on different aspects of Hellenistic thought:

[311] M. Schofield, M. Burnyeat and J. Barnes (edd.), *Doubt and Dogmatism: Studies in Hellenistic Epistemology* (Oxford, 1980)

[312] J. Barnes, J. Brunschwig, M. Burnyeat and M. Schofield (edd.), *Science and Speculation: Studies in Hellenistic Theory and Practice* (Cambridge/Paris, 1982)

[313] M. Schofield and G. Striker (edd.), *The Norms of Nature: Studies in Hellenistic Ethics* (Cambridge/Paris, 1986)

[314] J. Barnes and M. Mignucci (edd.), *Matter and Metaphysics* (Naples, 1987)

[315] J. Brunschwig and M. C. Nussbaum (edd.), *Passions and Perceptions* (Cambridge/Paris, 1993)

[316] H. Flashar and O. Gigon (edd.), *Aspects de la philosophie hellénistique.* Fondation Hardt, *Entretiens sur l'antiquité classique* 32 (Vandœuvres Geneva, 1986)

[317] J. M. Dillon and A. A. Long (edd.), *The Question of 'Eclecticism': Studies in Later Greek Philosophy* (Berkeley/Los Angeles/London, 1988).

Epicurus

The most comprehensive edition of Epicurus, including the papyrus fragments, is

[318] G. Arrighetti, *Epicuro opere* (Turin, 1960; 2nd edn, 1973), which has an Italian translation and commentary.
[319] C. Bailey, *Epicurus: The Extant Remains* (Oxford, 1926) does not contain papyrus fragments but does have an English translation.
[320] M. Isnardi Parente, *Opere di Epicuro* (Turin, 1974) has an Italian translation of and commentary on the surviving works and the more important testimonia.
For those with Greek,
[321] H. Usener, *Epicurea* (Leipzig, 1887) remains an essential collection of texts and reports of Epicurean doctrines.

Editions of papyrus fragments of the important *de Natura* can be found in

[322] G. Leone, 'Epicuro, *Della Natura*, libro XIV', *Cronache Ercolanesi* 14 (1984), 17–107
[323] C. Millot, 'Epicure *de la Nature* Livre XV', *Cronache Ercolanesi* 7 (1977), 9–39
[324] D. Sedley, 'Epicurus, *On Nature* Book XXVIII', *Cronache Ercolanesi* 3 (1973), 5–83.
Book XXV is discussed in
[325] S. Laursen, 'Epicurus, *On Nature* Book XXV', *Cronache Ercolanesi* 17 (1987), 77–8
[326] S. Laursen, 'Epicurus *On Nature*, Book XXV (Long–Sedley 20, B, C and j)', *Cronache Ercolanesi* 18 (1988), 7–18.

Apart from what survives of Epicurus' own work, our principal source for Epicurean philosophy is Lucretius' Latin poem, *de Rerum Natura*, written in the first century B.C. The standard edition of Lucretius is still

[327] C. Bailey, *Titi Lucreti De Rerum Natura Libri Sex*, 3 vols. (Oxford, 1947).
[328] W. H. D. Rouse, *Lucretius De Rerum Natura*, revised with new text, introduction, notes and index by M. F. Smith, Loeb Classical Library (Cambridge, Mass. and London, 1975) provides a text and translation.

The relation between Epicurus and Lucretius is discussed in

[329] D. Clay, *Lucretius and Epicurus* (Ithaca/London, 1983)
and that between Epicureanism and scepticism is discussed in
[330] M. Gigante, *Scetticismo e Epicureismo* (Naples, 1981).

For discussion of Philodemus, another important first-century Epicurean and source of Epicurean views, see [332], Supplementary Essays I, and

[331] M. Gigante, *La Bibliothèque de Philodème et l'épicurisme romain* (Paris, 1987).

Philodemus' work on sign inferences is edited and translated in

[332] P. and E. De Lacy, *Philodemus, On Methods of Inference* (Naples, 1978),

on which, see

[333] D. Sedley, 'On Signs', in [312], 239–72

[334] J. Barnes, 'Epicurean Signs', *Oxford Studies in Ancient Philosophy*, supplementary volume (1988), 91–134

[335] A. A. Long, 'Reply to Jonathan Barnes, "Epicurean Signs"', *Oxford Studies in Ancient Philosophy*, supplementary volume (1988), 135–44.

See also

[336] D. Sedley, 'Diodorus Cronus and Hellenistic Philosophy', *Proceedings of the Cambridge Philological Society* 23 (1977), 74–120.

A perhaps surprising source of Epicurean doctrine is the second-century A.D. Diogenes of Oenoanda, who had his writings inscribed on a public colonnade in Turkey. The standard edition of the fragments of this discovered before 1970 is

[337] C. W. Chilton, *Diogenes Oenoandensis* (Leipzig, 1967),

of which

[338] C. W. Chilton, *Diogenes of Oenoanda. The Fragments* (London/New York/ Toronto, 1971)

is a translation and commentary.

For the 'new fragments' see

[339] M. F. Smith, 'Fragments of Diogenes of Oenoanda Discovered and Rediscovered', *American Journal of Archaeology* 74 (1970), 51–62 [new frr. 1–4]

[340] M. F. Smith, 'New Fragments of Diogenes of Oenoanda', *American Journal of Archaeology* 75 (1971), 357–89 [new frr. 5–16]

[341] M. F. Smith, 'Two New Fragments of Diogenes of Oenoanda', *Journal of Hellenic Studies* 92 (1972), 147–55 [new frr. 17–18]

[342] M. F. Smith, 'Thirteen New Fragments of Diogenes of Oenoanda', in *Denkschrift Akad. Wien* 117 (1974) [new frr. 19–31]

[343] M. F. Smith, 'Seven New Fragments of Diogenes of Oenoanda', *Hermathena* 118 (1974), 110–29 [new frr. 32–8]

[344] M. F. Smith, 'More New Fragments of Diogenes of Oenoanda', in [353], 279–318 [new frr. 39–51]

[345] M. F. Smith, 'Fifty-five New Fragments of Diogenes of Oenoanda', *Anatolian Studies* 28 (1978), 39–92 [new frr. 52–106]

[346] M. F. Smith, 'Eight New Fragments of Diogenes of Oenoanda', *Anatolian Studies* 29 (1979), 69–89 [new frr. 107–14]

[347] M. F. Smith, 'Diogenes of Oenoanda, New Fragments 115–121', *Prometheus* 8 (1982), 193–212

[348] M. F. Smith, 'Diogenes of Oenoanda, New Fragments 122–124', *Anatolian Studies* 34 (1984), 43–57.

An introduction to Epicurus' philosophy is

[349] J. M. Rist, *Epicurus: An Introduction* (Cambridge, 1972).

The fullest study of Epicurus' epistemology and philosophy of science is
[350] E. Asmis, *Epicurus' Scientific Method* (Ithaca/London, 1984).

See also
[351] P. Merlan, *Studies in Aristotle and Epicurus* (Wiesbaden, 1960).

A valuable collection of essays is
[352] *SYZETESIS: Studi sull'Epicureismo Greco e Latino offerti a Marcello Gigante*, 2 vols. (Naples, 1983).

See also
[353] J. Bollack and A. Laks (edd.), *Etudes sur l'Epicurisme Antique*, in *Cahiers de Philologie* 1 (1976).

The soul and psychology

[354] G. Kerferd, 'Epicurus' doctrine of the soul', *Phronesis* 16 (1971), 80–96
[355] D. Konstan, *Some Aspects of Epicurean Psychology* (Leiden, 1973)
[356] D. Sedley, 'Epicurean Anti-reductionism', in [314], 295–328
[357] S. Everson, 'Epicurus on the Truth of the Senses', in [13], 161–83

Prolēpsis

See [364] and
[358] D. K. Glidden, 'Epicurean Prolepsis', *Oxford Studies in Ancient Philosophy* 3 (1985), 175–218
[359] V. Goldschmidt, 'Remarques sur l'origine épicurienne de la prénotion', in [376], 155–69
[360] F. Jurss, 'Epikur und das Problem des Begriffs (Prolepse)', *Philologus* 121 (1977), 211–25
[361] A. Manuwald, *Die Prolepsislehre Epikurs* (Bonn, 1972).

Semantic theory

[362] P. H. De Lacy, 'The Epicurean Analysis of Language', *American Journal of Philology* 60 (1939), 85–92
[363] D. K. Glidden, 'Epicurean Semantics', in [352], 185–226
[364] A. A. Long, 'Aisthesis, Prolepsis and Linguistic Theory in Epicurus', *Bulletin of the Institute of Classical Studies* 18 (1971), 114–33

See also
[365] J. Brunschwig, 'Epicure et le problème du langage privé, *Revue des Sciences Humaines* 43 (1977), 157–77

The origin of language

[366] C. W. Chilton, 'The Epicurean Theory of the Origin of Language', *American Journal of Philology* 83 (1962), 139–67
[367] P. H. Schrijvers, 'La Pensée de Lucrèce sur l'origine du langage', *Mnemosyne* 27 (1974), 337–64

The Stoics

The fragments of the Stoics are collected in
[368] H. von Arnim, *Stoicorum Veterum Fragmenta*, 3 vols. (Leipzig, 1903–5); vol. 4, indexes by M. Adler (Leipzig, 1924).

A much more comprehensive collection of fragments of Stoic dialectic (which included language, logic and epistemology) is

[369] K. Hülser, *Die Fragmente zur Dialektik der Stoiker – neue Sammlung der Texte mit deutscher Übersetzung und Kommentar*, 4 vols. (Stuttgart/Bad Cannstatt, 1987–9).

The following are introductions to Stoic thought:

[370] E. Brehier, *Chrysippe et l'ancien stoïcisme*, 2nd edn Paris, 1951)
[371] J. Christensen, *An Essay on the Unity of Stoic Philosophy* (Copenhagen, 1962)
[372] L. Edelstein, *The Meaning of Stoicism* (Cambridge, Mass., 1966)
[373] M. Pohlenz, *Die Stoa: Geschichte einer geistigen Bewegung*, 2nd edn (Göttingen, 1959)
[374] J. M. Rist, *Stoic Philosophy* (Cambridge, 1969)
[375] F. H. Sandbach, *The Stoics* (London, 1975).

The following contain articles on various aspects of Stoic philosophy:

[376] J. Brunschwig (ed.), *Les Stoïciens et leur logique* (Paris, 1978)
[377] R. Epp (ed.), *Spindel Conference 1984: Recovering the Stoics*. (*Southern Journal of Philosophy*, XXIII suppl., 1985)
[378] A. A. Long (ed.), *Problems in Stoicism* (London, 1971)
[379] J. M. Rist, *The Stoics* (Berkeley/Los Angeles/London, 1978).
[380] A.-J. Voelke (ed.), *Le Stoïcisme* (*Revue internationale de Philosophie*, forthcoming)

For a discussion of contemporary interpretations of the Stoics, see

[381] J. M. Rist, 'Stoicism: Some Reflections on the State of the Art', in [377], 1–11.

Useful monographs on Stoic philosophy are

[382] M. Frede, *Die stoische Logik* (Göttingen, 1974)
[383] J. Gould, *The Philosophy of Chrysippus* (Leiden, 1971)
[384] B. Inwood, *Ethics and Human Action in Early Stoicism* (Oxford, 1985)
[385] B. Mates, *Stoic Logic* (Berkeley/Los Angeles, 1953)
[386] M. Mignucci, *Il significato della logica Stoica*, 2nd edn (Bologna, 1967)
[387] M. A. Reesor, *The Nature of Man in Early Stoic Philosophy* (London, 1989).

Lekta

See [32] as well as

[388] W. Detel, R. Hülser, G. Krüger, W. Lorenz, '*Lekta ellipē* in der stoischen Sprachphilosophie', *Archiv für Geschichte der Philosophie* 62 (1980), 276–88
[389] U. Egli, 'Stoic syntax and semantics', in [376], 135–54
[390] A. Graeser, 'The Stoic Theory of Meaning', in [379], 77–100
[391] A. A. Long, 'The Stoic Distinction between Truth and the True', in [376], 297–316.

See also

[392] M. Frede, 'Stoics and Sceptics on Clear and Distinct Impressions', in [11], 65–93 and in [15], 151–76

[393] G. B. Kerferd, 'The Problem of *Synkatathesis* and *Katalepsis*', in [376], 251–72.

Propositions

[394] J. Gould, 'Chrysippus: On the Criteria for the Truth of a Conditional Proposition', *Phronesis* 12 (1967), 153–61

[395] R. Goulet, 'La Classification stoïcienne des propositions simples', in [376], 171–98

[396] A. C. Lloyd, 'Definite Propositions and the Concept of Reference', in [376], 285–96

See also

[397] P. Pachet, 'La Deixis selon Zénon et Chrysippe', *Phronesis* 20 (1975), 241–6.

Thought

[398] M. Daraki-Mallett, 'Les Fonctions psychologiques du logos' in [376], 87–119

[399] A. A. Long, 'Language and Thought in Stoicism', in [378], 75–113

See also

[400] K. Hülser, 'Expression and Content in Stoic Linguistic Theory', in [474], 287–306

[401] C. H. Kahn, 'Stoic Logic and Stoic Logos', *Archiv für Geschichte der Philosophie* 51 (1969), 158–72.

Grammar

[402] K. Barwick, *Probleme der stoischen Sprachlehre und Rhetorik* (Berlin, 1957)

[403] M. Frede, 'Some Remarks on the Origin of Traditional Grammar', in [478], 609–37 and [15], 338–59

[404] M. Frede, 'Principles of Stoic Grammar', in [379], 27–76

[405] P. Hadot, 'La Notion de "cas" dans la logique stoïcienne', *Actes du XXXme congrès des sociétés de langue française* (Geneva, 1966), 109–12

[406] A. C. Lloyd, 'Grammar and Metaphysics in the Stoa', in [378], 58–74

[407] R. T. Schmidt, *Die Grammatik der Stoiker* (Wiesbaden, 1979) contains a translation by K. Hülser of Schmidt's 1839 Latin text together with an introduction and bibliography by U. Egli.

Signs

[408] M. F. Burnyeat, 'The Origins of Non-deductive Inference', in [312], 193–238

[409] T. Ebert, 'The Origin of the Stoic Theory of Signs in Sextus Empiricus', *Oxford Studies in Ancient Philosophy* 5 (1987), 83–126

[410] G. Pretri, 'Sulla dottrina del *sēmeion* nella logica Stoica', *Rivista Critica di Storia della Filosofia* 11 (1956), 5–16
[411] G. Verbeke, 'La Philosophie du signe chez les stoïcens', in [376], 401–24

The sceptics

General accounts of ancient scepticism can be found in

[412] J. Annas and J. Barnes, *The Modes of Scepticism* (Cambridge, 1985)
[413] V. Brochard, *Les Sceptiques grecs* (2nd edn, Paris, 1923)
[414] M. F. Burnyeat, 'The Sceptic in His Place and Time', in [524], 225–54
[415] G. Giannantoni (ed.), *Lo scetticismo antico*, 2 vols. (Rome, 1981)
[416] M. dal Pra, *Lo scetticismo Greco*, 2 vols., 2nd edn (Rome/Bari, 1975)
[417] D. Sedley, 'The Motivation of Greek Scepticism', in [477], 9–30
[418] C. Stough, *Greek Skepticism* (Berkeley/Los Angeles, 1969).

A valuable general discussion of Sextus is

[419] K. Janáček, *Sextus Empiricus' Sceptical Methods* (Prague, 1972).

See also

[420] W. Heintz, *Studien zu Sextus Empiricus* (Halle, 1932).

Relevant papers on scepticism are

[421] S. Everson, 'The Objective Appearance of Pyrrhonism', in [14], 121–47
[422] D. K. Glidden, 'Skeptic Semiotics', *Phronesis* 28 (1983), 213–55
[423] C. Stough, 'Sextus Empiricus on Non-assertion', *Phronesis* 29 (1984), 137–64.

Medical writers

A general introduction to ancient medicine is

[424] A. J. Brock, *Greek Medicine* (London, 1929).

Good discussions of many aspects of ancient medicine are to be found in

[425] L. Edelstein (ed. O. Temkin and C. L. Temkin), *Ancient Medicine* (Baltimore, 1967)
[426] H. Diller, *Kleine Schriften zur antike Medizin* (Berlin, 1973)
[427] R. J. Hankinson (ed.), *Method, Medicine and Metaphysics: Studies in the Philosophy of Ancient Science* (Alberta, 1988)
[428] E. D. Philips, *Aspects of Greek Medicine* (New York, 1973).

The relation between ancient philosophy and medicine is discussed in

[429] L. Edelstein, 'The Relation of Ancient Philosophy to Medicine', *Bulletin of the History of Medicine* 26 (1952), 299–316 and in [425], 349–66
[430] M. Frede, 'Philosophy and Medicine in Antiquity', in [15], 225–42
[431] W. H. S. Jones, *Philosophy and Medicine in Ancient Greece, Bulletin of the History of Medicine* , supplement (Baltimore, 1946).

The empiricists

Fragments of the empiricists are collected in

[432] K. Deichgräber, *Die griechische Empirikerschule: Sammlung der Fragmente und Darstellung der Lehre* (Berlin, 1930, 2nd, enlarged edn, 1965).

For a general discussion of the method of the empiricists, see
[433] M. Frede, 'The Ancient Empiricists', in [15], 243–60.

Galen

Galen's works are collected in the monumental
[434] C. G. Kühn, *Galeni Opera Omnia*, 20 vols. (in 22) (Leipzig, 1821–33).

Shorter works are edited in
[435] J. Marquardt, *Galeni Scripta Minora*, vol. 1 (Leipzig, 1884)
[436] I. Müller, *Galeni Scripta Minora* vol. 2 (Leipzig, 1891)
[437] G. Helmreich, *Galeni Scripta Minora* vol. 3 (Leipzig, 1893).
[438] M. Frede (ed.), *Galen: Three Treatises on the Nature of Science* (Indianapolis, 1985)
contains translations of *de sectis Ingredientibus* (*On the Sects for Beginners*), the *Subfiguratio Empirica* (*Outline of Empiricism*) and *On Medical Experience*, together with a very useful introduction to Galen's work.

There is now a translation of the first two books of *On the Therapeutic Method* with a philosophical commentary:
[439] R. J. Hankinson, *Galen on the Therapeutic Method* (Oxford, 1991).

The important work *On the Views of Hippocrates and Plato* has been edited with a translation in
[440] P. H. de Lacy (ed.), *Galeni de Placitis Hippocratis et Platonis, Corpus Medicorum Graecorum* v.4.1.2, 3 vols. (Berlin, 1981–4).

Various short treatises are edited and translated in
[441] D. J. Furley and J. S. Wilkie, *Galen on Respiration and the Arteries* (Princeton, 1984),
which also contains essays on various aspects of Galen's doctrines.
[442] V. Nutton (ed.), *Galen: Problems and Prospects* (London, 1981), and
[443] R. Durling and F. Kudlien (edd.), *Galen's Method of Healing* (Leiden, 1992)
contain papers on Galen.

Two introductions to Galen are
[444] L. G. Ballester, *Galeno* (Madrid, 1972)
[445] G. Sarton, *Galen of Pergamon* (Kansas, 1954).

Galen's standing as a philosopher is examined in
[446] P. Moraux, 'Galien comme philosophe', in [442]
and his epistemology in
[447] M. Frede, 'On Galen's Epistemology', in [442], 65–86 and in [15], 279–98.

See also

[448] R. J. Hankinson, 'A Purely Verbal Dispute? Galen on Stoic and Academic Epistemology', in [380].

Galen's psychology is discussed in

[449] R. J. Hankinson, 'Actions and Passions: Affection, Emotion and Moral Self-management in Galen's Philosophical Psychology', in [315], 184–222

[450] R. J. Hankinson, 'Greek Medical Models of the Mind', in [14], 194–217

[451] R. J. Hankinson, 'Galen's Anatomy of the Soul', *Phronesis* 36 (1991), 197–233.

Galen's discussions on language are reviewed in

[452] M. Edlow, *Galen on Language and Ambiguity* (Leiden, 1977)

[453] M. Meyerhof and J. Schacht, *Galen über die medizinischen Namen, Abhandlung der Preussische Akademie der Wissenschaft, Phil-Hist. Kl.* (1931).

See also

[454] J. Barnes, 'Galen on Logic and Therapy', in [443], 50–102.

Grammarians

[455] D. Blank, *Ancient Philosophy and Grammar, American Classical Studies* 10 (Chico, Calif., 1982)

[456] D. L. Blank, 'Some Remarks on Nicanor, the Stoics, and the Ancient Theory of Punctuation', *Glotta* 61 (1983), 48–67

[457] D. L. Blank, 'Apollonius and Maximus on the Order and Meaning of the Oblique Cases', *Historiographica Linguistica* 13 (1986), 241–57

[458] D. Fehling, 'Varron und die grammatische Lehre von der Analogie und der Flexion', *Glotta* 35 (1956), 214–70 and 36 (1957), 48–100

[459] W. Hörschelmann, 'Kritische Bemerkungen zu Apollonios Dyskolos *de Pronomine*', *Rheinisches Museum* 35 (1880), 271–89

[460] H. J. Mette, *Parateresis: Untersuchungen zur Sprachtheorie des Krates von Pergamon* (Halle, 1952), 10–55

[461] A. Thierfelder, *Beiträge zur Kritik und Erklärung des Apollonios Dyskolos, Abh. sächs. Ak. Wiss. Leipzig, Phil-Hist. Kl.* 43.2 (1953), 28 ff.

Augustine

A brief introduction to Augustine can be found in

[462] H. Chadwick, *Augustine* (Oxford, 1986)
as well as R. Markus' part v of

[463] A. H. Armstrong (ed.), *The Cambridge History of Later Greek and Early Medieval Philosophy* (Cambridge, 1970).

[464] C. Kirwan, *Augustine* (London, 1989)
provides a philosophical introduction to Augustine's work.

[465] R. A. Markus (ed.), *Augustine: A Collection of Critical Essays* (London, 1972)
contains papers on various aspects of Augustine.
The *de Magistro* is translated in

[466] J. H. S. Burleigh, *Augustine: Earlier Writings* (London, and Philadelphia, 1953).

The *de Dialectica* is edited with a translation and commentary in
[467] J. Pinborg (ed.), *Augustine De Dialectica* (Leiden, 1975).
The *de Doctrina Christiana* is translated in
[468] D. W. Robertson, Jr, *Augustine, On Christian Doctrine* (New York, 1958).

For Augustine's theory of signs, see
[469] M. Baratin, 'Les Origines stoïciennes de la théorie Augustinienne du signe', *Revue des Etudes Latines* LIX (1981), 260–8
[470] B. D. Jackson, 'The Theory of Signs in the *De Doctrina Christiana*', in [465].
[471] R. A. Markus, 'St. Augustine on Signs', in [465].
Wittgenstein's treatment of Augustine is discussed in
[472] M. F. Burnyeat, 'Wittgenstein and Augustine *de Magistro*', *Proceedings of the Aristotelian Society*, supplementary volume (1987), 1–24.

Modern works

[473] G. Baker and P. M. S. Hacker, *Wittgenstein: Meaning and Understanding* (Oxford, 1983)
[474] R. Bäuerle, U. Egli, A. von Stechow (edd.), *Semantics from Different Points of View* (Heidelberg, 1979)
[475] D. Bell, *Husserl* (London, 1990)
[476] J. Boden and J. E. McGuire (edd.), *How Things Are* (Dordrecht, 1985)
[477] M. F. Burnyeat (ed.), *The Skeptical Tradition* (Berkeley/Los Angeles/London, 1983)
[478] R. Butts and J. Hintikka (edd.), *Logic, Methodology, and Philosophy of Science* (Dordrecht, 1976)
[479] R. Chisholm, *Perceiving* (Ithaca, 1957)
[480] J. Cohen, *The Dialogue of Reason* (Oxford, 1986)
[481] D. Davidson, 'Truth and Meaning', in his [484], 17–36
[482] D. Davidson, 'Thought and Talk', in his [484], 155–70
[483] D. Davidson, 'The Method of Truth in Metaphysics', in his [484], 199–214
[484] D. Davidson, *Inquiries into Truth and Interpretation* (Oxford, 1984)
[485] F. Dretske, *Knowledge and the Flow of Information* (Oxford, 1981)
[486] M. Dummett, *Frege: Philosophy of Language* (London, 1973)
[487] M. Dummett, *The Interpretation of Frege's Philosophy* (London, 1981)
[488] M. Dummett, 'Language and Communication', in [503], 192–212
[489] M. Dummett, 'The Relative Priority of Thought and Language', in his [490], 315–25
[490] M. Dummett, *Frege and Other Philosophers* (Oxford, 1991)
[491] M. Dummett, *Frege: Philosophy of Mathematics* (London, 1991)
[492] M. Dummett, *The Logical Basis of Metaphysics* (London, 1991)
[493] G. Evans and J. McDowell (edd.), *Truth and Meaning* (Oxford, 1976)
[494] G. Evans, 'The Causal Theory of Names', in his [495], 1–25
[495] G. Evans, *Collected Papers* (Oxford, 1985)
[496] G. Evans, *The Varieties of Reference* (Oxford, 1983)
[497] J. Fodor, *The Language of Thought* (Cambridge, Mass., 1975)
[498] G. Frege, 'Review of E. G. Husserl, *Philosophie der Arithmetik* I', *Zeitschrift*

für Philosophie und philosophische Kritik 103 (1894), 313–32, translated by H. Kaal in McGuinness [515], 195–209
[499] G. Frege 'Über Sinn und Bedeutung', in [517], 40–65
[500] P. A. French, T. E. Uehling, Jr, and H. K. Wettstein (edd.), *Contemporary Perspectives in the Philosophy of Language* (Minneapolis, 1977)
[501] P. T. Geach, 'Is it Right to Say Or is a Conjunction?', *Analysis* 19 (1958–9), and in [502], 204–5
[502] P. T. Geach, *Logic Matters* (Oxford, 1972)
[503] A. George (ed.), *Reflections on Chomsky* (Oxford, 1989)
[504] N. Goodman, *Fact, Fiction and Forecast* (Indianapolis, 1973)
[505] R. E. Grandy and R. Warner (edd.), *Philosophical Grounds of Rationality* (Oxford, 1986)
[506] H. P. Grice, 'Utterer's Meaning, Sentence-meaning and Word-meaning', in his [505], 117–37
[507] H. P. Grice, *Studies in the Way of Words* (Cambridge, Mass., 1989)
[508] D. Hume, *An Abstract of a Treatise of Human Nature*, in L. A. Selby-Bigge (ed.), *Hume's Treatise of Human Nature*, 2nd edn (Oxford, 1978)
[509] R. Jackendoff, *Semantics and Cognition* (Cambridge, Mass., 1990)
[510] D. Kaplan, 'Words', *Proceedings of the Aristotelian Society*, supplementary volume 64 (1990), 93–119
[511] J. M. Keynes and P. Staffa (edd.), *An Abstract of a Treatise of Human Nature* (Cambridge, 1938)
[512] S. Kripke, 'Speaker Reference and Semantic Reference', in [500], 6–27
[513] S. Kripke, *Wittgenstein on Rules and Private Language* (Oxford, 1982)
[514] J. McDowell, 'Truth Conditions, Bivalence and Verificationism', in [493], 42–66
[515] J. McDowell, 'On the Sense and Reference of a Proper Name', *Mind* 86 (1977), 159–85 and in [520], 141–66
[516] J. McDowell, 'Anti-realism and the Epistemology of Understanding', in [518], 225–48
[517] B. McGuinness (ed.), *Gottlob Frege, Collected Papers on Mathematics, Logic and Philosophy* (Oxford, 1984)
[518] H. Parret and J. Bouveresse (edd.), *Meaning and Understanding* (Berlin/New York, 1981)
[519] G. Patzig (ed.), *G. Frege: Funktion, Begriff, Bedeutung* (Göttingen, 1986)
[520] M. Platts (ed.), *Reference, Truth and Reality* (London, 1980)
[521] H. Putnam, 'The Meaning of "Meaning"', in [522], 215–71
[522] H. Putnam, *Mind, Language and Reality* (Cambridge, 1975)
[523] W. V. O. Quine, *Word and Object* (Boston, 1960)
[524] R. Rorty, J. B. Schneewind and Q. Skinner (edd.), *Philosophy in History* (Cambridge, 1984)
[525] B. Russell, *The Philosophy of Logical Atomism*, in [533], 157–244
[526] B. Russell, *An Introduction to Mathematical Philosophy* (London, 1919)
[527] G. Ryle, 'Discussion of Rudolf Carnap: *Meaning and Necessity*', *Philosophy* (1949), and in [528], 225–35
[528] G. Ryle, *Collected Papers*, vol. 1 (London, 1971)
[529] N. Salmon, *Frege's Puzzle* (Cambridge, Mass., 1986)
[530] S. Schiffer, *Remnants of Meaning* (Cambridge, Mass., 1987)

[531] M. Schirn (ed.), *Studien zu Frege*, 3 vols. (Stuttgart/Bad Cannstatt, 1976)
[532] J. Searle, *Intentionality: An Essay in the Philosophy of Mind* (Cambridge, 1983)
[533] J. G. Slater (ed.), *The Philosophy of Logical Atomism and Other Essays* (London/Boston/Sydney, 1986)
[534] T. Smiley, 'Syllogism and Quantification', *Journal of Symbolic Logic* (1962), 58–72
[535] F. Sommers, 'Do we Need Identity?' *Journal of Philosophy* 66 (499–504)
[536] D. Wiggins, 'On Frege's Problem of the Morning and the Evening Star', in [531], III, 221–55
[537] D. Wiggins, 'The Sense and Reference of Predicates: A Running Repair to Frege's Doctrine and a Plea for the Copula', in [538], 126–43
[538] C. Wright (ed.), *Frege: Influence and Tradition* (Oxford, 1984)

*Index of names**

Ancients

* I am grateful to Hugh Johnstone for preparing the references in the index of names and the index of passages discussed and to David Blank for supplying information on the ancient grammarians.

Moderns

Index of passages discussed

Index of subjects